Introduction

In *The Minister's Wooing* (1859), her third novel, Harriet Beecher Stowe holds a mirror to the "Two worlds" of life in late 18th- and early 19th-century New England — to "the great and the little, the solemn and the trivial." If her characters are concerned with household efficiency, with how to restore a wedding dress or to repair a neighbor's farming tools, they are more deeply concerned with the state of their souls and their minister's various interpretations of Scripture. Philosophical and theological debate was as much a part of New England as were hoeing and baking. "Two worlds must mingle," Mrs. Stowe explains to her reader in Chapter XII, "wreathing in and out, like the grotesque carvings on a Gothic shrine; — only, did we know it rightly, nothing is trivial; since the human soul, with its awful shadow, makes all things sacred."

The Minister's Wooing, then, is first of all a glimpse of the everyday. Mrs. Stowe relates such details as the hours meals were eaten and the proper time for retiring, the normal preparations for quiltings and wedding celebrations, and a list of characteristic topics at parties, such as "how best to keep moths out of blankets, — how to make fritters of Indian corn undistinguishable from oysters," and "how to put down the Democratic party." She presents these homely details only partly to establish her New England setting. To her, the orderly, hospitable home represents heaven on earth. The Christian home is as much a center of redemptive enterprise as the church because model acts of sacrifice begin there.

In the novel's treatment of the great and solemn aspects of life, Mrs. Stowe's image of the Gothic shrine is appropriate. Descriptions inevitably turn to considerations of religion. In Chapter I an invitation to tea becomes the occasion for a consideration of one man's religious ideals. At the gathering itself there is heated discussion of the minister's latest Sunday sermon. Chapter II, which begins with a description of a New England kitchen, leads to a discussion of the theology of one of the major characters. The novel deals with two religious views, two distinct ways of understanding God and the nature of man and how the Creator and his creation may be correctly related. It portrays a conflict between New Divinity, or New Light, theology — a Calvinist interpretation of Scripture as taught by Dr. Samuel Hopkins, a friend and follower of Jonathan Edwards — and the freedom of the individual to conduct his own quest for God and to interpret spiritual reality for himself. The book examines the question of religious authority, a question that concerned many 19th-century American thinkers, including Emerson as well as such mitigators of Calvinist theology as Nathaniel Taylor and Lyman Beecher, Mrs. Stowe's father.

Mrs. Stowe draws the novel's basic conflict between Calvinism and a less authoritarian interpretation of Scripture not only from then current debate but also from personal experience, from an emotional conflict resulting from two tragic incidents. The first, which occurred in her childhood, was the drowning of Alexander Metcalf Fisher, the fiance of her sister, Catharine. Fisher had never had what was termed a "conversion experience." After his death Catharine journeyed to Fisher's home to look for evidence of a conversion. She found that, though he had sought since childhood to give himself to God, he could not.[1] Since Calvinism denied any hope for the unregenerate apart from the transmission of a "divine and supernatural light,"[2] which was wholly God's doing, Fisher's soul was assumed to be condemned. Eventually, after a quarter-century of alternately accepting and re-

Alexander Metcalf Fisher (1794-1822), a Yale mathematics professor, drowned at sea.

futing these ideas in her books, Catharine renounced Calvinist theology and joined the Episcopal Church.

Nearly 40 years after the drowning and its aftermath, Mrs. Stowe incorporated similar incidents into her novel. As Charles Foster points out in his study of Mrs. Stowe, the supposed fate of the young hero of *The Minister's Wooing*, James Marvyn, parallels that of Fisher's. Marvyn's mother's revolt against Calvinist doctrine parallels that of Catharine's.[3] Although *The Minister's Wooing* appeared too late to console Catharine, Mrs. Stowe does speak in the novel to the skeptical and the bitter, to those who consider adopting the pagan philosophy of "eat and drink, for tomorrow we die." Self-forgetting love, she says, is "the noblest capability of your eternal inheritance ... made known to you." One's capacity to love another unselfishly is, to Mrs. Stowe, symbolic of divine love, a kind of intimation of immortality.

It was not only her sister's experience that Mrs. Stowe was remembering, however. A more immediate sorrow and impulse for questioning God's ways to man was the drowning, in 1857, of her eldest son, Henry. Henry, like Fisher, had never experienced regeneration, although he had written his mother from college that he would live nobly and as a Christian should. Mrs. Stowe was at first untroubled by doubts about his eternal state, but subsequently doubts were aroused. She allayed these through the writing of this novel.[4] Mrs. Stowe's anxiety over the uncertainty of the state of her son's soul is reflected in Chapter XXIV by Mary Scudder's questioning of the fate of her lover, who was supposedly drowned at sea. The description of Mary's spiritual anguish is deeply moving. If Mrs. Stowe finally did come to terms with her son's death through this novel, it was not simply by questioning, as her sister had, the ultimate authority of Calvinist doctrine, but by adopting the idea that God in his mercy might accommodate himself to human weakness or to individual personality. The young hero's experience of conversion suggests that man's relationship with God may begin not only with the recognition of one's total depravity and infinite distance from God but also with the realization of his benevolence.

The extent of Mrs. Stowe's departure from Calvinism becomes clear in her correspondence of this period. In an 1860 letter to a friend she

Henry Ellis Stowe (1838-1857), a student at Dartmouth
College, drowned while swimming the Connecticut
River.

states that God may extend grace to the individual soul even in the next world, that there are healing means beyond this life. Although continuous rejection will result finally in separation from God, "No soul will be lost till all the resources of omnipotent love and wisdom have been exhausted on it."[5] So great is her confidence in Christ's mediation that she even suggests "the lost, if any shall be, are as nothing."[6]

Were the conflict only a personal matter, however, *The Minister's Wooing* might have little claim on the reader's attention. As it is, the novel is historically significant and aesthetically worthy. Mrs. Stowe, as a reform writer and visionary, shapes details of late 18th-century New England in order to create art that she hoped would serve as a reference for future society. Among the book's historical analogues is Dr. Samuel Hopkins, a major character. Much of Mrs. Stowe's information about him was gleaned from discussions with her friend and neighbor, Dr. Edwards Amasa Park, president of Andover Theological Seminary, and from his biography, *Memoir of the Life and Character of Samuel Hopkins, D.D.* (1854). According to Dr. Park's account, from 1770 to 1803, except for five years during the Revolutionary War, Hopkins was a leading figure in the bustling community of Newport, Rhode Island, the setting of *The Minister's Wooing*. Newport included traffic in slaves among its commercial enterprises, and Hopkins became noted as much for the zeal with which he attacked the slave trade as for his rigorous theological system. Dr. Park's book includes the incident, related by Mrs. Stowe in Chapter XI, in which Hopkins suggests to one of his parishioners that he question his slaves about their desire to be free. Also, as Mrs. Stowe relates in Chapter XV, Hopkins did, in fact, severely admonish his slaveholding congregation at the risk of his own popularity. Some notable families subsequently left his church. (Mrs. Stowe's dating of Hopkins's sermon is, however, inaccurate by several years.) Hopkins's ability to play on the ideals of the patriots to help them see the injustice of slavery no doubt appealed greatly to Mrs. Stowe. Her message to America in *Uncle Tom's Cabin* had been published seven years before *The Minister's Wooing*. Yet little had changed. Thus, this novel was, in part, a reminder of a moral imperative.

Hopkins's clerical rivalry with Dr. Ezra Stiles is also historically based, although, as Foster ex-

Rev. SAMUEL HOPKINS, D.D.

The Rev. Samuel Hopkins (1721-1803) was minister of the First Congregational Church of Newport, R.I., from 1770 until his death. *Courtesy The Connecticut Historical Society*

plains, Stiles became president of Yale in 1778 and was not in Newport during the 1790s. Nor was Stiles proslavery, as Mrs. Stowe represents him for dramatic purposes.[7] Hopkins's concern for the soul of Aaron Burr, who serves as the villain in the subplot of this novel and who was, in actuality, the grandson of Jonathan Edwards, is also based on fact. Mrs. Stowe takes her ideas for Hopkins's encounters with Burr, in part at least, from a letter Hopkins wrote when he was more than 80 years old. In it he reminds the then vice president of the United States of the hopes that his distinguished ancestry held for him and of the dangers of basing one's happiness in this world only.[8]

The book is not historical in every detail, however. The account of Hopkins's romance with Mary Scudder is fictional. In his youth, Hopkins had experienced a rejection similar to the one described in this love story, but he was not a middle-aged bachelor and he had married young. Also, it seems unlikely that the real Dr. Hopkins would have been changed by hearing a conversion story as, in the novel, he is changed by Marvyn's recital of conversion.

Though broadly historical in its tracing of the

decline of the concepts of God's unquestionable sovereignty and the special merit of clerical authority, *The Minister's Wooing* does more than mirror New England life and thought. The novel grants credence to a new order in which there is a recognition of man's individual authority in religious matters as well as in political ones. As Forrest Wilson observes, the novel was "almost as revolutionary in the religious life of the nation as was *Uncle Tom's Cabin* in its political life. ... It marked the beginning of a more liberal and emotional type of religious observance."[9]

To demonstrate and achieve this quiet revolution, Mrs. Stowe chooses an aesthetic pattern that reflects her hope for mankind. History is here turned to the heart's desire or rather, since Mrs. Stowe believes in Scripture, to a reflection of her view of God's intent in history. It is through a kind of evolution or the changing of men's hearts and minds to accommodate each other (as God, in Christ, had accepted man) that Mrs. Stowe hopes to foster in America a religious community founded upon democratic principles. Hopkins believed that the various religious sects would war with each other before the millennium. In contrast, Mrs. Stowe views the various beliefs, as did Horace Bushnell, a prominent 19th-century theologian, as healthy balances to one another and as creating opportunities for mediation and understanding. The kind of resolution of the central conflict she achieves in her novel and the manner in which she achieves it, as well as her characters' actions, can best be comprehended in terms of an artistic analogue to historic Christianity, the aesthetic pattern of comedy.

In their classic concern with correcting human error through appeals to a standard or to an ideal order, the works of Mrs. Stowe reflect the comic structure. In tragedy, evil and error are surmounted and standards attained only after death and sweeping change. Tragedy's effects are irrevocable. In comedy, on the other hand, change is gradual and orderly. Comedy presents a faith in man's ability to function within society as well as a faith in supernatural assistance. Above all, comedy is optimistic. It affirms that justice will be done — if not in this world, though Mrs. Stowe hoped that it would be, then in the next or at the millennium. In *The Minister's Wooing,* as in her other novels, Mrs. Stowe's characters are comic as they give up their rights in order to soothe quarrels; to insist on their own way would be to harm others. The novel examines and dismisses the tragic view of life.

It is in the pattern of conflict that Mrs. Stowe's comedy, her Christian hope for man, can best be analyzed and understood. As in other comedies, this conflict results in a mitigation of the older generation's ruling philosophy, a reformation brought about by the young hero's discovery. James Marvyn has a "contempt of orthodox opinion." He looks at himself rather than at God as a starting point for a changed life, a view, as he notes, that Dr. Hopkins would have regarded as selfish. The two points of view are not easy to resolve, however, and Mrs. Stowe makes sure that the reader understands all of the negative implications of the older man's ideology.

Like Jonathan Edwards, who believed in the Calvinist doctrine of unconditional election, Dr. Hopkins believes that God will save whomever he chooses, that man cannot aid in his own salvation. This view forbids man to create rituals or symbolism. It is represented by Mrs. Stowe in the image of the rungless ladder in Chapter VI and is sharply contrasted to her own belief in the soul's gradual ascent to perfection. Unlike Dr. Hopkins,

Mrs. Stowe thought that a redemptive capacity might exist in the human experience. The ability to love, to create symbols and rituals — to recognize relationships — is part of that experience. By comparison, Dr. Hopkins's expectations for the soul's salvation and his ignoring of man's temporal dimensions are made to seem disregardful of God's creation.

Mrs. Stowe is at pains to illustrate how Dr. Hopkins's system fails to capture the redemptive intention of Scripture. According to her and others who appealed to the moral argument against Calvinism, the system is inimical to the human spirit. Man can do nothing to achieve God's acceptance without the aid of the Holy Spirit; yet man is regarded as a free agent and is thus responsible for his own salvation. The system, she points out in Chapter XXIII, is tyrannical; it "had, on minds of a certain class, the effect of a slow poison, producing life-habits of morbid action very different from any which ever followed the simple reading of the Bible." The mother of James Marvyn is a member of the "certain class" poisoned by Dr. Hopkins's interpretation. Incapable of resignation to her son's reported death and to the possibility that he may be in hell, she voices

the utter despair such a view could cause: "' —
Oh, my wedding-day! Why did they rejoice?
Brides should wear mourning, — the bells should
toll for every wedding; every new family is built
over this awful pit of despair, and only one in a
thousand escapes!'" Mrs. Marvyn nearly goes
mad until Candace, a Negro slave, bids her to
remember the Christ of the cross and persuades
her of his intercessory love.

Mrs. Marvyn begins to heal after this encoun-
ter. But for the society to be changed, the minister or the ruling power must be persuaded of the
centrality of God's love for man and the value he
places on each individual. Man must be converted
to this position; it is not enough simply to repu-
diate his original stance.[10] James, Mrs. Marvyn's
son, a rebel against the beliefs of the older generation, is responsible for the beginning of the
minister's transformation.

This "young heir of life and hope" represents
the younger generation that must triumph. In
Chapter VII, James is described as a headstrong,
independent youth, more unmanageable than his
older brothers and sisters. It is hardly surprising
that he should leave home because of a "miscellaneous assortment of influences" — monotony,

the call of the sea, acquaintance with sailors, dislike of the farm, and, most significant to comedy, "a bitter break with his father, in which came that last wrench for an individual existence which some time or other the young growing mind will give to old authority." His independence thus becomes a condition for his conversion. And, paradoxically, it is at sea that he realizes his dependence on someone outside himself. As in other novels of Mrs. Stowe — *Uncle Tom's Cabin, The Pearl of Orr's Island* — the sea is symbolic of the sin and despair from which a character is saved. In what he describes as "'the crisis'" of his life, a time as "'dreadful as the Day of Judgment,'" James is literally saved from shipwreck and casts himself on God.

When he is first at sea, he bargains with God, much like the Old Testament Jacob. James's relationship with God is appropriately symbolized by a ladder. Unlike the image used to describe Dr. Hopkins's system in Chapter XXXVI, this ladder possesses rungs and mediators. It was Jacob's vision of God's concern for him that prompted that young renegade to vow allegiance to God. Just so, James states that the possibility that God might befriend and protect him "'was something that looked to me like a tangible foundation to begin upon.'" Initially, then, James's belief in God is self-centered. His conversion begins as he discovers a God who will aid him. The Old Testament schools him to desire to be helped to "'carry out those higher aspirations.'" Later, after reading the New Testament, he prays to become "'noble, and patient, and self-denying, and constant in my duty, than for any other kind of help.'"

Described early in the book as "an infant of moods and tenses, and those not of any regular verb," James surprises those who question him about his conversion. He "'didn't talk in the regular way'" at his examination for church membership, writes Miss Prissy, the seamstress, in a letter to her sister. "'Jim always did have his own way of talking, and never could say things in other people's words; and sometimes he makes folks laugh, when he himself don't know what they laugh at, because he hits the nail on the head in some strange way they aren't expecting.'" He told of "'the loving kindness of the Lord, till the Doctor's spectacles got all blinded with tears, and he couldn't see the notes he made to examine him by.'" Dr. Hopkins's system is rendered inoperable by James's conversion. The Doctor is persuaded by James's experience, by his undictated response to God. The Doctor has heard a new language, James's unorthodox language, which mediates James's experience of God and makes it available to the Doctor. The philosophy of predetermination and election is shown to be of no use.

James's winning of the Doctor, his marriage to Mary, and the traditional happy ending are not entirely his own doing. He has a necessary aide in the seamstress, Miss Prissy, who reveals his and Mary's love for each other to Dr. Hopkins. She is a type familiar to comedy, the type of the "tricky slave," the "scheming valet," the "Female confidantes."[11] Miss Prissy dares tell the Doctor the truth. A kind of resident miracle worker in the novel, Miss Prissy redesigns things into a new pattern. She is the one who can uncover the truth as well as create masquerade. When talking with Mrs. Scudder, Mary's mother, she disguises her feelings about the propriety of the match between Mary and the Doctor; however, when she and Candace discuss James's return, they agree that he should become engaged to Mary. She can reveal as well as conceal: "'I always told folks that I should spoil a novel before it got half-way through the first volume, by blurting out some of those things that they let go trailing on so, till everybody gets so mixed up they don't know what they're doing.'"

Through her speech, Miss Prissy changes the direction of the novel. She describes revelation as a "'mercy'" and tells the Doctor the truth about Mary's long-standing love for James. Later she compares this same revelation to an act of violence: "'Poor man! such a good man, too! I declare, I feel just like Herod taking off John the Baptist's head. Well, well! it's done, and can't be helped.'" Her reference to herself is ironic. She, of course, has not committed the violence that the Doctor's systematized language allowed people to inflict upon themselves. His system claims to define — and therefore to limit — the hidden, but it robs life of possibility. Miss Prissy, by delivering her message, restores life to its proper course. Revelation renews a possibility for living the truth. Mary will not have to mask her real affections, as she would have had she married Dr Hopkins.

Since Miss Prissy reveals the truth, which allows for the expansion of human experience, it is appropriate that, after Mrs. Stowe shows the

Doctor giving Mary to James and writes "thus ended THE MINISTER'S WOOING," the book should continue in a letter by Miss Prissy. She writes to her sister, concluding with her plan to study Dr. Hopkins's system because of his character and despite the fact that she cannot understand it. Her last statement in the book indicates that finally, like James, she interprets the Bible for herself.

James's discovery of new possibilities for conversion and Miss Prissy's unmasking of the truth are not the only reasons for the young hero's success. Within the comic construction the supernatural may influence events. Sacrifice or self-denial imitates divine action and guides the outcome of this novel. Within a week of James's arrival home, Mary is to become the wife of Dr. Hopkins. She has made a vow to him, which, in a covenant society, cannot be broken. It is the Doctor himself who releases Mary from her vow. Mrs. Stowe carefully delineates in Chapter XL the intensity of the Doctor's struggle with himself. He does not want to give up his young bride and struggles with himself until he can exchange happiness for blessedness. His own system of control, however rational, is inadequate to the situation. It is not the proper means to an end. "Numbering all the proof-texts for one of the chapters of his theological system" only calms him until he can pray and imitate Christ. He concludes "that blessedness, which was all the portion his Master had on earth, might do for him also; and therefore he kissed and blessed that silver dove of happiness, which he saw was weary of sailing in his clumsy old ark, and let it go out of his hand without a tear."

The Doctor watches James and Mary leave — the ostensible end of the story. But the novel continues, as has been seen, redefining its own limits, just as James through his experience has broadened the possibilities for conversion. Now, too, its title can be reinterpreted. The minister himself has been wooed from strict enforcement of the covenant to an imitation of Christ's Passion, a self-sacrifice. The novel closes with a reconciliation. If James has overcome the Doctor, the Doctor, changed, has won James. The release of Mary from her vow, James tells the Doctor, "'tells on my heart more than any sermon you ever preached.'"

In works of comedy, even those characters who must relinquish their authority are reconciled to the new way. So it is that Dr. Hopkins later marries and continues to work and to write. His theological system is published and "proved a success, not only in public acceptance and esteem, but even in a temporal view," although it is no longer the exclusive reference it might have been. It is, as Miss Prissy's plan of study suggests, more compelling as a memorial of Hopkins's character than it is as an authority. Hopkins continues to work, too, with James's help to free the slaves. Their joint effort in this particular task is especially significant. Just as their partnership symbolizes their freedom from an enslaving theological system, so their new work shows their goodwill extending into the political sphere.

The Doctor is completely reconciled, but one major figure in the book, Aaron Burr, is not. The primary task of James, Miss Prissy, and Dr. Hopkins — to form an ideal community by dispelling illusion — is counterpointed by the example of one character who stubbornly refuses to reveal his true self. Burr alone is practically irredeemable. This unregenerate grandson of Jonathan Edwards is deliberately juxtaposed with Dr. Hopkins in Chapter XXXII. Whereas Hopkins is sacrificial and watchful of his worse self, Burr is selfish and suspicious of his sentiment or his better nature. That they both should be guided through life by "an inflexible rigidity" makes them liable to censure, but the Doctor is more malleable than Burr. At one point, Hopkins says that he would give up his theological system if it should keep him from his duty of freeing the slaves. He is, moreover, capable of seeing that interpretations other than his own are possible. He changes. Burr refuses change, however, and is rejected by society.

Unlike Dr. Hopkins, who is convinced that it is wrong to keep a covenant that would have compelled Mary and him to live in a fictional universe of forced love, Burr willfully creates a fiction in which he must live. When Burr receives a letter from Madame de Frontignac, the woman who fascinates him and who loves him, he momentarily sees "what he might be, and what he was."

Burr's denial of his highest potential is what dooms him. His death is anticlimatic. That he should be denied a memorial — as is consistent with history — is hardly surprising. Madame de Frontignac's son does later memorialize him, but in silence, by placing "a plain granite slab" over his grave. Burr cannot be given a name, cannot be remembered, because he has denied his own better nature and through that denial the possibility of reform or change. He hides his feelings, and for this reason the comic vision cannot embrace him. Only Madame de Frontignac, who knows that he can feel, can forgive him. She writes, "'I was almost shipwrecked,'" which, as in James's case, means that she barely escaped the world of sin and despair. But she continues, "'yet I will still say to the last that what I loved in him was a better self, — something really noble and good, however concealed and perverted by pride, ambition, and self-will.'" She has seen through his "habitual mask," still has "'faith in this better nature, and [offers] prayers that he will be led right at last. There is at least one heart that will always intercede with God for him.'"

At the end, as in all comedies, society is unified, but only as its members are noble and brave and merciful. Both Dr. Hopkins and Madame de Frontignac, in self-denial and forgiveness, imitate the graciousness of Christ and so help to save society, which comes to mirror the cohesion of an eternal order. In this new society, man-made systems that have come to be accepted as absolute are found to be unsatisfactory, indeed detrimental. James reverses the starting point of conversion, from God to man, and interprets the Bible for himself. This experiment with tradition validates a higher truth: James makes reinterpretation possible as his own experience leads him on to knowledge of self and of God. His language, neither rigid like Dr. Hopkins's, nor contrived like Burr's, can free society without wreaking vengeance. Only as one can learn and create and "work out his own salvation" can one be saved from self-destruction. "Thus the movement from . . . a society controlled by habit, ritual bondage, arbitrary law and the older characters to a society controlled by youth and pragmatic freedom is fundamentally . . . a movement from illusion to reality. Illusion is whatever is fixed or definable, and reality is best understood as its negation: whatever reality is, it's not *that*."[12]

Mrs. Stowe's later New England novels, *The Pearl of Orr's Island, Oldtown Folks, Poganuc People*, as well as two books set in New York City during the Gilded Age, repeat the pattern set in this novel. Mrs. Stowe continues to unmask philosophies, such as materialism, to advocate a new kind of society based on freedom and mutual acceptance. She envisions America as a theological democracy in which mediating love is the "rule," and responsibility is taken by members of the community rather than devolving from leaders.

Hers is a vision of brotherhood similar to the one Mark Twain later realized in *Adventures of Huckleberry Finn,* written while he was her neighbor in Hartford, Connecticut. Huckleberry Finn's decision to help Jim on his way to freedom at the peril of his own soul typifies the attitude Mrs. Stowe endorses. That Huck must act totally outside of family and society is where the philosophies of the two writers differ. Mrs. Stowe desires the ultimate reform of individual relationships and not irrevocable sacrifice outside society — as the fictional Huck and the historical Dr. Hopkins envisioned. In *Huckleberry Finn* Mark Twain approaches a tragic view. Mrs. Stowe's philosophy is typically comic. Her vision of a reformed America, beginning with individual change, resembles that of Walt Whitman's. Mrs. Stowe celebrates the 19th-century idea of individualism; but, unlike Mark Twain, she remains sympathetic to religious origins.

Mrs. Stowe's vision advocates change; yet, it is conservative. She would keep individuals from harmful subservience, yet keep them also from acting on whim. With the clarity resulting from careful observation and from a keen understanding of New England thought, she is able in *The Minister's Wooing* to shape her materials to conform to the Scriptures she revered. Thus, the new individual freedom of her characters is attended by a shared sense of life's significance and purpose. Her offer of this ideal of community, so radical in her own day and still attractive today — though from how different a perspective! — is the greatest appeal of *The Minister's Wooing*.

Footnotes

1. Charles H. Foster, *The Rungless Ladder*, p. 95.
2. Foster, p. 98.
3. Foster, p.89.
4. Foster, p. 91 ff.
5. Harriet Beecher Stowe, *The Stowe, Beecher, Hooker, Seymour, Day Foundation Bulletin for September, 1961*, p. 11.
6. Stowe, p. 12.
7. Foster, pp. 88-89.
8. Edwards A. Park, *Memoir of the Life and Character of Samuel Hopkins, D. D..*, pp. 257, 258.
9. Forrest Wilson, *Crusader in Crinoline*, p. 452.
10. Northrop Frye, "The Mythos of Spring: Comedy," p. 143.
11. Frye, p. 151.
12. Frye, p. 147.

Bibliography

Foster, Charles H. *The Rungless Ladder: Harriet Beecher Stowe and New England Puritanism.* Durham, N.C.: Duke University Press, 1954.

Frye, Northrop, "The Mythos of Spring: Comedy," *Comedy: Meaning and Form,* edited by Robert W. Corrigan. San Francisco: Chandler Publishing Company, 1965.

Lauter, Paul, ed. *Theories of Comedy.* Garden City, N.Y.: Anchor Books, 1964.

Park, Edwards A, *Memoir of the Life and Character of Samuel Hopkins, D. D.* 2nd ed. Boston: Doctrinal Tract and Book Society, 1854.

Smith, H. Shelton, ed. *Horace Bushnell.* New York: Oxford University Press, 1965.

Stowe, Harriet Beecher. *The Stowe, Beecher, Hooker, Seymour, Day Foundation Bulletin for September, 1961,* edited by Joseph S. Van Why. Hartford: Stowe, Beecher, Hooker, Seymour, Day Foundation, 1961.

Wilson, Forrest. *Crusader in Crinoline: The Life of Harriet Beecher Stowe.* Philadelphia: J. B. Lippincott Co., 1941.

THE MINISTER'S WOOING.

CHAPTER I.

PRE-RAILROAD TIMES.

Mrs. Katy Scudder had invited Mrs. Brown, and Mrs. Jones, and Deacon Twitchel's wife to take tea with her on the afternoon of June second, A. D. 17—.

When one has a story to tell, one is always puzzled which end of it to begin at. You have a whole corps of people to introduce that *you* know and your reader doesn't; and one thing so presupposes another, that, whichever way you turn your patchwork, the figures still seem ill-arranged. The small item which I have given will do as well as any other to begin with, as it certainly will lead you to ask, "Pray, who was Mrs. Katy Scudder?"—and this will start me systematically on my story.

You must understand that in the then small seaport-town of Newport, at that time unconscious of its present fashion and fame, there lived nobody in those days who did not know "the Widow Scudder."

1

In New England settlements a custon. has obtain-
ed, which is wholesome and touching, of ennobling
the woman whom God has made desolate, by a sort
of brevet rank which continually speaks for her as a
claim on the respect and consideration of the community. The Widow Jones, or Brown, or Smith, is
one of the fixed institutions of every New England
village,—and doubtless the designation acts as a
continual plea for one whom bereavement, like the
lightning of heaven, has made sacred.

The Widow Scudder, however, was one of the
sort of women who reign queens in whatever society they move; nobody was more quoted, more
deferred to, or enjoyed more unquestioned position
than she. She was not rich,—a small farm, with a
modest, "gambrel-roofed," one-story cottage, was her
sole domain; but she was one of the much-admired
class who, in the speech of New England, are said
to have "faculty,"—a gift which, among that shrewd
people, commands more esteem than beauty, riches,
learning, or any other worldly endowment. *Faculty*
is Yankee for *savoir faire*, and the opposite virtue
to shiftlessness. Faculty is the greatest virtue, and
shiftlessness the greatest vice, of Yankee man and
woman. To her who has faculty nothing shall be
impossible. She shall scrub floors, wash, wring,
bake, brew, and yet her hands shall be small and
white; she shall have no perceptible income, yet
always be handsomely dressed; she shall have not a

servant in her house, — with a dairy to manage, hired men to feed, a boarder or two to care for, unheard-of pickling and preserving to do, — and yet you commonly see her every afternoon sitting at her shady parlor-window behind the lilacs, cool and easy, hemming muslin cap-strings, or reading the last new book. She who hath faculty is never in a hurry, never behindhand. She can always step over to distressed Mrs. Smith, whose jelly won't come, — and stop to show Mrs. Jones how she makes her pickles so green, — and be ready to watch with poor old Mrs. Simpkins, who is down with the rheumatism.

Of this genus was the Widow Scudder, — or, as the neighbors would have said of her, she that *was* Katy Stephens. Katy was the only daughter of a shipmaster, sailing from Newport harbor, who was wrecked off the coast one cold December night, and left small fortune to his widow and only child. Katy grew up, however, a tall, straight, black-eyed girl, with eyebrows drawn true as a bow, a foot arched like a Spanish woman's, and a little hand which never saw the thing it could not do, — quick of speech, ready of wit, and, as such girls have a right to be, somewhat positive withal. Katy could harness a chaise, or row a boat; she could saddle and ride any horse in the neighborhood; she could cut any garment that ever was seen or thought of, make cake, jelly, and wine, from her earliest years,

in most precocious style ;—all without seeming to
derange a sort of trim, well-kept air of ladyhood
that sat jauntily on her.

Of course, being young and lively, she had her
admirers, and some well-to-do in worldly affairs laid
their lands and houses at Katy's feet; but, to the
wonder of all, she would not even pick them up to
look at them. People shook their heads, and wondered whom Katy Stephens expected to get, and
talked about going through the wood to pick up a
crooked stick,—till one day she astonished· her
world by marrying a man that nobody ever thought
of her taking.

George Scudder was a grave, thoughtful young
man,—not given to talking, and silent in the
society of women, with that kind of reverential
bashfulness which sometimes shows a pure, unworldly nature. How Katy came to fancy him
everybody wondered,—for he never talked to her,
never so much as picked up her glove when it fell,
never asked her to ride or sail; in short, everybody
said she must have wanted him from sheer wilfulness, because he of all the young men of the neighborhood never courted her. But Katy, having very
sharp eyes, saw some things that nobody else saw.
For example, you must know she discovered by
mere accident that George Scudder always was
looking at her, wherever she moved, though he
looked away in a moment, if discovered,—and that

an accidental touch of her hand or brush of her dress would send the blood into his cheek like the spirit in the tube of a thermometer; and so, as women are curious, you know, Katy amused herself with investigating the causes of these little phenomena, and, before she knew it, got her foot caught in a cobweb that held her fast, and constrained her, whether she would or no, to marry a poor man that nobody cared much for but herself.

George was, in truth, one of the sort who evidently have made some mistake in coming into this world at all, as their internal furniture is in no way suited to its general courses and currents. He was of the order of dumb poets,—most wretched when put to the grind of the hard and actual; for if he who would utter poetry stretches out his hand to a gainsaying world, he is worse off still who is possessed with the desire of living it. Especially is this the case, if he be born poor, and with a dire necessity upon him of making immediate efforts in the hard and actual. George had a helpless invalid mother to support; so, though he loved reading and silent thought above all things, he put to instant use the only convertible worldly talent he possessed, which was a mechanical genius, and shipped at sixteen as a ship-carpenter. He studied navigation in the forecastle, and found in its calm diagrams and tranquil eternal signs food for his thoughtful nature, and a refuge from the brutality and coarseness of sea-life. He had a healthful, kindly animal nature, and so his inwardness did not ferment and turn to Byronic sourness and bitterness; nor did he needlessly parade to everybody in his vicinity the great gulf which lay between him and them. He was called a good fellow, — only a little lumpish, — and as he was brave and faithful, he rose in time to be a ship-master. But when came the business of making money, the aptitude for accumulating, George found himself distanced by many a one with not half his general powers.

What shall a man do with a sublime tier of moral faculties, when the most profitable business out of his port is the slave-trade? So it was in Newport in those days. George's first voyage was on a slaver, and he wished himself dead many a time before it was over, — and ever after would talk like a man beside himself, if the subject was named. He declared that the gold made in it was distilled from human blood, from mothers' tears, from the agonies and dying groans of gasping, suffocating men and women, and that it would sear and blister the soul of him that touched it; in short, he talked as whole-souled, unpractical fellows are apt to talk about what respectable people sometimes do. Nobody had ever instructed him that a slave-ship, with a procession of expectant sharks in its wake, is a missionary institution, by which closely-packed heathens are brought over to enjoy the light of the gospel.

So, though George was acknowledged to be a good fellow, and honest as the noon-mark on the kitchen floor, he let slip so many chances of making money as seriously to compromise his reputation among thriving folks. He was wastefully gener-ous, — insisted on treating every poor dog that came in his way, in any foreign port, as a brother, — absolutely refused to be party in cheating or deceiving the heathen on any shore, or in skin of any color, — and also took pains, as far as in him lay, to spoil any bargains which any of his subor-dinates founded on the ignorance or weakness of his fellow-men. So he made voyage after voyage, and gained only his wages and the reputation among his employers of an incorruptibly honest fellow.

To be sure, it was said that he carried out books in his ship, and read and studied, and wrote obser-vations on all the countries he saw, which Parson Smith told Miss Dolly Persimmon would really do credit to a printed book ; but then they never *were* printed, or, as Miss Dolly remarked of them, they never seemed to come to anything, — and coming to anything, as she understood it, meant standing in definite relations to bread and butter.

George never cared, however, for money. He

made enough to keep his mother comfortable, and
tnat was enough for him, till he fell in love with
Katy Stephens. He looked at her through those
glasses which such men carry in their souls, and
she was a mortal woman no longer, but a transfigured, glorified creature,—an object of awe and
wonder. He was actually afraid of her; her glove,
her shoe, her needle, thread, and thimble, her bonnet-
string, everything, in short, she wore or touched, became invested with a mysterious charm. He wondered at the impudence of men that could walk up
and talk to her,— that could ask her to dance with
such an assured air. *Now* he wished he were rich;
he dreamed impossible chances of his coming home
a millionnaire to lay unknown wealth at Katy's feet;
and when Miss Persimmon, the ambulatory dressmaker of the neighborhood, in making up a new
black gown for his mother, recounted how Captain
Blatherem had sent Katy Stephens " 'most the
splendidest India shawl that ever she did see," he
was ready to tear his hair at the thought of his
poverty. But even in that hour of temptation he
did not repent that he had refused all part and lot
in the ship by which Captain Blatherem's money
was made, for he knew every timber of it to be
seasoned by the groans and saturated with the
sweat of human agony. True love is a natural
sacrament; and if ever a young man thanks God
for having saved what is noble and manly in his

soul, it is when he thinks of offering it to the woman he loves. Nevertheless, the India-shawl story cost him a night's rest; nor was it till Miss Persimmon had ascertained, by a private confabulation with Katy's mother, that she had indignantly rejected it, and that she treated the Captain "real ridiculous," that he began to take heart. "He ought not," he said, "to stand in her way now, when he had nothing to offer. No, he would leave Katy free to do better, if she could; he would try his luck; and if, when he came home from the next voyage, Katy was disengaged, why, then he would lay all at her feet."

And so George was going to sea with a secret shrine in his soul, at which he was to burn unsuspected incense.

But, after all, the mortal maiden whom he adored suspected this private arrangement, and contrived — as women will — to get her own key into the lock of his secret temple; because, as girls say, "she was *determined* to know what was there." So, one night, she met him quite accidentally on the sea-sands, struck up a little conversation, and begged him in such a pretty way to bring her a spotted shell from the South Sea, like the one on his mother's mantel-piece, and looked so simple and childlike in saying it, that our young man very imprudently committed himself by remarking, that, "When people had rich friends to bring them all

the world from foreign parts, he never dreamed of
her wanting so trivial a thing."

Of course Katy " didn't know what he meant, —
she hadn't heard of any rich friends." And then
came something about Captain Blatherem ; and
Katy tossed her head, and said, " If anybody
wanted to insult her, they might talk to her about
Captain Blatherem," — and then followed this, that,
and the other, till finally, as you might expect, out
came all that never was to have been said ; and
Katy was almost frightened at the terrible earnestness of the spirit she had evoked. She tried to
laugh, and ended by crying, and saying she hardly
knew what ; but when she came to herself in her
own room at home, she found on her finger a ring of
African gold that George had put there, which she
did not send back like Captain Blatherem's presents.

Katy was like many intensely matter-of-fact and
practical women, who have not in themselves a bit
of poetry or a particle of ideality, but who yet worship these qualities in others with the homage which
the Indians paid to the unknown tongue of the
first whites. They are secretly weary of a certain
conscious dryness of nature in themselves, and this
weariness predisposes them to idolize the man who
brings them this unknown gift. Naturalists say that
every defect of organization has its compensation,
and men of ideal natures find in the favor of women
the equivalent for their disabilities among men.

Do you remember, at Niagara, a little cataract on the American side, which throws its silver sheeny veil over a cave called the Grot of Rainbows? Whoever stands on a rock in that grotto sees himself in the centre of a rainbow-circle, above, below, around. In like manner, merry, chatty, positive, busy, housewifely, Katy saw herself standing in a rainbow-shrine in her lover's inner soul, and liked to see herself so. A woman, by-the-by, must be very insensible, who is not moved to come upon a higher plane of being, herself, by seeing how undoubtingly she is insphered in the heart of a good and noble man. A good man's faith in you, fair lady, if you ever have it, will make you better and nobler even before you know it.

Katy made an excellent wife; she took home her husband's old mother and nursed her with a dutifulness and energy worthy of all praise, and made her own keen outward faculties and deft handiness a compensation for the defects in worldly estate. Nothing would make Katy's black eyes flash quicker than any reflections on her husband's want of luck in the material line. "She didn't know whose business it was, if *she* was satisfied. She hated these sharp, gimlet, gouging sort of men that would put a screw between body and soul for money. George had that in him that nobody understood. She would rather be his wife on bread and water than to take Captain Blatherem's house carriages, and horses, and all, — and she *might* have had 'em fast enough, dear knows. She was sick of making money when she saw what sort of men could make it," — and so on. All which talk did her infinite credit, because after all she *did* care, and was naturally as proud and ambitious a little minx as ever breathed, and was thoroughly grieved at heart at George's want of worldly success; but, like a nice little Robin Redbreast, she covered up the grave of her worldliness with the leaves of true love, and sung a " Who cares for that?" above it.

Her thrifty management of the money her husband brought her soon bought a snug little farm, and put up the little brown gambrel-roofed cottage to which we directed your attention in the first of our story. Children were born to them; and George found, in short intervals between voyages, his home an earthly paradise. He was still sailing, with the fond illusion, in every voyage, of making enough to remain at home, — when the yellow fever smote him under the line, and the ship returned to Newport without its captain.

George was a Christian man; — he had been one of the first to attach himself to the unpopular and unworldly ministry of the celebrated Dr. Hopkins, and to appreciate the sublime ideality and unselfishness of those teachings which then were awakening new sensations in the theological mind of New England. Katy, too, had become a professor with her husband in the same church, and her husband's death in the midst of life deepened the power of her religious impressions. She became absorbed in religion, after the fashion of New England, where devotion is doctrinal, not ritual. As she grew older, her energy of character, her vigor and good judgment, caused her to be regarded as a mother in Israel; the minister boarded at her house, and it was she who was first to be consulted in all matters relating to the well-being of the church. No woman could more manfully breast a long sermon, or bring a more determined faith to the reception of a difficult doctrine. To say the truth, there lay at the bottom of her doctrinal system this stable corner-stone, — "Mr. Scudder used to believe it, — *I* will." And after all that is said about independent thought, isn't the fact, that a just and good soul has thus or thus believed, a more respectable argument than many that often are adduced? If it be not, more's the pity, — since two thirds of the faith in the world is built on no better foundation.

In time, George's old mother was gathered to her son, and two sons and a daughter followed their father to the invisible, — one only remaining of the flock, and she a person with whom you and I, good reader, have joint concern in the further unfolding of our story.

CHAPTER II.

THE KITCHEN.

As I before remarked, Mrs. Katy Scudder had in
vited company to tea.   Strictly speaking, it is neces
sary to begin with the creation of the world, in order
to give a full account of anything.   But, for popular
use, something less may serve one's turn, and therefore I shall let the past chapter suffice to introduce
my story, and shall proceed to arrange my scenery
and act my little play, on the supposition that you
know enough to understand things and persons.

Being asked to tea in our New England in the
year 17— meant something very different from the
same invitation in our more sophisticated days.   In
those times, people held to the singular opinion that
the night was made to sleep in; they inferred it
from a general confidence they had in the wisdom
of Mother Nature, supposing that she did not put
out her lights and draw her bed-curtains and hush
all noise in her great world-house without strongly
intending that her children should go to sleep; and
the consequence was, that very soon after sunset the
whole community very generally set their faces bed-

ward, and the tolling of the nine-o'clock evening-bell had an awful solemnity in it, announcing the end of all respectable proceedings in life for that day. Good society in New England in those days very generally took its breakfast at six, its dinner at twelve, and its tea at six. " Company tea," how-ever, among thrifty, industrious folk, was often taken an hour earlier, because each of the *invitées* had children to put to bed, or other domestic cares at home; and, as in those simple times people were invited because you wanted to see them, a tea-party assembled themselves at three and held session till sundown, when each matron rolled up her knitting-work and wended soberly home.

Though Newport, even in those early times, was not without its families which affected state and splendor, rolled about in carriages with armorial em-blazonments, and had servants in abundance to every turn within-doors, yet there, as elsewhere in New England, the majority of the people lived with the wholesome, thrifty simplicity of the olden time, when labor and intelligence went hand in hand in perhaps a greater harmony than the world has ever seen.

Our scene opens in the great, old-fashioned kitch-en, which, on ordinary occasions, is the family din-ing and sitting-room of the Scudder family I know fastidious moderns think that the working-room wherein are carried on the culinary operations of a large family, must necessarily be an untidy and comfortless sitting-place; but it is only because they are ignorant of the marvellous workings which pertain to the organ of " faculty," on which we have before insisted. The kitchen of a New England matron was her throne-room, her pride; it was the habit of her life to produce the greatest possible results there with the slightest possible discomposure; and what any woman could do, Mrs. Katy Scudder could do *par excellence*. Everything there seemed to be always done and never doing. Washing and baking, those formidable disturbers of the composure of families, were all over with in those two or three morning-hours when we are composing ourselves for a last nap,—and only the fluttering of linen over the green yard, on Monday mornings, proclaimed that the dreaded solemnity of a wash had transpired. A breakfast arose there as by magic; and in an incredibly short space after, every knife, fork, spoon, and trencher, clean and shining, was looking as innocent and unconscious in its place as if it never had been used and never expected to be.

The floor,— perhaps, Sir, you remember your grandmother's floor, of snowy boards sanded with whitest sand; you remember the ancient fireplace stretching quite across one end,—a vast cavern, in each corner of which a cozy seat might be found, distant enough to enjoy the crackle of the great jolly

wood-fire; across the room ran a dresser, on which
was displayed great store of shining pewter dishes
and plates, which always shone with the same mysterious brightness; and by the side of the fire, a
commodious wooden "settee," or settle, offered repose to people too little accustomed to luxury to ask
for a cushion.   Oh, that kitchen of the olden times,
the old, clean, roomy New England kitchen!— who
that has breakfasted, dined, and supped in one has
not cheery visions of its thrift, its warmth, its coolness?   The noon-mark on its floor was a dial that
told off some of the happiest days; thereby did we
right up the short-comings of the solemn old clock
that tick-tacked in the corner, and whose ticks
seemed mysterious prophecies of unknown good yet
to arise out of the hours of life.   How dreamy the
winter twilight came in there,—when as yet the
candles were not lighted,—when the crickets chirped
around the dark stone hearth, and shifting tongues
of flame flickered and cast dancing shadows and elf-
ish lights on the walls, while grandmother nodded
over her knitting-work, and puss purred, and old
Rover lay dreamily opening now one eye and then
the other on the family group!   With all our ceiled
houses, let us not forget our grandmothers' kitchens!

  But we must pause, however, and back to our
subject-matter, which is in the kitchen of Mrs. Katy
Scudder, who has just put into the oven, by the fireplace, some wondrous tea-rusks, for whose composi-

tion she is renowned. She has examined and pro
nounced perfect a loaf of cake, which has been
prepared for the occasion, and which, as usual, is
done exactly right. The best room, too, has been
opened and aired,— the white window-curtains saluted with a friendly little shake, as when one says,
" How d'ye do ? " to a friend ;— for you must know,
clean as our kitchen is, we are genteel, and have
something better for company. Our best room in
here has a polished little mahogany tea-table, and
six mahogany chairs, with claw talons grasping
balls; the white sanded floor is crinkled in curious
little waves, like those on the seabeach ; and right
across the corner stands the " buffet," as it is called,
with its transparent glass doors, wherein are displayed the solemn appurtenances of company tea-
table. There you may see a set of real China
teacups, which George bought in Canton, and had
marked with his and his wife's joint initials, — a
small silver cream-pitcher, which has come down
as an heirloom from unknown generations, — silver
spoons and delicate China cake-plates, which have
been all carefully reviewed and wiped on napkins of
Mrs. Scudder's own weaving.

Her cares now over, she stands drying her hands
on a roller-towel in the kitchen, while her only
daughter, the gentle Mary, stands in the doorway
with the afternoon sun streaming in spots of flickering golden light on her smooth pale-brown hair,—

a *petite* figure in a full stuff petticoat and white short gown, she stands reaching up one hand and cooing to something among the apple-blossoms,— and now a Java dove comes whirring down and settles on her finger,— and we, that have seen pictures, think, as we look on her girlish face, with its lines of statuesque beauty, on the tremulous, half-infantine expression of her lovely mouth, and the general air of simplicity and purity, of some old pictures of the girlhood of the Virgin. But Mrs. Scudder was thinking of no such Popish matter, I can assure you,— not she! I don't think you could have done her a greater indignity than to mention her daughter in any such connection. She had never seen a painting in her life, and therefore was not to be reminded of them; and furthermore, the dove was evidently, for some reason, no favorite,— for she said, in a quick, imperative tone, " Come, come, child! don't fool with that bird,— it's high time we were dressed and ready," — and Mary, blushing, as it would seem, even to her hair, gave a little toss, and sent the bird, like a silver fluttering cloud, up among the rosy apple-blossoms. And now she and her mother have gone to their respective little bedrooms for the adjustment of their toilettes; and while the door is shut and nobody hears us, we shall talk to you about Mary.

Newport at the present day blooms like a flower-garden with young ladies of the best *ton*,— lovely girls, hopes of their families, possessed of amiable tempers and immensely large trunks, and capable of sporting ninety changes of raiment in thirty days and otherwise rapidly emptying the purses of distressed fathers, and whom yet travellers and the world in general look upon as genuine specimens of the kind of girls formed by American institutions.

We fancy such a one lying in a rustling silk *négligée*, and, amid a gentle generality of rings, ribbons, puffs, laces, beaux, and dinner-discussion, reading our humble sketch;— and what favor shall our poor heroine find in her eyes? For though her mother was a world of energy and "faculty," in herself considered, and had bestowed on this one little lone chick all the vigor and all the care and all the training which would have sufficed for a family of sixteen, there were no results produced which could be made appreciable in the eyes of such company. She could not waltz or polk, or speak bad French, or sing Italian songs; but, nevertheless, we must proceed to say what was her education and what her accomplishments.

Well, then, she could both read and write fluently in the mother-tongue. She could spin both on the little and the great wheel; and there were numberless towels, napkins, sheets, and pillow-cases in the household store that could attest the skill of her pretty fingers. She had worked several samplers of such rare merit, that they hung framed in different rooms of the house, exhibiting every variety and style of possible letter in the best marking-stitch. She was skilful in all sewing and embroidery, in all shaping and cutting, with a quiet and deft handiness that constantly surprised her energetic mother, who could not conceive that so much could be done with so little noise. In fact, in all household lore she was a veritable good fairy; her knowledge seemed unerring and intuitive; and whether she washed or ironed, or moulded biscuit or conserved plums, her gentle beauty seemed to turn to poetry all the prose of life.

There was something in Mary, however, which divided her as by an appreciable line from ordinary girls of her age. From her father she had inherited a deep and thoughtful nature, predisposed to moral and religious exaltation. Had she been born in Italy, under the dissolving influences of that sunny dreamy clime, beneath the shadow of cathedrals, and where pictured saints and angels smiled in clouds of painting from every arch and altar, she might, like fair St. Catherine of Siena, have seen beatific visions in the sunset skies, and a silver dove descending upon her as she prayed; but, unfolding in the clear, keen, cold New England clime, and nurtured in its abstract and positive theologies, her religious faculties took other forms. Instead of lying entranced in mysterious raptures at the foot of altars, she read and pondered treatises on the Will, and listened in rapt attention, while her spiritual guide, the venerated Dr. Hopkins, unfolded to her the theories of the great Edwards on the nature of true virtue. Womanlike, she felt the subtile poetry of these sublime abstractions which dealt with such infinite and unknown quantities, — which spoke of the universe, of its great Architect, of man, of angels, as matters of intimate and daily contemplation; and her teacher, a grand-minded and simple-hearted man as ever lived, was often amazed at the tread with which this fair young child walked through these high regions of abstract thought, — often comprehending through an ethereal clearness of nature what he had laboriously and heavily reasoned out; and sometimes, when she turned her grave, childlike face upon him with some question or reply, the good man started as if an angel had looked suddenly out upon him from a cloud. Unconsciously to himself, he often seemed to follow her, as Dante followed the flight of Beatrice, through the ascending circles of the celestial spheres.

When her mother questioned him, anxiously, of her daughter's spiritual estate, he answered, that she was a child of a strange graciousness of nature, and of a singular genius; to which Katy responded with a woman's pride, that she was all her father' over again. It is only now and then that a matter-of-fact woman is sublimated by a real love; but if she is, it is affecting to see how impossible it is for death to quench it; for in the child the mother feels that she has a mysterious and undying repossession of the father.

But, in truth, Mary was only a recast in feminine form of her father's nature. The elixir of the spirit that sparkled within her was of that quality of which the souls of poets and artists are made ; but the keen New England air crystalizes emotions into ideas, and restricts many a poetic soul to the necessity of expressing itself only in practical living.

The rigid theological discipline of New England is fitted to produce rather strength and purity than enjoyment. It was not fitted to make a sensitive and thoughtful nature happy, however it might ennoble and exalt.

The system of Dr. Hopkins was one that could have had its origin in a soul at once reverential and logical — a soul, moreover, trained from its earliest years in the habits of thought engendered by monarchical institutions. For although he, like other ministers, took an active part as a patriot in the Revolution, still he was brought up under the shadow of a throne, and a man cannot ravel out the stitches in which early days have knit him. His theology was, in fact, the turning to an invisible Sovereign of that spirit of loyalty and unquestioning subjugation which is one of the noblest capabilities of our nature. And as a gallant soldier renounces life and personal aims in the cause of his

king and country, and holds himself ready to be
drafted for a forlorn hope, to be shot down, or help
make a bridge of his mangled body, over which the
more fortunate shall pass to victory and glory, so he
regarded himself as devoted to the King Eternal,
ready in His hands to be used to illustrate and build
up an Eternal Commonwealth, either by being sacri-
ficed as a lost spirit or glorified as a redeemed one,
ready to throw not merely his mortal life, but his immortality even, into the forlorn hope, to bridge with
a never-dying soul the chasm over which white-robed
victors should pass to a commonwealth of glory and
splendor whose vastness should dwarf the misery of
all the lost to an infinitesimal.

It is not in our line to imply the truth or the falsehood of those systems of philosophic theology which
seem for many years to have been the principal out-
let for the proclivities of the New England mind,
but as psychological developments they have an intense interest. He who does not see a grand side to
these strivings of the soul cannot understand one of
the noblest capabilities of humanity.

No real artist or philosopher ever lived who has
not at some hours risen to the height of utter self-
abnegation for the glory of the invisible. There
have been painters who would have been crucified
to demonstrate the action of a muscle, — chemists
who would gladly have melted themselves and all
humanity in their crucible, if so a new discovery

might arise out of its fumes. Even persons of mere artistic sensibility are at times raised by music, painting, or poetry to a momentary trance of self-oblivion, in which they would offer their whole being before the shrine of an invisible loveliness. These hard old New England divines were the poets of metaphysical philosophy, who built systems in an artistic fervor, and felt self exhale from beneath them as they rose into the higher regions of thought. But where theorists and philosophers tread with sublime assurance, woman often follows with bleeding footsteps;—women are always turning from the abstract to the individual, and feeling where the philosopher only thinks.

It was easy enough for Mary to believe in *self-*renunciation, for she was one with a born vocation for martyrdom; and so, when the idea was put to her of suffering eternal pains for the glory of God and the good of being in general, she responded to it with a sort of sublime thrill, such as it is given to some natures to feel in view of uttermost sacrifice. But when she looked around on the warm, living faces of friends, acquaintances and neighbors, viewing them as possible candidates for dooms so fearfully different, she sometimes felt the walls of her faith closing round her as an iron shroud,—she wondered that the sun could shine so brightly, that lowers could flaunt such dazzling colors, that sweet airs could breathe, and little children play, and youth

love and hope, and a thousand intoxicating influences combine to cheat the victims from the thought
that their next step might be into an abyss of hor-
rors without end. The blood of youth and hope was
saddened by this great sorrow, which lay ever on her
heart, — and her life, unknown to herself, was a
sweet tune in the minor key ; it was only in prayer,
or deeds of love and charity, or in rapt contemplation of that beautiful millennial day, which her
spiritual guide most delighted to speak of, that the
tone of her feelings ever rose to the height of joy.

Among Mary's young associates was one who
had been as a brother to her childhood. He was
her mother's cousin's son, — and so, by a sort of
family immunity, had always a free access to her
mother's house. He took to the ·sea, as the most
bold and resolute young men will, and brought
home from foreign parts those new modes of
speech, those other eyes for received opinions and
established things, which so often shock established
prejudices, — so that he was held as little better
than an infidel and a castaway by the stricter religious circles in his native place. Mary's mother,
now that Mary was grown up to woman's estate,
looked with a severe eye on her cousin. She
warned her daughter against too free an association with him, — and so —— We all know what
comes to pass when girls are constantly warned
not to think of a man. The most conscientious

and obedient little person in the world, Mary resolved to be very careful. She never would think
of James, except, of course, in her prayers; but as
these were constant, it may easily be seen it was
not easy to forget him.

All that was so often told her of his carelessness,
his trifling, his contempt of orthodox opinions, and
his startling and bold expressions, only wrote his
name deeper in her heart,—for was not his soul in
peril? Could she look in his frank, joyous face and
listen to his thoughtless laugh, and then think that
a fall from mast-head, or one night's storm, might
—— Ah, with what images her faith filled the blank!
Could she believe all this and forget him?

You see, instead of getting our tea ready, as we
promised at the beginning of this chapter, we have
filled it with descriptions and meditations,—and
now we foresee that the next chapter will be equally
far from the point. But have patience with us; for
we can write only as we are driven, and never know
exactly where we are going to land.

CHAPTER III.

THE INTERVIEW.

A QUIET, maiden-like place was Mary's little
room.   The window looked out under the over-
arching boughs of a thick apple-orchard, now all
in a blush with blossoms and pink-tipped buds, and
the light came golden-green, strained through flickering leaves, — and an ever-gentle rustle and whirr of
branches and blossoms, a chitter of birds, and an
indefinite whispering motion, as the long heads of
orchard-grass nodded and bowed to each other under
the trees, seemed to give the room the quiet hush of
some little side-chapel in a cathedral, where green
and golden glass softens the sunlight, and only the
sigh and rustle of kneeling worshippers break the stillness of the aisles.   It was small enough for a nun's
apartment, and dainty in its neatness as the waxen
cell of . a bee.   The bed and low window were
draped in spotless white, with fringes of Mary's own
knotting.   A small table under the looking-glass
bore the library of a well-taught young woman of
those times.   " The Spectator," " Paradise Lost,"
Shakspeare, and " Robinson Crusoe," stood for the

admitted secular literature, and beside them the Bible and the works then published of Mr. Jonathan Edwards. Laid a little to one side as if of doubtful reputation, was the only novel which the stricter people in those days allowed for the reading of their daughters: that seven-volumed, trailing, tedious, delightful old bore, " Sir Charles Grandison," — a book whose influence in those times was so universal, that it may be traced in the epistolary style even of the gravest divines. Our little heroine was mortal, with all her divinity, and had an imagination which sometimes wandered to the things of earth; and this glorious hero in lace and embroidery, who blended rank, gallantry, spirit, knowledge of the world, disinterestedness, constancy, and piety, sometimes stepped before her, while she sat spinning at her wheel, till she sighed, she hardly knew why, that no such men walked the earth now. Yet it is to be confessed, this occasional raid of the romantic into Mary's balanced and well-ordered mind was soon energetically put to rout, and the book, as we have said, remained on her table under protest, — protected by being her father's gift to her mother during their days of courtship. The small looking-glass was curiously wreathed with corals and foreign shells, so disposed as to indicate an artistic eye and skilful hand; and some curious Chinese paintings of birds and flowers gave rather a piquant and foreign air to the otherwise homely neatness of the apartment.

Hére in this little retreat Mary spent those few hours which her exacting conscience would allow her to spare from her busy-fingered household-life here she read and wrote and thought and prayed; — and here she stands·now, arraying herself for the tea company that afternoon. Dress, which in our day is becoming in some cases the whole of woman, was in those times a remarkably simple affair. True, every person of a certain degree of respectability had state and festival robes; and a certain camphor-wood brass-bound trunk, which was always kept solemnly locked in Mrs. Katy Scudder's apartment, if it could have spoken, might have given off quite a catalogue of brocade satin and laces. The wedding-suit there slumbered in all the unsullied whiteness of its stiff ground broidered with heavy knots of flowers; and there were scarfs of wrought India muslin and embroidered crape, each of which had its history, — for each had been brought into the door with beating heart on some return voyage of one who, alas, should return no more! The old trunk stood with its histories, its imprisoned remembrances, — and a thousand tender thoughts seemed to be shaken out of every rustling fold of silk and embroidery, on the few yearly occasions when all were brought out to be aired, their history related, and then solemnly locked up again. Nevertheless, the possession of these things gave to the women of an establishment a certain innate dignity, like a good conscience; so that in that larger portion of existence commonly denominated among them "every day," they were content with plain stuff and homespun. Mary's toilette, therefore, was sooner made than those of Newport belles of the present day; it simply consisted in changing her ordinary "short gown and petticoat" for another of somewhat nicer materials, — a skirt of India chintz and a striped jacconet short-gown. Her hair was of the kind which always lies like satin; but, nevertheless, girls never think their toilette complete unless the smoothest hair has been shaken down and rearranged. A few moments, however, served to braid its shining folds and dispose them in their simple knot on the back of the head; and having given a final stroke to each side with her little dimpled hands, she sat down a moment at the window, thoughtfully watching where the afternoon sun was creeping through the slats of the fence in long lines of gold among the tall, tremulous orchard-grass, and unconsciously she began warbling, in a low, gurgling voice, the words of a familiar hymn, whose grave earnestness accorded well with the general tone of her life and education : —

> "Life is the time to serve the Lord,
> The time to insure the great reward."

There was a swish and rustle in the orchard-grass, and a tramp of elastic steps; then the branches were brushed aside, and a young man suddenly emerged from the trees a little behind Mary. He was apparently about twenty-five, dressed in the holiday rig of a sailor on shore, which well set off his fine athletic figure, and accorded with a sort of easy, dashing, and confident air which sat not unhandsomely on him. For the rest, a high forehead shaded by rings of the blackest hair, a keen, dark eye, a firm and determined mouth, gave the impression of one who had engaged to do battle with life, not only with a will, but with shrewdness and ability.

He introduced the colloquy by stepping deliberately behind Mary, putting his arms round her neck, and kissing her.

" Why, James!" said Mary, starting up, and blushing. " Come, now!"

" I have come, haven't I?" said the young man, leaning his elbow on the window-seat and looking at her with an air of comic determined frankness, which yet had in it such wholesome honesty that it was scarcely possible to be angry. " The fact is, Mary," he added, with a sudden earnest darkening of the face, " I won't stand this nonsense any longer. Aunt Katy has been holding me at arm's length ever since I got home; and what have I done? Haven't I been to every prayer-meeting and lecture and sermon, since I got into port, just as regular as a psalm-book? and not a bit of a word could I get with you, and no chance even so much as to give you my arm. Aunt Kate always comes between us and says, ' Here, Mary, you take my arm.' What does she think I go to meeting for, and almost break my jaws keeping down the gapes? I never even go to sleep, and yet I'm treated in this way! It's too bad! What's the row? What's anybody been saying about me? I always have waited on you ever since you were that high. Didn't I always draw you to school on my sled? didn't we always use to do our sums together? didn't I always wait on you to singing-school? and I've been made free to run in and out as if I were your brother; — and now she is as glum and stiff, and always stays in the room every minute of the time that I am there, as if she was afraid I should be in some mischief. It's too bad!"

" Oh, James, I am sorry that you only go to meeting for the sake of seeing me; you feel no real interest in religious things; and besides, mother thinks now I'm grown so old, that—— Why, you know things are different now, — at least, we mustn't, you know, always do as we did when we were children. But I wish you did feel more interested in good things."

" I *am* interested in one or two good things, Mary, — principally in you, who are the best I know of. Besides," he said quickly, and scanning her face attentively to see the effect of his words,

2 *

"don't you think there is more merit in my sit-ting out all these meetings, when they bore me so confoundedly, than there is in your and Aunt Katy's doing it, who really seem to find something to like in them? I believe you have a sixth sense, quite unknown to me; for it's all a maze, — I can't find top, nor bottom, nor side, nor up, nor down to it,—it's you can and you can't, you shall and you sha'n't, you will and you won't,"——

"James!"

"You needn't look at me so. I'm not going to say the rest of it. But, seriously, it's all anywhere and nowhere to me; it don't touch me, it don't help me, and I think it rather makes me worse; and then they tell me it's because I'm a natural man, and the natural man understandeth not the things of the Spirit. Well, I *am* a natural man, — how's a fellow to help it?"

"Well, James, why need you talk everywhere as you do? You joke, and jest, and trifle, till it seems to everybody that you don't believe in anything. I'm afraid mother thinks you are an infidel. but I *know* that can't be; yet we hear of all sorts of things that you say."

"I suppose you mean my telling Deacon Twitch-el that I had seen as good Christians among the Mahometans as any in Newport. *Didn't* I make him open his eyes? It's true, too!"

"In every nation, he that feareth God and worketh righteousness is accepted of Him," said Mary; " and if there are better Christians than we are among the Mahometans, I am sure I'm glad of it. But, after all, the great question is, ' Are we Christians ourselves ? ' Oh, James, if you only were a real, true, noble Christian!"

" Well, Mary, you have got into that harbor, through all the sandbars and rocks and crooked channels; and now do you think it right to leave a fellow beating about outside, and not go out to help him in? This way of drawing up, among you good people, and leaving us sinners to ourselves, isn't generous. You might care a little for the soul of an old friend, anyhow!"

" And don't I care, James ? How many days and nights have been one prayer for you! If I could take my hopes of heaven out of my own heart and give them to you, I would. Dr. Hopkins preached last Sunday on the text, 'I could wish myself accursed from Christ for my brethren, my kinsmen'; and he went on to show how we must be willing to give up even our own salvation, if necessary, for the good of others. People said it was hard doctrine, but I could feel my way through it very well. Yes, I would give my soul for yours; I wish I could."

There was a solemnity and pathos in Mary's manner which checked the conversation. James was the more touched because he felt it all so real.

from one whose words were always yea and nay
so true, so inflexibly simple. Her eyes filled with
tears, her face kindled with a sad earnestness, and
James thought, as he looked, of a picture he
had once seen in a European cathedral, where
the youthful Mother of Sorrows is represented,

> " Radiant and grave, as pitying man's decline;
> All youth, but with an aspect beyond time;
> Mournful, but mournful of another's crime;
> She looked as if she sat by Eden's door,
> And grieved for those who should return no more."

James had thought he loved Mary; he had admired her remarkable beauty, he had been proud
of a certain right in her before that of other young
men, her associates; he had thought of her as the
keeper of his home; he had wished to appropriate
her wholly to himself; — but in all this there had
been, after all, only the thought of what she was
to be to him; and, for this poor measure of what
he called love, she was ready to offer, an infinite
sacrifice.

As a subtile flash of lightning will show in a
moment a whole landscape, tower, town, winding
stream, and distant sea, so that one subtile ray of
feeling seemed in a moment to reveal to James
the whole of his past life; and it seemed to him
so poor, so meagre, so shallow, by the side of that
childlike woman, to whom the noblest of feelings

were unconscious matters of course, that a sort of awe awoke in him; like the Apostles of old, he "feared as he entered into the cloud"; it seemed as if the deepest string of some eternal sorrow had vibrated between them.

After a moment's pause, he spoke in a low and altered voice:—

"Mary, I am a sinner. No psalm or sermon ever taught it to me, but I see it now. Your mother is quite right, Mary; you are too good for me; I am no mate for you. Oh, what would you think of me, if you knew me wholly? I have lived a mean, miserable, shallow, unworthy life. You are worthy, you are a saint, and walk in white! Oh, what upon earth could ever make you care so much for me?"

"Well, then, James, you will be good? Won't you talk with Dr. Hopkins?"

"Hang Dr. Hopkins!" said James. "Now, Mary, I beg your pardon, but I can't make head or tail of a word Dr. Hopkins says. I don't get hold of it, or know what he would be at. You girls and women don't know your power. Why, Mary, you are a living gospel. You have always had a strange power over us boys. You never talked religion much, but I have seen high fellows come away from being with you as still and quiet as one feels when one goes into a church. I can't understand all the hang of predestination, and moral ability and natural ability, and God's efficiency, and man's agency, which Dr. Hopkins is so engaged about; but I can understand *you,*—*you* can do me good!"

"Oh, James, can I?"

"Mary, I'm going to confess my sins. I saw, that, somehow or other, the wind was against me in Aunt Katy's quarter, and you know we fellows who take up the world in both fists don't like to be beat. If there's opposition, it sets us on. Now I confess I never did care much about religion, but I thought, without being really a hypocrite, I'd just let you try to save my soul for the sake of getting you; for there's nothing surer to hook a woman than trying to save a fellow's soul. It's a dead-shot, generally, that. Now our ship sails to-night, and I thought I'd just come across this path in the orchard to speak to you. You know I used always to bring you peaches and juneatings across this way, and once I brought you a ribbon."

"Yes, I've got it yet, James."

"Well, now, Mary, all this seems mean to me, —mean, to try and trick and snare you, who are so much too good for me. I felt very proud this morning that I was to go out first mate this time, and that I should command a ship next voyage. I meant to have asked you for a promise, but I don't. Only, Mary, just give me your little Bible, and I'll promise to read it all through soberly, and

see what it all comes to. And pray for me; and
if, while I'm gone, a good man comes who loves
you, and is worthy of you, why, take him, Mary,
—that's my advice."

"James, I am not thinking of any such things;
I don't ever mean to be married. And I'm glad
you don't ask me for any promise,—because it
would be wrong to give it; mother doesn't even
like me to be much with you. But I'm sure all
I have said to you to-day is right; I shall tell her
exactly all I have said."

"If Aunt Katy knew what things we fellows are
pitched into, who take the world headforemost, she
wouldn't be so selfish. Mary, you girls and women
don't know the world you live in; you ought to be
pure and good; you are not tempted as we are. You
don't know what men, what women,—no, they're
not women!—what creatures, beset us in every
foreign port, and boarding-houses that are gates
of hell; and then, if a fellow comes back from all
this and don't walk exactly straight, you just draw
up the hems of your garments and stand close to
the wall, for fear he should touch you when he
passes. I don't mean you, Mary, for you are different from most; but if you would do what you
could, you might save us.—But it's no use talking, Mary. Give me the Bible; and please be kind
to my dove,—for I had a hard time getting him
across the water, and I don't want him to die."

If Mary had spoken all that welled up in her little heart at that moment, she might have said too much; but duty had its habitual seal upon her lips. She took the little Bible from her table and gave it with a trembling hand, and James turned to go. In a moment he turned back, and stood irresolute.

"Mary," he said, "we are cousins; I may never come back; you might kiss me this once."

The kiss was given and received in silence, and James disappeared among the thick trees.

"Come, child," said Aunt Katy, looking in, "there is Deacon Twitchel's chaise in sight,—are you ready?"

"Yes, mother."

CHAPTER IV.

THEOLOGICAL TEA.

Ar the call of her mother, Mary hurried into the " best room," with a strange discomposure of spirit she had never felt before. From childhood, her love for James had been so deep, equable, and intense, that it had never disturbed her with thrills and yearnings; it had grown up in sisterly calmness, and, quietly expanding, had taken possession of her whole nature, without her once dreaming of its power. But this last interview seemed to have struck some great nerve of her being,—and calm as she usually was, from habit, principle, and good health, she shivered and trembled, as she heard his retreating footsteps, and saw the orchard-grass fly back from under his feet. It was as if each step trod on a nerve,—as if the very sound of the rustling grass was stirring something living and sensitive in her soul. And, strangest of all, a vague impression of guilt hovered over her. *Had* she done anything wrong? She did not ask him there; she had not spoken love to him; no, she had only talked to him of his soul, and how she would give hers for his,—oh, so willingly!—and that was not love; it was only what Dr. Hopkins said Christians must always feel.

"Child, what *have* you been doing?" said Aunt Katy, who sat in full flowing chintz petticoat and spotless dimity short-gown, with her company knitting-work in her hands; "your cheeks are as red as peonies. Have you been crying? What's the matter?"

"There is the Deacon's wife, mother," said Mary, turning confusedly, and darting to the entry-door.

Enter Mrs. Twitchel,—a soft, pillowy little elderly lady, whose whole air and dress reminded one of a sack of feathers tied in the middle with a string. A large, comfortable pocket, hung upon the side, disclosed her knitting-work ready for operation; and she zealously cleansed herself with a checked handkerchief from the dust which had accumulated during her ride in the old "one-hoss shay," answering the hospitable salutation of Katy Scudder in that plaintive, motherly voice which belongs to certain nice old ladies, who appear to live in a state of mild chronic compassion for the sins and sorrows of this mortal life generally.

"Why, yes, Miss Scudder, I'm pretty tol'able. I keep goin', and goin'. That's my way. I's a-tellin' the Deacon, this mornin', I didn't see how I *was* to come here this afternoon; but then I *did* want to see Miss Scudder and talk a little about that precious sermon, Sunday. How *is* the Doctor? blessed man! Well, his reward must be great in heaven, if not on earth, as I was a-tellin' the Deacon; and he says to me, says he, 'Polly, we mustn't be man-worshippers.' There, dear," (*to Mary*,) "don't trouble yourself about my bonnet; it a'n't my Sunday one, but I thought 'twould do. Says I to Cerinthy Ann, ' Miss Scudder won't mind, 'cause her heart's set on better things.' I always like to drop a word in season to Cerinthy Ann, 'cause she's clean took up with vanity and dress. Oh, dear! oh, dear me! so different from your blessed daughter, Miss Scudder! Well, it's a great blessin' to be called in one's youth, like Samuel and Timothy; but then we doesn't know the Lord's ways. Sometimes I gets clean discouraged with my children,—but then ag'in I don't know; none on us does. Cerinthy Ann is one of the most master hands to turn off work; she takes hold and goes along like a woman, and nobody never knows when that gal finds the time to do all she does do; and I don't know nothin' what I *should* do without her. Deacon was saying, if ever she was called, she'd be a Martha, and not a Mary; but then she's dreadful opposed to the doctrines. Oh, dear me! oh, dear me! Somehow they seem to rile her all up; and she was a-tellin' me yesterday, when she was a-hangin' out clothes, that she never should get reconciled to Decrees and 'Lection, 'cause she can't see, if things is certain, how folks is to help 'emselves. Says I, ' Cerinthy Ann, folks a'n't to help themselves; they's to submit unconditional.' And she jest slammed down the clothes-basket and went into the house."

When Mrs. Twitchel began to talk, it flowed a steady stream, as when one turns a faucet, that never ceases running till some hand turns it back again; and the occasion that cut the flood short at present was the entrance of Mrs. Brown.

Mr. Simeon Brown was a thriving ship-owner of Newport, who lived in a large house, owned several negro-servants and a span of horses, and affected some state and style in his worldly appearance. A passion for metaphysical Orthodoxy had drawn Simeon to the congregation of Dr. Hopkins, and his wife of course stood by right in a high place there. She was a tall, angular, somewhat hard-favored body, dressed in a style rather above the simple habits of her neighbors, and her whole air spoke the great woman, who in right of her thousands expected to have her say in all that was going on in the world, whether she understood it or not.

On her entrance, mild little Mrs. Twitchel fled from the cushioned rocking-chair, and stood with the quivering air of one who feels she has no business to be anywhere in the world, until Mrs.

Brown's bonnet was taken and she was seated, when Mrs. Twitchel subsided into a corner and rattled her knitting-needles to conceal her emotion.

New England has been called the land of equality; but what land upon earth is wholly so? Even the mites in a bit of cheese, naturalists say, have great tumblings and strivings about position and rank; he who has ten pounds will always be a nobleman to him who has but one, let him strive as manfully as he may; and therefore let us forgive meek little Mrs. Twitchel for melting into nothing in her own eyes when Mrs. Brown came in, and let us forgive Mrs. Brown that she sat down in the rocking-chair with an easy grandeur, as one who thought it her duty to be affable and meant to be. It was, however, rather difficult for Mrs. Brown, with her money, house, negroes, and all, to patronize Mrs. Katy Scudder, who was one of those women whose natures seem to sit on thrones, and who dispense patronage and favor by an inborn right and aptitude, whatever be their social advantages. It was one of Mrs. Brown's trials of life, this secret, strange quality in her neighbor, who stood apparently so far below her in worldly goods. Even the quiet, positive style of Mrs. Katy's knitting made her nervous; it was an implication of independence of her sway; and though on the present occasion every customary courtesy was bestowed, she still felt, as she always did when Mrs. Katy's guest, a secret uneasiness. She mentally contrasted the neat little parlor, with its white sanded floor and muslin curtains, with her own grand front-room, which boasted the then uncommon luxuries of Turkey carpet and Persian rug, and wondered if Mrs. Katy did really feel as cool and easy in receiving her as she appeared.

You must not understand that this was what Mrs. Brown *supposed* herself to be thinking about; oh, no! by no means! All the little, mean work of our nature is generally done in a small dark closet just a little back of the subject we are talking about, on which subject we suppose ourselves of course to be thinking; — of course we *are* thinking of it; how else could we talk about it?

The subject in discussion, and what Mrs. Brown supposed to be in her own thoughts, was the last Sunday's sermon on the doctrine of entire Disinterested Benevolence, in which good Doctor Hopkins had proclaimed to the citizens of Newport their duty of being so wholly absorbed in the general good of the universe as even to acquiesce in their own final and eternal destruction, if the greater good of the whole might thereby be accomplished.

" Well, now, dear me! " said Mrs. Twitchel, while her knitting-needles trotted contentedly to the mournful tone of her voice, — " I was tellin'

the Deacon, if we only could get there! Sometimes I think I get a little way,—but then ag'in
I don't know; but the Deacon he's quite down,—
he don't see no evidences in himself. Sometimes
he says he don't feel as if he ought to keep his
place in the church,—but then ag'in he don't know.
He keeps a-turnin' and turnin' on't over in his
mind, and a-tryin' himself this way and that way;
and he says he don't see nothin' but what's selfish,
no way.

"'Member one night last winter, after the Deacon got warm in bed, there come a rap at the
door; and who should it be but old Beulah Ward,
wantin' to see the Deacon?—'twas her boy she sent,
and he said Beulah was sick and hadn't no more
wood nor candles. Now I know'd the Deacon had
carried that crittur half a cord of wood, if he had
one stick, since Thanksgivin', and I'd sent her two
o' my best moulds of candles,—nice ones that
Cerinthy Ann run when we killed a crittur; but
nothin' would do but the Deacon must get right
out his warm bed and dress himself, and hitch up
his team to carry over some wood to Beulah.
Says I, 'Father, you know you'll be down with
the rheumatis for this; besides, Beulah is real
aggravatin'. I know she trades off what we send
her to the store for rum, and you never get no
thanks. She expects, 'cause we has done for her,
we always must; and more we do more we may

do.' And says he to me, says he, ' That's jest the
way we sarves the Lord, Polly; and what if He
shouldn't hear us when we call on Him in our
troubles?' So I shet up; and the next day he
was down with the rheumatis. And Cerinthy Ann,
says she, ' Well, father, *now* I hope you'll own
you have got *some* disinterested benevolence,' says
she; and the Deacon he thought it over a spell,
and then he says, ' I'm 'fraid it's all selfish. I'm
jest a-makin' a righteousness of it.' And Cerinthy
Ann she come out, declarin' that the best folks
never had no comfort in religion; and for her part
she didn't mean to trouble her head about it, but
have jest as good a time as she could while she's
young, 'cause if she was 'lected to be saved she
should be, and if she wa'n't she couldn't help it,
any how."

" Mr. Brown says he came on to Dr. Hopkins's
ground years ago," said Mrs. Brown, giving a nervous twitch to her yarn, and speaking in a sharp,
hard, didatic voice, which made little Mrs. Twitchel
give a gentle quiver, and look humble and apologetic. " Mr. Brown's a master thinker; there's
nothing pleases that man better than a hard doctrine; he says you can't get 'em too hard for him.
He don't find any difficulty in bringing his mind
up; he just reasons it out all plain; and he says,
people have no need to be in the dark; and that's
my opinion. ' If folks know they ought to come

up to anything, why *don't* they?' he says; and I say so too."

" Mr. Scudder used to say that it took great afflictions to bring his mind to that place," said Mrs. Katy. " He used to say that an old paper-maker told him once, that paper that was shaken only one way in the making would tear across the other, and the best paper had to be shaken every way; a:d so he said we couldn't tell, till we had been turned and shaken and tried every way, where we should tear."

Mrs. Twitchel responded to this sentiment with a gentle series of groans, such as were her general expression of approbation, swaying herself backward and forward; while Mrs. Brown gave a sort of toss and snort, and said that for her part she always thought people knew what they did know, —but she guessed she was mistaken.

The conversation was here interrupted by the civilities attendant on the reception of Mrs. Jones, —a broad, buxom, hearty soul, who had come on horseback from a farm about three miles distant.

Smiling with rosy content, she presented Mrs. Katy a small pot of golden butter,—the result of her forenoon's churning.

There are some people so evidently broadly and heartily of this world, that their coming into a room always materializes the conversation. We wish to be understood that we mean no disparaging reflection on such persons;—they are as necessary to make up a world as cabbages to make up a garden; the great healthy principles of cheerfulness and animal life seem to exist in them in the gross; they are wedges and ingots of solid, contented vitality. Certain kinds of virtues and Christian graces thrive in such people as the first crop of corn does in the bottom-lands of the Ohio Mrs. Jones was a church-member, a regular church-goer, and planted her comely person plump in front of Dr. Hopkins every Sunday, and listened to his searching and discriminating sermons with broad, honest smiles of satisfaction. Those keen distinctions as to motives, those awful warnings and urgent expostulations, which made poor Deacon Twitchel weep, she listened to with great, round, satisfied eyes, making to all, and after all, the same remark,—that it was good, and she liked it, and the Doctor was a good man; and on the present occasion, she announced her pot of butter as one fruit of her reflections after the last discourse.

"You see," she said, "as I was a-settin' in the spring-house, this mornin', a-workin' my butter, I says to Dinah,—'I'm goin' to carry a pot of this down to Miss Scudder for the Doctor,—I got so much good out of his Sunday's sermon.' And Dinah she says to me, says she,—'Laws, Miss Jones, I thought you was asleep, for sartin!'

But I wasn't; only 1 forgot to take any caraway-seed in the mornin', and so I kinder missed it; you know it 'livens one up. But I never lost myself so but what I kinder heerd him goin' on, on, sort o' like,—and it sounded *all* sort o' *good;* and so I thought of the Doctor to-day."

" Well, I'm sure," said Aunt Katy, " this will be a treat; we all know about your butter, Mrs. Jones. I sha'n't think of putting any of mine on table to-night, I'm sure."

" Law, now don't! " said Mrs. Jones. " Why, you re'lly make me ashamed, Miss Scudder. To be sure, folks does like our butter, and it always fetches a pretty good price,—*he's* very proud on't. I tell him he oughtn't to be,—we oughtn't to be proud of anything."

And now Mrs. Katy, giving a look at the old clock, told Mary it was time to set the tea-table; and forthwith there was a gentle movement of expectancy. The little mahogany tea-table opened its brown wings, and from a drawer came forth the snowy damask covering. It was etiquette, on such occasions, to compliment every article of the establishment successively, as it appeared; so the Deacon's wife began at the table-cloth.

" Well, I do declare, Miss Scudder beats us all in her table-cloths," she said, taking up a corner of the damask, admiringly; and Mrs. Jones forth-with jumped up and seized the other corner.

"Why, this 'ere must have come from the Old Country. It's 'most the beautiflest thing I ever did see."

"It's my own spinning," replied Mrs. Katy, with conscious dignity. "There was an Irish weaver came to Newport the year before I was married, who wove beautifully,—just the Old-Country patterns,—and I'd been spinning some uncommonly fine flax then. I remember Mr. Scudder used to read to me while I was spinning,"—and Aunt Katy looked afar, as one whose thoughts are in the past, and dropped out the last words with a little sigh, unconsciously, as if speaking to herself.

"Well, now, I must say," said Mrs. Jones, "this goes quite beyond me. I thought I could spin some; but I sha'n't never dare to show mine."

"I'm sure, Mrs. Jones, your towels that you had out bleaching, this spring, were wonderful," said Aunt Katy. "But I don't pretend to do much now," she continued, straightening her trim figure. "I'm getting old, you know; we must let the young folks take up these things. Mary spins better now than I ever did. Mary, hand out those napkins."

And so Mary's napkins passed from hand to hand.

"Well, well," said Mrs. Twitchel to Mary, "it's easy to see that *your* linen-chest will be pretty full by the time *he* comes along; won't it, Miss Jones?"

—and Mrs. Twitchel looked pleasantly facetious, as elderly ladies generally do, when suggesting such possibilities to younger ones.

Mary was vexed to feel the blood boil up in her cheeks in a most unexpected and provoking way at the suggestion; whereat Mrs. Twitchel nodded knowingly at Mrs. Jones, and whispered something in a mysterious aside, to which plump Mrs. Jones answered,—" Why, do tell! now I never!"

" It's strange," said Mrs. Twitchel, taking up her parable again, in such a plaintive tone that all knew something pathetic was coming, " what mis· takes some folks will make, a-fetchin' up girls. Now there's your Mary, Miss Scudder,—why, there a'n't nothin' she can't do; but law, I was down to Miss Skinner's, last week, a-watchin' with her, and re'lly it 'most broke my heart to see her. Her mother was a most amazin' smart woman; but she brought Suky up, for all the world, as if she'd been a wax doll, to be kept in the drawer,—and sure enough, she was a pretty creetur,—and now she's married, what is she? She ha'n't no more idee how to take hold than nothin'. The poor child means well enough, and she works so hard she most kills herself; but then she is in the suds from mornin' till night,—she's one the sort whose work's never done,—and poor George Skinner's clean discouraged."

" There's everything in *knowing how*," said Mrs Katy. " Nobody ought to be always working; it's a bad sign. I tell Mary,—' Always do up your work in the forenoon.' Girls must learn that. I never work afternoons, after my dinner-dishes are got away; I never did and never would."

" Nor I, neither," chimed in Mrs. Jones and Mrs. Twitchel,—both anxious to show themselves clear on this leading point of New England housekeeping.

" There's another thing I always tell Mary," said Mrs. Katy, impressively. "' Never say there isn't time for a thing that ought to be done. If a thing is *necessary*, why, life is long enough to find a place for it. That's my doctrine. When anybody tells me they can't *find time* for this or that, I don't think much of 'em. I think they don't know how to work,—that's all.' "

Here Mrs. Twitchel looked up from her knitting, with an apologetic giggle, at Mrs. Brown.

" Law, now, there's Miss Brown, she don't know nothin' about it, 'cause she's got her servants to every turn. I s'pose she thinks it queer to hear us talkin' about our work. Miss Brown must have her time all to herself. I was tellin' the Deacon the other day that she was a privileged woman."

" I'm sure, those that have servants find work enough following 'em 'round," said Mrs. Brown,—who, like all other human beings, resented the implication of not having as many trials in life as her neighbors. "As to getting the work done up in the forenoon, that's a thing I never can teach 'em; they'd rather not. Chloe likes to keep her work 'round, and do it by snacks, any time, day or night, when the notion takes her."

"And it was just for that reason I never would have one of those creatures 'round," said Mrs. Katy. "Mr. Scudder was principled against buying negroes, — but if he had *not* been, I should not have wanted any of *their* work. I know what's to be done, and most help is no help to me. I want people to stand out of my way and let me get done. I've tried keeping a girl once or twice, and I never worked so hard in my life. When Mary and I do all ourselves, we can calculate everything to a minute; and we get our time to sew and read and spin and visit, and live just as we want to."

Here, again, Mrs. Brown looked uneasy. To what use was it that she was rich and owned servants, when this Mordecai in her gate utterly despised her prosperity? In her secret heart she thought Mrs. Katy must be envious, and rather comforted herself on this view of the subject, — sweetly unconscious of any inconsistency in the feeling with her views of utter self-abnegation just announced.

Meanwhile the tea-table had been silently gathering on its snowy plateau the delicate china, the golden butter, the loaf of faultless cake, a plate of crullers or wonders, as a sort of sweet fried cake was commonly called,—tea-rusks, light as a puff, and shining on top with a varnish of egg,—jellies of apple and quince quivering in amber clearness, —whitest and purest honey in the comb,—in short; everything that could go to the getting-up of a most faultless tea.

"I don't see," said Mrs. Jones, resuming the gentle pæans of the occasion, "how Miss Scudder's loaf-cake always comes out jest so. It don't rise neither to one side nor t'other, but jest even all 'round; and it a'n't white one side and burnt the other, but jest a good brown all over; and it don't have no heavy streak in it."

"Jest what Cerinthy Ann was sayin', the other day," said Mrs. Twitchel. "She says she can't never be sure how hers is a-comin' out. Do what she can, it will be either too much or too little; but Miss Scudder's is always jest so. 'Law,' says I, 'Cerinthy Ann, it's *faculty*,—that's it;—them that has it has it, and them that hasn't—why, they've got to work hard, and not do half so well, neither.'"

Mrs. Katy took all these praises as matter of course. Since she was thirteen years old, she had never put her hand to anything that she had not been held to do better than other folks, and therefore she accepted her praises with the quiet repose and serenity of assured reputation; though, of course, she used the usual polite disclaimers of " Oh, it's nothing, nothing at all; I'm sure I don't know how I do it, and was not aware it was so good,"—and so on. All which things are proper for gentle-women to observe in like cases, in every walk of life.

" Do you think the Deacon will be along soon?" said Mrs. Katy, when Mary, returning from the kitchen, announced the important fact, that the tea-kettle was boiling.

" Why, yes," said Mrs. Twitchel. " I'm a-lookin' for him every minute. He told me, that he and the men should be plantin' up to the eight-acre lot, but he'd keep the colt up there to come down on; and so I laid him out a clean shirt, and says I, ' Now, Father, you be sure and be there by five, so that Miss Scudder may know when to put her tea a-drawin'.' — There he is, I believe," she added, as a horse's tramp was heard without, and, after a few moments, the desired Deacon entered.

He was a gentle, soft-spoken man, low, sinewy, thin, with black hair showing lines and patches of silver. His keen, thoughtful, dark eye marked the nervous and melancholic temperament. A mild and pensive humility of manner seemed to brood over him, like the shadow of a cloud. Everything in his dress, air, and motions indicated punctilious

3*

exactness and accuracy, at times rising to the point of nervous anxiety.

Immediately after the bustle of his entrance had subsided, Mr. Simeon Brown followed. He was a tall, lank individual, with high cheek-bones, thin, sharp features, small, keen, hard eyes, and large hands and feet.

Simeon was, as we have before remarked, a keen theologian, and had the scent of a hound for a metaphysical distinction. True, he was a man of business, being a thriving trader to the coast of Africa, whence he imported negroes for the American market; and no man was held to understand that branch of traffic better,—he having, in his earlier days, commanded ships in the business, and thus learned it from the root. In his private life, Simeon was severe and dictatorial. He was one of that class of people who, of a freezing day, will plant themselves directly between you and the fire, and there stand and argue to prove that selfishness is the root of all moral evil. Simeon said he always had thought so; and his neighbors sometimes supposed that nobody could enjoy better experimental advantages for understanding the subject. He was one of those men who suppose themselves submissive to the Divine will, to the uttermost extent demanded by the extreme theology of that day, simply because they have no nerves to feel, no imagination to conceive what endless happiness or suffering is, and who deal therefore with the great question of the salvation or damnation of myriads as a problem of theological algebra, to be worked out by their inevitable x, y, z.

But we must not spend too much time with our analysis of character, for matters at the tea-table are drawing to a crisis. Mrs. Jones has announced that she does not think "*he*" can come this afternoon, by which significant mode of expression she conveyed the dutiful idea that there was for her but one male person in the world. And now Mrs. Katy says, "Mary, dear, knock at the Doctor's door and tell him that tea is ready."

The Doctor was sitting in his shady study, in the room on the other side of the little entry. The windows were dark and fragrant with the shade and perfume of blossoming lilacs, whose tremulous shadow, mingled with spots of afternoon sunlight, danced on the scattered papers of a great writing-table covered with pamphlets and heavily-bound volumes of theology, where the Doctor was sitting.

A man of gigantic proportions, over six feet in height, and built every way with an amplitude corresponding to his height, he bent over his writing, so absorbed that he did not hear the gentle sound of Mary's entrance.

"Doctor," said the maiden, gently, "tea is ready."

No motion, no sound, except the quick racing of the pen over the paper.

"Doctor! Doctor!"—a little louder, and with another step into the apartment,—"tea is ready."

The Doctor stretched his head forward to a paper which lay before him, and responded in a low, murmuring voice, as reading something.

"Firstly,—if underived virtue be peculiar to the Deity, can it be the duty of a creature to have it?"

Here a little waxen hand came with a very gentle tap on his huge shoulder, and "Doctor, tea is ready," penetrated drowsily to the nerve of his ear, as a sound heard in sleep. He rose suddenly with a start, opened a pair of great blue eyes, which shone abstractedly under the dome of a capacious and lofty forehead, and fixed them on the maiden, who by this time was looking up rather archly, and yet with an attitude of the most profound respect, while her venerated friend was assembling together his earthly faculties.

"Tea is ready, if you please. Mother wished me to call you."

"Oh!—ah!—yes!—indeed!" he said, looking confusedly about, and starting for the door, in his study-gown.

"If you please, Sir," said Mary, standing in his way, "would you not like to put on your coat and wig?"

The Doctor gave a hurried glance at his study-gown, put his hand to his head, which, in place of the ample curls of his full-bottomed wig, was decked only with a very ordinary cap, and seemed to come at once to full comprehension. He smiled a kind of conscious, benignant smile, which adorned his high cheek-bones and hard features as sunshine adorns the side of a rock, and said, kindly, " Ah, well, child, I understand now; I'll be out in a moment."

And Mary, sure that he was now on the right track, went back to the tea-room with the announcement that the Doctor was coming.

In a few moments he entered, majestic and proper, in all the dignity of full-bottomed, powdered wig, full, flowing coat, with ample cuffs, silver knee- and shoe-buckles, as became the gravity and majesty of the minister of those days.

He saluted all the company with a benignity which had a touch of the majestic, and also of the rustic in it; for at heart the Doctor was a bashful man, — that is, he had somewhere in his mental camp that treacherous fellow whom John Bunyan anathematizes under the name of Shame. The company rose on his entrance ; the men bowed and the women curtsied, and all remained standing while he addressed to each with punctilious decorum those inquiries in regard to health and well-being which preface a social interview. Then,

at a dignified sign from Mrs. Katy, he advanced
to the table, and, all following his example, stood,
while, with one hand uplifted, he went through a
devotional exercise which, for length, more resembled a prayer than a grace,—after which the company were seated.

"Well, Doctor," said Mr. Brown, who, as a
householder of substance, felt a conscious right to
be first to open conversation with the minister,
"people are beginning to make a noise about your
views. I was talking with Deacon Timmins the
other day down on the wharf, and he said Dr.
Stiles said that it was entirely new doctrine,—
entirely so,—and for his part he wanted the good
old ways."

"They say so, do they?" said the Doctor, kindling up from an abstraction into which he seemed
to be gradually subsiding. "Well, let them. I
had rather publish *new* divinity than any other,
and the more of it the better,—*if it be but true.*
I should think it hardly worth while to write, if I
had nothing *new* to say."

"Well," said Deacon Twitchel,—his meek face
flushing with awe of his minister,—"Doctor, there's
all sorts of things said about you. Now the other
day I was at the mill with a load of corn, and
while I was a-waitin', Amariah Wadsworth came
along with his'n; and so while we were waitin',
he says to me, 'Why they say your minister is

gettin' to be an Armenian'; and he went on a-tellin' how old Ma'am Badger told him that you interpreted some parts of Paul's Epistles clear on the Arminian side. You know Ma'am Badger's a master-hand at doctrines, and she's 'most an uncommon Calvinist."

" That does not frighten me at all," said the sturdy Doctor. " Supposing I do interpret some texts like the Arminians. Can't Arminians have anything right about them? Who wouldn't rather go with the Arminians when they are *right*, than with the Calvinists when they are wrong?"

" That's it,—you've hit it, Doctor," said Simeon Brown. " That's what I always say. I say, ' Don't he *prove* it? and how are you going to answer him?' That gravels 'em."

" Well," said Deacon Twitchel, " Brother Seth, —you know Brother Seth,—he says you deny depravity. He's all for imputation of Adam's sin, you know; and I have long talks with Seth about it, every time he comes to see me; and he says, that, if we did not sin in Adam, it's givin' up the whole ground altogether; and then he insists you're clean wrong about the unregenerate doings."

" Not at all,—not in the least," said the Doctor, promptly.

" I wish Seth could talk with you sometime, Doctor. Along in the spring, he was down helpin' me to lay stone fence,—it was when we was fencin' off the south-pastur' lot,—and we talked pretty nigh all day; and it re'lly did seem to me that the longer we talked, the sotter Seth grew. He's a master-hand at readin'; and when he heard that your remarks on Dr. Mayhew had come out, Seth tackled up o' purpose and come up to Newport to get them, and spent all his time, last winter, studyin' on it and makin' his remarks; and I tell you, Sir, he's a tight fellow to argue with. Why, that day, what with layin' stone wall and what with arguin' with Seth, I come home quite beat out,—Miss Twitchel will remember."

"That he was!" said his helpmeet. "I 'member, when he came home, says I, 'Father, you seem clean used up'; and I stirred 'round lively like, to get him his tea. But he jest went into the bedroom and laid down afore supper; and I says to Cerinthy Ann, 'That's a thing I ha'n't seen your father do since he was took with the typhus.' And Cerinthy Ann, she said she knew 'twa'n't anything but them old doctrines,—that it was always so when Uncle Seth come down. And after tea Father was kinder chirked up a little, and he and Seth sot by the fire, and was a-beginnin' it ag'in, and I jest spoke out and said,—'Now, Seth, these 'ere things doesn't hurt you; but the Deacon is weakly, and if he gets his mind riled after supper, he don't sleep none all night. So,' says I, 'you'd better jest let matters stop where they be; 'cause,' says I, ' 'twon't make no difference, for to-night, which on ye's got the right on't;—reckon the Lord 'll go on his own way without you; and we shall find out, by'm-by, what that is.'"

"Mr. Scudder used to think a great deal on these points," said Mrs. Katy, "and the last time he was home he wrote out his views. I haven't ever shown them to you, Doctor; but I should be pleased to know what you think of them."

"Mr. Scudder was a good man, with a clear head," said the Doctor; "and I should be much pleased to see anything that he wrote."

A flush of gratified feeling passed over Mrs. Katy's face;—for one flower laid on the shrine which we keep in our hearts for the dead, is worth more than any gift to our living selves.

We will not now pursue our party further, lest you, reader, get more theological tea than you can drink. We will not recount the numerous nice points raised by Mr. Simeon Brown and adjusted by the Doctor,—and how Simeon invariably declared, that that was the way in which he disposed of them himself, and how he had thought it out ten years ago.

We will not relate, either, too minutely, how Mary changed color and grew pale and red in quick succession, when Mr. Simeon Brown incidentally remarked, that the "Monsoon" was going to set sail that very afternoon, for her three-years' voyage. Nobody noticed it in the busy amenities, —the sudden welling and ebbing of that one poor little heart-fountain.

So we go,—so little knowing what we touch and what touches us as we talk! We drop out a common piece of news,—" Mr. So-and-so is dead,—Miss Such-a-one is married,—such a ship has sailed,"—and lo, on our right hand or our left, some heart has sunk under the news silently, —gone down in the great ocean of Fate, without even a bubble rising to tell its drowning pang. And this—God help us!—is what we call living!

CHAPTER V.

THE LETTER.

MARY returned to the quietude of her room. The red of twilight had faded, and the silver moon, round and fair, was rising behind the thick boughs of the apple-trees. She sat down in the window, thoughtful and sad, and listened to the crickets. whose ignorant jollity often sounds as mournfully to us mortals as ours may to superior beings. There the little hoarse, black wretches were scraping and creaking, as if life and death were invented solely for their pleasure, and the world were created only to give them a good time in it. Now and then a little wind shivered among the boughs and brought down a shower of white petals which shimmered in the slant beams of the moonlight; and now a ray touched some tall head of grass, and forthwith it blossomed into silver, and stirred itself with a quiet joy, like a new-born saint just awakening in paradise. And ever and anon came on the still air the soft eternal pulsations of the distant sea,—sound mournfulest, most mysterious,

of all the harpings of Nature. It was the sea,—
the deep, eternal sea,—the treacherous, soft, dreadful, inexplicable sea; and *he* was perhaps at this
moment being borne away on it,—away, away,—
to what sorrows, to what temptations, to what
dangers, she knew not. She looked along the old,
familiar, beaten path by which he came, by which
he went, and thought, "What if he *never* should
come back?" There was a little path through
the orchard out to a small elevation in the pasture lot behind, whence the sea was distinctly visible, and Mary had often used her low-silled window as a door when she wanted to pass out
thither; so now she stepped out, and, gathering
her skirts back from the dewy grass, walked thoughtfully along the path and gained the hill. Newport
harbor lay stretched out in the distance, with the
rising moon casting a long, wavering track of silver upon it; and vessels, like silver-winged moths,
were turning and shifting slowly to and fro upon
it, and one stately ship in full sail passing fairly
out under her white canvas, graceful as some
grand, snowy bird. Mary's beating heart told her
that *there* was passing away from her one who
carried a portion of her existence with him. She
sat down under a lonely tree that stood there, and,
resting her elbow on her knee, followed the ship
with silent prayers, as it passed, like a graceful
cloudy dream, out of her sight.

Then she thoughtfully retraced her way to her chamber; and as she was entering, observed in the now clearer moonlight what she had not seen before,— something white, like a letter, lying on the floor. Immediately she struck a light, and there, sure enough, it was,— a letter in James's handsome, dashing hand; and the little puss, before she knew what she was about, actually kissed it, with a fervor which would much have astonished the writer, could he at that moment have been clairvoyant. But Mary felt as one who finds, in the emptiness after a friend's death, an unexpected message or memento; and all alone in the white, calm stillness of her little room her heart took sudden possession of her. She opened the letter with trembling hands, and read what of course we shall let you read. We got it out of a bundle of old, smoky, yellow letters, years after all the parties concerned were gone on the eternal journey beyond earth.

" My dear Mary,—

" I cannot leave you so. I have about two hun dred things to say to you, and it's a shame I could not have had longer to see you; but blessed be ink and paper! I am writing and seeing to fifty things besides; so you mustn't wonder if my letter has rather a confused appearance.

" I have been thinking that perhaps I gave you

a wrong impression of myself, this afternoon. I am going to speak to you from my heart, as if I were confessing on my death-bed. Well, then, I do not confess to being what is commonly called a bad young man. I should be willing that men of the world generally, even strict ones, should look my life through and know all about it. It is only in your presence, Mary, that I feel that I am bad and low and shallow and mean, because you represent to me a sphere higher and holier than any in which I have ever moved, and stir up a sort of sighing and longing in my heart to come towards it. In all countries, in all temptations, Mary, your image has stood between me and low, gross vice. When I have been with fellows roaring drunken, beastly songs, — suddenly I have seemed to see you as you used to sit beside me in the singing-school, and your voice has been like an angel's in my ear, and I have got up and gone out sick and disgusted. Your face has risen up calm and white and still, between the faces of poor lost creatures who know no better way of life than to tempt us to sin. And sometimes, Mary, when I have seen girls that, had they been cared for by good pious mothers, might have been like you, I have felt as if I could cry for them. Poor women are abused all the world over; and it's no wonder they turn round and re venge themselves on us.

" No, I have not been bad, Mary, as the world

calls badness. I have been kept by you. But do you remember you told me once, that, when the snow first fell and lay so dazzling and pure and soft, all about, you always felt as if the spreads and window-curtains that seemed white before were not clean? Well, it's just like that with me. Your presence makes me feel that I am not pure,—that I am low and unworthy,—not worthy to touch the hem of your garment. Your good Dr. Hopkins spent a whole half-day, the other Sunday, trying to tell us about the beauty of holiness; and he cut, and pared, and peeled, and sliced, and told us what it wasn't, and what was *like* it, and wasn't; and then he built up an exact definition, and fortified and bricked it up all round; and I thought to myself that he'd better tell 'em to look at Mary Scudder, and they'd understand all about it. That was what I was thinking when you talked to me for looking at you in church instead of looking towards the pulpit. It really made me laugh in myself to see what a good little ignorant, unconscious way you had of looking up at the Doctor, as if he knew more about that than you did.

"And now as to your Doctor that you think so much of, I like him for certain things, in certain ways. He is a great, grand, large pattern of a man,—a man who isn't afraid to think, and to speak anything he does think; but then I do believe, if he would take a voyage round the world

in the forecastle of a whaler, he would know more
about what to say to people than he does now ;
it would certainly give him several new points to
be considered. Much of his preaching about men
is as like live men as Chinese pictures of trees
and rocks and gardens,—no nearer the reality than
that. All I can say is, ' It isn't so ; and you'd
know it, Sir, if you knew men.' He has got what
they call a *system*,—just so many bricks put together just so ; but it is too narrow to take in all
I see in my wanderings round this world of ours.
Nobody that has a soul, and goes round the world
as I do, can help feeling it at times, and thinking,
as he sees all the races of men and their ways,
who made them, and what they were made for.
To doubt the existence of a God seems to me
like a want of common sense. There is a Maker
and a Ruler, doubtless ; but then, Mary, all this
invisible world of religion is unreal to me. I can
see we must be good, somehow,—that if we are
not, we shall not be happy here or hereafter. As
to all the metaphysics of your good Doctor, you
can't tell how they tire me. I'm not the sort of
person that they can touch. I must have real
things,—real people ; abstractions are nothing to
me. Then I think that he systematically contra-
dicts on one Sunday what he preaches on another.
One Sunday he tells us that God is the immediate efficient Author of every act of will ; the next

he tolls us that we are entire free agents. I see no sense in it, and can't take the trouble to put it together. But then he and you have something in you that I call religion,—something that makes you *good*. When I see a man working away on an entirely honest, unworldly, disinterested pattern, as he does, and when I see you, Mary, as I said before, I should like at least to *be* as you are, whether I can believe as you do or not.

" How could you so care for me, and waste on one so unworthy of you such love? Oh, Mary, some better man must win you; I never shall and never can; but then you must not quite forget me; you must be my friend, my saint. If, through your prayers, your Bible, your friendship, you can bring me to your state, I am willing to be brought there,—nay, desirous. God has put the key of my soul into your hands.

" So, dear Mary, good-by! Pray still for your naughty, loving

" COUSIN JAMES."

Mary read this letter and re-read it, with more pain than pleasure. To feel the immortality of a beloved soul hanging upon us, to feel that its only communications with Heaven must be through us, is the most solemn and touching thought that can pervade a mind. It was without one particle of gratified vanity, with even a throb of pain, that

4

she read such exalted praises of herself from one
blind to the glories of a far higher loveliness.

Yet was she at that moment, unknown to herself, one of the great company scattered through
earth who are priests unto God,—ministering between the Divine One, who has unveiled himself
unto them, and those who as yet stand in the
outer courts of the great sanctuary of truth and
holiness. Many a heart, wrung, pierced, bleeding
with the sins and sorrows of earth, longing to depart, stands in this mournful and beautiful ministry, but stands unconscious of the glory of the
work in which it waits and suffers. God's kings
and priests are crowned with thorns, walking the
earth with bleeding feet, and comprehending not
the work they are performing.

Mary took from a drawer a small pocket-book,
from which dropped a lock of black hair,—a glossy
curl, which seemed to have a sort of wicked, wilful life in every shining ring, just as she had often
seen it shake naughtily on the owner's head. She
felt a strange tenderness towards the little wilful
thing, and, as she leaned over it, made in her
heart a thousand fond apologies for every fault and
error.

She was standing thus when Mrs. Scudder entered the room to see if her daughter had yet retired.

"What are you doing there, Mary?" she said,

as her eye fell on the letter. "What is it you are reading?"

Mary felt herself grow pale; it was the first time in her whole life that her mother had asked her a question that she was not from the heart ready to answer. Her loyalty to her only parent had gone on even-handed with that she gave to her God; she felt, somehow, that the revelations of that afternoon had opened a gulf between them, and the consciousness overpowered her.

Mrs. Scudder was astonished at her evident embarrassment, her trembling, and paleness. She was a woman of prompt, imperative temperament, and the slightest hesitation in rendering to her a full, outspoken confidence had never before occurred in their intercourse. Her child was the core of her heart, the apple of her eye; and intense love is always near neighbor to anger; there was, therefore, an involuntary flash from her eye and a heightening of her color, as she said, — "Mary, are you concealing anything from your mother?"

In that moment, Mary had grown calm again. The wonted serene, balanced nature had found its habitual poise, and she looked up innocently, though with tears in her large, blue eyes, and said, —

"No, mother, — I have nothing that I do not mean to tell you fully. This letter came from James Marvyn he came here to see me this afternoon."

" Here ? — when ? I did not see him "

" After dinner.   I was sitting here in the win·
dow, and suddenly he came up behind me through
the orchard-path."

Mrs. Katy sat down with a flushed cheek and a
discomposed air; but Mary seemed actually to bear
her down by the candid clearness of the large, blue
eye which she turned on her, as she stood perfectly
collected, with her deadly pale face and a brilliant
spot burning on each cheek.

" James came to say good-by.   He complained
that he had not had a chance to see me alone
since he came home."

" And what should he want to see you alone
for ? " said Mrs. Scudder, in a dry, disturbed tone.

" Mother, — everybody has things at times which
they would like to say to some one person alone,"
said Mary.

" Well, tell me what he said."

" I will try.   In the first place, he said that he
always had been free, all his life, to run in and
out of our house, and to wait on me like a
brother."

" Hum ! " said Mrs. Scudder; " but he isn't your
brother, for all that."

" Well, then, he wanted to know why you were
so cold to him, and why you never let him walk
with me from meetings or see me alone, as he of·
ten used to.   And I told him why, — that we were

not children now, and that you thought it was not best; and then I talked with him about religion, and tried to persuade him to attend to the concerns of his soul, and I never felt so much hope for him as I do now."

Aunt Katy looked skeptical, and remarked, — "If he really felt a disposition for religious instruction, Dr. Hopkins could guide him much better than you could."

"Yes, — so I told him, and I tried to persuade him to talk with Dr. Hopkins; but he was very unwilling. He said, I could have more influence over him than anybody else, — that nobody could do him any good but me."

"Yes, yes, — I understand all that," said Aunt Katy, — "I have heard young men say *that* before, and I know just what it amounts to."

"But, mother, I do think James was moved very much, this afternoon. I never heard him speak so seriously; he seemed really in earnest, and he asked me to give him my Bible."

"Couldn't he read any Bible but yours?"

"Why, naturally, you know, mother, he would like my Bible better, because it would put him in mind of me. He promised faithfully to read it all through."

"And then, it seems, he wrote you a letter."

"Yes, mother."

Mary shrank from showing this letter, from the

natural sense of honor which makes us feel it in-
delicate to expose to an unsympathizing eye the
confidential outpourings of another heart; and then
she felt quite sure that there was no such inter-
cessor for James in her mother's heart as in her
own. But over all this reluctance rose the determined force of duty; and she handed the letter in
silence to her mother.

Mrs. Scudder took it, laid it deliberately in her
lap, and then began searching in the pocket of her
chintz petticoat for her spectacles. These being
found, she wiped them, accurately adjusted them,
opened the letter and spread it on her lap, brushing out its folds and straightening it, that she
might read with the greater ease. After this she
read it carefully and deliberately; and all this while
there was such a stillness, that the sound of the
tall varnished clock in the best room could be
heard through the half-opened door.

After reading it with the most tiresome, tortur-
ing slowness, she rose, and laying it on the table
under Mary's eye, and pressing down her finger on
two lines in the letter, said, " Mary, have you told
James that you loved him ? "

" Yes, mother, always. I always loved him, and
he always knew it."

" But, Mary, this that he speaks of is something
different. What has passed between —— "

" Why, mother, he was saying that we who were

Christians drew to ourselves and did not care for the salvation of our friends; and then I told him how I had always prayed for him, and how I should be willing even to give up my hopes in heaven, if he might be saved."

" Child,—what do you mean?"

" I mean, if only one of us two could go to heaven, I had rather it should be him than me," said Mary.

" Oh, child! child!" said Mrs. Scudder, with a sort of groan,—"has it gone with you so far as this? Poor child!—after all my care, you *are* in love with this boy,—your heart is set on him."

" Mother, I am not. I never expect to see him much,—never expect to marry him or anybody else;—only he seems to me to have so much more life and soul and spirit than most people,—I think him so noble and grand,—that is, that he *could* be if he were all he ought to be,—that, somehow, I never think of myself in thinking of him, and his salvation seems worth more than mine;—men can do so much more!—they can live such splendid lives!—oh, a real noble man is so glorious!"

" And you would like to see him well married, would you not?" said Mrs. Scudder, sending, with a true woman's aim, this keen arrow into the midst of the cloud of enthusiasm which enveloped her daughter. " I think," she added, " that Jane Spencer would make him an excellent wife."

Mary was astonished at a strange, new pain that shot through her at these words. She drew in her breath and turned herself uneasily, as one who had literally felt a keen dividing blade piercing between soul and spirit. Till this moment, she had never been conscious of herself; but the shaft had torn the veil. She covered her face with her hands; the hot blood flushed scarlet over neck and brow; at last, with a beseeching look, she threw herself into her mother's arms.

"Oh, mother, mother, I am selfish, after all!"

Mrs. Scudder folded her silently to her heart, and said, "My daughter, this is not at all what I wished it to be; I see how it is;—but then you have been a good child; I don't blame you. We can't always help ourselves. We don't always really know how we do feel. I didn't know, for a long while, that I loved your father. I thought I was only curious about him, because he had a strange way of treating me, different from other men; but, one day, I remember, Julian Simons told me that it was reported that his mother was making a match for him with Susan Emery, and I was astonished to find how I felt. I saw him that evening, and the moment he looked at me I saw it wasn't true; all at once I knew something I never knew before,—and that was, that I should be very unhappy if he loved any one else better than me. But then, my child, your father was a different man from

James;—he was as much better than I was as you are than James. I was a foolish, thoughtless young thing then. I never should have been any thing at all, but for him. Somehow, when I loved him, I grew more serious, and then he always guided and led me. Mary, your father was a wonderful man; he was one of the sort that the world knows not of;—sometime I must show you his letters. I always hoped, my daughter, that you would marry such a man."

" Don't speak of marrying, mother. I never shall marry."

" You certainly should not, unless you can marry in the Lord. Remember the words, 'Be ye not unequally yoked together with unbelievers. For what fellowship hath righteousness with unrighteousness? and what communion hath light with darkness? and what concord hath Christ with Belial? or what part hath he that believeth with an infidel?'"

" Mother, James is not an infidel."

" He certainly is an *unbeliever*, Mary, by his own confession;—but then God is a Sovereign and hath mercy on whom he will. You do right to pray for him; but if he does not come out on the Lord's side, you must not let your heart mislead you. He is going to be gone three years, and you must try to think as little of him as possible;—put your mind upon your duties, like a good girl, and God

4 *

will bless you. Don't believe too much in your
power over him;—young men, when they are in
love, will promise anything, and really think they
mean it; but nothing is a saving change, except
what is wrought in them by sovereign grace."

"But, mother, does not God use the love we
have to each other as a means of doing us good?
Did you not say that it was by your love to father
that you first were led to think seriously?"

"That is true, my child," said Mrs. Scudder,
who, like many of the rest of the world, was surprised to meet her own words walking out on a
track where she had not expected them, but was
yet too true of soul to cut their acquaintance because they were not going the way of her wishes.
"Yes, all that is true; but yet, Mary, when one
has but one little ewe lamb in the world, one is
jealous of it.   I would give all the world, if you
had never seen James.   It is dreadful enough for a
woman to love anybody as you can, but it is more
to love a man of unsettled character and no religion.   But then the Lord appoints all our goings;
it is not in man that walketh to direct his steps;—
I leave you, my child, in His hands."   And, with
one solemn and long embrace, the mother and
daughter parted for the night.

It is impossible to write a story of New England
life and manners for a thoughtless, shallow-minded
person   If we represent things as they are, their

intensity, their depth, their unworldly gravity and earnestness, must inevitably repel lighter spirits, as the reverse pole of the magnet drives off sticks and straws.

In no other country were the soul and the spiritual life ever such intense realities, and everything contemplated so much (to use a current New England phrase) "in reference to eternity." Mrs. Scudder was a strong, clear-headed, practical woman. No one had a clearer estimate of the material and outward life, or could more minutely manage its smallest item; but then a tremendous, eternal future had so weighed down and compacted the fibres of her very soul, that all earthly things were but as dust in comparison to it. That her child should be one elected to walk in white, to reign with Christ when earth was a forgotten dream, was her one absorbing wish; and she looked on all the events of life only with reference to this. The way of life was narrow, the chances in favor of any child of Adam infinitely small; the best, the most seemingly pure and fair, was by nature a child of wrath, and could be saved only by a sovereign decree, by which it should be plucked as a brand from the burning. Therefore it was, that, weighing all things in one balance, there was the sincerity of her whole being in the dread which she felt at the thought of her daughter's marriage with an unbeliever.

Mrs. Scudder, after retiring to her room, took her
Bible, in preparation for her habitual nightly exercise of devotion, before going to rest. She read
and re-read a chapter, scarce thinking what she was
reading,—aroused herself,—and then sat with the
book in her hand in deep thought. James Marvyn
was her cousin's son, and she had a strong feeling
of respect and family attachment for his father.
She had, too, a real kindness for the young man,
whom she regarded as a well-meaning, wilful young-
ster; but that *he* should touch her saint, her Mary,
that *he* should take from her the daughter who was
her all, really embittered her heart towards him.

"After all," she said to herself, "there are three
years,—three years in which there will be no letters, or perhaps only one or two,—and a great deal
may be done in three years, if one is wise";—and
she felt within herself an arousing of all the shrewd
womanly and motherly tact of her nature to meet
this new emergency.

CHAPTER VI.

THE DOCTOR.

I⊤ is seldom that man and woman come to-gether in intimate association, unless influences are at work more subtile and mysterious than the subjects of them dream. Even in cases where the strongest ruling force of the two sexes seems out of the question, there is still something peculiar and insidious in their relationship. A fatherly old gentleman, who undertakes the care of a sprightly young girl, finds, to his astonishment, that little Miss spins all sorts of cobwebs round him. Grave professors and teachers cannot give lessons to their female pupils just as they give them to the coarser sex, and more than once has the fable of " Cadenus and Vanessa " been acted over by the most unlikely performers.

The Doctor was a philosopher, a metaphysician, a philanthropist, and in the highest and most earnest sense a minister of good on earth. The New England clergy had no sentimental affectation of sanctity that segregated them from wholesome hu-

man relations; and consequently our good Doctor
had always resolved, in a grave and thoughtful
spirit, at a suitable time in his worldly affairs, to
choose unto himself a helpmeet. Love, as treated
of in romances, he held to be a foolish and pro-
fane matter, unworthy the attention of a serious
and reasonable creature. All the language of poetry on this subject was to him an unknown tongue.
He contemplated the entrance on married life somewhat in this wise : — That at a time and place
suiting, he should look out unto himself a woman
of a pleasant countenance and of good repute, a
zealous, earnest Christian, and well skilled in the
items of household management, whom, accosting
as a stranger and pilgrim to a better life, he should
loyally and lovingly entreat, as Isaac did Rebekah,
to come under the shadow of his tent and be a
helpmeet unto him in what yet remained of this
mortal journey. But straitened circumstances, and
the unsettled times of the Revolution, in which he
had taken an earnest and zealous part, had delayed
to a late bachelorhood the fulfilment of this resolution.

When once received under the shadow of Mrs.
Scudder's roof, and within the provident sphere of
her unfailing housekeeping, all material necessity
for an immediate choice was taken away; for he
was exactly in that situation dearest to every schol-
arly and thoughtful man, in which all that per-

tained to the outward life appeared to rise under his hand at the moment he wished for it, without his knowing how or why.

He was not at the head of a prosperous church and society, rich and well-to-do in the world,—but, as the pioneer leader of a new theology, in a country where theology was the all-absorbing interest, he had to breast the reaction that ever attends the advent of new ideas. His pulpit talents, too, were unattractive. His early training had been all logical, not in the least æsthetic; for, like the ministry of his country generally, he had been trained always to think more of what he should say than of how he should say it. Consequently, his style, though not without a certain massive greatness, which always comes from largeness of nature, had none of those attractions by which the common masses are beguiled into thinking. He gave only the results of thought, not its incipient processes; and the consequence was, that few could follow him. In like manner, his religious teachings were characterized by an ideality so high as quite to discourage ordinary virtue.

There is a ladder to heaven, whose base God has placed in human affections, tender instincts, symbolic feelings, sacraments of love, through which the soul rises higher and higher, refining as she goes, till she outgrows the human, and changes, as she rises, into the image of the divine. At the very top of this ladder, at the threshold of paradise, blazes dazzling and crystalline that celestial grade where the soul knows self no more, having learned, through a long experience of devotion, how blest it is to lose herself in that eternal Love and Beauty of which all earthly fairness and grandeur are but the dim type, the distant shadow. This highest step, this saintly elevation, which but few selectest spirits ever on earth attain, to raise the soul to which the Eternal Father organized every relation of human existence and strung every cord of human love, for which this world is one long discipline, for which the soul's human education is constantly varied, for which it is now torn by sorrow, now flooded by joy, to which all its multiplied powers tend with upward hands of dumb and ignorant aspiration, — this Ultima Thule of virtue had been seized upon by our sage as the *all* of religion. He knocked out every round of the ladder but the highest, and then, pointing to its hope·less splendor, said to the world, " Go up thither and be saved!"

Short of that absolute self-abnegation, that unconditional surrender to the Infinite, there was nothing meritorious,—because, if *that* were commanded, every moment of refusal was rebellion. Every prayer, not based on such consecration, he held to be an insult to the Divine Majesty;—the reading of the Word, the conscientious conduct of life, the performance of the duties of man to man, being, without this, the deeds of a creature in conscious rebellion to its Eternal Sovereign, were all vitiated and made void. Nothing was to be preached to the sinner, but his ability and obligation to rise immediately to this height.

It is not wonderful that teaching of this sort should seem to many unendurable, and that the multitude should desert the preacher with the cry, "This is an hard saying; who can hear it?" The young and gay were wearied by the dryness of metaphysical discussions which to them were as unintelligible as a statement of the last results of the mathematician to the child commencing the multiplication table. There remained around him only a select circle,—shrewd, hard thinkers, who delighted in metaphysical subtilties,—deep-hearted, devoted natures, who sympathized with the unworldly purity of his life, his active philanthropy and untiring benevolence,—courageous men, who admired his independence of thought and freedom in breasting received opinion,—and those unperceiving, dull, good people who are content to go to church anywhere as convenience and circumstance may drift them,—people who serve, among the keen feeling and thinking portion of the world, much the same purpose as adipose matter in the human system, as a soft cushion between the nerves of feeling and the muscles of activity.

There was something affecting in the pertinacity with which the good Doctor persevered in saying his say to his discouraging minority of hearers. His salary was small; his meeting-house, damaged during the Revolutionary struggle, was dilapidated and forlorn,—fireless in winter, and in summer admitting a flood of sun and dust through those great windows which formed so principal a feature in those first efforts of Puritan architecture.

Still, grand in his humility, he preached on,— and as a soldier never asks why, but stands at apparently the most useless post, so he went on from Sunday to Sunday, comforting himself with the reflection that no one could think more meanly of his ministrations than he did himself. " I am like Moses only in not being eloquent," he said, in his simplicity. " My preaching is barren and dull, my voice is hard and harsh; but then the Lord is a Sovereign, and may work through me. He fed Elijah once through a raven, and he may feed some poor wandering soul through me."

The only mistake made by the good man was that of supposing that the elaboration of theology was preaching the gospel. The gospel he was preaching constantly, by his pure, unworldly living, by his visitations to homes of poverty and sorrow, by his searching out of the lowly African slaves, his teaching of those whom no one else in those days had thought of teaching, and by the grand

humanity, outrunning his age, in which he protested against the then admitted system of slavery
and the slave-trade. But when, rising in the pulpit, he followed trains of thought suited only to
the desk of the theological lecture-room, he did it
blindly, following that law of self-development by
which minds of a certain amount of fervor *must*
utter what is in them, whether men will hear or
whether they will forbear.

But the place where our Doctor was happiest
was his study. There he explored, and wandered,
and read, and thought, and lived a life as wholly
ideal and intellectual as heart could conceive.

And could *Love* enter a reverend doctor's study,
and find his way into a heart empty and swept
of all those shreds of poetry and romance in which
he usually finds the material of his incantations?
Even so;—but he came so thoughtfully, so reverently, with so wise and cautious a footfall, that
the good Doctor never even raised his spectacles
to see who was there. The first that he knew,
poor man, he was breathing an air of strange and
subtile sweetness,—from what paradise he never
stopped his studies to inquire. He was like a
great, rugged elm, with all its lacings and archings
of boughs and twigs, which has stood cold and
frozen against the metallic blue of winter sky, for-
getful of leaves, and patient in its bareness, calmly
content in its naked strength and crystalline defi-

niteness of outline. But in April there is a 1.sing
and stirring within the grand old monster, — a whispering of knotted buds, a mounting of sap coursing
ethereally from bough to bough with a warm and
gentle life ; and though the old elm knows it not,
a new creation is at hand. Just so, ever since
the good man had lived at Mrs. Scudder's, and
had the gentle Mary for his catechumen, a richer
life seemed to have colored his thoughts, — his
mind seemed to work with a pleasure as never
before.

Whoever looked on the forehead of the good
Doctor must have seen the squareness of ideality
giving marked effect to its outline. As yet ideality
had dealt only with the intellectual and invisible,
leading to subtile refinements of argument and
exalted ideas of morals. But there was lying in
him, crude and unworked, a whole mine of those
artistic feelings and perceptions which are awakened and developed only by the touch of beauty.
Had he been born beneath the shadow of the great
Duomo of Florence, where Giotto's Campanile rises
like the slender stalk of a celestial lily, where varied
marbles and rainbow-glass and gorgeous paintings
and lofty statuary call forth, even from childhood,
the soul's reminiscences of the bygone glories of
its pristine state, his would have been a soul as
rounded and full in its sphere of faculties as that
of Da Vinci or Michel Angelo. But oi all that

he was as ignorant as a child; and the first revelation of his dormant nature was to come to him
through the face of woman,—that work of the
Mighty Master which is to be found in all lands
and ages.

What makes the love of a great mind something
fearful in its inception is, that it is often the un-
sealing of a hitherto undeveloped portion of a large
and powerful being; the woman may or may not
seem to other eyes adequate to the effect produced,
but the man cannot forget her, because with her
came a change which makes him forever a different being. So it was with our friend. A woman
it was that was destined to awaken in him all
that consciousness which music, painting, poetry
awaken in more evenly developed minds; and it
is the silent breathing of her creative presence that
is even now creating him anew, while as yet he
knows it not.

He never thought, this good old soul, whether
Mary were beautiful or not; he never even knew
that he looked at her; nor did he know why it
was that the truths of his theology, when uttered
by her tongue, had such a wondrous beauty as
he never felt before. He did not know why it
was, that, when she silently sat by him, copying
tangled manuscript for the press, as she sometimes
did, his whole study seemed so full of some divine
influence, as if, like St. Dorothea, she had worn

in her bosom, invisibly, the celestial roses of paradise. He recorded honestly in his diary what marvellous freshness of spirit the Lord had given him,
and how he seemed to be uplifted in his communings with heaven, without once thinking from the
robes of what angel this sweetness had exhaled.

On Sundays, when he saw good Mrs. Jones
asleep, and Simeon Brown's hard, sharp eyes, and
Deacon Twitchel mournfully rocking to and fro,
and his wife handing fennel to keep the children
awake, his eye glanced across to the front gallery,
where one earnest young face, ever kindling with
feeling and bright with intellect, followed on his
way, and he felt uplifted and comforted. On Sunday mornings, when Mary came out of her little
room, in clean white dress, with her singing-book
and psalm-book in her hands, her deep eyes solemn
from recent prayer, he thought of that fair and
mystical bride, the Lamb's wife, whose union with
her Divine Redeemer in a future millennial age
was a frequent and favorite subject of his musings;
yet he knew not that this celestial bride, clothed
in fine linen, clean and white, veiled in humility
and meekness, bore in his mind those earthly features. No, he never had dreamed of that! But
only after she had passed by, that mystical vision
seemed to him more radiant, more easy to be con-
ceived.

It is said, that, if a grape-vine be planted in the

neighborhood of a well, its roots, running silently underground, wreathe themselves in a network around the cold, clear waters, and the vine's putting on outward greenness and unwonted clusters and fruit is all that tells where every root and fibre of its being has been silently stealing. So those loves are most fatal, most absorbing, in which, with unheeded quietness, every thought and fibre of our life twines gradually around some human soul, to us the unsuspected wellspring of our being. Fearful it is, because so often the vine must be uprooted, and all its fibres wrenched away; but till the hour of discovery comes, how is it transfigured by a new and beautiful life!

There is nothing in life more beautiful than that trance-like quiet dawn which precedes the rising of love in the soul. When the whole being is pervaded imperceptibly and tranquilly by another being, and we are happy, we know not and ask not why, the soul is then receiving all and asking nothing. At a later day she becomes self-conscious, and then come craving exactions, endless questions,— the whole world of the material comes in with its hard counsels and consultations, and the beautiful trance fades forever.

Of course, all this is not so to *you*, my good friends, who read it without the most distant idea what it can mean; but there are people in the world to whom it has meant and will mean much and who will see in the present happiness of our respectable friend something even ominous and sorrowful.

It had not escaped the keen eye of the mother how quickly and innocently the good Doctor was absorbed by her daughter, and thereupon had come long trains of practical reflections.

The Doctor, though not popular indeed as a preacher, was a noted man in his age. Her deceased husband had regarded him with something of the same veneration which might have been accorded to a divine messenger, and Mrs. Scudder had received and kept this veneration as a precious legacy. Then, although not handsome, the Doctor had decidedly a grand and imposing appearance. There was nothing common or insignificant about him. Indeed, it had been said, that, when, just after the declaration of peace, he walked through the town in the commemorative procession side by side with General Washington, the minister, in the majesty of his gown, bands, cocked hat, and full flowing wig, was thought by many to be the more majestic and personable figure of the two.

In those days, the minister united in himself all those ideas of superior position and cultivation with which the theocratic system of the New England community had invested him. Mrs. Scudder's notions of social rank could reach no higher than to place her daughter on the throne of such pre-eminence.

Her Mary, she pondered, was no common girl. In those days, it was a rare thing for young persons to devote themselves to religion or make any professions of devout life. The church, or that body of people who professed to have passed through a divine regeneration, was almost entirely confined to middle-aged and elderly people, and it was looked upon as a singular and unwonted call of divine grace when young persons came forward to attach themselves to it. When Mary, therefore, at quite an early age, in all the bloom of her youthful beauty, arose, according to the simple and impressive New England rite, to consecrate herself publicly to a religious life, and to join the company of professing Christians, she was regarded with a species of deference amounting even to awe. Had it not been for the childlike, unconscious simplicity of her manners, the young people of her age would have shrunk away from her, as from one entirely out of their line of thought and feeling; but a certain natural and innocent playfulness and amiable self-forgetfulness made her a general favorite.

Nevertheless, Mrs. Scudder knew no young man whom she deemed worthy to have and hold a heart which she prized so highly. As to James, he stood at double disadvantage, because, as her cousin's

5

son, he had grown up from childhood under her eye, and all those sins and iniquities into which gay and adventurous youngsters will be falling had come to her knowledge. She felt kindly to the youth; she wished him well; but as to giving him her Mary!—the very suggestion made her dislike him. She was quite sure he must have tried to beguile her,—he must have tampered with her feelings, to arouse in her pure and well-ordered mind so much emotion and devotedness as she had witnessed.

How encouraging a Providence, then, was it that he was gone to sea for three years!—how fortu-nate that Mary had been prevented in any way from committing herself with him!—how encourag-ing that the only man in those parts, in the least fitted to appreciate her, seemed so greatly pleased and absorbed in her society!—how easily might Mary's dutiful reverence be changed to a warmer sentiment, when she should find that so great a man could descend from his lofty thoughts to think of her!

In fact, before Mrs. Scudder had gone to sleep the first night after James's departure, she had set-tled upon the house where the minister and his young wife were to live, had reviewed the window-curtains and bed-quilts for each room, and glanced complacently at an improved receipt for wedding-cake which might be brought out to glorify a cer tain occasion!

CHAPTER VII.

THE FRIENDS AND RELATIONS OF JAMES.

Mr. Zebedee Marvyn, the father of James, was the sample of an individuality so purely the result of New England society and education, that he must be embodied in our story as a representative man of the times.

He owned a large farm in the immediate vicinity of Newport, which he worked with his own hands and kept under the most careful cultivation. He was a man past the middle of life, with a white head, a keen blue eye, and a face graven deeply with the lines of energy and thought. His was one of those clearly-cut minds which New England forms among her farmers, as she forms quartz crystals in her mountains, by a sort of gradual influence flowing through every pore of her soil and system.

His education, properly so called, had been merely that of those common schools and academies with which the States are thickly sown, and which are the springs of so much intellectual activity. Here he had learned to think and to inquire,— a process which had not ceased with his school-days. Though toiling daily with his sons and hired man in all the minutiæ of a farmer's life, he kept an observant eye on the field of literature, and there was not a new publication heard of which he did not immediately find means to add to his yearly increasing stock of books. In particular was he a well-read and careful theologian, and all the controversial tracts, sermons, and books, with which then, (as ever since,) New England abounded, not only lay on his shelves, but had his pencilled annotations, queries, and comments thickly scattered along their margins. There was scarce an office of public trust which had not at one time or another been filled by him. He was deacon of the church, chairman of the school-committee, justice of the peace, had been twice representative in the State legislature, and was in permanence a sort of adviser-general in all cases between neighbor and neighbor. Among other acquisitions, he had gained some knowledge of the general forms of law, and his advice was often asked in preference to that of the regular practitioners.

His dwelling was one of those large, square, white, green-blinded mansions, cool, clean, and roomy, wherein the respectability of New England in those days rejoiced. The windows were shaded by clumps of lilacs; the deep yard with its white

fence inclosed a sweep of clean, short grass, and
a few fruit-trees.   Opposite the house was a small
blacksmith's-shed, which, of a wet day, was sparkling and lively with bellows and ringing forge,
while Mr. Zebedee and his sons were hammering
and pounding and putting in order anything that
was out of the way in farming-tools or establishments.   Not unfrequently the latest scientific work
or the last tractate of theology lay open by his
side, the contents of which would be discussed
with a neighbor or two as they entered; for, to
say the truth, many a neighbor, less forehanded
and thrifty, felt the benefit of this arrangement of
Mr. Zebedee, and would drop in to see if he
"wouldn't just tighten that rivet," or "kind o' ease
out that 'ere brace," or "let a feller have a turn
with his bellows, or a stroke or two on his anvil,"
—to all which the good man consented with a
grave obligingness.   The fact was, that, as nothing
in the establishment of Mr. Marvyn was often
broken or lost or out of place, he had frequent
applications to lend to those less fortunate persons,
always to be found, who supply their own lack of
considerateness from the abundance of their neighbors.

He who is known always to be in hand, and
always obliging, in a neighborhood, stands the
chance sometimes of having nothing for himself.
Mr. Zebedee reflected quietly on this subject, tak-

ing it, as he did all others, into grave and orderly
consideration, and finally provided a complete set
of tools, which he kept for the purpose of lending;
and when any of these were lent, he told the next
applicant quietly, that the axe or the hoe was already out, and thus he reconciled the Scripture
which commanded him " to do good and lend"
with that law of order which was written in his
nature.

Early in life Mr. Marvyn had married one of the
handsomest girls of his acquaintance, who had
brought him a thriving and healthy family of children, of whom James was the youngest. Mrs. Marvyn was, at this time, a tall, sad-eyed, gentle-man-
nered woman, thoughtful, earnest, deep-natured,
though sparing in the matter of words. In all her
household arrangements, she had the same thrift
and order which characterized her husband; but
hers was a mind of a finer and higher stamp than
his.

In her bedroom, near by her work-basket, stood
a table covered with books, — and so systematic
were her household arrangements, that she never
any day missed her regular hours for reading. One
who should have looked over this table would have
seen there how eager and hungry a mind was hid
behind the silent eyes of this quiet woman. History, biography, mathematics, volumes of the encyclopædia, poetry, novels, all alike found their

time and place there,—and while she pursued her
household labors, the busy, active soul within travelled cycles and cycles of thought, few of which
ever found expression in words. What might be
that marvellous music of the *Miserere*, of which
she read, that it convulsed crowds and drew groans
and tears from the most obdurate? What might
be those wondrous pictures of Raphael and Leonardo da Vinci? What would it be to see the
Apollo, the Venus? What was the charm that
enchanted the old marbles,— charm untold and in-
conceivable to one who had never seen even the
slightest approach to a work of art? Then those
glaciers of Switzerland, that grand, unapproachable mixture of beauty and sublimity in her mountains!—what would it be to one who could see
it? Then what were all those harmonies of which
she read,—masses, fugues, symphonies? Oh, could
she once hear the Miserere of Mozart, just to know
what music was like! And the cathedrals, what
were they? How wonderful they must be, with
their forests of arches, many-colored as autumn-
woods with painted glass, and the chants and an-
thems rolling down their long aisles! On all these
things she pondered quietly, as she sat often on
Sundays in the old staring, rattle-windowed meeting-house, and looked at the uncouth old pulpit,
and heard the choir faw-sol-la-ing or singing fu-
guing tunes; but of all this she said nothing.

Sometimes, for days, her thoughts would turn from these subjects and be absorbed in mathematical or metaphysical studies. "I have been following that treatise on Optics for a week, and never understood it till to-day," she once said to her husband. "I have found now that there has been a mistake in drawing the diagrams. I have corrected it, and now the demonstration is complete. Dinah, take care, that wood is hickory, and it takes only seven sticks of that size to heat the oven."

It is not to be supposed that a woman of this sort was an inattentive listener to preaching so stimulating to the intellect as that of Dr. Hopkins. No pair of eyes followed the web of his reasonings with a keener and more anxious watchfulness than those sad, deep-set, hazel ones; and as she was drawn along the train of its inevitable logic, a close observer might have seen how the shadows deepened over them. For, while others listened for the clearness of the thought, for the acuteness of the argument, she listened as a soul wide, fine-strung, acute, repressed, whose every fibre is a nerve, listens to the problem of its own destiny, — listened as the mother of a family listens, to know what were the possibilities, the probabilities, of this mysterious existence of ours to herself and those dearer to her than herself.

The consequence of all her listening was a history of deep inward sadness. That exultant joy, or that entire submission, with which others seemed to view the scheme of the universe, as thus unfolded, did not visit her mind. Everything to her seemed shrouded in gloom and mystery; and that darkness she received as a token of unregeneracy, as a sign that she was one of those who are destined, by a mysterious decree, never to receive the light of the glorious gospel of Christ. Hence, while her husband was a deacon of the church, she, for years, had sat in her pew while the sacramental elements were distributed, a mournful spectator. Punctilious in every duty, exact, reverential, she still regarded herself as a child of wrath, an enemy to God, and an heir of perdition; nor could she see any hope of remedy, except in the sovereign, mysterious decree of an Infinite and Unknown Power, a mercy for which she waited with the sickness of hope deferred.

Her children had grown up successively around her, intelligent and exemplary. Her eldest son was mathematical professor in one of the leading colleges of New England. Her second son, who jointly with his father superintended the farm, was a man of wide literary culture and of fine mathematical genius; and not unfrequently, on winter evenings, the son, father, and mother worked together, by their kitchen fireside, over the calculations for the almanac for the ensuing year, which the son had been appointed to edit.

5 *

Everything in the family arrangements was marked by a sober precision, a grave and quiet self-possession. There was little demonstrativeness of affection between parents and children, brothers and sisters, though great mutual love and confidence. It was not pride, nor sternness, but a sort of habitual shamefacedness, that kept far back in each soul those feelings which are the most beautiful in their outcome; but after a while, the habit became so fixed a nature, that a caressing or affectionate expression could not have passed the lips of one to another without a painful awkwardness. Love was understood, once for all, to be the basis on which their life was built. Once for all, they loved each other, and after that, the less said, the better. It had cost the woman's heart of Mrs. Marvyn some pangs, in the earlier part of her wedlock, to accept of this *once for all* in place of those daily outgushings which every woman desires should be like God's loving-kindnesses, " new every morning; " but hers, too, was a nature strongly inclining inward, and, after a few tremulous movements, the needle of her soul settled, and her life-lot was accepted,— not as what she would like or could conceive, but as a reasonable and good one. Life was a picture painted in low, cool tones, but in perfect keeping; and though another and brighter style might have pleased better, she did not quarrel with this.

Into this steady, decorous, highly-respectable circle the youngest child, James, made a formidable
irruption. One sometimes sees launched into a
family-circle a child of so different a nature from
all the rest, that it might seem as if, like an aëro-
lite, he had fallen out of another sphere. All the
other babies of the Marvyn family had been of
that orderly, contented sort, who sleep till it is con-
venient to take them up, and while awake suck
their thumbs contentedly and look up with large,
round eyes at the ceiling when it is not conven-
ient for their elders and betters that they should
do anything else. In farther advanced childhood,
they had been quiet and decorous children, who
could be all dressed and set up in chairs, like so
many dolls, of a Sunday morning, patiently await-
ing the stroke of the church-bell to be carried out
and put into the wagon which took them over the
two-miles' road to church. Possessed of such tranquil, orderly, and exemplary young offshoots, Mrs.
Marvyn had been considered eminent for her "faculty" in bringing up children.

But James was destined to put "faculty," and
every other talent which his mother possessed, to
rout. He was an infant of moods and tenses, and
those not of any regular verb. He would cry of
nights, and he would be taken up of mornings,
and he would not suck his thumb, nor a bundle
of caraway-seed tied in a rag and dipped in sweet

milk, with which the good gossips in vain endeav-
ored to pacify him. He fought manfully with his
two great fat fists the battle of babyhood, utterly
reversed all nursery maxims, and reigned as baby
over the whole prostrate household. When old
enough to run alone, his splendid black eyes and
glossy rings of hair were seen flashing and bob-
bing in every forbidden place and occupation.
Now trailing on his mother's gown, he assisted
her in salting her butter by throwing in small con-
tributions of snuff or sugar, as the case might be;
and again, after one of those mysterious periods
of silence which are of most ominous significance
in nursery experience, he would rise from the dem-
olition of her indigo-bag, showing a face ghastly
with blue streaks, and looking more like a gnome
than the son of a respectable mother. There was
not a pitcher of any description of contents left
within reach of his little tiptoes and busy fingers
that was not pulled over upon his giddy head
without in the least seeming to improve its steadiness. In short, his mother remarked that she was
thankful every night when she had fairly gotten
him into bed and asleep; James had really got
through one more day and killed neither himself
nor any one else.

As a boy, the case was little better. He did not
take to study,—yawned over books, and cut out
moulds for running anchors when he should have

been thinking of his columns of words in four syllables. No mortal knew how he learned to read, for he never seemed to stop running long enough to learn anything; and yet he did learn and used the talent in conning over travels, sea-voyages, and lives of heroes and naval commanders Spite of father, mother, and brother, he seemed to possess the most extraordinary faculty of running up unsavory acquaintances. He was hale-fellow well-met with every Tom and Jack and Jim and Ben and Dick that strolled on the wharves, and astonished his father with minutest particulars of every ship, schooner, and brig in the harbor, together with biographical notes of the different Toms, Dicks, and Harrys by whom they were worked.

There was but one member of the family that seemed to know at all what to make of James, and that was their negro servant, Candace.

In those days, when domestic slavery prevailed in New England, it was quite a different thing in its aspects from the same institution in more southern latitudes. The hard soil, unyielding to any but the most considerate culture, the thrifty, close, shrewd habits of the people, and their untiring activity and industry, prevented, among the mass of the people, any great reliance on slave labor.

Added to this, there were from the very first,

in New England, serious doubts in the minds of thoughtful and conscientious people in reference to the lawfulness of slavery; this scruple prevented many from availing themselves of it, and proved a restraint on all, so that nothing like plantation-life existed, and what servants were owned were scattered among different families, of which they came to be regarded and to regard themselves as a legitimate part and portion. Slavery was something foreign, grotesque, and picturesque in a life of the most matter-of-fact sameness; it was even as if one should see clusters of palm-trees scattered here and there among Yankee wooden meeting-houses, or open one's eyes on clumps of yellow-striped aloes growing among hardhack and huckleberry bushes in the pastures.

Mr. Marvyn, as a man of substance, numbered two or three in his establishment, among whom Candace reigned chief. The presence of these tropical specimens of humanity, with their wide, joyous, rich, physical abundance of nature, and their hearty *abandon* of outward expression, was a relief to the still clear-cut lines in which the picture of New England life was drawn, that an artist must appreciate.

No race has ever shown such infinite and rich capabilities of adaptation to varying soil and circumstances as the negro. Alike to them the snows of Canada, the hard, rocky land of New

England, with its set lines and orderly ways, or the gorgeous profusion and loose abundance of the Southern States. Sambo and Cuffy expand under them all. New England yet preserves among her hills and valleys the lingering echoes of the jokes and jollities of various sable worthies, who saw alike in orthodoxy and heterodoxy, in Dr. This-side and Dr. That-side, only food for more abundant merriment; — in fact, the minister of those days not unfrequently had his black shadow, a sort of African Boswell, who powdered his wig, brushed his boots, defended and patronized his sermons, and strutted complacently about as if through virtue of his blackness he had absorbed every ray of his master's dignity and wisdom. In families, the presence of these exotics was a god-send to the children, supplying from the abundant outwardness and demonstrativeness of their nature that aliment of sympathy so dear to childhood, which the repressed and quiet habits of New England education denied. Many and many a New Englander counts among his pleasantest early recol-'ections the memory of some of these genial creatures, who by their warmth of nature were the first and most potent mesmerizers of his childish mind.

Candace was a powerfully built, majestic black woman, corpulent, heavy, with a swinging majesty of motion like that of a ship in a ground-swell. Her shining black skin and glistening white teeth

were indications of perfect physical vigor which
had never known a day's sickness; her turban, of
broad red and yellow bandanna stripes, had even
a warm tropical glow; and her ample skirts were
always ready to be spread over every childish
transgression of her youngest pet and favorite,
James.

She used to hold him entranced long winter-
evenings, while she sat knitting in the chimney-
corner, and crooned to him strange, wild African
legends of the things that she had seen in her
childhood and early days,—for she had been stolen when about fifteen years of age; and these
weird, dreamy talks increased the fervor of his
roving imagination, and his desire to explore the
wonders of the wide and unknown world. When
rebuked or chastised, it was she who had secret
bowels of mercy for him, and hid doughnuts in
her ample bosom to be secretly administered to
him in mitigation of the sentence that sent him
supperless to bed; and many a triangle of pie,
many a wedge of cake, had conveyed to him surreptitious consolations which his more conscientious mother longed, but dared not, to impart. In
fact, these ministrations, if suspected, were winked
at by Mrs. Marvyn, for two reasons: first, that
mothers are generally glad of any loving-kindness
to an erring boy, which they are not responsible
for; and second, that Candace was so set in her

ways and opinions that one might as well come
in front of a ship under full sail as endeavor to
stop her in a matter where her heart was engaged.

To be sure, she had her own private and special quarrels with "Massa James" when he dis-
puted any of her sovereign orders in the kitchen,
and would sometimes pursue him with uplifted
rolling-pin and floury hands when he had snatched
a gingernut or cookey without suitable deference
or supplication, and would declare, roundly, that
there "never was sich an aggravatin' young un."
But if, on the strength of this, any one else ven-
tured a reproof, Candace was immediately round
on the other side:—"Dat ar' chile gwin' to be
spiled, 'cause dey's allers a-pickin' at him;—he's
well enough, on'y let him alone."

Well, under this miscellaneous assortment of
influences,—through the order and gravity and
solemn monotone of life at home, with the un-
ceasing tick-tack of the clock forever resounding
through clean, empty-seeming rooms,—through the
sea, ever shining, ever smiling, dimpling, soliciting,
like a magical charger who comes saddled and
bridled and offers to take you to fairyland,—
through acquaintance with all sorts of foreign, out-
landish ragamuffins among the ships in the harbor,—from disgust of slow-moving oxen, and long-
drawn, endless furrows round the fifteen-acre lot,

—from misunderstandings with grave elder brothers, and feeling somehow as if, he knew not why,
he grieved his mother all the time just by being
what he was and couldn't help being, — and,
finally, by a bitter break with his father, in which
came that last wrench for an individual existence
which some time or other the young growing
mind will give to old authority,—by all these
united, was the lot at length cast; for one evening James was missing at supper, missing by the
fireside, gone all night, not at home to breakfast,
—till, finally, a strange, weird, most heathenish-
ooking cabin-boy, who had often been forbidden
the premises by Mr. Marvyn, brought in a letter,
half-defiant, half-penitent, which announced that
James had sailed in the " Ariel " the evening before.

Mr. Zebedee Marvyn set his face as a flint, and
said, " He went out from us because he was not
of us," — whereat old Candace lifted her great
floury fist from the kneading-trough, and, shaking
it like a large snowball, said, " Oh, you go 'long,
Massa Marvyn; ye'll live to count dat ar' boy for
de staff o' your old age yet, now I tell ye; got
de makin' o' ten or'nary men in him; kittles dat's
full allers will bile over; good yeast will blow out
de cork,—lucky ef it don't bust de bottle. Tell
ye, der's angels has der hooks in sich, and when
de Lord wants him dey'll haul him in safe and

sound." And Candace concluded her speech by giving a lift to her whole batch of dough and flinging it down in the trough with an emphasis that made the pewter on the dresser rattle.

This apparently irreverent way of expressing her mind, so contrary to the deferential habits studiously inculcated in family discipline, had grown to be so much a matter of course to all the family that nobody ever thought of rebuking it. There was a sort of savage freedom about her which they excused in right of her having been born and bred a heathen, and of course not to be expected to come at once under the yoke of civilization. In fact, you must all have noticed, my dear readers, that there are some sorts of people for whom everybody turns out as they would for a railroad-car, without stopping to ask why; and Candace was one of them.

Moreover, Mr. Marvyn was not displeased with this defence of James, as might be inferred from his mentioning it four or five times in the course of the morning, to say how foolish it was,—wondering why it was that Candace and everybody else got so infatuated with that boy,—and ending, at last, after a long period of thought, with the remark, that these poor African creatures often seemed to have a great deal of shrewdness in them, and that he was often astonished at the penetration that Candace showed.

At the end of the year James came home, more quiet and manly than he had ever been before,—so handsome with his sunburnt face, and his keen, dark eyes, and glossy curls, that half the girls in the front gallery lost their hearts the first Sunday he appeared in church. He was tender as a woman to his mother, and followed her with his eyes, like a lover, wherever she went; he made due and manly acknowledgments to his father, but declared his fixed and settled intention to abide by the profession he had chosen; and he brought home all sorts of strange foreign gifts for every member of the household. Candace was glorified with a flaming red and yellow turban of Moorish stuff, from Mogadore, together with a pair of gorgeous yellow morocco slippers with peaked toes, which, though there appeared no call to wear them in her common course of life, she would put on her fat feet and contemplate with daily satisfaction. She became increasingly strengthened thereby in the conviction that the angels who had their hooks in Massa James's jacket were already beginning to shorten the line.

CHAPTER VIII.

WHICH TREATS OF ROMANCE.

THERE is no word in the English language more unceremoniously and indefinitely kicked and cuffed about, by what are called sensible people, than the word *romance*. When Mr. Smith or Mr. Stubbs has brought every wheel of life into such range and order that it is one steady, daily grind,—when they themselves have come into the habits and attitudes of the patient donkey, who steps round and round the endlessly turning wheel of some machinery, then they fancy that they have gotten " the victory that overcometh the world."

All but this dead grind, and the dollars that come through the mill, is by them thrown into one waste " catch-all " and labelled *romance*. Perhaps there was a time in Mr. Smith's youth,—he remembers it now,—when he read poetry, when his cheek was wet with strange tears, when a little song, ground out by an organ-grinder in the street, had power to set his heart beating and bring a mist before his eyes. Ah, in those days he had a vision!—a pair of soft eyes stirred him strangely; a little weak hand was laid on his manhood, and it shook and trembled; and then came all the humility, the aspiration, the fear, the hope, the high desire, the troubling of the waters by the descending angel of love,—and a little more and Mr. Smith might have become a man, instead of a banker! He thinks of it now, sometimes, as he looks across the fireplace after dinner and sees Mrs. Smith asleep, innocently shaking the bouquet of pink bows and Brussels lace that waves over her placid red countenance.

Mrs. Smith wasn't his first love, nor, indeed, any love at all; but they agree reasonably well. And as for poor Nellie,—well, she is dead and buried,—all that was stuff and romance. Mrs. Smith's money set him up in business, and Mrs. Smith is a capital manager, and he thanks God that he isn't romantic, and tells Smith Junior not to read poetry or novels, and to stick to realities.

" This is the victory that overcometh the world," —to learn to be fat and tranquil, to have warm fires and good dinners, to hang your hat on the same peg at the same hour every day, to sleep soundly all night, and never to trouble your head with a thought or imagining beyond.

But there are many people besides Mr. Smith who have gained this victory,—who have stran gled their higher nature and buried it, and built over its grave the structure of their life, the better to keep it down.

The fascinating Mrs. T., whose life is a whirl between ball and opera, point-lace, diamonds, and schemings of admiration for herself, and of establishments for her daughters,—there was a time, if you will believe me, when that proud, worldly woman was so humbled, under the touch of some mighty power, that she actually thought herself capable of being a poor man's wife. She thought she could live in a little, mean house on no-matter-what-street, with one servant, and make her own bonnets and mend her own clothes, and sweep the house Mondays, while Betty washed,— all for what? All because she thought that there was a man so noble, so true, so good, so high-minded, that to live with him in poverty, to be guided by him in adversity, to lean on him in every rough place of life, was a something no-bler, better, purer, more satisfying, than French laces, opera-boxes, and even Madame Roget's best gowns.

Unfortunately, this was all romance,— there was no such man. There was, indeed, a person of very common, self-interested aims and worldly na-ture, whom she had credited at sight with an un-limited draft on all her better nature; and when the hour of discovery came, she awoke from her dream with a start and a laugh, and ever since has despised aspiration, and been busy with the *realities* of life, and feeds poor little Mary Jane, who sits by her in the opera-box there, with all the fruit which she has picked from the bitter tree of knowledge. There is no end of the epigrams and witticisms which she can throw out, this elegant Mrs. T., on people who marry for love, lead prosy, worky lives, and put on their best cap with pink ribbons for Sunday. " Mary Jane shall never make a fool of herself;" but, even as she speaks, poor Mary Jane's heart is dying within her at the vanishing of a pair of whiskers from an opposite box,—which whiskers the poor little fool has credited with a *résumé* drawn from her own imaginings of all that is grandest and most heroic, most worshipful in man. By-and-by, when Mrs. T. finds the glamour has fallen on her daughter, she wonders ; she has " tried to keep novels out of the girl's way,—where did she get these notions ? "

All prosaic, and all bitter, disenchanted people talk as if poets and novelists *made* romance. They do, —just as much as craters make volcanoes,— no more. What is romance ? whence comes it ? Plato spoke to the subject wisely, in his quaint way, some two thousand years ago, when he said, " Man's soul, in a former state, was winged and soared among the gods and so it comes to pass, that, in this life, when the soul, by the power of music or poetry, or the sight of beauty, hath her remembrance quickened, forthwith there is a strug·gling and a pricking pain as of wings trying to come forth, — even as children in teething." And if an old heathen, two thousand years ago, discoursed thus gravely of the romantic part of our nature, whence comes it that in Christian lands we think in so pagan a way of it, and turn the whole care of it to ballad-makers, romancers, and opera-singers?

Let us look up in fear and reverence and say, " GOD is the great maker of romance. HE, from whose hand came man and woman, — HE, who strung the great harp of Existence with all its wild and wonderful and manifold chords, and attuned them to one another, — HE is the great Poet of life." Every impulse of beauty, of heroism, and every craving for purer love, fairer perfection, nobler type and style of being than that which closes like a prison-house around us, in the dim, daily walk of life, is God's breath, God's impulse, God's reminder to the soul that there is something higher, sweeter, purer, yet to be attained.

Therefore, man or woman, when thy ideal is shattered, — as shattered a thousand times it must be, — when the vision fades, the rapture burns out, turn not away in skepticism and bitterness, saying, " There is nothing better for a man than that

6

he should eat and drink," but rather cherish the revelations of those hours as prophecies and fore-shadowings of something real and possible, yet to be attained in the manhood of immortality. The scoffing spirit that laughs at romance is an apple of the Devil's own handing from the bitter tree of knowledge;—it opens the eyes only to see eternal nakedness.

If ever you have had a romantic, uncalculating friendship,—a boundless worship and belief in some hero of your soul,—if ever you have so loved, that all cold prudence, all selfish worldly considerations have gone down like drift-wood before a river flooded with new rain from heaven, so that you even forgot yourself, and were ready to cast your whole being into the chasm of existence, as an offer-ing before the feet of another, and all for nothing, —if you awoke bitterly betrayed and deceived, still give thanks to God that you have had one glimpse of heaven. The door now shut will open again. Rejoice that the noblest capability of your eternal inheritance has been made known to you; treasure it, as the highest honor of your being, that ever you could so feel,—that so divine a guest ever possessed your soul.

By such experiences are we taught the pathos, the sacredness of life; and if we use them wisely, our eyes will ever after be anointed to see what poems, what romances, what sublime tragedies lie around us in the daily walk of life, "written not with ink, but in fleshy tables of the heart." The dullest street of the most prosaic town has matter in it for more smiles, more tears, more intense excitement, than ever were written in story or sung in poem; the reality is there, of which the romancer is the second-hand recorder.

So much of a plea we put in boldly, because we foresee grave heads beginning to shake over our history, and doubts rising in reverend and discreet minds whether this history is going to prove anything but a love-story, after all.

We do assure you, right reverend Sir, and you, most discreet Madam, that it is not going to prove anything else; and you will find, if you will follow us, that there is as much romance burning under the snow-banks of cold Puritan preciseness as if Dr. Hopkins had been brought up to attend operas instead of metaphysical preaching, and Mary had been nourished on Byron's poetry instead of "Edwards on the Affections."

The innocent credulities, the subtle deceptions, that were quietly at work under the grave, white curls of the Doctor's wig, were exactly of the kind which have beguiled man in all ages, when near the sovereign presence of her who is born for his destiny;—and as for Mary, what did it avail her that she could say the Assembly's Catechism from end to end without tripping, and that every habit of her life beat time to practical realities, steadily as the parlor clock? The wildest Italian singer or dancer, nursed on nothing but excitement from her cradle, never was more thoroughly possessed by the awful and solemn mystery of woman's life than this Puritan girl.

It is quite true, that, the next morning after James's departure, she rose as usual in the dim gray, and was to be seen opening the kitchen-door just at the moment when the birds were giving the first little drowsy stir and chirp,— and that she went on setting the breakfast-table for the two hired men, who were bound to the fields with the oxen,— and that then she went on skimming cream for the butter, and getting ready to churn, and making up biscuit for the Doctor's breakfast, when he and they should sit down together at a somewhat later hour; and as she moved about, doing all these things, she sung various scraps of old psalm-tunes; and the good Doctor, who was then busy with his early exercises of devotion, listened, as he heard the voice, now here, now there, and thought about angels and the Millennium. Solemnly and tenderly there floated in at his open study-window, through the breezy lilacs, mixed with low of kine and bleat of sheep and hum of early wakening life, the little silvery ripples of that singing, somewhat mournful in its cadence, as if a gentle soul were striving to hush itself to rest.

The words were those of the rough old version of the Psalms then in use:—

> " Truly my waiting soul relies
>   In silence God upon;
>   Because from him there doth arise
>   All my salvation."

And then came the busy patter of the little foot-steps without, the moving •of chairs, the clink of plates, as busy hands were arranging the table; and then again there was a pause, and he thought she seemed to come near to the open window of the adjoining room, for the voice floated in clearer and sadder:—

> " O God, to me be merciful,
>   Be merciful to me!
>   Because my soul for shelter safe
>   Betakes itself to thee.
>
> " Yea, in the shadow of thy wings
>   My refuge have I placed,
>   Until these sore calamities
>   Shall quite be overpast."

The tone of life in New England, so habitually earnest and solemn, breathed itself in the grave and plaintive melodies of the tunes then sung in the churches; and so these words, though in the saddest minor key, did not suggest to the listen-ing ear of the auditor anything more than that pensive religious calm in which he delighted to repose. A contrast indeed they were, in their melancholy earnestness, to the exuberant carollings of a robin, who, apparently attracted by them, perched himself hard by in the lilacs, and struck up such a merry *roulade* as quite diverted the attention of the fair singer;—in fact, the intoxication breathed in the strain of this little messenger, whom God had feathered and winged and filled to the throat with ignorant joy, came in singular contrast with the sadder notes breathed by that creature of so much higher mould and fairer clay,—that creature born for an immortal life.

But the good Doctor was inly pleased when she sung,—and when she stopped, looked up from his Bible wistfully, as missing something, he knew not what; for he scarce thought how pleasant the little voice was, or knew he had been listening to it,—and yet he was in a manner enchanted by it, so thankful and happy that he exclaimed with fervor, " The lines are fallen unto me in pleasant places; yea, I have a goodly heritage."

So went the world with him, full of joy and praise, because the voice and the presence wherein lay his unsuspected life were securely near, so certainly and constantly a part of his daily walk that he had not even the trouble to wish for them. But in that other heart how was it?—how with the sweet saint that was talking to herself in psalms and hymns and spiritual songs?

The good child had remembered her mother's parting words the night before, — "Put your mind upon your duties," — and had begun her first conscious exercise of thought with a prayer that grace might be given her to do it. But even as she spoke, mingling and interweaving with that golden thread of prayer was another consciousness, a life in another soul, as she prayed that the grace of God might overshadow him, shield him from temptation, and lead him up to heaven; and this prayer so got the start of the other, that, ere she was aware, she had quite forgotten self, and was feeling, living, thinking in that other life.

The first discovery she made, when she looked out into the fragrant orchard, whose perfumes steamed in at her window, and listened to the first chirping of birds among the old apple-trees, was one that has astonished many a person before her; it was this: she found that all that had made life interesting to her was suddenly gone. She herself had not known, that, for the month past, since James came from sea, she had been living in an enchanted land, — that Newport harbor, and every rock and stone, and every mat of yellow seaweed on the shore, that the two-mile road between the cottage and the white house of Zebedee Marvyn, every mullein-stalk, every juniper-tree, had all had a light and a charm which were suddenly gone. There had not been an hour in the day for the last four weeks that had not had its unsuspected interest,—because he was at the white house, because, possibly, he might be going by, or coming in; nay, even in church, when she stood up to sing, and thought she was thinking only of God, had she not been conscious of that tenor voice that poured itself out by her side? and though afraid to turn her head that way, had she not felt that he was there every moment,—heard every word of the sermon and prayer for him? The very vigilant care which her mother had taken to prevent private interviews had only served to increase the interest by throwing over it the veil of constraint and mystery. Silent looks, involuntary starts, things indicated, not expressed,—these are the most dangerous, the most seductive aliment of thought to a delicate and sensitive nature. If things were said out, they might not be said wisely,—they might repel by their freedom, or disturb by their unfitness; but what is only looked is sent into the soul through the imagination, which makes of it all that the ideal faculties desire.

In a refined and exalted nature, it is very seldom that the feeling of love, when once thoroughly aroused, bears any sort of relation to the reality of the object. It is commonly an enkindling of the whole power of the soul's love for whatever she considers highest and fairest; it is,

in fact, the love of something divine and unearthly, which, by a sort of illusion, connects
itself with a personality. Properly speaking, there
is but One true, eternal Object of all that the
mind conceives, in this trance of its exaltation.
Disenchantment must come, of course; and in a
love which terminates in happy marriage; there is
a tender and gracious process, by which, without
shock or violence, the ideal is gradually sunk in
the real, which, though found faulty and earthly,
is still ever tenderly remembered as it seemed
under the morning light of that enchantment.

What Mary loved so passionately, that which
came between her and God in every prayer, was
not the gay, young, dashing sailor,—sudden in
anger, imprudent of speech, and, though generous
in heart, yet worldly in plans and schemings,—
but her own ideal of a grand and noble man,—
such a man as she thought he might become.
He stood glorified before her, an image of the
strength that overcomes things physical, of the
power of command which controls men and circumstances, of the courage which disdains fear, of
the honor which cannot lie, of constancy which
knows no shadow of turning, of tenderness which
protects the weak, and, lastly, of religious loyalty
which should lay the golden crown of its per-
fected manhood at the feet of a Sovereign Lord
and Redeemer. This was the man she loved, and

6 *

with this regal mantle of glories she invested the
person called James Marvyn; and all that she saw
and felt to be wanting she prayed for with the
faith of a believing woman.

Nor was she wrong;—for, as to every leaf and
every flower there is an ideal to which the growth
of the plant is constantly urging, so is there an
ideal to every human being,—a perfect form in
which it might appear, were every defect removed
and every characteristic excellence stimulated to
the highest point. Once in an age, God sends to
some of us a friend who loves in us, *not* a false
imagining, an unreal character, but, looking through
all the rubbish of our imperfections, loves in us
the divine ideal of our nature,—loves, not the
man that we are, but the angel that we may be.
Such friends seem inspired by a divine gift of
prophecy,—like the mother of St. Augustine, who,
in the midst of the wayward, reckless youth of
her son, beheld him in a vision, standing, clothed
in white, a ministering priest at the right hand
of God,—as he has stood for long ages since.
Could a mysterious foresight unveil to us this
resurrection form of the friends with whom we
daily walk, compassed about with mortal infirmity,
we should follow them with faith and reverence
through all the disguises of human faults and
weaknesses, " waiting for the manifestation of the
sons of God."

But these wonderful soul-friends, to whom God grants such perception, are the exceptions in life; yet sometimes are we blessed with one who sees through us, as Michel Angelo saw through a block of marble, when he attacked it in a divine fervor, declaring that an angel was imprisoned within it; and it is often the resolute and delicate hand of such a friend that sets the angel free.

There be soul-artists, who go through this world, looking among their fellows with reverence, as one looks amid the dust and rubbish of old shops for hidden works of Titian and Leonardo, and, finding them, however cracked or torn or painted over with tawdry daubs of pretenders, immediately recognize the divine original, and set themselves to cleanse and restore. Such be God's real priests, whose ordination and anointing are from the Holy Spirit; and he who hath not this enthusiasm is not ordained of God, though whole synods of bishops laid hands on him.

Many such priests there be among women;— for to this silent ministry their nature calls them, endowed, as it is, with fineness of fibre, and a subtile keenness of perception outrunning slow-footed reason;— and she of whom we write was one of these.

At this very moment, while the crimson wings of morning were casting delicate reflections on tree, and bush, and rock, they were also reddening innumerable waves round a ship that sailed alone, with a wide horizon stretching like an eternity around it; and in the advancing morning stood a young man thoughtfully looking off into the ocean, with a book in his hand,—James Marvyn,—as truly and heartily a creature of this material world as Mary was of the invisible and heavenly.

There are some who seem made to *live ;*—life is such a joy to them, their senses are so fully *en rapport* with all outward things, the world is so keenly appreciable, so much a part of themselves, they are so conscious of power and victory in the government and control of material things, — that the moral and invisible life often seems to hang tremulous and unreal in their minds, like the pale, faded moon in the light of a gorgeous sunrise. When brought face to face with the great truths of the invisible world, they stand related to the higher wisdom much like the gorgeous, gay Alcibiades to the divine Socrates, or like the young man in Holy Writ to Him for whose appearing Socrates longed;—they gaze, imperfectly comprehending, and at the call of ambition or riches turn away sorrowing.

So it was with James;— in the full tide of worldly energy and ambition, there had been forming over his mind that hard crust, that skepticism of the spiritual and exalted, which men of the world delight to call practical sense; he had been suddenly arrested and humbled by the revelation of a nature so much nobler than his own that he seemed worthless in his own eyes. He had asked for love; but when *such* love unveiled itself, he felt like the disciple of old in the view of a diviner tenderness,—" Depart from me, for I am a sinful man."

But it is not often that all the current of a life is reversed in one hour; and now, as James stood on the ship's deck, with life passing around him, and everything drawing upon the strings of old habits, Mary and her religion recurred to his mind as some fair, sweet, inexplicable vision. Where she stood he saw; but how *he* was ever to get there seemed as incomprehensible as how a mortal man should pillow his form on sunset clouds.

He held the little Bible in his hand as if it were some amulet charmed by the touch of a superior being; but when he strove to read it, his thoughts wandered, and he shut it, troubled and unsatisfied. Yet there were within him yearnings and cravings, wants never felt before, the beginning of that trouble which must ever precede the soul's rise to a higher plane of being.

There we leave him. We have shown you

now our three different characters, each one in its separate sphere, feeling the force of that strongest and holiest power with which it has pleased our great Author to glorify this mortal life.

CHAPTER IX.

WHICH TREATS OF THINGS SEEN.

As, for example, the breakfast. It is six o'clock, — the hired men and oxen are gone, — the breakfast-table stands before the open kitchen-door, snowy with its fresh cloth, the old silver coffee-pot steaming up a refreshing perfume, — and the Doctor sits on one side, sipping his coffee and looking across the table at Mary, who is innocently pleased at the kindly beaming in his placid blue eyes, — and Aunt Katy Scudder discourses of housekeeping, and fancies something must have disturbed the rising of the cream, as it is not so thick and yellow as wont.

Now the Doctor, it is to be confessed, was apt to fall into a way of looking at people such as pertains to philosophers and scholars generally, that is, as if he were looking through them into the infinite, — in which case his gaze became so earnest and intent that it would quite embarrass an uninitiated person ; but Mary, being used to this style of contemplation, was only quietly amused, and waited till some great thought should loom up before his mental vision,— in which case she hoped to hear from him.

The good man swallowed his first cup of coffee and spoke :—

"In the Millennium, I suppose, there will be such a fulness and plenty of all the necessaries and conveniences of life, that it will not be necessary for men and women to spend the greater part of their lives in labor in order to procure a living. It will not be necessary for each one to labor more than two or three hours a day, — not more than will conduce to health of body and vigor of mind; and the rest of their time they will spend in reading and conversation, and such exercises as are necessary and proper to improve their minds and make progress in knowledge."

New England presents probably the only example of a successful commonwealth founded on a theory, as a distinct experiment in the problem of society. It was for this reason that the minds of its great thinkers dwelt so much on the final solution of that problem in this world. The fact of a future Millennium was a favorite doctrine of the great leading theologians of New England, and Dr. Hopkins dwelt upon it with a peculiar partiality. Indeed, it was the solace and refuge of his soul, when oppressed with the discouragements which always attend things actual, to dwell upon and draw out in detail the splendors of this perfect future which was destined to glorify the world.

Nobody, therefore, at the cottage was in the least surprised when there dropped into the flow of their daily life these sparkling bits of ore, which their friend had dug in his explorations of a future Canaan,—in fact, they served to raise the hackneyed present out of the level of mere commonplace.

"But how will it be possible," inquired Mrs. Scudder, "that so much less work will suffice in those days to do all that is to be done?"

"Because of the great advance of arts and sciences which will take place before those days," said the Doctor, "whereby everything shall be performed with so much greater ease,—also the great increase of disinterested love, whereby the skill and talents of those who have much shall make up for the weakness of those who have less.

"Yes,"—he continued, after a pause,—"all the careful Marthas in those days will have no excuse for not sitting at the feet of Jesus; there will be no cumbering with much serving; the Church will have only Maries in those days."

This remark, made without the slightest personal intention, called a curious smile into Mrs. Scudder's face, which was reflected in a slight blush from Mary's, when the crack of a whip and the rattling of wagon-wheels disturbed the conversation and drew all eyes to the door.

There appeared the vision of Mr. Zebedee Marvyn's farm-wagon, stored with barrels, boxes, and baskets, over which Candace sat throned triumphant, her black face and yellow-striped turban glowing in the fresh morning with a hearty, joyous light, as she pulled up the reins, and shouted to the horse to stop with a voice that might have done credit to any man living.

" Dear me, if there isn't Candace ! " said Mary.

" Queen of Ethiopia," said the Doctor, who sometimes adventured a very placid joke.

The Doctor was universally known in all the neighborhood as a sort of friend and patron-saint of the negro race; he had devoted himself to their interests with a zeal unusual in those days. His church numbered more of them than any in Newport; and his hours of leisure from study were often spent in lowliest visitations among them, hearing their stories, consoling their sorrows, advising and directing their plans, teaching them reading and writing, and he often drew hard on his slender salary to assist them in their emergencies and distresses.

This unusual condescension on his part was repaid on theirs with all the warmth of their race ; and Candace, in particular, devoted herself to the Doctor with all the force of her being

There was a legend current in the neighborhood, that the first efforts to catechize Candace were not eminently successful, her modes of contemplating theological tenets being so peculiarly from her own individual point of view that it was hard to get her subscription to a received opinion. On the venerable clause in the Catechism, in particular, which declares that all men sinned in Adam and fell with him, Candace made a dead halt:—

"I didn't do dat ar', for one, I knows. I's got good mem'ry,—allers knows what I does,—nebber did eat dat ar' apple,—nebber eat a bit ob him. Don't tell me!"

It was of no use, of course, to tell Candace of all the explanations of this redoubtable passage, — of potential presence, and representative presence, and representative identity, and federal headship. She met all with the dogged, —

"Nebber did it, I knows; should 'ave 'membered, if I had. Don't tell me!"

And even in the catechizing class of the Doctor himself, if this answer came to her, she sat black and frowning in stony silence even in his reverend presence.

Candace was often reminded that the Doctor believed the Chatechism, and that she was differing from a great and good man; but the argument made no manner of impression on her, till, one day, a far-off cousin of hers, whose condition

under a hard master had often moved her compassion, came in overjoyed to recount to her how,
owing to Dr. Hopkins's exertions, he had gained
his freedom. The Doctor himself had in person
gone from house to house, raising the sum for his
redemption; and when more yet was wanting,
supplied it by paying half his last quarter's limited salary.

"He do dat ar'?" said Candace, dropping the
fork wherewith she was spearing doughnuts. "Den
I'm gwine to b'liebe ebery word *he* does!"

And accordingly, at the next catechizing, the
Doctor's astonishment was great when Candace
pressed up to him, exclaiming, —

"De Lord bress you, Doctor, for opening de
prison for dem dat is bound! I b'liebes in you
now, Doctor. I's gwine to b'liebe every word you
say. I'll say de Catechize now, — fix it any way
you like. I *did* eat dat ar' apple, — I eat de
whole tree, an' swallowed ebery bit ob it, if you
say so."

And this very thorough profession of faith was
followed, on the part of Candace, by years of the
most strenuous orthodoxy. Her general mode of
expressing her mind on the subject was short and
definitive.

"Law me! what's de use? I's set out to b'liebe
de Catechize, an' I'm gwine to b'liebe it, — so!"

While we have been telling you all this about

ner, she has fastened her horse, and is swinging eisurely up to the house with a basket on either arm.

"Good morning, Candace," said Mrs. Scudder. "What brings you so early?"

"Come down 'fore light to sell my chickens an' eggs,— got a lot o' money for 'em, too. Missy Marvyn she sent Miss Scudder some turkey-eggs, an' I brought down some o' my doughnuts for de Doctor. Good folks must lib, you know, as well as wicked ones,"— and Candace gave a hearty, unctuous laugh. "No reason why Doctors shouldn't hab good tings as well as sinners, is dere?"— and she shook in great billows, and showed her white teeth in the *abandon* of her laugh. "Lor' bress ye honey, chile!" she said, turning to Mary, "why ye looks like a new rose, ebery bit! Don't wondei *somebody* was allers pryin' an' spyin' about here!"

"How is your mistress, Candace?" said Mrs. Scudder, by way of changing the subject.

"Well, porly,—rader porly. When Massa Jim goes, 'pears like takin' de light right out her eyes. Dat ar' boy trains roun' arter his mudder like a cosset, he does. Lor', de house seems so still widout him!— can't a fly scratch his ear but it starts a body. Missy Marvyn she sent down, an' says, would you an' de Doctor an' Miss Mary please come to tea dis arternoon."

"Thank your mistress, Candace," said Mrs. Scud-

der; " Mary and I will come,— and the Doctor,
perhaps," looking at the good man, who had re-
lapsed into meditation, and was eating his breakfast without taking note of anything going on.
" It will be time enough to tell him of it," she
said to Mary, " when we have to wake him up to
dress; so we won't disturb him now."

To Mary the prospect of the visit was a pleasant one, for reasons which she scarce gave a definite form to. Of course, like a good girl, she had
come to a fixed and settled resolution to think of
James as little as possible; but when the path of
duty lay directly along scenes and among people
fitted to recall him, it was more agreeable than
if it had lain in another direction. Added to this,
a very tender and silent friendship subsisted between Mrs. Marvyn and Mary; in which, besides
similarity of mind and intellectual pursuits, there
was a deep, unspoken element of sympathy.

Candace watched the light in Mary's eyes with
the instinctive shrewdness by which her race seem
to divine the thoughts and feelings of their supe-
riors, and chuckled to herself internally. Without
ever having been made a *confidante* by any party,
or having a word said to or before her, still the
whole position of affairs was as clear to her as
if she had seen it on a map. She had appreciated at once Mrs. Scudder's coolness, James's devotion, and Mary's perplexity,—and inly resolved,

that, if the little maiden did not think of James in his absence, it should not be her fault.

"Laws, Miss Scudder," she said, "I's right glad you's comin'; 'cause you hasn't seen how we's kind o' splendified since Massa Jim come home. You wouldn't know it. Why, he's got mats from Mogadore on all de entries, and a great big 'un on de parlor; and ye ought to see de shawl he brought Missus, an' all de cur'us kind o' tings to de squire. 'Tell ye, dat ar' boy honors his fader and mudder, ef he don't do nuffin else,—an' dats de fus' commandment wid promise, Ma'am; an' to see him a-settin' up ebery day in prayer-time, so handsome, holdin' Missus's han', an' lookin' right into her eyes all de time! Why, dat ar' boy is one of de 'lect,—it's jest as clare to me; and de 'lect has got to come in,—dat's what I say. My faith's strong,—real clare, 'tell ye," she added, with the triumphant laugh which usually chorused her conversation, and turning to the Doctor, who, aroused by her loud and vigorous strain, was attending with interest to her.

"Well, Candace," he said, "we all hope you are right."

"*Hope*, Doctor!—I don't hope,—I *knows*. 'Tell ye, when I pray for him, don't I feel enlarged? 'Tell ye, it goes wid a rush. I can feel it gwine up like a rushin', mighty wind. I feels strong I do."

" That's right, Candace," said the Doctor, "keep on ; your prayers stand as much chance with God as if you were a crowned queen. The Lord is no respecter of persons."

" Dat's what he a'n't, Doctor,— an' dere's where I 'gree wid him," said Candace, as she gathered her baskets vigorously together, and, after a sweeping curtsy, went sailing down to her wagon, full laden with content, shouting a hearty " Good mornin', Missus," with the full power of her cheerful lungs, as she rode off.

As the Doctor looked after her, the simple, pleased expression with which he had watched her gradually faded, and there passed over his broad, good face a shadow, as of a cloud on a mountain-side.

" What a shame it is," he said, "what a scandal and disgrace to the Protestant religion, that Christians of America should openly practise and countenance this enslaving of the Africans ! I have for a long time holden my peace,— may the Lord forgive me !— but I believe the time is coming when I must utter my voice. I cannot go down to the wharves or among the shipping, without these poor dumb creatures look at me so that I am ashamed, — as if they asked me what I, a Christian minister, was doing, that I did not come to their help. I must testify."

Mrs. Scudder looked grave at this earnest announcement; she had heard many like it before, and they always filled her with alarm, because — — Shall we tell you why?

Well, then, it was not because she was not a thoroughly indoctrinated anti-slavery woman. Her husband, who did all her thinking for her, had been a man of ideas beyond his day, and never for a moment countenanced the right of slavery so far as to buy or own a servant or attendant of any kind; and Mrs. Scudder had always followed decidedly along the path of his opinions and practice, and never hesitated to declare the reasons for the faith that was in her. But if any of us could imagine an angel dropped down out of heaven, with wings, ideas, notions, manners, and customs all fresh from that very different country, we might easily suppose that the most pious and orthodox family might find the task of presenting him in general society and piloting him along the courses of this world a very delicate and embarrassing one. However much they might reverence him on their own private account, their hearts would probably sink within them at the idea of allowing him to expand himself according to his previous nature and habits in the great world without. In like manner, men of high, unworldly natures are often reverenced by those who are somewhat puzzled what to do with them practically.

7

Mrs. Scudder considered the Doctor as a superior being, possessed by a holy helplessness in all things material and temporal, which imposed on her the necessity of thinking and caring for him, and prevising the earthly and material aspects of his affairs.

There was not in Newport a more thriving and reputable business at that time than the slave-trade. Large fortunes were constantly being turned out in it, and what better providential witness of its justice could most people require?

Besides this, in their own little church, she reflected with alarm, that Simeon Brown, the richest and most liberal supporter of the society, had been, and was then, drawing all his wealth from this source; and rapidly there flashed before her mind a picture of one and another, influential persons, who were holders of slaves. Therefore, when the Doctor announced, "I must testify," she rattled her tea-spoon uneasily, and answered,—

"In what way, Doctor, do you think of bearing testimony? The subject, I think, is a very difficult one."

"Difficult? I think no subject can be clearer. If we were right in our war for liberty, we are wrong in making slaves or keeping them."

"Oh, I did not mean," said Mrs. Scudder, "that it was difficult to understand the subject; the *right* of the matter is clear, but what to *do* is the thing."

"I shall preach about it," said the Doctor; "my mind has run upon it some time. I shall show to the house of Judah their sin in this matter."

"I fear there will be great offence given," said Mrs. Scudder. "There's Simeon Brown, one of our largest supporters,—he is in the trade."

"Ah, yes,—but he will come out of it,—of course he will,—he is all right, all clear. I was delighted with the clearness of his views the other night, and thought then of bringing them to bear on this point,—only, as others were present, I deferred it. But I can show him that it follows logically from his principles; I am confident of that."

"I think you'll be disappointed in him, Doctor; —I think he'll be angry, and get up a commotion, and leave the church."

"Madam," said the Doctor, "do you suppose that a man who would be willing even to give up his eternal salvation for the greatest good of the universe could hesitate about a few paltry thousands that perish in the using?"

"He may feel willing to give up his soul," said Mrs. Scudder, naïvely, "but I don't think he'll give up his ships,—that's quite another matter,— he won't see it to be his duty."

"Then, Ma'am, he'll be a hypocrite, a gross hypocrite, if he won't," said the Doctor. "It is not Christian charity to think it of him. I shall call upon him this morning and tell him my intentions."

"But, Doctor," exclaimed Mrs. Scudder, with a start, "pray, think a little more of it. You know a great many things depend on him. Why! he has subscribed for twenty copies of your ' System of Theology.' I hope you'll remember that."

"And why should I remember that?" said the Doctor,—hastily turning round, suddenly enkindled, his blue eyes flashing out of their usual misty calm,—"what has my ' System of Theology' to do with the matter?"

"Why," said Mrs. Scudder, "it's of more importance to get right views of the gospel before the world than anything else, is it not?—and if, by any imprudence in treating influential people, this should be prevented, more harm than good would be done."

"Madam," said the Doctor, "I'd sooner my system should be sunk in the sea than it should be a millstone round my neck to keep me from my duty. Let God take care of my theology; I must do my duty."

And as the Doctor spoke, he straightened himself to the full dignity of his height, his face kindling with an unconscious majesty, and, as he turned, his eye fell on Mary, who was standing with her slender figure dilated, her large blue eye wide and bright, in a sort of trance of solemn feeling, half smiles, half tears,—and the strong, heroic man started, to see this answer to his higher soul in the sweet, tremulous mirror of womanhood. One of those lightning glances passed between his eyes and hers which are the freemasonry of noble spirits,—and, by a sudden impulse, they approached each other. He took both her outstretched hands, looked down into her face with a look full of admiration, and a sort of naïve wonder,—then, as if her inspired silence had been a voice to him, he laid his hand on her head, and said,—

"God bless you, child! 'Out of the mouth of babes and sucklings hast thou ordained strength because of thine enemies, that thou mightest still the enemy and the avenger!'"

In a moment he was gone.

"Mary," said Mrs. Scudder, laying her hand on her daughter's arm, "the Doctor loves you!"

"I know he does, mother," said Mary, innocently; "and I love him,—dearly!—he is a noble, grand man!"

Mrs. Scudder looked keenly at her daughter. Mary's eye was as calm as a June sky, and she began, composedly, gathering up the teacups.

"She did not understand me," thought the mother.

CHAPTER X.

THE TEST OF THEOLOGY.

The Doctor went immediately to his study and put on his best coat and his wig, and, surmounting them by his cocked hat, walked manfully out of the house, with his gold-headed cane in his hand.

"There he goes!" said Mrs. Scudder, looking regretfully after him. "He is *such* a good man! —but he has not the least idea how to get along in the world. He never thinks of anything but what is true; he hasn't a particle of management about him."

"Seems to me," said Mary, "that is like an Apostle. You know, mother, St. Paul says, 'In simplicity and godly sincerity, not with fleshly wisdom, but by the grace of God, we have had our conversation in the world.'"

"To be sure,—that is just the Doctor," said Mrs. Scudder; "that's as like him as if it had been written for him. But that kind of way, somehow, don't seem to do in our times; it won't

answer with Simeon Brown, — I know the man.
I know just as well, now, how it will all seem to
him, and what will be the upshot of this talk, if
the Doctor goes there! It won't do any good; if
it would, I would be willing. I feel as much desire to have this horrid trade in slaves stopped as
anybody; your father, I'm sure, said enough about
it in his time; but then I know it's no use trying.
Just as if Simeon Brown, when he is making his
hundreds of thousands in it, is going to be persuaded to give it up! He won't, — he'll only turn
against the Doctor, and won't pay his part of the
salary, and will use his influence to get up a
party against him, and our church will be broken
up and the Doctor driven away, — that's all that
will come of it; and all the good that he is
doing now to these poor negroes will be over-
thrown, — and they never will have so good a
friend. If he would stay here and work gradually, and get his System of Theology printed, —
and Simeon Brown would help at that, — and
only drop words in season here and there, till
people are brought along with him, why, by-and-
by something might be done; but now, it's just
the most imprudent thing a man could under-
take."

"But, mother, if it really is a sin to trade in
slaves and hold them, I don't see how he can
help himself. I quite agree with him. I don't

see how he came to let it go so long as he has."

"Well," said Mrs. Scudder, "if worst comes to worst, and he will do it, I, for one, shall stand by him to the last."

"And I, for another," said Mary.

"I would like him to talk with Cousin Zebedee about it," said Mrs. Scudder. "When we are up there this afternoon, we will introduce the conversation. He is a good, sound man, and the Doctor thinks much of him, and perhaps he may shed some light upon this matter."

Meanwhile the Doctor was making the best of his way, in the strength of his purpose to test the orthodoxy of Simeon Brown.

Honest old granite boulder that he was, no sooner did he perceive a truth than he rolled after it with all the massive gravitation of his being, inconsiderate as to what might lie in his way;— from which it is to be inferred, that, with all his intellect and goodness, he would have been a very clumsy and troublesome inmate of the modern American Church. How many societies, boards, colleges, and other good institutions, have reason to congratulate themselves that he has long been among the saints!

With him logic was everything, and to perceive a truth and not act in logical sequence from it a thing so incredible, that he had not yet enlarged his capacity to take it in as a possibility. That a man should refuse to hear truth, he could understand. In fact, he had good reason to think the majority of his townsmen had no leisure to give to that purpose. That men hearing truth should dispute it and argue stoutly against it, he could also understand; but that a man could admit a truth and not admit the plain practice resulting from it was to him a thing incomprehensible. Therefore, spite of Mrs. Katy Scudder's discouraging observations, our good Doctor walked stoutly and with a trusting heart.

At the moment when the Doctor, with a silent uplifting of his soul to his invisible Sovereign, passed out of his study, on this errand, where was the disciple whom he went to seek?

In a small, dirty room, down by the wharf, the windows veiled by cobwebs and dingy with the accumulated dust of ages, he sat in a greasy, leathern chair by a rickety office-table, on which was a great pewter inkstand, an account-book, and divers papers tied with red tape.

Opposite to him was seated a square-built individual,—a man of about forty, whose round head, shaggy eyebrows, small, keen eyes, broad chest, and heavy muscles showed a preponderance of the animal and brutal over the intellectual and spiritual. This was Mr. Scroggs, the agent of a rice-plantation, who had come on, bringing an

7 *

order for a new relay of negroes to supply the deficit occasioned by fever, dysentery, and other causes, in their last year's stock.

"The fact is," said Simeon, "this last ship-load wasn't as good a one as usual; we lost more than a third of it, so we can't afford to put them a penny lower."

"Ay," said the other,—"but then there are so many women!"

"Well," said Simeon, "women a'n't so strong, perhaps, to start with,— but then they stan' it out, perhaps, in the long run, better. They're more patient;—some of these men, the Mandingoes, particularly, are pretty troublesome to manage. We lost a splendid fellow, coming over, on this very voyage. Let 'em on deck for air, and this fellow managed to get himself loose and fought like a dragon. He settled one of our men with his fist, and another with a marlinspike that he caught,— and, in fact, they had to shoot him down. You'll have his wife; there's his son, too, —fine fellow, fifteen year old by his teeth."

"What! that lame one?"

"Oh, he a'n't lame!—it's nothing but the cramps from stowing. You know, of course, they are more or less stiff. He's as sound as a nut."

'Don't much like to buy relations, on account of their hatching up mischief together," said Mr. Scroggs.

" Oh, that's all humbug! You must keep 'em from coming together, anyway. It's about as broad as 'tis long. There'll be wives and husbands and children among 'em before long, start 'em as you will. And then this woman will work better for having the boy; she's kinder set on him; she jabbers lots of lingo to him, day and night."

" Too much, I doubt," said the overseer, with a shiug.

" Well, well,— I'll tell you," said Simeon, rising. " I've got a few errands up-town, and you just step over with Matlock and look over the stock; —just set aside any that you want, and when I see 'em all together, I'll tell you just what you shall have 'em for. I'll be back in an hour or two."

And so saying, Simeon Brown called an underling from an adjoining room, and, committing his customer to his care, took his way up-town, in a serene frame of mind, like a man who comes from the calm performance of duty.

Just as he came upon the street where was situated his own large and somewhat pretentious mansion, the tall figure of the Doctor loomed in sight, sailing majestically down upon him, making a signal to attract his attention.

" Good morning, Doctor," said Simeon.

" Good morning, Mr. Brown," said the Doctor. " I was looking for you. I did not quite finish the subject we were talking about at Mrs. Scudder's table last night. I thought I should like to go on with it a little."

"With all my heart, Doctor," said Simeon, not a little flattered. "Turn right in. Mrs. Brown will be about her house-business, and we will have the keeping-room all to ourselves. Come right in."

The "keeping-room" of Mr. Simeon Brown's house was an intermediate apartment between the ineffable glories of the front-parlor and that court of the gentiles, the kitchen; for the presence of a large train of negro servants made the latter apartment an altogether different institution from the throne-room of Mrs. Katy Scudder.

This keeping-room was a low-studded apartment, finished with the heavy oaken beams of the wall left full in sight, boarded over and painted. Two windows looked out on the street, and another into a sort of court-yard, where three black wenches, each with a broom, pretended to be sweeping, but were, in fact, chattering and laughing, like so many crows.

On one side of the room stood a heavy mahogany sideboard, covered with decanters, labelled Gin, Brandy, Rum, etc., — for Simeon was held to be a provider of none but the best, in his house-keeping. Heavy mahogany chairs, with crewel coverings, stood sentry about the room; and the fireplace was flanked by two broad arm-chairs, covered with stamped leather.

On ushering the Doctor into this apartment, Simeon courteously led him to the sideboard.

"We mus'n't make our discussions too *dry*, Doctor," he said. "What will you take?"

"Thank you, Sir," said the Doctor, with a wave of his hand, — "nothing this morning."

And depositing his cocked hat in a chair, he settled himself into one of the leathern easy-chairs, and, dropping his hands upon his knees, looked fixedly before him, like a man who is studying how to enter upon an inwardly absorbing subject.

"Well, Doctor," said Simeon, seating himself opposite, sipping comfortably at a glass of rum-and-water, "our views appear to be making a noise in the world. Everything is preparing for your volumes; and when they appear, the battle of New Divinity, I think, may fairly be considered as won."

Let us consider, that, though a woman may forget her first-born, yet a man cannot forget his own system of theology, — because therein, if he be a true man, is the very elixir and essence of all that is valuable and hopeful to the universe; and considering this, let us appreciate the settled purpose of our friend, whom even this tempting bait did not swerve from the end which he had in view.

"Mr. Brown," he said, "all our theology is as

a drop in the ocean of God's majesty, to whose glory we must be ready to make any and every sacrifice."

" Certainly," said Mr. Brown, not exactly comprehending the turn the Doctor's thoughts were taking.

" And the glory of God consisteth in the happiness of all his rational universe, each in his proportion, according to his separate amount of being; so that, when we devote ourselves to God's glory, it is the same as saying that we devote ourselves to the highest happiness of his created universe.

" That's clear, Sir," said Simeon, rubbing his hands, and taking out his watch to see the time.

The Doctor hitherto had spoken in a laborious manner, like a man who is slowly lifting a heavy bucket of thought out of an internal well.

" I am glad to find your mind so clear on this all-important point, Mr. Brown,— the more so as I feel that we must immediately proceed to apply our principles, at whatever sacrifice of worldly goods ; and I trust, Sir, that you are one who at the call of your Master would not hesitate even to lay down all your worldly possessions for the greater good of the universe."

" I trust so, Sir," said Simeon, rather uneasily, and without the most distant idea what could be coming next in the mind of his reverend friend.

" Did it never occur to you, my friend," said

the Doctor, "that the enslaving of the African race is a clear violation of the great law which commands us to love our neighbor as ourselves,— and a dishonor upon the Christian religion, more particularly in us Americans, whom the Lord hath so marvellously protected, in our recent struggle for our own liberty?"

Simeon started at the first words of this address, much as if some one had dashed a bucket of water on his head, and after that rose uneasily, walking the room and playing with the seals of his watch.

"I—I never regarded it in this light," he said.

"Possibly not, my friend," said the Doctor,— "so much doth established custom blind the minds of the best of men. But since I have given more particular attention to the case of the poor negroes here in Newport, the thought has more and more labored in my mind,— more especially as our own struggles for liberty have turned my attention to the rights which every human creature hath before God,— so that I find much in my former blindness and the comparative dumbness I have heretofore maintained on this subject wherewith to reproach myself; for, though I have borne somewhat of a testimony, I have not given it that force which so important a subject required. I am humbled before God for my neglect, and resolved now, by His grace, to leave no stone unturned till this iniquity be purged away from our Zion."

"Well, Doctor," said Simeon, "you are certainly touching on a very dark and difficult subject, and one in which it is hard to find out the path of duty. Perhaps it will be well to bear it in mind, and by looking at it prayerfully some light may arise. There are such great obstacles in the way, that I do not see at present what can be done; do you, Doctor?"

"I intend to preach on the subject next Sunday, and hereafter devote my best energies in the most public way to this great work," said the Doctor.

"You, Doctor? — and now, immediately? Why, it appears to me you cannot do it. You are the most unfit man possible. Whosoever duty it may be, it does not seem to me to be yours. You already have more on your shoulders than you can carry; you are hardly able to keep your ground now, with all the odium of this new theology upon you. Such an effort would break up your church, — destroy the chance you have to do good here, — prevent the publication of your system."

"If it's nobody's system but mine, the world won't lose much, if it never be published; but if it be God's system, nothing can hinder its appearing. Besides, Mr. Brown, I ought not to be one man alone. I count on your help. I hold it as a special providence, Mr. Brown, that in our own church an opportunity will be given to testify to the reality of disinterested benevolence. How glorious the opportunity for a man to come out and testify by sacrificing his worldly living and business! If you, Mr. Brown, will at once, at whatever sacrifice, quit all connection with this detestable and diabolical slave-trade, you will exhibit a spectacle over which angels will rejoice, and which will strengthen and encourage me to preach and write and testify."

Mr. Simeon Brown's usual demeanor was that of the most leathery imperturbability. In calm theological reasoning, he could demonstrate, in the dryest tone, that, if the eternal torment of six bodies and souls were absolutely the necessary means for preserving the eternal blessedness of thirty-six, benevolence would require us to rejoice in it, not in itself considered, but in view of greater good. And when he spoke, not a nerve quivered; the great mysterious sorrow with which the creation groaneth and travaileth, the sorrow from which angels veil their faces, never had touched one vibrating chord either of body or soul; and he laid down the obligations of man to unconditional submission in a style which would have affected a person of delicate sensibility much like being mentally sawn in sunder. Benevolence, when Simeon Brown spoke of it, seemed the grimmest and unloveliest of Gorgons; for his mind seemed to resemble those fountains which petrify everything that falls into them. But the hardest-shelled animals have a vital and sensitive part, though only so large as the point of a needle; and the Doctor's innocent proposition to Simeon, to abandon his whole worldly estate for his principles, touched this spot.

When benevolence required but the acquiescence in certain possible things which might be supposed to happen to his soul, which, after all, he was comfortably certain never would happen, or the acquiescence in certain suppositious sacrifices for the good of that most intangible of all abstractions, Being in general, it was a dry, calm subject. But when it concerned the immediate giving-up of his slave-ships and a transfer of business, attended with all that confusion and loss which he foresaw at a glance, then he *felt*, and felt too much to see clearly. His swarthy face flushed, his little blue eye kindled, he walked up to the Doctor and began speaking in the short, energetic sentences of a man thoroughly awake to what he is talking about.

"Doctor, you're too fast. You are not a practical man, Doctor. You are good in your pulpit; —nobody better. Your theology is clear;—nobody can argue better. But come to practical matters, why, business has its laws, Doctor. Ministers are the most unfit men in the world to talk on such subjects; it's departing from their sphere; they talk about what they don't understand. Besides, you take too much for granted. I'm not sure that this trade is an evil. I want to be convinced of it. I'm sure it's a favor to these poor creatures to bring them to a Christian land. They are a thousand times better off. Here they can hear the gospel and have some chance of salvation."

"If we want to get the gospel to the Africans," said the Doctor, "why not send whole ship-loads of missionaries to them, and carry civilization and the arts and Christianity to Africa, instead of stirring up wars, tempting them to ravage each other's territories, that we may get the booty? Think of the numbers killed in the wars, — of all that die on the passage? Is there any need of killing ninety-nine men to give the hundredth one the gospel, when we could give the gospel to them all? Ah, Mr. Brown, what if all the money spent in fitting out ships to bring the poor negroes here, so prejudiced against Christianity that they regard it with fear and aversion, had been spent in sending it to them, Africa would have been covered with towns and villages, rejoicing in civilization and Christianity?"

"Doctor, you are a dreamer," replied Simeon,

" an unpractical man. Your situation prevents your knowing anything of real life."

" Amen! the Lord be praised therefor!" said the Doctor, with a slowly increasing flush mounting to his cheek, showing the burning brand of a smouldering fire of indignation.

" Now let me just talk common-sense, Doctor, — which has its time and place, just as much as theology ; — and if you have the most theology, I flatter myself I have the most common-sense ; a business-man must have it. Now just look at your situation, — how you stand. You've got a most important work to do. In order to do it, you must keep your pulpit, you must keep our church together. We are few and weak. We are a minority. Now there's not an influential man in your society that don't either hold slaves or engage in the trade ; and if you open upon this subject as you are going to do, you'll just divide and destroy the church. All men are not like you ; — men are men, and will be, till they are thoroughly sanctified, which never happens in this life, — and there will be an instant and most unfavorable agitation. Minds will be turned off from the discussion of the great saving doctrines of the gospel to a side issue. You will be turned out, — and you know, Doctor, you are not appreciated as you ought to be, and it won't be easy for you to get a new settlement ; and then subscriptions will all drop off from your book, and you won't be able to get that out; and all this good will be lost to the world, just for want of common-sense."

"There is a kind of wisdom in what you say, Mr. Brown," replied the Doctor, naïvely; "but I fear much that it is the wisdom spoken of in James, iii. 15, which 'descendeth not from above, but is earthly, sensual, devilish.' You avoid the very point of the argument, which is, Is this a sin against God? That it is, I am solemnly convinced; and shall I 'use lightness? or the things that I purpose do I purpose according to the flesh, that with me there should be yea, yea, and nay, nay?' No, Mr. Brown, immediate repentance, unconditional submission, these are what I must preach as long as God gives me a pulpit to stand in, whether men will hear or whether they will forbear."

"Well, Doctor," said Simeon, shortly, "you can do as you like; but I give you fair warning, that I, for one, shall stop my subscription, and go to Dr. Stiles's church."

"Mr. Brown," said the Doctor, solemnly, rising, and drawing his tall figure to its full height, while a vivid light gleamed from his blue eye, "as to that, you can do as you like; but I think it my duty, as your pastor, to warn you that I have perceived, in my conversation with you this morn-

ing, such a want of true spiritual illumination
and discernment as leads me to believe that you
are yet in the flesh, blinded by that 'carnal mind'
which 'is not subject to the law of God, neither
indeed can be.' I much fear you have no part
nor lot in this matter, and that you have need,
seriously, to set yourself to search into the foundations of your hope; for you may be like him
of whom it is written, (Isaiah, xliv. 20,) 'he feedeth on ashes: a deceived heart hath turned him
aside, that he cannot deliver his soul, nor say, Is
there not a lie in my right hand?'"

The Doctor delivered this address to his man
of influence with the calmness of an ambassador
charged with a message from a sovereign, for
which he is no otherwise responsible than to
speak it in the most intelligible manner; and
then, taking up his hat and cane, he bade him
good morning, leaving Simeon Brown in a tumult
of excitement which no previous theological discussion had ever raised in him.

CHAPTER XI.

THE PRACTICAL TEST.

THE hens cackled drowsily in the barnyard of the white Marvyn-house; in the blue June-afternoon sky sported great sailing islands of cloud, whose white, glistening heads looked in and out through the green apertures of maple and blossoming apple-boughs; the shadows of the trees had already turned eastward, when the one-horse wagon of Mrs. Katy Scudder appeared at the door, where Mrs. Marvyn stood, with a pleased, quiet welcome in her soft, brown eyes. Mrs. Scudder herself drove, sitting on a seat in front, while the Doctor, apparelled in the most faultless style, with white wrist-ruffles, plaited shirt-bosom, immaculate wig, and well-brushed coat, sat by Mary's side, serenely unconscious how many feminine cares had gone to his getting-up. He did not know of the privy consultations, the sewings, stitchings, and starchings, the ironings, the brushings, the foldings and unfoldings and timely arrangements, that gave such dignity and respectability to his outer man, any more than the serene moon rising tranquilly behind a purple mountain-top troubles her calm head with treatises on astronomy; it is enough for her to shine,—she thinks not how or why.

There is a vast amount of latent gratitude to women lying undeveloped in the hearts of men, which would come out plentifully, if they only knew what they did for them. The Doctor was so used to being well dressed, that he never asked why. That his wig always sat straight and even around his ample forehead, not facetiously poked to one side, nor assuming rakish airs, unsuited to clerical dignity, was entirely owing to Mrs. Katy Scudder. That his best broadcloth coat was not illustrated with shreds and patches, fluff and dust, and hanging in ungainly folds, was owing to the same. That his long silk stockings never had a treacherous stitch allowed to break out into a long running ladder was due to her watchfulness; and that he wore spotless ruffles on his wrists or at his bosom was her doing also. The Doctor little thought, while he, in common with good ministers generally, gently traduced the Scriptural Martha and insisted on the duty of heavenly abstractedness, how much of his own leisure for spiritual contemplation was due to the Martha-like talents of his hostess. But then, the good soul had it in him to be grateful,

and would have been unboundedly so, if he had
known his indebtedness,—as, we trust, most of
our magnanimous masters would be.

Mr. Zebedee Marvyn was quietly sitting in the
front summer parlor, listening to the story of two
of his brother church-members, between whom some
difficulty had arisen in the settling of accounts:
Jim Bigelow, a small, dry, dapper little individual,
known as general jobber and factotum, and Abram
Griswold, a stolid, wealthy, well-to-do farmer. And
the fragments of conversation we catch are not
uninteresting, as showing Mr. Zebedee's habits of
thought and mode of treating those who came to
him for advice.

" I could 'ave got along better, if he'd 'a' paid
me regular every night," said the squeaky voice
of little Jim;—"but he was allers puttin' me off
till it come even change, he said."

" Well, 'ta'n't always handy," replied the other,
"one doesn't like to break into a five-pound note
for nothing; and I like to let it run till it comes
even change."

" But, brother," said Mr. Zebedee, turning over
the great Bible that lay on the mahogany stand
in the corner, "we must go to the law and to
the testimony,"—and, turning over the leaves, he
read from Deuteronomy, xxiv.:—

" Thou shalt not oppress an hired servant that
is poor and needy, whether he be of thy brethren

8

or of thy strangers that are in thy land within thy gates. At his day thou shalt give him his hire, neither shall the sun go down upon it; for he is poor, and setteth his heart upon it: lest he cry against thee unto the Lord, and it be sin unto thee."

" You see what the Bible has to say on the matter," he said.

" Well, now, Deacon, I rather think you've got me in a tight place," said Mr. Griswold, rising; and turning confusedly round, he saw the placid figure of the Doctor, who had entered the room unobserved in the midst of the conversation, and was staring with that look of calm, dreamy abstraction which often led people to suppose that he heard and saw nothing of what was going forward.

All rose reverently; and while Mr. Zebedee was shaking hands with the Doctor, and welcoming him to his house, the other two silently withdrew, making respectful obeisance.

Mrs. Marvyn had drawn Mary's hand gently under her arm and taken her to her own sleeping-room, as it was her general habit to do, that she might show her the last book she had been reading, and pour into her ear the thoughts that had been kindled up by it.

Mrs. Scudder, after carefully brushing every speck of dust from the Doctor's coat and seeing him seated in an arm-chair by the open window, took out a long stocking of blue-mixed yarn which she was knitting for his winter wear, and, pinning her knitting-sheath on her side, was soon trotting her needles contentedly in front of him.

The ill-success of the Doctor's morning attempt at enforcing his theology in practice rather depressed his spirits. There was a noble innocence of nature in him which looked at hypocrisy with a puzzled and incredulous astonishment. How a man *could* do so and be so was to him a problem at which his thoughts vainly labored. Not that he was in the least discouraged or hesitating in regard to his own course. When he had made up his mind to perform a duty, the question of success no more entered his thoughts than those of the granite boulder to which we have before compared him. When the time came for him to roll, he did roll with the whole force of his being; — where he was to land was not his concern.

Mildly and placidly he sat with his hands resting on his knees, while Mr. Zebedee and Mrs. Scudder compared notes respecting the relative prospects of corn, flax, and buckwheat, and thence passed to the doings of Congress and the last proclamation of General Washington, pausing once in a while, if, peradventure, the Doctor might take up the conversation. Still he sat dreamily eyeing the flies as they fizzed down the panes of the half-open window.

"I think," said Mr. Zebedee, " the prospects of the Federal party were never brighter."

The Doctor was a stanch Federalist, and generally warmed to this allurement; but it did not serve this time.

Suddenly drawing himself up, a light came into his blue eyes, and he said to Mr. Marvyn, —

"I'm thinking, Deacon, if it is wrong to keep back the wages of a servant till after the going down of the sun, what those are to do who keep them back all their lives."

There was a way the Doctor had of hearing and seeing when he looked as if his soul were afar off, and bringing suddenly into present conversation some fragment of the past on which he had been leisurely hammering in the quiet chambers of his brain, which was sometimes quite startling.

This allusion to a passage of Scripture which Mr. Marvyn was reading when he came in, and which nobody supposed he had attended to, startled Mrs. Scudder, who thought, mentally, " Now for it!" and laid down her knitting-work, and eyed her cousin anxiously. Mrs. Marvyn and Mary, who had glided in and joined the circle, looked interested; and a slight flush rose and overspread the thin cheeks of Mr. Marvyn, and his blue eyes deepened in a moment with a thoughtful shadow, as he looked inquiringly at the Doctor, who proceeded : —

"My mind labors with this subject of the enslaving of the Africans, Mr. Marvyn. We have
just been declaring to the world that all men are
born with an inalienable right to liberty. We
have fought for it, and the Lord of Hosts has
been with us; and can we stand before Him
with our foot upon our brother's neck?"

A generous, upright nature is always more sensitive to blame than another, — sensitive in proportion to the amount of its reverence for good,
— and Mr. Marvyn's face flushed, his eye kindled,
and his compressed respiration showed how deeply
the subject moved him. Mrs. Marvyn's eyes turned
on him an anxious look of inquiry. He answered,
however, calmly: —

"Doctor, I have thought of the subject myself.
Mrs. Marvyn has lately been reading a pamphlet
of Mr. Thomas Clarkson's on the slave-trade, and
she was saying to me only last night, that she
did not see but the argument extended equally to
holding slaves. One thing, I confess, stumbles
me: — Was there not an express permission given
to Israel to buy and hold slaves of old?"

"Doubtless," said the Doctor; "but many per-
missions were given to them which were local
and temporary; for if we hold them to apply to
the human race, the Turks might quote the Bible
for making slaves of us, if they could, — and the
Algerines have the Scripture all on their side, —

and our own blacks, at some future time, if they
can get the power, might justify themselves in
making slaves of us."

"I assure you, Sir," said Mr. Marvyn, "if I
speak, it is not to excuse myself. But I am
quite sure my servants do not desire liberty, and
would not take it, if it were offered."

"Call them in and try it," said the Doctor.
"If they refuse, it is their own matter."

There was a gentle movement in the group at
the directness of this personal application; but
Mr. Marvyn replied, calmly, —

"Cato is up at the eight-acre lot, but you may
call in Candace. My dear, call Candace, and let
the Doctor put the question to her."

Candace was at this moment sitting before the
ample fireplace in the kitchen, with two iron ket-
tles before her, nestled each in its bed of hickory
coals, which gleamed out from their white ashes
like sleepy, red eyes, opening and shutting. In
one was coffee, which she was burning, stirring
vigorously with a pudding-stick, — and in the other,
puffy doughnuts, in shapes of rings, hearts, and
marvellous twists, which Candace had such a special proclivity for making, that Mrs. Marvyn's
table and closets never knew an intermission of
their presence.

"Candace, the Doctor wishes to see you," said
Mrs. Marvyn.

"Bress his heart!" said Candace, looking up, perplexed. "Wants to see me, does he? Can't nobody hab me till dis yer coffee's done; a minnit's a minnit in coffee;—but I'll be in dereckly," she added, in a patronizing tone. "Missis, you jes' go 'long in, an' I'll be dar dereckly."

A few moments after, Candace joined the group in the sitting-room, having hastily tied a clean, white apron over her blue linsey working-dress, and donned the brilliant Madras which James had lately given her, and which she had a barbaric fashion of arranging so as to give to her head the air of a gigantic butterfly. She sunk a dutiful curtsy, and stood twirling her thumbs, while the Doctor surveyed her gravely.

"Candace," said he, "do you think it right that the black race should be slaves to the white?"

The face and air of Candace presented a curious picture at this moment; a sort of rude sense of delicacy embarrassed her, and she turned a deprecating look, first on Mrs. Marvyn and then on her master.

"Don't mind us, Candace," said Mrs. Marvyn; "tell the Doctor the exact truth."

Candace stood still a moment, and the spectators saw a deeper shadow roll over her sable face, like a cloud over a dark pool of water, and her immense person heaved with her labored breathing.

"Ef I must speak, I must," she said. "No,—

I neber did tink 'twas right. When Gineral Washington was here, I hearn 'em read de Declaration ob Independence and Bill o' Rights; an' I tole Cato den, says I, 'Ef dat ar' true, you an' I are as free as anybody.' It stands to reason. Why, look at me, — I a'n't a critter. I's neider huffs nor horns. I's a reasonable bein', — a woman, — as much a woman as anybody," she said, holding up her head with an air as majestic as a palm-tree; — " an' Cato, — he's a man, born free an' equal, ef dar's any truth in what you read, — dat's all."

" But, Candace, you've always been contented and happy with us, have you not?" said Mr. Marvyn.

" Yes, Mass'r, — I ha'n't got nuffin to complain ob in dat matter. I couldn't hab no better friends 'n you an' Missis."

" Would you like your liberty, if you could get it, though?" said Mr. Marvyn. " Answer me honestly."

" Why, to be sure I should! Who wouldn't? Mind ye," she said, earnestly raising her black, heavy hand, " 'ta'n't dat I want to go off, or want to shirk work; but I want to *feel free*. Dem dat isn't free has nuffin to gib to nobody; — dey can't show what dey would do."

" Well, Candace, from this day you are free," said Mr. Marvyn, solemnly.

Candace covered her face with both her fat hands, and shook and trembled, and, finally, throwing her apron over her head, made a desperate rush for the door, and threw herself down in the kitchen in a perfect tropical torrent of tears and sobs.

"You see," said the Doctor, "what freedom is to every human creature. The blessing of the Lord will be on this deed, Mr. Marvyn. 'The steps of a just man are ordered by the Lord, and he delighteth in his way.'"

At this moment, Candace reappeared at the door, her butterfly turban somewhat deranged with the violence of her prostration, giving a whimsical air to her portly person.

"I want ye all to know," she said, with a clearing-up snuff, "dat it's my will an' pleasure to go right on doin' my work jes' de same; an', Missis, please, I'll allers put three eggs in de crullers, now; an' I won't turn de wash-basin down in de sink, but hang it jam-up on de nail; an' I won't pick up chips in a milk-pan, ef I'm in ever so big a hurry;—I'll do eberyting jes' as ye tells me. Now you try me an' see ef I won't!"

Candace here alluded to some of the little private wilfulnesses which she had always obstinately cherished as reserved rights, in pursuing domestic matters with her mistress.

"I intend," said Mr. Marvyn, "to make the

8*

same offer to your husband, when he returns from work to-night."

"Laus, Mass'r, — why, Cato he'll do jes' as I do, — dere a'n't no kind o' need o' askin' him. 'Course he will."

A smile passed round the circle, because between Candace and her husband there existed one of those whimsical contrasts which one sometimes sees in married life. Cato was a small-built, thin, softly-spoken negro, addicted to a gentle chronic cough; and, though a faithful and skilful servant, seemed, in relation to his better half, much like a hill of potatoes under a spreading apple-tree. Candace held to him with a vehement and patronizing fondness, so devoid of conjugal reverence as to excite the comments of her friends.

"You must remember, Candace," said a good deacon to her one day, when she was ordering him about at a catechizing, "you ought to give honor to your husband; the wife is the weaker vessel."

"*I* de weaker vessel?" said Candace, looking down from the tower of her ample corpulence on the small, quiet man whom she had been fledging with the ample folds of a worsted comforter, out of which his little head and shining bead-eyes looked, much like a blackbird in a nest, — "*I* de weaker vessel? Umph!"

A whole woman's-rights' convention could not

have expressed more in a day than was given in that single look and word. Candace considered a husband as a thing to be taken care of, — a rather inconsequent and somewhat troublesome species of pet, to be humored, nursed, fed, clothed, and guided in the way that he was to go, — an animal that was always losing off buttons, catching colds, wearing his best coat every day, and getting on his Sunday hat in a surreptitious manner for week-day occasions; but she often condescended to express it as her opinion that he was a blessing, and that she didn't know what she should do, if it wasn't for Cato. In fact, he seemed to supply her that which we are told is the great want in woman's situation, — an object in life. She sometimes was heard expressing herself very energetically in disapprobation of the conduct of one of her sable friends, named Jinny Stiles, who, after being presented with her own freedom, worked several years to buy that of her husband, but became afterwards so disgusted with her acquisition that she declared she would " nebcr buy anoder nigger."

" Now Jinny don't know what she's talkin' about," she would say. " S'pose he does cough and keep her awake nights, and take a little too much sometimes, a'n't he better'n no husband at all? A body wouldn't seem to hab nuffin to lib for, ef dey hadn't an ole man to look arter. Men is nate'lly foolish about some tings,—but dey's good deal better'n nuffin."

And Candace, after this condescending remark, would lift off with one hand a brass kettle in which poor Cato might have been drowned, and fly across the kitchen with it as if it were a feather.

CHAPTER XII.

MISS PRISSY.

WILL our little Mary really fall in love with the Doctor? — The question reaches us in anxious tones from all the circle of our readers; and what especially shocks us is, that grave doctors of divinity, and serious, stocking-knitting matrons seem to be the class who are particularly set against the success of our excellent orthodox hero, and bent on reminding us of the claims of that unregenerate James, whom we have sent to sea on purpose that our heroine may recover herself of that foolish partiality for him which all the Christian world seems bent on perpetuating.

"Now, really," says the Rev. Mrs. Q., looking up from her bundle of Sewing-Society work, "you are *not* going to let Mary marry the Doctor?"

My dear Madam, is not that just what you did, yourself, after having turned off three or four fascinating young sinners as good as James any day? Don't make us believe that you are sorry for it now!

" Is it possible," says Dr. Theophrastus, who is himself a stanch Hopkinsian divine, and who is at present recovering from his last grand effort on Natural and Moral Ability, — " is it possible that you are going to let Mary forget that poor young man and marry Dr. Hopkins? That will never do in the world!"

Dear Doctor, consider what would have become of you, if some lady at a certain time had not had the sense and discernment to fall in love with the *man* who came to her disguised as a theologian.

" But he's so old!" says Aunt Maria.

Not at all. Old? What do you mean? Forty is the very season of ripeness, — the very meridian of manly lustre and splendor.

" But he wears a wig."

My dear Madam, so did Sir Charles Grandison, and Lovelace, and all the other fine fellows of those days; the wig was the distinguishing mark of a gentleman.

No, — spite of all you may say and declare, we do insist that our Doctor is a very proper and probable subject for a young lady to fall in love with.

If women have one weakness more marked than another, it is towards veneration. They are born worshippers, — makers of silver shrines for some divinity or other, which, of course, they always think fell straight down from heaven.

The first step towards their falling in love with

an ordinary mortal is generally to dress him out with all manner of real or fancied superiority; and having made him up, they worship him.

Now a truly great man, a man really grand and noble in heart and intellect, has this advantage with women, that he is an idol ready-made to hand; and so that very painstaking and ingenious sex have less labor in getting him up, and can be ready to worship him on shorter notice.

In particular is this the case where a sacred profession and a moral supremacy are added to the intellectual. Just think of the career of celebrated preachers and divines in all ages. Have they not stood like the image that " Nebuchadnezzar the king set up," and all womankind, coquettes and flirts not excepted, been ready to fall down and worship, even before the sound of cornet, flute, harp, sackbut, and so forth? Is not the faithful Paula, with her beautiful face, prostrate in reverence before poor, old, lean, haggard, dying St. Jerome, in the most splendid painting of the world, an emblem and sign of woman's eternal power of self-sacrifice to what she deems noblest in man? Does not old Richard Baxter tell us, with delightful single-heartedness, how his wife fell in love with him first, spite of his long, pale face, — and how she confessed, dear soul, after many years of married life, that she had found him *less* sour and bitter than she had expected?

The fact is, women are burdened with fealty, faith, reverence, more than they know what to do with; they stand like a hedge of sweet-peas, throwing out fluttering tendrils everywhere for something high and strong to climb by,— and when they find it, be it ever so rough in the bark, they catch upon it. And instances are not wanting of those who have turned away from the flattery of admirers to prostrate themselves at the feet of a genuine hero who never wooed them, except by heroic deeds and the rhetoric of a noble life.

Never was there a distinguished man whose greatness could sustain the test of minute domestic inspection better than our Doctor. Strong in a single hearted humility, a perfect unconsciousness of self an honest and sincere absorption in high and holy themes and objects, there was in him what we so seldom see,— a perfect logic of life; his minutest deeds were the true results of his sublimest principles. His whole nature, moral, physical and intellectual, was simple, pure, and cleanly. He was temperate as an anchorite in all matters of living, — avoiding, from a healthy instinct, all those intoxicating stimuli then common among the clergy. In his early youth, indeed, he had formed an attachment to the almost universal clerical pipe, — but, observing a delicate woman once nauseated by coming into the atmosphere which he and his brethren had polluted, he set himself gravely to re-

flect that that which could so offend a woman
must needs be uncomely and unworthy a Christian
man; wherefore he laid his pipe on the mantel-
piece, and never afterwards resumed the indulgence.

In all his relations with womanhood he was delicate and reverential, forming his manners by that
old precept, " The elder women entreat as mothers,
the younger as sisters," — which rule, short and simple as it is, is, nevertheless, the most perfect *résumé*
of all true gentlemanliness. Then, as for person,
the Doctor was not handsome, to be sure; but he
was what sometimes serves with woman better, —
majestic and manly; and, when animated by thought
and feeling, having even a commanding grandeur
of mien. Add to all this, that our valiant hero is
now on the straight road to bring him into that
situation most likely to engage the warm partisan-
ship of a true woman, — namely, that of a man
unjustly abused for right-doing, — and one may
see that it is ten to one our Mary may fall in love
with him yet before she knows it.

If it were not for this mysterious selfness-and-
sameness which makes this wild, wandering, unca-
nonical sailor, James Marvyn, so intimate and internal, — if his thread were not knit up with the
thread of her life, — were it not for the old habit
of feeling for him, thinking for him, praying for
him, hoping for him, fearing for him, which — wo

is us ! — is the unfortunate habit of womankind, — if it were not for that fatal something which neither judgment, nor wishes, nor reason, nor common sense shows any great skill in unravelling, — we are quite sure that Mary would be in love with the Doctor within the next six months ; as it is, we leave you all to infer from your own heart and consciousness what his chances are.

A new sort of scene is about to open on our heroine, and we shall show her to you, for an evening at least, in new associations, and with a different background from that homely and rural one in which she has fluttered as a white dove amid leafy and congenial surroundings.

As we have before intimated, Newport presented a *résumé* of many different phases of society, all brought upon a social level by the then universally admitted principle of equality.

There were scattered about in the settlement lordly mansions, whose owners rolled in emblazoned carriages, and whose wide halls were the scenes of a showy and almost princely hospitality. By her husband's side, Mrs. Katy Scudder was allied to one of these families of wealthy planters, and often recognized the connection with a quiet undertone of satisfaction, as a dignified and self-respecting woman should. She liked, once in a while, quietly to let people know, that, although they lived in the plain little cottage, and made no

pretensions, yet they had good blood in their veins,
—that Mr. Scudder's mother was a Wilcox, and
that the Wilcoxes were, she supposed, as high as
anybody, — generally ending the remark with the
observation, that "all these things, to be sure, were
matters of small consequence, since at last it would
be of far more importance to have been a true
Christian than to have been connected with the
highest families of the land."

Nevertheless, Mrs. Scudder was not a little pleased to have in her possession a card of invitation
to a splendid wedding-party that was going to be
given, on Friday, at the Wilcox Manor. She
thought it a very becoming mark of respect to the
deceased Mr. Scudder that his widow and daughter should be brought to mind, — so becoming and
praiseworthy, in fact, that, "though an old woman,"
as she said, with a complacent straightening of her
tall, lithe figure, she really thought she must make
an effort to go.

Accordingly, early one morning, after all domestic duties had been fulfilled, and the clock, loudly
ticking through the empty rooms, told that all
needful bustle had died down to silence, Mrs.
Katy, Mary, and Miss Prissy Diamond, the dressmaker, might have been observed sitting in solemn
senate around the camphor-wood trunk, before
spoken of, and which exhaled vague foreign and
Indian perfumes of silk and sandal-wood.

You may have heard of dignitaries, my good reader, — but, I assure you, you know very little of a situation of trust or importance compared to that of *the* dressmaker in a small New England town.

What important interests does she hold in her hands! How is she besieged, courted, deferred to! Three months beforehand, all her days and nights are spoken for; and the simple statement, that *only* on that day you can have Miss Clippers, is of itself an apology for any omission of attention elsewhere, — it strikes home at once to the deepest consciousness of every woman, married or single. How thoughtfully is everything arranged, weeks beforehand, for the golden, important season when Miss Clippers can come! On that day, there is to be no extra sweeping, dusting, cleaning, cooking, no visiting, no receiving, no reading or writing, but all with one heart and soul are to wait upon her, intent to forward the great work which she graciously affords a day's leisure to direct. Seated in her chair of state, with her well-worn cushion bristling with pins and needles at her side, her ready roll of patterns and her scissors, she hears, judges, and decides *ex cathedrá* on the possible or not possible, in that important art on which depends the right of presentation of the floral part of Nature's great horticultural show. She alone is competent to say whether there is any available remedy for the stained breadth in Jane's dress, — whether the fatal spot by any magical hocus-pocus can be cut out from the fulness, or turned up and smothered from view in the gathers, or concealed by some new fashion of trimming falling with generous appropriateness exactly across the fatal weak point. She can tell you whether that remnant of velvet will make you a basque, — whether Mamma's old silk can reappear in juvenile grace for Miss Lucy. What marvels follow her, wherever she goes! What wonderful results does she contrive from the most unlikely materials, as everybody after her departure wonders to see old things become so much better than new!

Among the most influential and happy of her class was Miss Prissy Diamond, — a little, dapper, doll-like body, quick in her motions and nimble in her tongue, whose delicate complexion, flaxen curls, merry flow of spirits, and ready abundance of gayety, song, and story, apart from her professional accomplishments, made her a welcome guest in every family in the neighborhood. Miss Prissy laughingly boasted being past forty, sure that the avowal would always draw down on her quite a storm of compliments, on the freshness of her sweet-pea complexion and the brightness of her merry blue eyes. She was well pleased to hear dawning girls wondering why, with so many advantages, she had never married. At such remarks,

Miss Prissy always laughed loudly, and declared
that she had always had such a string of engage-
ments with the women that she never found half
an hour to listen to what any *man* living would
say to her, supposing she could stop to hear him.
" Besides, if I were to get married, nobody else
could," she would say. " What would become of
all the wedding-clothes for everybody else ? " But
sometimes, when Miss Prissy felt extremely gracious, she would draw out of her little chest just
the faintest tip-end of a sigh, and tell some young
lady, in a confidential undertone, that one of these
days she would tell her something, — and then there
would come a wink of her blue eyes and a fluttering of the pink ribbons in her cap quite stimulating to youthful inquisitiveness, though we have
never been able to learn by any of our antiqua-
rian researches that the expectations thus excited
were ever gratified.

In her professional prowess she felt a pardonable pride. What feats could she relate of wonderful dresses got out of impossibly small patterns
of silk! what marvels of silks turned that could
not be told from new! what reclaimings of waists
that other dressmakers had hopelessly spoiled. Had
not Mrs. General Wilcox once been obliged to call
in her aid on a dress sent to her from Paris ? and
did not Miss Prissy work three days and nights
on that dress, and make every stitch of that trim-

ming over with her own hands, before it was fit to be seen? And when Mrs. Governor Dexter's best silver-gray brocade was spoiled by Miss Pimlico, and there wasn't another scrap to pattern it with, didn't she make a new waist out of the cape and piece one of the sleeves twenty-nine times, and yet nobody would ever have known that there was a joining in it?

In fact, though Miss Prissy enjoyed the fair average plain-sailing of her work, she might be said to *revel* in difficulties. A full pattern with trimming, all ample and ready, awoke a moderate enjoyment; but the resurrection of anything half-worn or imperfectly made, the brilliant success, when, after turning, twisting, piecing, contriving, and, by unheard-of inventions of trimming, a dress faded and defaced was restored to more than pristine splendor, — *that* was a triumph worth enjoying.

It was true, Miss Prissy, like most of her no-madic compeers, was a little given to gossip; but, after all, it was innocent gossip, — not a bit of malice in it; it was only all the particulars about Mrs. Thus-and-So's wardrobe, — all the statistics of Mrs. That-and-T'other's china-closet, — all the minute items of Miss Simkins's wedding-clothes, — and how her mother cried, the morning of the wedding, and said that she didn't know anything how she could spare Louisa Jane, only that Edward was such a good boy that she felt she could

love him like an own son,— and what a providence
it seemed that the very ring that was put into the
bride-loaf was the one that he gave her when he
first went to sea, when she wouldn't be engaged
to him because she thought she loved Thomas
Strickland better, but that was only because she
hadn't found him out, you know,— and so forth,
and so forth. Sometimes, too, her narrations assumed a solemn cast, and brought to mind the
hush of funerals, and told the words spoken in
faint whispers, when hands were clasped for the
last time,— and of utterances crushed out from
hearts, when the hammer of a great sorrow strikes
out sparks of the divine, even from common stone;
and there would be real tears in the little blue
eyes, and the pink bows would flutter tremulously,
like the last three leaves on a bare scarlet maple
in autumn.   In fact, dear reader, *gossip*, like romance, has its noble side to it. How can you
love your neighbor as yourself and not feel a little
curiosity as to how he fares, what he wears, where
he goes, and how he takes the great life tragi-
comedy at which you and he are both more than
spectators ? Show me a person who lives in a
country village absolutely without curiosity or interest on these subjects, and I will show you a
cold, fat oyster, to whom the tide-mud of propriety
is the whole of existence.

As one of our esteemed collaborators in the AT-

LANTIC remarks,—"A dull town, where there is neither theatre nor circus nor opera, must have some excitement, and the real tragedy and comedy of life *must* come in place of the second-hand. Hence the noted gossiping propensities of country-places, which, so long as they are not poisoned by envy or ill-will, have a respectable and picturesque side to them,—an undoubted leave to be, as probably has almost everything, which obstinately and always insists on being, except sin!"

As it is, it must be confessed that the arrival of Miss Prissy in a family was much like the setting up of a domestic show-case, through which you could look into all the families of the neighborhood, and see the never-ending drama of life,—births, marriages, deaths,—joy of new-made mothers, whose babes weighed just eight pounds and three quarters, and had hair that would part with a comb,—and tears of Rachels who wept for their children, and would not be comforted because they were not. Was there a tragedy, a mystery, in all Newport, whose secret closet had not been unlocked by Miss Prissy? She thought not; and you always wondered, with an uncertain curiosity, what those things might be over which she gravely shook her head, declaring, with such a look,—"Oh, if you only *could* know!"—and ending with a general sigh and lamentation, like the confidential chorus of a Greek tragedy.

9

We have been thus minute in sketching Miss
Prissy's portrait, because we rather like her. She
has great power, we admit; and were she a sour-
faced, angular, energetic body, with a heart whose
secretions had all become acrid by disappointment
and dyspepsia, she might be a fearful gnome,
against whose family visitations one ought to
watch and pray. As it was, she came into the
house rather like one of those breezy days of
spring, which burst all the blossoms, set all the
doors and windows open, make the hens cackle
and the turtles peep,— filling a solemn Puritan
dwelling with as much bustle and chatter as if
a box of martins were setting up housekeeping
in it.

Let us now introduce you to the sanctuary of
Mrs. Scudder's own private bedroom, where the
committee of exigencies, with Miss Prissy at their
head, are seated in solemn session around the
camphor-wood trunk.

"Dress, you know, is of *some* importance, after
all," said Mrs. Scudder, in that apologetic way in
which sensible people generally acknowledge a
secret leaning towards anything so very mundane.
While the good lady spoke, she was reverentially
unpinning and shaking out of their fragrant folds
creamy crape shawls of rich Chinese embroidery,
—India muslin, scarfs, and aprons; and already
her hands were undoing the pins of a silvery

damask linen in which was wrapped her own wedding-dress. "I have always told Mary," she continued, "that, though our hearts ought not to be set on these things, yet they had their impor tance."

"Certainly, certainly, Ma'am," chimed in Miss Prissy. "I was saying to Miss General Wilcox, the other day, *I* didn't see how we could 'con- sider the lilies of the field,' without seeing the impoitance of looking pretty. I've got a flower- de-luce in my garden now, from one of the new roots that old Major Seaforth brought over from France, which is just the most beautiful thing you ever did see; and I was thinking, as I looked at it to-day, that, if women's dresses only grew on 'em as handsome and well-fitting as that, why, there wouldn't be any need of me; but as it is, why, we *must think*, if we want to look well. Now, peach-trees, I s'pose, might bear just as good peaches without the pink blows, but then who would want 'em to? Miss Deacon Twitchel, when I was up there the other day, kept kind o' sighin' 'cause Cerintha Ann is getting a new pink silk made up, 'cause she said it was such a dying world it didn't seem right to call off our atten- tion: but I told her it wasn't any pinker than the apple-blossoms; and what with robins and blue-birds and one thing or another, the Lord is always calling off our attention; and I think we

ought to observe the Lord's works and take a les-
son from 'em."

"Yes, you are quite right," said Mrs. Scudder,
rising and shaking out a`splendid white brocade,
on which bunches of moss-roses were looped to
bunches of violets by graceful fillets of blue ribbons. "This was my wedding-dress," she said.

Little Miss Prissy sprang up and clapped her
hands in an ecstasy.

"Well, now, Miss Scudder, really!—did I ever
see anything more beautiful? It really goes beyond anything *I* ever saw. I don't think, in all
the brocades I ever made up, I ever saw so pretty
a pattern as this."

"Mr. Scudder chose it for me, himself, at the
silk-factory in Lyons," said Mrs. Scudder, with
pardonable pride, "and I want it tried on to
Mary."

"Really, Miss Scudder, this ought to be kept
for *her* wedding-dress," said Miss Prissy, as she
delightedly bustled about the congenial task. "I
was up to Miss Marvyn's, a-working, last week,"
she said, as she threw the dress over Mary's head,
"and she said that James expected to make his
fortune in that voyage, and come home and settle
down."

Mary's fair head emerged from the rustling folds
of the brocade, her cheeks crimson as one of the
moss-roses,—while her mother's face assumed a

severe gravity, as she remarked that she believed James had been much pleased with Jane Spencer, and that, for her part, she should be very glad, when he came home, if he could marry such a steady, sensible girl, and settle down to a useful, Christian life.

"Ah, yes,—just so,—a very excellent idea, certainly," said Miss Prissy. "It wants a little taken in here on the shoulders, and a little under the arms. The biases are all right; the sleeves will want altering, Miss Scudder. I hope you will have a hot iron ready for pressing."

Mrs. Scudder rose immediately, to see the command obeyed; and as her back was turned, Miss Prissy went on in a low tone,—

"Now, *I*, for my part, don't think there's a word of truth in that story about James Marvyn and Jane Spencer; for I was down there at work one day when he called, and I *know* there couldn't have been anything between them,— besides, Miss Spencer, her mother, told me there wasn't.— There, Miss Scudder, you see that is a good fit. It's astonishing how near it comes to fitting, just as it was. I didn't think Mary was so near what you were, when you were a girl, Miss Scudder. The other day, when I was up to General Wilcox's, the General he was in the room when I was a-trying on Miss Wilcox's cherry velvet, and she was asking couldn't I come this week for her, and I mentioned I was coming to Miss Scudder, and the General says he,—'I used to know her when she was a girl. I tell you, she was one of the handsomest girls in Newport, by George!' says he. And says I,—'General, you ought to see her daughter.' And the General,—you know his jolly way,—he laughed, and says he,—'If she is as handsome as her mother was, I don't want to see her,' says he. 'I tell you, wife,' says he, 'I but just missed falling in love with Katy Stephens.'"

"I could have told her more than that," said Mrs. Scudder, with a flash of her old coquette girlhood for a moment lighting her eyes and straightening her lithe form. "I guess, if I should show a letter he wrote me once —— But what am I talking about?" she said, suddenly stiffening back into a sensible woman. "Miss Prissy, do you think it will be necessary to cut it off at the bottom? It seems a pity to cut such rich silk."

"So it does, I declare. Well, I believe it will do to turn it up."

"I depend on you to put it a little into modern fashion, you know," said Mrs. Scudder. "It is many a year, you know, since it was made."

"Oh, never you fear! You leave all that to me," said Miss Prissy. "Now, there never was anything so lucky as, that, just before all these wedding-dresses had to be fixed, I got a letter

from my sister Martha, that works for all the first
families of Boston. And Martha she is really un
usually privileged, because she works for Miss
Cranch, and Miss Cranch gets letters from Miss
Adams,— you know Mr. Adams is Ambassador
now at the Court of St. James, and Miss Adams
writes home all the particulars about the court-
dresses; and Martha she heard one of the letters
read, and she told Miss Cranch that she would
give the best five-pound-note she had, if she could
just copy that description to send to Prissy. Well,
Miss Cranch let her do it, and I've got a copy of
the letter here in my work-pocket. I read it up to
Miss General Wilcox's, and to Major Seaforth's,
and I'll read it to you."

Mrs. Katy Scudder was a born subject of a
crown, and, though now a republican matron, had
not outlived the reverence, from childhood implant-
ed, for the high and stately doings of courts, lords,
ladies, queens, and princesses, and therefore it was
not without some awe that she saw Miss Prissy
produce from her little black work-bag the well-
worn epistle.

"Here it is," said Miss Prissy, at last. "I only
copied out the parts about being presented at
Court. She says:—

"'One is obliged here to attend the circles of
the Queen, which are held once a fortnight; and
what renders it very expensive is, that you cannot

go twice in the same dress, and a court-dress you cannot make use of elsewhere. I directed my mantua-maker to let my dress be elegant, but plain as I could possibly appear with decency. Accordingly, it is white lutestring, covered and full-trimmed with white crape, festooned with lilac ribbon and mock point-lace, over a hoop of enormous size. There is only a narrow train, about three yards in length to the gown-waist, which is put into a ribbon on the left side, — the Queen only having her train borne. Ruffled cuffs for married ladies, — treble lace ruffles, a very dress cap with long lace lappets, two white plumes, and a blonde lace handkerchief. This is my rigging.'"

Miss Prissy here stopped to adjust her spectacles. Her audience expressed a breathless interest.

"You see," she said, "I used to know her when she was Nabby Smith. She was Parson Smith's daughter, at Weymouth, and as handsome a girl as ever I wanted to see, — just as graceful as a sweet-brier bush. I don't believe any of those English ladies looked one bit better than she did. She was always a master-hand at writing. Everything she writes about, she puts it right before you. You feel as if you'd been there. Now, here she goes on to tell about her daughter's dress. She says : —

"'My head is dressed for St. James's, and in

my opinion looks very tasty. Whilst my daughter is undergoing the same operation, I set myself
down composedly to write you a few lines. Well,
methinks I hear Betsey and Lucy say, "What is
cousin's dress?" *White*, my dear girls, like your
aunt's, only differently trimmed and ornamented,—
her train being wholly of white crape, and trimmed with white ribbon ; the petticoat, which is
the most showy part of the dress, covered and
drawn up in what are called festoons, with light
wreaths of beautiful flowers ; the sleeves, white
crape drawn over the silk, with a row of lace
round the sleeve near the shoulder, another half-
way down the arm, and a third upon the top of
the ruffle,— a little stuck between,— a kind of
hat-cap with three large feathers and a bunch of
flowers,— a wreath of flowers on the hair.' "

Miss Prissy concluded this relishing description
with a little smack of the lips, such as people
sometimes give when reading things that are particularly to their taste.

"Now, I was a-thinking," she added, "that it
would be an excellent way to trim Mary's sleeves,
—three rows of lace, with a sprig to each row."

All this while, our Mary, with her white short-
gown and blue stuff-petticoat, her shining pale
brown hair and serious large blue eyes, sat innocently looking first at her mother, then at Miss
Prissy, and then at the finery.

We do not claim for her any superhuman exemption from girlish feelings. She was innocently dazzled with the vision of courtly halls and princely splendors, and thought Mrs. Adams's descriptions almost a perfect realization of things she had read in " Sir Charles Grandison." If her mother thought it right and proper she should be dressed and made fine, she was glad of it; only there came a heavy, leaden feeling in her little heart, which she did not understand, but we who know womankind will translate it for you; it was, that a certain pair of dark eyes would not see her after she was dressed; and so, after all, what was the use of looking pretty?

" I wonder what James *would* think," passed through her head; for Mary had never changed a ribbon, or altered the braid of her hair, or pinned a flower in her bosom, that she had not quickly seen the effect of the change mirrored in those dark eyes. It was a pity, of course, now she had found out that she ought not to think about him, that so many thought-strings were twisted round him.

So while Miss Prissy turned over her papers, and read out of others extracts about Lord Caermarthen and Sir Clement Cotterel Dormer and the Princess Royal and Princess Augusta, in black and silver, with a silver netting upon the coat, and a head stuck full of diamond pins, — and Lady

Salisbury and Lady Talbot and the Duchess of
Devonshire, and scarlet satin sacks and diamonds
and ostrich-plumes, and the King's kissing Mrs.
Adams, — little Mary's blue eyes grew larger and
larger, seeing far off on the salt green sea, and her
ears heard only the ripple and murmur of those
waters that carried her heart away, — till, by-and-
by, Miss Prissy gave her a smart little tap, which
awakened her to the fact that she was wanted
again to try on the dress which Miss Prissy's nimble fingers had basted.

So passed the day, — Miss Prissy busily chattering, clipping, basting, — Mary patiently trying on
to an unheard-of extent, — and Mrs. Scudder's neat
room whipped into a perfect froth and foam of
gauze, lace, artificial flowers, linings, and other
aids, accessories, and abetments.

At dinner, the Doctor, who had been all the
morning studying out his Treatise on the Millennium, discoursed tranquilly as usual, innocently ignorant of the unusual cares which were distract-
ing the minds of his listeners. What should he
know of dress-makers, good soul ? Encouraged
by the respectful silence of his auditors, he calmly
expanded and soliloquized on his favorite topic,
the last golden age of Time, the Marriage-Supper
of the Lamb, when the purified Earth, like a re-
pentant Psyche, shall be restored to the long-lost
favor of a celestial Bridegroom, and glorified saints

and angels shall walk familiarly as wedding-guests among men.

"Sakes alive!" said little Miss Prissy, after dinner, "did I ever hear any one go on like that blessed man? — such a spiritual mind! Oh, Miss Scudder, how you are privileged in having him here! I do really think it is a shame such a blessed man a'n't thought more of. Why, I could just sit and hear him talk all day. Miss Scudder, I wish sometimes you'd just let me make a ruffled shirt for him, and do it all up myself, and put a stitch in the hem that I learned from my sister Martha, who learned it from a French young lady who was educated in a convent;—nuns, you know, poor things, can do *some* things right; and I think *I* never saw such hemstitching as they do there; — and I should like to hemstitch the Doctor's ruffles; he is *so* spiritually-minded, it really makes me love him. Why, hearing him talk put me in mind of a real beautiful song of Mr. Watts, — I don't know as I could remember the tune."

And Miss Prissy, whose musical talent was one of her special *fortes*, tuned her voice, a little cracked and quavering, and sang, with a vigorous accent on each accented syllable, —

> "From *the* third heaven, where God resides,
>   That holy, happy place,
> The New Jerusalem comes down,
>   Adorned with shining grace.

" Attending angels shout for joy,
And the bright armies sing, —
' Mortals! behold the sacred seat
Of your descending King!'"

" Take care, Miss Scudder! — that silk must be cut exactly on the bias"; and Miss Prissy, hastily finishing her last quaver, caught the silk and the scissors out of Mrs. Scudder's hand, and fell down at once from the Millennium into a discourse on her own particular way of covering piping-cord.

So we go, dear reader, — so long as we have a body and a soul. Two worlds must mingle, — the great and the little, the solemn and the trivial, wreathing in and out, like the grotesque carvings on a Gothic shrine ; — only, did we know it rightly, nothing is trivial; since the human soul, with its awful shadow, makes all things sacred. Have not ribbons, cast-off flowers, soiled bits of gauze, trivial, trashy fragments of millinery, sometimes had an awful meaning, a deadly power, when they belonged to one who should wear them no more, and whose beautiful form, frail and crushed as they, is a hidden and a vanished thing for all time? For so sacred and individual is a human being, that, of all the million-peopled earth, no one form ever restores another. The mould of each mortal type is broken at the grave; and never, never, though you look through all the faces on earth, shall the exact form you mourn ever meet your eyes again! You are living your daily life among trifles that one death-stroke may make relics. One false step, one luckless accident, an obstacle on the track of a train, the tangling of the cord in shifting a sail, and the penknife, the pen, the papers, the trivial articles of dress and clothing, which to-day you toss idly and jestingly from hand to hand, may become dread memorials of that awful tragedy whose deep abyss ever underlies our common life.

CHAPTER XIII.

THE PARTY.

WELL, let us proceed to tell how the eventful evening drew on, — how Mary, by Miss Prissy's care, stood at last in a long-waisted gown flowered with rose-buds and violets, opening in front to display a white satin skirt trimmed with lace and flowers, — how her little feet were put into high-heeled shoes, and a little jaunty cap with a wreath of moss-rose-buds was fastened over her shining hair, — and how Miss Prissy, delighted, turned her round and round, and then declared that she must go and get the Doctor to look at her. She knew he must be a man of taste, he talked so beautifully about the Millennium ; and so, bursting into his study, she actually chattered him back into the visible world, and, leading the blushing Mary to the door, asked him, point-blank, if he ever saw anything prettier.

The Doctor, being now wide awake, gravely gave his mind to the subject, and, after some consideration, said, gravely, " No, — he didn't think he

ever did." For the Doctor was not a man of compliment, and had a habit of always thinking, before he spoke, whether what he was going to say
was exactly true; and having lived some time in
the family of President Edwards, renowned for
beautiful daughters, he naturally thought them
over.

The Doctor looked innocent and helpless, while
Miss Prissy, having got him now quite into her
power, went on volubly to expatiate on the difficulties overcome in adapting the ancient wedding-
dress to its present modern fit. He told her that
it was very nice,—said, "Yes, Ma'am," at proper
places,— and, being a very obliging man, looked
at whatever he was directed to, with round, blank
eyes; but ended all with a long gaze on the laughing, blushing face, that, half in shame and half in
perplexed mirth, appeared and disappeared as Miss
Prissy in her warmth turned her round and showed
her.

"Now don't she look beautiful?" Miss Prissy
reiterated for the twentieth time, as Mary left the
room.

The Doctor, looking after her musingly, said to
himself,—"'The king's daughter is all glorious
within; her clothing is of wrought gold; she shall
be brought unto the king in raiment of needle-
work.'"

"Now, did I ever?" said Miss Prissy, rushing

out. " How that good man does turn everything!
I believe you couldn't get anything, that he wouldn't
find a text right out of the Bible about it. I mean
to get the linen for that shirt this very week, with
the Miss Wilcox's money ; they always pay well,
those Wilcoxes,—and I've worked for them, off
and on, sixteen days and a quarter. To be sure,
Miss Scudder, there's no real need of my doing it,
for I must say you keep him looking like a pink,—
but only I feel as if I must do something for such
a good man."

The good doctor was brushed up for the evening with zealous care and energy; and if he did
not look like a pink, it was certainly no fault of
his hostess.

Well, we cannot reproduce in detail the faded
glories of that entertainment, nor relate how the
Wilcox Manor and gardens were illuminated,—
how the bride wore a veil of real point-lace,— how
carriages rolled and grated on the gravel walks,
and negro servants, in white kid gloves, handed
out ladies in velvet and satin.

To Mary's inexperienced eye it seemed like an
enchanted dream, — a realization of all she had
dreamed of grand and high society. She had her
little triumph of an evening ; for everybody asked
who that beautiful girl was, and more than one
gallant of the old Newport first families felt himself adorned and distinguished to walk with her

on his arm. Busy, officious dowagers repeated to Mrs. Scudder the applauding whispers that followed her wherever she went.

"Really, Mrs. Scudder," said gallant old General Wilcox, "where have you kept such a beauty all this time? It's a sin and a shame to hide such a light under a bushel."

And Mrs. Scudder, though, of course, like you and me, sensible reader, properly apprised of the perishable nature of such fleeting honors, was, like us, too, but a mortal, and smiled condescendingly on the follies of the scene.

The house was divided by a wide hall opening by doors, the front one upon the street, the back into a large garden, the broad central walk of which, edged on each side with high clipped hedges of box, now resplendent with colored lamps, seemed to continue the prospect in a brilliant vista.

The old-fashioned garden was lighted in every part, and the company dispersed themselves about it in picturesque groups.

We have the image in our mind of Mary as she stood with her little hat and wreath of rose-buds, her fluttering ribbons and rich brocade, as it were a picture framed in the door-way, with her back to the illuminated garden, and her calm, innocent face regarding with a pleased wonder the unaccustomed gayeties within.

Her dress, which, under Miss Prissy's forming

hand, had been made to assume that appearance of style and fashion which more particularly char acterized the mode of those times, formed a singular, but not unpleasing contrast to the sort of dewy freshness of air and mien which was characteristic of her style of beauty. It seemed so to represent a being who was in the world, yet not of it,— who, though living habitually in a higher region of thought and feeling, was artlessly curious, and innocently pleased with a fresh experience in an altogether untried sphere. The feeling of being in a circle to which she did not belong, where her presence was in a manner an accident, and where she felt none of the responsibilities which come from being a component part of a society, gave to her a quiet, disengaged air, which produced all the effect of the perfect ease of high breeding.

While she stands there, there comes out of the door of the bridal reception-room a gentleman with a stylishly-dressed lady on either arm, with whom he seems wholly absorbed. He is of middle height, peculiarly graceful in form and moulding, with that indescribable air of high breeding which marks the polished man of the world. His beautifully-formed head, delicate profile, fascinating sweetness of smile, and, above all, an eye which seemed to have an almost mesmeric power of attraction, were traits which distinguished one of the most celebrated men of the time, and one whose peculiar history yet lives not only in our national records, but in the private annals of many an American family.

" Good Heavens! " he said, suddenly pausing in conversation, as his eye accidentally fell upon Mary. " Who is that lovely creature? "

" Oh, that," said Mrs. Wilcox,—"why, that is Mary Scudder. Her father was a family connection of the General's. The family are in rather modest circumstances, but highly respectable."

After a few moments more of ordinary chit-chat, in which from time to time he darted upon her glances of rapid and piercing observation, the gentleman might have been observed to disembarrass himself of one of the ladies on his arm, by passing her with a compliment and a bow to another gallant, and, after a few moments more, he spoke something to Mrs. Wilcox, in a low voice, and with that gentle air of deferential sweetness which always made everybody well satisfied to do his will. The consequence was, that in a few moments Mary was startled from her calm speculations by the voice of Mrs. Wilcox, saying at her elbow, in a formal tone,—

" Miss Scudder, I have the honor to present to your acquaintance Colonel Burr, of the United States Senate."

CHAPTER XIV.

AARON BURR.

At the period of which we are speaking, no
name in the New Republic was associated with
ideas of more brilliant promise, and invested with
a greater *prestige* of popularity and success, than
that of Colonel Aaron Burr.

Sprung of a line distinguished for intellectual
ability, the grandson of a man whose genius has
swayed New England from that day to this, the
son of parents eminent in their day for influential and popular talents, he united in himself the
quickest perceptions and keenest delicacy of fibre
with the most diamond hardness and unflinching steadiness of purpose ;— apt, subtle, adroit, dazzling, no man in his time ever began life with
fairer chances of success and fame.

His name, as it fell on the ear of our heroine,
carried with it the suggestion of all this ; and
when, with his peculiarly engaging smile, he
offered his arm, she felt a little of the flutter natural to a modest young person unexpectedly hon-

ored with the notice of one of the great ones of
the earth, whom it is seldom the lot of humble
individuals to know, except by distant report.

But, although Mary was a blushing and sensitive person, she was not what is commonly called
a diffident girl; — her nerves had that healthy,
steady poise which gave her presence of mind in
the most unwonted circumstances.

The first few sentences addressed to her by her
new companion were in a tone and style altogether different from any in which she had ever
been approached, — different from the dashing frankness of her sailor lover, and from the rustic gallantry of her other admirers.

That indescribable mixture of ease and deference, guided by refined tact, which shows the
practised, high-bred man of the world, made its
impression on her immediately, as a breeze on the
chords of a wind-harp. She felt herself pleasantly
swayed and breathed upon; — it was as if an atmosphere were around her in which she felt a
perfect ease and freedom, an assurance that her
lightest word might launch forth safely, as a tiny
boat, on the smooth, glassy mirror of her listener's
pleased attention.

"I came to Newport only on a visit of business," he said, after a few moments of introduc-
tory conversation. "I was not prepared for its
many attractions."

"Newport has a great deal of beautiful scenery," said Mary.

"I have heard that it was celebrated for the beauty of its scenery, and of its ladies," he answered; "but," he added, with a quick flash of his dark eye, "I never realized the fact before."

The glance of the eye pointed and limited the compliment, and, at the same time, there was a wary shrewdness in it;—he was measuring how deep his shaft had sunk, as he always instinctively measured the person he talked with.

Mary had been told of her beauty since her childhood, notwithstanding her mother had essayed all that transparent, respectable hoaxing by which discreet mothers endeavor to blind their daughters to the real facts of such cases; but, in her own calm, balanced mind, she had accepted what she was so often told, as a quiet verity; and therefore she neither fluttered nor blushed on this occasion, but regarded the speaker with a pleased attention, as one who was saying obliging things.

"Cool!" he thought to himself,— "hum!— a little rustic belle, I suppose,— well aware of her own value;—rather piquant, on my word!"

"Shall we walk in the garden?" he said,— 'the evening is so beautiful."

They passed out of the door and began promenading the long walk. At the bottom of the alley he stopped, and, turning, looked up the vista of box ending in the brilliantly-lighted rooms, where gentlemen, with powdered heads, lace ruffles, and glittering knee-buckles, were handing ladies in stiff brocades, whose towering heads were shaded by ostrich-feathers and sparkling with gems.

"Quite court-like, on my word!" he said. "Tell me, do you often have such brilliant entertainments as this?"

"I suppose they do," said Mary. "I never was at one before, but I sometimes hear of them."

"And *you* do not attend?" said the gentleman, with an accent which made the inquiry a marked compliment.

"No, I do not," said Mary; "these people generally do not visit us."

"What a pity," he said, "that their parties should want such an ornament! But," he added, "this night must make them aware of their oversight;— if you are not always in society after this, it will surely not be for want of solicitation."

"You are very kind to think so," replied Mary; "but even if it were to be so, I should not see my way clear to be often in such scenes as this."

Her companion looked at her with a glance a little doubtful and amused, and said, "And pray, why not? if the inquiry be not too presumptuous."

"Because," said Mary, "I should be afraid they would take too much time and thought, and lead me to forget the great object of life."

The simple gravity with which this was said, as if quite assured of the sympathy of her auditor, appeared to give him a secret amusement. His bright, dark eyes danced, as if he suppressed some quick repartee; but, drooping his long lashes deferentially, he said, in gentle tones, "I should like to know what so beautiful a young lady considers the great object of life."

Mary answered reverentially, in those words then familiar from infancy to every Puritan child, "To glorify God, and enjoy Him forever."

"*Really?*" he said, looking straight into her eyes with that penetrating glance with which he was accustomed to take the gauge of every one with whom he conversed.

"Is it *not?*" said Mary, looking back, calm and firm, into the sparkling, restless depths of his eyes.

At that moment, two souls, going with the whole force of their being in opposite directions, looked out of their windows at each other with a fixed and earnest recognition.

Burr was practised in every art of gallantry,— he had made womankind a study,— he never saw a beautiful face and form without a sort of restless desire to experiment upon it and try his

10

power over the interior inhabitant; but, just at
this moment, something streamed into his soul
from those blue, earnest eyes, which brought back
to his mind what pious people had so often told
him of his mother, the beautiful and early-sainted
Esther Burr. He was one of those persons who
systematically managed and played upon himself
and others, as a skilful musician, and on an in
strument. Yet one secret of his fascination was
the *naïveté* with which, at certain moments, he
would abandon himself to some little impulse of
a nature originally sensitive and tender. Had the
strain of feeling which now awoke in him come
over him elsewhere, he would have shut down
some spring in his mind, and excluded it in a
moment; but, talking with a beautiful creature
whom he wished to please, he gave way at once
to the emotion;—real tears stood in his fine eyes,
and he raised Mary's hand to his lips, and kissed
it, saying,—

"Thank you, my beautiful child, for so good a
thought. It is truly a noble sentiment, though
practicable only to those gifted with angelic natures."

"Oh, I trust not," said Mary, earnestly touched
and wrought upon, more than she herself knew,
by the beautiful eyes, the modulated voice, the
charm of manner, which seemed to enfold her
like an Italian summer.

Burr sighed, — a real sigh of his better nature, but passed out with all the more freedom that he felt it would interest his fair companion, who, for the time being, was the one woman of the world to him.

"Pure and artless souls like yours," he said, "cannot measure the temptations of those who are called to the real battle of life in a world like this. How many nobler aspirations fall withered in the fierce heat and struggle of the conflict!"

He was saying then what he really felt, often bitterly felt, — but *using* this real feeling advisedly, and with skilful tact, for the purpose of the hour.

What was this purpose? To win the regard, the esteem, the tenderness of a religious, exalted nature shrined in a beautiful form, — to gain and hold ascendency. It was a life-long habit, — one of those forms of refined self-indulgence which he pursued, thoughtless and reckless of consequences. He had found now the key-note of the character; it was a beautiful instrument, and he was well pleased to play on it.

"I think, Sir," said Mary, modestly, "that you forget the great provision made for our weakness."

"How?" he said.

"They that *wait on the Lord* shall renew their strength," she replied, gently.

He looked at her, as she spoke these words, with a pleased, artistic perception of the contrast between her worldly attire and the simple, religious earnestness of her words.

" She is entrancing ! " he thought to himself, — " so altogether fresh and *naïve !* "

" My sweet saint," he said, " such as you are the appointed guardians of us coarser beings. The prayers of souls given up to worldliness and ambition effect little. You must intercede for us. I am very orthodox, you see," he added, with that subtle smile which sometimes irradiated his features. " I am fully aware of all that your reverend doctor tells you of the worthlessness of unregenerate doings ; and so, when I see angels walking below, I try to secure 'a friend at court.'"

He saw that Mary looked embarrassed and pained at this banter, and therefore added, with a delicate shading of earnestness, —

" In truth, my fair young friend, I hope you *will* sometimes pray for me. I am sure, if I have any chance of good, it will come in such a way."

" Indeed I will," said Mary, fervently, — her little heart full, tears in her eyes, her breath coming quick, — and she added, with a deepening color, " I am sure, Mr. Burr, that there should be a covenant blessing for you, if for any one, for you are the son of a holy ancestry."

" *Eh, bien, mon ami, qu'est ce que tu fais ici ?* " said a gay voice behind a clump of box ; and immediately there started out, like a French picture from its frame, a dark-eyed figure, dressed like a Marquise of Louis XIV.'s time, with powdered hair, sparkling with diamonds.

"*Rien que m'amuser*," he replied, with ready presence of mind, in the same tone, and then added, — " Permit me, Madame, to present to you a charming specimen of our genuine New England flowers. Miss Scudder, I have the honor to present you to the acquaintance of Madame de Frontignac."

" I am very happy," said the lady, with that sweet, lisping accentuation of English which well became her lovely mouth. " Miss Scudder, I hope, is very well."

Mary replied in the affirmative, — her eyes resting the while with pleased admiration on the graceful, animated face and diamond-bright eyes which seemed looking her through.

" *Monsieur la trouve bien séduisante apparemment*," said the stranger, in a low, rapid voice, to the gentleman, in a manner which showed a mingling of pique and admiration.

" *Petite jalouse ! rassure-toi*," he replied, with a look and manner into which, with that mobile force which was peculiar to him, he threw the most tender and passionate devotion. " *Ne suis-je pas à toi tout à fait ?* " — and as he spoke, he offered her his other arm. " Allow me to be an unworthy link between the beauty of France and America."

The lady swept a proud curtsy backward, bridled her beautiful neck, and signed for them to pass her. " I am waiting here for a friend," she said.

" Whatever is your will is mine," replied Burr, bowing with proud humility, and passing on with Mary to the supper-room.

Here the company were fast assembling, in that high tide of good-humor which generally sets in at this crisis of the evening.

The scene, in truth, was a specimen of a range of society which in those times could have been assembled nowhere else but in Newport. There stood Dr. Hopkins in the tranquil majesty of his lordly form, and by his side, the alert, compact figure of his contemporary and theological opponent, Dr. Stiles, who, animated by the social spirit of the hour, was dispensing courtesies to right and left with the debonair grace of the trained gentleman of the old school. Near by, and engaging from time to time in conversation with them, stood a Jewish Rabbin, whose olive complexion, keen eye, and flowing beard gave a picturesque and foreign grace to the scene. Colonel Burr, one of the most brilliant and distinguished men of the New Republic, and Colonel de Frontignac, who had won for himself laurels in the corps of La Fayette, during the recent revolutionary struggle, with his brilliant, accomplished wife, were all unexpected and distinguished additions to the circle.

Burr gently cleared the way for his fair companion, and, purposely placing her where the full light of the wax chandeliers set off her beauty to the best advantage, devoted himself to her with a subserviency as deferential as if she had been a goddess.

For all that, he was not unobservant, when, a few moments after, Madame de Frontignac was led in, on the arm of a Senator, with whom she was presently in full flirtation.

He observed, with a quiet, furtive smile, that, while she rattled and fanned herself, and listened with apparent attention to the flatteries addressed to her, she darted every now and then a glance, keen as a steel blade towards him and his companion. He was perfectly adroit in playing off one woman against another, and it struck him with a pleasant sense of oddity, how perfectly unconscious his sweet and saintly neighbor was of the position in which she was supposed to stand by her rival; and poor Mary, all this while, in her simplicity, really thought that she had seen traces of what she would have called the "strivings of the spirit" in his soul. Alas! that a phrase weighed down with such mysterious truth and meaning should ever come to fall on the ear as mere empty cant!

With Mary it was a living form, — as were all her words ; for in nothing was the Puritan education more marked than in the earnest *reality* and truthfulness which it gave to language ; and even now, as she stands by his side, her large blue eye is occasionally fixed in dreamy reverie as she thinks what a triumph of Divine grace it would be, if these inward movings of her companion's mind *should* lead him, as all the pious of New England hoped, to follow in the footsteps of President Edwards, and forms wishes that she could see him some time when she could talk to him undisturbed.

She was too humble and too modest fully to accept the delicious flattery which he had breathed, in implying that her hand had had power to unseal the fountains of good in his soul ; but still it thrilled through all the sensitive strings of her nature a tremulous flutter of suggestion.

She had read instances of striking and wonderful conversions from words dropped by children and women, — and suppose some such thing should happen to her! and that this so charming and distinguished and powerful being should be called into the fold of Christ's Church by her means! No it was too much to be hoped, — but the very possibility was thrilling.

When, after supper, Mrs. Scudder and the Doctor made their adieus, Burr's devotion was still unabated. With an enchanting mixture of reverence and fatherly protection, he waited on her to the last,—shawled her with delicate care, and handed her into the small, one-horse wagon,—as if it had been the coach of a duchess.

"I have pleasant recollections connected with this kind of establishment," he said, as, after looking carefully at the harness, he passed the reins into Mrs. Scudder's hands. "It reminds me of school-days and old times. I hope your horse is quite safe, Madam."

"Oh, yes," said Mrs. Scudder, "I perfectly understand him."

"Pardon the suggestion," he replied;—"what is there that a New England matron does *not* understand? Doctor, I must call by-and-by, and have a little talk with you,—my theology, you know, needs a little straightening."

"We should all be happy to see you, Colonel Burr," said Mrs. Scudder; "we live in a very plain way, it is true,"——

"But can always find place for a friend,—that, I trust, is what you meant to say," he replied, bowing, with his own peculiar grace, as the carriage drove off.

"Really, a most charming person is this Colonel Burr," said Mrs. Scudder.

"He seems a very frank, ingenuous young person," said the Doctor; "one cannot but mourn

that the son of such gracious parents should be
left to wander into infidelity."

"Oh, he is not an infidel," said Mary; "he is
far from it, though I think his mind is a little
darkened on some points."

"Ah," said the Doctor, "have you had any special religious conversation with him?"

"A little," said Mary blushing; "and it seems
to me that his mind is perplexed somewhat in regard to the doings of the unregenerate,— I fear that
it has rather proved a stumbling-block in his way;
but he showed *so* much feeling!— I could really
see the tears in his eyes!"

"His mother was a most godly woman, Mary,"
said the Doctor. "She was called from her youth,
and her beautiful person became a temple for the
indwelling of the Holy Spirit. Aaron Burr is a
child of many prayers, and therefore there is hope
that he may yet be effectually called. He studied
awhile with Bellamy," he added, musingly, "and I
have often doubted whether Bellamy took just the
right course with him."

"I hope he *will* call and talk with you," said
Mary, earnestly; "what a blessing to the world,
if such talents as his could become wholly consecrated!"

"Not many wise, not many mighty, not many
noble are called," said the Doctor; "yet if it would
please the Lord to employ my instrumentality and

prayers, how much should I rejoice! I was struck," he added, "to-night, when I saw those Jews present, with the thought that it was, as it were, a type of that last ingathering, when both Jew and Gentile shall sit down lovingly together to the gospel feast. It is only by passing over and forgetting these present years, when so few are called and the gospel makes such slow progress, and looking unto that glorious time, that I find comfort. If the Lord but use me as a dumb stepping-stone to that heavenly Jerusalem, I shall be content."

Thus they talked while the wagon jogged soberly homeward, and the frogs and the turtles and the distant ripple of the sea made a drowsy, mingling concert in the summer-evening air.

Meanwhile Colonel Burr had returned to the lighted rooms, and it was not long before his quick eye espied Madame de Frontignac standing pensively in a window-recess, half hid by the curtain. He stole softly up behind her and whispered something in her car.

In a moment she turned on him a face glowing with anger, and drew back haughtily; but Burr remarked the glitter of tears, not quite dried even by the angry flush of her eyes.

"In what have I had the misfortune to offend?" he said, crossing his arms upon his breast. "I stand at the bar, and plead, Not guilty."

He spoke in French, and she replied in the same smooth accents, —

"It was not for her to dispute Monsieur's right to amuse himself."

Burr drew nearer, and spoke in those persuasive, pleading tones which he had ever at command, and in that language whose very structure in its delicate *tutoiement* gives such opportunity for gliding on through shade after shade of intimacy and tenderness, till gradually the haughty fire of the eyes was quenched in tears, and, in the sudden revulsion of a strong, impulsive nature, she said what she called words of friendship, but which carried with them all the warmth of that sacred fire which is given to woman to light and warm the temple of home, and which sears and scars when kindled for any other shrine.

And yet this woman was the wife of his friend and associate!

Colonel de Frontignac was a grave and dignified man of forty-five. Virginie de Frontignac had been given him to wife when but eighteen, — a beautiful, generous, impulsive, wilful girl. She had accepted him gladly, for very substantial reasons. First, that she might come out of the convent where she was kept for the very purpose of educating her in ignorance of the world she was to live in. Second, that she might wear velvet, lace, cashmere, and jewels. Third, that she might be a Madame, free to go and come, ride, walk, and talk, without surveillance. Fourth,—and consequent upon this,—that she might go into company and have admirers and adorers.

She supposed, of course, that she loved her husband;—whom else should she love? He was the only man, except her father and brothers, that she had ever seen; and in the fortnight that preceded their marriage did he not send her the most splendid *bon-bons* every day, with bouquets of every pattern that ever taxed the brain of a Parisian *artiste?*—was not the *corbeille de mariage* a wonder and an envy to all her acquaintance?—and after marriage had she not found him always a steady, indulgent friend, easy to be coaxed as any grave papa?

On his part, Monsieur de Frontignac cherished his young wife as a beautiful, though somewhat absurd little pet, and amused himself with her frolics and gambols, as the gravest person often will with those of a kitten.

It was not until she knew Aaron Burr that poor Virginie de Frontignac came to that great awakening of her being which teaches woman what she is, and transforms her from a careless child to a deep-hearted, thinking, suffering human being.

For the first time, in his society she became aware of the charm of a polished and cultivated

mind, able with exquisite tact to adapt itself to
hers, to draw forth her inquiries, to excite her
tastes, to stimulate her observation. A new world
awoke around her,—the world of literature and
taste, of art and of sentiment; she felt somehow,
as if she had gained the growth of years in a
few months. She felt within herself the stirring
of dim aspiration, the uprising of a new power of
self-devotion and self-sacrifice, a trance of hero-
worship, a cloud of high ideal images,—the lighting up, in short, of all that God has laid, ready
to be enkindled, in a woman's nature, when the
time comes to sanctify her as the pure priestess
of a domestic temple. But, alas! it was kindled
by one who did it only for an experiment, because
he felt an artistic pleasure in the beautiful light
and heat, and cared not, though it burned a soul
away.

Burr was one of those men willing to play with
any charming woman the game of those navi-
gators who give to simple natives glass beads
and feathers in return for gold and diamonds,—
to accept from a woman her heart's blood in return for such odds and ends and clippings as he
can afford her from the serious ambition of life

Look in with us one moment, now that the party
is over, and the busy hum of voices and blaze of
lights has died down to midnight silence and dark
ness; we make you clairvoyant, and you may look

through the walls of this stately old mansion, still known as that where Rochambeau held his head-quarters, into this room, where two wax candles are burning on a toilette table, before an old-fashioned mirror. The slumberous folds of the curtains are drawn with stately gloom around a high bed, where Colonel de Frontignac has been for many hours quietly asleep; but opposite, resting with one elbow on the toilette table, her long black hair hanging down over her night-dress, and the brush lying list-lessly in her hand, sits Virginie, looking fixedly into the dreamy depths of the mirror.

Scarcely twenty yet, all unwarned of the world of power and passion that lay slumbering in her girl's heart, led in the meshes of custom and society to utter vows and take responsibilities of whose na-ture she was no more apprised than is a slumbering babe, and now at last fully awake, feeling the whole power of that mysterious and awful force which we call love, yet shuddering to call it by its name, but by its light beginning to understand all she is capa-ble of, and all that marriage should have been to her! She struggles feebly and confusedly with her fate, still clinging to the name of duty, and baptizing as friendship this strange new feeling which makes her tremble through all her being. How can she dream of danger in such a feeling, when it seems to her the awakening of all that is highest and no-blest within her? She remembers when she thought of nothing beyond an opera-ticket or a new dress and now she feels that there might be to her a friend for whose sake she would try to be noble and great and good,—for whom all self-denial, all high endeavor, all difficult virtue would become possible,— who would be to her life, inspiration, order, beauty.

She sees him as woman always sees the man she loves,—noble, great, and good;—for when did a loving woman ever believe a man otherwise?—too noble, too great, too high, too good, she thinks, for her,—poor, trivial, ignorant coquette,—poor, childish, trifling Virginie! Has he not commanded armies? she thinks,—is he not eloquent in the senate? and yet what interest he has taken in her, a poor, unformed, ignorant creature!—she never tried to improve herself till since she knew him. And he is so considerate, too,—so respectful, so thoughtful and kind, so manly and honorable, and has such a tender friendship for her, such a brotherly and fatherly solicitude! and yet, if she is haughty or imperious or severe, how humbled and grieved he looks! How strange that she could have power over such a man!

It is one of the saddest truths of this sad mystery of life, that woman is, often, never so much an angel as just the moment before she falls into an unsounded depth of perdition. And what shall we say of the man who leads her on as an experiment,—who amuses himself with taking woman after woman up these dazzling, delusive heights, knowing, as he certainly must, where they lead?

We have been told, in extenuation of the course of Aaron Burr, that he was not a man of gross passions or of coarse indulgence, but, in the most consummate and refined sense, *a man of gallantry*. This, then, is the descriptive name which polite society has invented for the man who does this thing!

Of old, it was thought that one who adminis-tered poison in the sacramental bread and wine had touched the very height of impious sacrilege; but this crime is white, by the side of his who poisons God's eternal sacrament of love and destroys a woman's soul through her noblest and purest af-fections.

We have given you the after-view of most of the actors of our little scene to-night, and there-fore it is but fair that you should have a peep over the Colonel's shoulder, as he sums up the evening in a letter to a friend.

"MY DEAR ———

"As to the business, it gets on rather slowly L—— and S—— are away, and the coalition cannot be formed without them; they set out a week ago from Philadelphia, and are yet on the road.

" Meanwhile, we have some providential allevia-
tions,— as, for example, a wedding-party to-night,
at the Wilcoxes', which was really quite an affair.
I saw the prettiest little Puritan there that I have
set eyes on for many a day. I really couldn't
help getting up a flirtation with her, although it
was much like flirting with a small copy of the
' Assembly's Catechism,'— of which last I had
enough years ago, Heaven knows.

" But, really, such a *naïve*, earnest little saint,
who has such real deadly belief, and opens such
pitying blue eyes on one, is quite a stimulating
novelty. I got myself well scolded by the fair
Madame, (as angels scold,) and had to plead like
a lawyer to make my peace ;— after all, that
woman really enchains me. Don't shake your
head wisely,—' What's going to be the end of
it ? ' I'm sure I don't know; we'll see, when the
time comes.

" Meanwhile, push the business ahead with all
your might. I shall not be idle. D—— must
canvass the Senate thoroughly. I wish I could
be in two p aces at once,—I would do it myself.
Au revoir.

" Ever yours,

" Burr."

CHAPTER XV.

THE SERMON.

"AND now, Mary," said Mrs. Scudder, at five o'clock the next morning, "to-day, you know, is the Doctor's fast; so we won't get any regular dinner, and it will be a good time to do up all our little odd jobs. Miss Prissy promised to come in for two or three hours this morning, to alter the waist of that black silk; and I shouldn't be surprised if we should get it all done and ready to wear by Sunday."

We will remark, by way of explanation to a part of this conversation, that our Doctor, who was a specimen of life in earnest, made a practice, through the greater part of his pulpit course, of spending every Saturday as a day of fasting and retirement, in preparation for the duties of the Sabbath.

Accordingly, the early breakfast things were no sooner disposed of than Miss Prissy's quick footsteps might have been heard pattering in the kitchen.

"Well, Miss Scudder, how *do* you do this morning? and how do you do, Mary? Well, if you a'n't the beaters! up just as early as ever, and everything cleared away! I was telling Miss Wilcox there didn't ever seem to be anything done in Miss Scudder's kitchen, and I did verily believe you made your beds before you got up in the morning.

"Well, well, wasn't that a party last night?" she said, as she sat down with the black silk and prepared her ripping-knife.—"I must rip this myself, Miss Scudder; for there's a great deal in ripping silk so as not to let anybody know where it has been sewed.—You didn't know that I was at the party, did you? Well, I was. You see, I thought I'd just step round there, to see about that money to get the Doctor's shirt with, and there I found Miss Wilcox with so many things on her mind, and says she, 'Miss Prissy, you don't know how much it would help me, if I had somebody like you just to look after things a little here.' And says I, 'Miss Wilcox, you just go right to your room and dress, and don't you give yourself one minute's thought about anything, and you see if I don't have everything just right.' And so, there I was, in for it; and I just staid through, and it was well I did,—for Dinah, she wouldn't have put near enough egg into the coffee, if it hadn't been for me; why, I just went and beat up four eggs with my own hands and stirred 'em into the grounds.

"Well, — but, really, wasn't I behind the door, and didn't I peep into the supper-room? I saw who was a-waitin' on Miss Mary. Well, they do say he's the handsomest, most fascinating man. Why, they say all the ladies in Philadelphia are in a perfect quarrel about him; and I heard he said he hadn't seen such a beauty he didn't remember when."

"We all know that beauty is of small consequence," said Mrs. Scudder. "I hope Mary has been brought up to feel that."

"Oh, of course," said Miss Prissy, "it's just like a fading flower; all is to be good and useful, — and that's what she is. I told 'em that her beauty was the least part of her; though I must say, that dress did fit like a biscuit, — if 'twas my own fitting.

"But, Miss Scudder, what do you think I heard 'em saying about the good Doctor?"

"I'm sure I don't know," said Mrs. Scudder; "I only know they couldn't say anything bad."

"Well, not bad exactly," said Miss Prissy, — "but they say he's getting such strange notions in his head. Why, I heard some of 'em say, he's going to come out and preach against the slave-trade; and I'm sure I don't know what Newport folks will do, if that's wicked. There a'n't hardly

any money here that's made any other way; and
I hope the Doctor a'n't a-going to do anything of
that sort."

"I believe he is," said Mrs. Scudder; "he thinks
it's a great sin, that ought to be rebuked;—and
I think so too," she added, bracing herself resolutely; "that was Mr. Scudder's opinion when I
first married him, and it's mine."

"Oh,—ah,—yes,—well,—if it's a sin, of course,"
said Miss Prissy; "but then—dear me!—it don't
seem as if it could be. Why, just think how
many great houses are living on it;—why, there's
General Wilcox himself, and he's a very nice man;
and then there's Major Seaforth; why, I could
count you off a dozen,—all our very first people.
Why, Doctor Stiles doesn't think so, and I'm sure
he's a good Christian. Doctor Stiles thinks it's
a dispensation for giving the light of the gospel
to the Africans. Why, now I'm sure, when I
was a-working at Deacon Stebbins's, I stopped
over Sunday once 'cause Miss Stebbins she was
weakly,—'twas when she was getting up, after
Samuel was born,—no, on the whole, I believe
it was Nehemiah,—but, any way, I remember I
staid there, and I remember, as plain as if 'twas
yesterday, just after breakfast, how a man went
driving by in a chaise, and the Deacon he went
out and stopped him ('cause you know he was
justice of the peace) for travelling on the Lord's

day, and who should it be but Tom Seaforth?—
he told the Deacon his father had got a ship-load
of negroes just come in,— and the Deacon he
just let him go; 'cause I remember he said that
was a plain work of necessity and mercy.* Well,
now who would 'a' thought it? I believe the
Doctor is better than most folks, but then the best
people may be mistaken, you know."

"The Doctor has made up his mind that it's
his duty," said Mrs. Scudder. "I'm afraid it will
make him very unpopular; but I, for one, shall
stand by him."

"Oh, certainly, Miss Scudder, you are doing
just right exactly. Well, there's one comfort, he'll
have a great crowd to hear him preach; 'cause as
I was going round through the entries last night,
I heard 'em talking about it,— and Colonel Burr
said he should be there, and so did the General,
and so did Mr. What's-his-name there, that Senator from Philadelphia. I tell you, you'll have a
full house."

It was to be confessed that Mrs. Scudder's heart
rather sunk than otherwise at this announcement;
and those who have felt what it is to stand
almost alone in the right, in the face of all the
first families of their acquaintance, may perhaps
find some compassion for her,— since, after all,
truth is invisible, but "first families" are very evi

* A fact.

dent. First families are often very agreeable, un-
deniably respectable, fearfully virtuous, and it takes
great faith to resist an evil principle which incar-
nates itself in the suavities of their breeding and
amiability; and therefore it was that Mrs. Scudder felt her heart heavy within her, and could
with a very good grace have joined in the Doctor's Saturday fast.

As for the Doctor, he sat the while tranquil in
his study, with his great Bible and his Concordance open before him, culling, with that patient
assiduity for which he was remarkable, all the terrible texts which that very unceremonious and old-
fashioned book rains down so unsparingly on the
sin of oppressing the weak.

First families, whether in Newport or elsewhere,
were as invisible to him as they were to Moses
during the forty days that he spent with God on
the mount; he was merely thinking of his message, — thinking only how he should shape it, so
as not to leave one word of it unsaid, — not even
imagining in the least what the result of it was
to be. He was but a voice, but an instrument.—
the passive instrument through which an almighty
will was to reveal itself; and the sublime fatal-
ism of his faith made him as dead to all human
considerations as if he had been a portion of the
immutable laws of Nature herself.

So, the next morning, although all his friends

trembled for him when he rose in the pulpit, he never thought of trembling for himself; he had come in the covered way of silence from the secret place of the Most High, and felt himself still abiding under the shadow of the Almighty. It was alike to him, whether the house was full or empty,— whoever were decreed to hear the message would be there; whether they would hear or forbear was already settled in the counsels of a mightier will than his,—he had the simple duty of utterance.

The ruinous old meeting-house was never so radiant with station and gentility as on that morning. A June sun shone brightly; the sea sparkled with a thousand little eyes; the birds sang all along the way; and all the notables turned out to hear the Doctor. Mrs. Scudder received into her pew, with dignified politeness, Colonel Burr and Colonel and Madame de Frontignac. General Wilcox and his portly dame, Major Seaforth, and we know not what of Vernons and De Wolfs, and other grand old names, were represented there; stiff silks rustled, Chinese fans fluttered, and the last court fashions stood revealed in bonnets.

Everybody was looking fresh and amiable,— a charming and respectable set of sinners, come to hear what the Doctor would find to tell them about their transgressions.

11

Mrs. Scudder was calculating consequences; and, shutting her eyes on the too evident world about her, prayed *that the Lord would overrule all for good. The Doctor prayed that he might have grace to speak the truth, and the whole truth. We have yet on record, in his published works, the great argument of that day, through which he moved with that calm appeal to the reason which made his results always so weighty.

" If these things be true," he said, after a condensed statement of the facts of the case, " then the following terrible consequences, which may well make all shudder and tremble who realize them, force themselves upon us, namely: that all who have had any hand in this iniquitous business, whether directly or indirectly, or have used their influence to promote it, or have consented to it, or even connived at it, or have not opposed it by all proper exertions of which they are capable, —all these are, in a greater or less degree, chargeable with the injuries and miseries which millions have suffered and are suffering, and are guilty of the blood of millions who have lost their lives by this traffic in the human species. Not only the merchants who have been engaged in this trade, and the captains who have been tempted by the love of money to engage in this cruel work, and the slave-holders of every description, are guilty of shedding rivers of blood, but all the legislatures who have authorized, encouraged, or even neglected to suppress it to the utmost of their power, and all the individuals in private stations who have in any way aided in this business, consented to it, or have not opposed it to the utmost of their ability, have a share in this guilt.

" This trade in the human species has been the first wheel of commerce in Newport, on which every other movement in business has chiefly depended; this town has been built up, and flourished in times past, at the expense of the blood, the liberty, and the happiness of the poor Africans; and the inhabitants have lived on this, and by it have gotten most of their wealth and riches. If a bitter woe is pronounced on him 'that buildeth his house by unrighteousness and his chambers by wrong,' Jer. xxii. 13, — to him 'that buildeth a town with blood, and stablisheth a city by iniquity,' Hab. ii. 12, — to 'the bloody city,' Ezek. xxiv. 6, — what a heavy, dreadful woe hangs over the heads of all those whose hands are defiled by the blood of the Africans, especially the inhabitants of this State and this town, who have had a distinguished share in this unrighteous and bloody commerce! "

He went over the recent history of the country, expatiated on the national declaration so lately made, that all men are born equally free and independent and have natural and inalienable rights

to liberty, and asked with what face a nation declaring such things could continue to hold thousands of their fellow-men in abject slavery. He
pointed out signs of national disaster which fore-
boded the wrath of Heaven, — the increase of public and private debts, the spirit of murmuring and
jealousy of rulers among the people, divisions and
contentions and bitter party alienations, the jealous
irritation of England constantly endeavoring to
hamper our trade, the Indians making war on the
frontiers, the Algerines taking captive our ships
and making slaves of our citizens, — all evident
tokens of the displeasure and impending judgment
of an offended Justice.

The sermon rolled over the heads of the gay
audience, deep and dark as a thunder-cloud, which
in a few moments changes a summer sky into
heaviest gloom. Gradually an expression of intense interest and deep concern spread over the
listeners; it was the magnetism of a strong mind,
which held them for a time under the shadow of
his own awful sense of God's almighty justice.

It is said that a little child once described his
appearance in the pulpit by saying, " I saw God
there, and I was afraid."

Something of the same effect was produced on
his audience now; and it was not till after sermon,
prayer, and benediction were all over, that the re-
spectables of Newport began gradually to unstiffen

themselves from the spell, and to look into each other's eyes for comfort, and to reassure themselves that after all they were the first families, and going on the way the world had always gone, and that the Doctor, of course, was a radical and a fanatic.

When the audience streamed out, crowding the broad aisle, Mary descended from the singers, and stood with her psalm-book in hand, waiting at the door to be joined by her mother and the Doctor. She overheard many hard words from people who, an evening or two before, had smiled so graciously upon them. It was therefore with no little determination of manner that she advanced and took the Doctor's arm, as if anxious to associate herself with his well-earned unpopularity, — and just at this moment she caught the eye and smile of Colonel Burr, as he bowed gracefully, yet not without a suggestion of something sarcastic in his eye.

CHAPTER XVI.

THE GARRET-BOUDOIR.

WE suppose the heroine of a novel, among other privileges and immunities, has a prescriptive right to her own private boudoir, where, as a French writer has it, "she appears like a lovely picture in its frame."

Well, our little Mary is not without this luxury, and to its sacred precincts we will give you this morning a ticket of admission. Know, then, that the garret of this gambrel-roofed cottage had a projecting window on the seaward side, which opened into an immensely large old apple-tree, and was a look-out as leafy and secluded as a robin's nest.

Garrets are delicious places in any case, for people of thoughtful, imaginative temperament. Who has not loved a garret in the twilight days of childhood, with its endless stores of quaint, cast-off, suggestive antiquity, — old worm-eaten chests, — rickety chairs, — boxes and casks full of odd comminglings, out of which, with tiny, childish hands, we fished wonderful hoards of fairy treasure? What peep-holes, and hiding-places, and undiscoverable retreats we made to ourselves,— where we sat rejoicing in our security, and bidding defiance to the vague, distant cry which summoned us to school, or to some unsavory every-day task! How deliciously the rain came pattering on the roof over our head, or the red twilight streamed in at the window, while we sat snugly ensconced over the delicious pages of some romance, which careful aunts had packed away at the bottom of all things, to be sure we should never read it! If you have anything, beloved friends, which you wish your Charley or your Susie to be sure and read, pack it mysteriously away at the bottom of a trunk of stimulating rubbish, in the darkest corner of your garret;— in that case, if the book be at all readable, one that by any possible chance can make its way into a young mind, you may be sure that it will not only be read, but remembered to the longest day they have to live.

Mrs. Katy Scudder's garret was not an exception to the general rule. Those quaint little people who touch with so airy a grace all the lights and shadows of great beams, bare rafters, and unplastered walls, had not failed in their work there. Was there not there a grand easy-chair of stamped-leather, minus two of its hinder legs, which had

genealogical associations through the Wilcoxes
with the Vernons and through the Vernons quite
across the water with Old England? and was
there not a dusky picture, in an old tarnished
frame, of a woman of whose tragic end strange
stories were whispered, — one of the sufferers in
the time when witches were unceremoniously helped
out of the world, instead of being, as now-a-days,
helped to make their fortune in it by table-turn-
ing?

Yes, there were all these things, and many more
which we will not stay to recount, but bring you to
the boudoir which Mary has constructed for herself
around the dormer-window which looks into the
whispering old apple-tree.

The inclosure was formed by blankets and bed-
spreads, which, by reason of their antiquity, had
been pensioned off to an undisturbed old age in
the garret, — not *common* blankets or bed-spreads,
either, — bought, as you buy yours, out of a shop,
— spun or woven by machinery, — without individuality or history. Every one of these curtains
had its story. The one on the right, nearest the
window, and already falling into holes, is a Chinese
linen, and even now displays unfaded, quaint patterns of sleepy-looking Chinamen, in conical hats,
standing on the leaves of most singular herbage,
and with hands forever raised in act to strike bells,
which never are struck and never will be till the

end of time. These, Mrs. Katy Scudder had often instructed Mary, were brought from the Indies by her great-great-grandfather, and were her grand-mother's wedding-curtains, — the grandmother who had blue eyes like hers and was just about her height.

The next spread was spun and woven by Mrs. Katy's beloved Aunt Eunice, — a mythical person-age, of whom Mary gathered vague accounts that she was disappointed in love, and that this very article was part of a bridal outfit, prepared in vain, against the return of one from sea, who never came back, — and she heard of how she sat wearily and patiently at her work, this poor Aunt Eunice, month after month, starting every time she heard the gate shut, every time she heard the tramp of a horse's hoof, every time she heard the news of a sail in sight, — her color, meanwhile, fading and fading as life and hope bled away at an inward wound, — till at last she found comfort and reunion beyond the veil.

Next to this was a bed-quilt pieced in tiny blocks, none of them bigger than a sixpence, containing, as Mrs. Katy said, pieces of the gowns of all her grandmothers, aunts, cousins, and female relatives for years back, — and mated to it was one of the blankets which had served Mrs. Scudder's uncle in his bivouac at Valley Forge, when the American soldiers went on the snows with bleeding feet, and had scarce anything for daily bread except a morning message of patriotism and hope from George Washington.

Such were the memories woven into the tapestry of our little boudoir. Within, fronting the window, stands the large spinning-wheel, one end adorned with a snowy pile of fleecy rolls,—and beside it, a reel and a basket of skeins of yarn,—and open, with its face down on the beam of the wheel, lay always a book, with which the intervals of work were beguiled.

The dusky picture of which we have spoken hung against the rough wall in one place, and in another appeared an old engraved head of one of the Madonnas of Leonardo da Vinci, a picture which to Mary had a mysterious interest, from the fact of its having been cast on shore after a furious storm, and found like a waif lying in the seaweed; and Mrs. Marvyn, who had deciphered the signature, had not ceased exploring till she found for her, in an Encyclopædia, a life of that wonderful man, whose greatness enlarges our ideas of what is possible to humanity,—and Mary pondering thereon, felt the seaworn picture as a constant vague inspiration.

Here our heroine spun for hours and hours,—with intervals, when, crouched on a low seat in the window, she pored over her book, and then, returning again to her work, thought of what she had read to the lulling burr of the sounding wheel.

By chance a robin had built its nest so that from her retreat she could see the five little blue eggs, whenever the patient brooding mother left them for a moment uncovered. And sometimes, as she sat in dreamy reverie, resting her small, round arms on the window-sill, she fancied that the little feathered watcher gave her familiar nods and winks of a confidential nature,—cocking the small head first to one side and then to the other, to get a better view of her gentle human neighbor.

I dare say it seems to you, reader, that we have travelled in our story, over a long space of time, because we have talked so much and introduced so many personages and reflections; but, in fact, it is only Wednesday week since James sailed, and the eggs which were brooded when he went are still unhatched in the nest, and the apple-tree has changed only in having now a majority of white blossoms over the pink buds.

This one week has been a critical one to our Mary;—in it, she has made the great discovery, that she loves; and she has made her first step into the gay world; and now she comes back to her retirement to think the whole over by herself. It seems a dream to her, that she who sits there now reeling yarn in her stuff petticoat and white short-gown is the same who took the arm of

Colonel Burr amid the blaze of wax-lights and the sweep of silks and rustle of plumes. She wonders dreamily as she remembers the dark, lovely face of the foreign Madame, so brilliant under its powdered hair and flashing gems,—the sweet, foreign accents of the voice,—the tiny, jewelled fan, with its glancing pictures and sparkling tassels, whence exhaled vague and floating perfumes; then she hears again that manly voice, softened to tones so seductive, and sees those fine eyes with the tears in them, and wonders within herself that *he* could have kissed her hand with such veneration, as if she had been a throned queen.

But here the sound of busy, pattering footsteps is heard on the old, creaking staircase, and soon the bows of Miss Prissy's bonnet part the folds of the boudoir drapery, and her merry, May-day face looks in.

" Well, really, Mary, how do you do, to be sure? You wonder to see me, don't you? but I thought I must just run in, a minute, on my way up to Miss Marvyn's. I promised her at least a half-a-day, though I didn't see how I was to spare it,— for I tell Miss Wilcox I just run and run till it does seem as if my feet would drop off; but I thought I must just step in to say, that I, for my part, *do admire* the Doctor more than ever, and I was telling your mother we mus'n't mind too much what people say. I 'most made Miss Wil-

cox angry, standing up for him; but I put it right
to her, and says I, ' Miss Wilcox, you know folks
must speak what's on their mind,—in particular
ministers must; and you know, Miss Wilcox,' I
says, ' that the Doctor *is* a good man, and lives up
to his teaching, if anybody in this world does, and
gives away every dollar he can lay hands on to
those poor negroes, and works over 'em and teaches
'em as if they were his brothers' ; and says I,
' Miss Wilcox, you know I don't spare myself, night
nor day, trying to please you and do your work
to give satisfaction ; but when it comes to my
conscience,' says I, ' Miss Wilcox, you know I always must speak out, and if it was the last word
I had to say on my dying bed, I'd say that I think
the Doctor is right.' Why! what things he told
about the slave-ships, and packing those poor creatures so that they couldn't move nor breathe!—
why, I declare, every time I turned over and
stretched in bed, I thought of it;—and says I,
' Miss Wilcox, I do believe that the judgments of
God will come down on us, if something a'n't
done, and I shall always stand by the Doctor,'
says I;—and, if you'll believe me, just then I turned
round and saw the General; and the General, he
just haw-hawed right out, and says he, ' Good for
you, Miss Prissy! that's real grit,' says he, ' and I
like you better for it.'—Laws," added Miss Prissy,
reflectively, " I sha'n't lose by it, for Miss Wilcox

know.s she never can get anybody to do the work
for her that I will."

"Do you think," said Mary, "that there are a
great many made angry?"

"Why, bless your heart, child, haven't you heard?
— Why, there never was such a talk in all Newport. Why, you know Mr. Simeon Brown is gone
clear off to Dr. Stiles; and Miss Brown, I was
making up her plum-colored satin o' Monday, and
you ought to 'a' heard her talk. But, I tell you,
I fought her. She used to talk to me," said Miss
Prissy, sinking her voice to a mysterious whisper,
"'cause I never could come to it to say that I
was willin' to be lost, if it was for the glory of
God; and she always told me folks could just
bring their minds right up to anything they knew
they must; and I just got the tables turned on
her, for they talked and abused the Doctor till
they fairly wore me out, and says I, 'Well, Miss
Brown, I'll give in, that you and Mr. Brown *do*
act up to your principles; you certainly *act* as if
you were willing to be damned';—and so do all
those folks who will live on the blood and groans
of the poor Africans, as the Doctor said; and I
should think, by the way Newport people are making their money, that they were all pretty willing
to go that way,—though, whether it's for the glory
of God, or not, I'm doubting.—But you see,
Mary," said Miss Prissy, sinking her voice again

to a solemn whisper, " I never was *clear* on that point; it always did seem to me a dreadful high place to come to, and it didn't seem to be given to me; but I thought, perhaps, if it *was* necessary, it would be given, you know,—for the Lord always has been so good to me that I've faith to believe that, and so I just say, ' The Lord is my shepherd, I shall not want' ";—and Miss Prissy hastily whisked a little drop out of her blue eye with her handkerchief.

At this moment, Mrs. Scudder came into the boudoir with a face expressive of some anxiety.

" I suppose Miss Prissy has told you," she said, " the news about the Browns. That'll make a great falling off in the Doctor's salary; and I feel for him, because I know it will come hard to him not to be able to help and do, especially for these poor negroes, just when he will. But then we must put everything on the most economical scale we can, and just try, all of us, to make it up to him. I was speaking to Cousin Zebedee about it, when he was down here, on Monday, and he is all clear;—he has made out free papers for Candace and Cato and Dinah, and they couldn't, one of 'em, be hired to leave him; and he says, from what he's seen already, he has no doubt but they'll do enough more to pay for their wages."

" Well," said Miss Prissy, " I haven't got anybody to care for but myself. I was telling sister

Elizabeth, one time, (she's married and got four children,) that I could take a storm a good deal easier than she could, 'cause I hadn't near so many sails to pull down; and now, you just look to me for the Doctor's shirts, 'cause, after this, they shall all come in ready to put on, if I have to sit up till morning. And I hope, Miss Scudder, you can trust me to make them; for if I do say it myself, I a'n't afraid to do fine stitching 'longside of anybody, — and hemstitching ruffles, too; and I haven't shown you yet that French stitch I learned of the nuns; — but you just set your heart at rest about the Doctor's shirts. I always thought," continued Miss Prissy, laughing, "that I should have made a famous hand about getting up that tabernacle in the wilderness, with the blue and the purple and fine-twined linen; it's one of my favorite passages, that is; — different things, you know, are useful to different people."

"Well," said Mrs. Scudder, "I see that it's our call to be a remnant small and despised, but I hope we sha'n't shrink from it. I thought, when I saw all those fashionable people go out Sunday, tossing their heads and looking so scornful, that I hoped grace would be given me to be faithful."

"And what does the Doctor say?" said Miss Prissy.

"He hasn't said a word; his mind seems to be very much lifted above all these things."

"La, yes," said Miss Prissy, "that's one comfort; he'll never know where his shirts come from; and besides that, Miss Scudder," she said, sinking her voice to a whisper, "as you know, I haven't any children to provide for, — though I was telling Elizabeth t'other day, when I was making up frocks for her children, that I believed old maids, first and last, did more providing for children than married women ; but still I do contrive to slip away a pound-note, now and then, in my little old silver tea-pot that was given to me when they settled old Mrs. Simpson's property, (I nursed her all through her last sickness, and laid her out with my own hands,) and, as I was saying, if ever the Doctor should want money, you just let me know."

"Thank you, Miss Prissy," said Mrs. Scudder; "we all know where your heart is."

"And now," added Miss Prissy, "what do you suppose they say? Why, they say Colonel Burr is struck dead in love with our Mary; and you know his wife's dead, and he's a widower; and they do say that he'll get to be the next President. Sakes alive! Well, Mary must be careful, if she don't want to be carried off; for they do say that there can't any woman resist him, that sees enough of him. Why, there's that poor French woman, Madame —— what do you call her, that's staying with the Vernons? — they say she's over head and ears in love with him."

"But she's a married woman," said Mary; "it can't be possible."

Mrs. Scudder looked reprovingly at Miss Prissy, and for a few moments there was great shaking of heads and a whispered conference between the two ladies, ending in Miss Prissy's going off, saying, as she went down stairs, —

"Well, if women will do so, I, for my part, can't blame the men."

In a few moments Miss Prissy rushed back as much discomposed as a clucking hen who has seen a hawk.

"Well, Miss Scudder, what do you think? Here's Colonel Burr come to call on the ladies!"

Mrs. Scudder's first movement, in common with all middle-aged gentlewomen, was to put her hand to her head and reflect that she had not on her best cap; and Mary looked down at her dimpled hands, which were blue from the contact with mixed yarn she had just been spinning.

"Now, I'll tell you what," said Miss Prissy, — "wasn't it lucky you had me here? for I first saw him coming in at the gate, and I whipped in quick as a wink and opened the best-room window-shutters, and then I was back at the door, and he bowed to me as if I'd been a queen, and says he, 'Miss Prissy, how fresh you're looking this morning!' You see, I was in working at the Vernons', but I never thought as he'd noticed me.

And then he inquired in the handsomest way for the ladies and the Doctor, and so I took him into the parlor and settled him down, and then I ran into the study, and you may depend upon it I flew round lively for a few minutes. I got the Doctor's study-gown off, and got his best coat on, and put on his wig for him, and started him up kinder lively, — you know it takes me to get him down into this world, — and so there he's in talking with him; and so you can just slip down and dress yourselves, — easy as not.

Meanwhile Colonel Burr was entertaining the simple-minded Doctor with all the grace of a young neophyte come to sit at the feet of superior truth. There are some people who receive from Nature as a gift a sort of graceful facility of sympathy, by which they incline to take on, for the time being, the sentiments and opinions of those with whom they converse, as the chameleon was fabled to change its hue with every surrounding. Such are often supposed to be wilfully acting a part, as exerting themselves to flatter and deceive, when in fact they are only framed so sensitive to the sphere of mental emanation which surrounds others that it would require an exertion *not* in some measure to harmonize with it. In approaching others in conversation, they are like a musician who joins a performer on an instrument, it is impossible for them to strike a discord;

their very nature urges them to bring into play faculties according in vibration with those which another is exerting. It was as natural as possible for Burr to commence talking with the Doctor on scenes and incidents in the family of President Edwards, and his old tutor, Dr. Bellamy, — and thence to glide on to the points of difference and agreement in theology, with a suavity and deference which acted on the good man like a June sun on a budding elm-tree. The Doctor was soon wide awake, talking with fervent animation on the topic of disinterested benevolence, — Burr the mean while studying him with the quiet interest of an observer of natural history, who sees a new species developing before him. At all the best possible points he interposed suggestive questions, and set up objections in the quietest manner for the Doctor to knock down, smiling ever the while as a man may who truly and genuinely does not care a *sou* for truth on any subject not practically connected with his own schemes in life. He therefore gently guided the Doctor to sail down the stream of his own thoughts till his bark glided out into the smooth waters of the Millennium, on which, with great simplicity, he gave his views at length.

It was just in the midst of this that Mary and her mother entered. Burr interrupted the conversation to pay them the compliments of the morning, — to inquire for their health, and hope they suffered no inconvenience from their night-ride from the party; then, seeing the Doctor still looking eager to go on, he contrived with gentle dexterity to tie again the broken thread of conversation.

"Our excellent friend," he said, "was explaining to me his views of a future Millennium. I assure you, ladies, that we sometimes find ourselves in company which enables us to believe in the perfectibility of the human species. We see family retreats, so unaffected, so charming in their simplicity, where industry and piety so go hand in hand! One has only to suppose all families such, to imagine a Millennium."

There was no disclaiming this compliment, because so delicately worded, that, while perfectly clear to the internal sense, it was, in a manner, veiled and unspoken.

Meanwhile the Doctor, who sat ready to begin where he left off, turned to his complaisant listener and resumed an exposition of the Apocalypse.

"To my mind, it is certain," he said, "as it is now three hundred years since the fifth vial was poured out, there is good reason to suppose that the sixth vial began to be poured out at the beginning of the last century, and has been running for a hundred years or more, so that it is run nearly out; the seventh and last vial will begin to run early in the next century."

" You anticipate, then, no rest for the world for some time to come ? " said Burr.

" Certainly not," said the Doctor, definitively; " there will be no rest from overturnings till He whose right it is shall come.

"The passage," he added, " concerning the drying up of the river Euphrates, under the sixth vial, has a distinct reference, I think, to the account in ancient writers of the taking of Babylon, and prefigures, in like manner, that the resources of that modern Babylon, the Popish power, shall continue to be drained off, as they have now been drying up for a century or more, till, at last, there will come a sudden and final downfall of that power. And after that will come the first triumphs of truth and righteousness, — the marriage-supper of the Lamb."

" These investigations must undoubtedly possess a deep interest for you, Sir," said Burr; " the hope of a future as well as the tradition of a past age of gold seems to have been one of the most cherished conceptions of the human breast."

" In those times," continued the Doctor, " the whole earth will be of one language."

" Which language, Sir, do you suppose will be considered worthy of such preëminence ? " inquired his listener.

"That will probably be decided by an amicable conference of all nations," said the Doctor; "and the one universally considered most valuable will be adopted; and the literature of all other nations being translated into it, they will gradually drop all other tongues. Brother Stiles thinks it will be the Hebrew. I am not clear on that point. The Hebrew seems to me too inflexible, and not sufficiently copious. I do not think," he added, after some consideration, "that it will be the Hebrew tongue."

"I am most happy to hear it, Sir," said Burr, gravely; "I never felt much attracted to that language. But, ladies," he added, starting up with animation, "I must improve this fine weather to ask you to show me the view of the sea from this little hill beyond your house, it is evidently so fine; — I trust I am not intruding too far on your morning?"

"By no means, Sir," said Mrs. Scudder, rising; "we will go with you in a moment."

And soon Colonel Burr, with one on either arm, was to be seen on the top of the hill beyond the house, — the very one from which Mary, the week before, had seen the retreating sail we all wot of. Hence, though her companion contrived, with the adroitness of a practised man of gallantry, to direct his words and looks as constantly to her as if they had been in a *tête-a-tête*, and although nothing could be more graceful, more delicately flattering, more engaging, still the little heart kept equal poise; for where a true love has once bolted the door, a false one serenades in vain under the window.

Some fine, instinctive perceptions of the real character of the man beside her seemed to have dawned on Mary's mind in the conversation of the morning; — she had felt the covert and subtle irony that lurked beneath his polished smile, felt the utter want of faith or sympathy in what she and her revered friend deemed holiest, and therefore there was a calm dignity in her manner of receiving his attentions which rather piqued and stimulated his curiosity. He had been wont to boast that he could subdue any woman, if he could only see enough of her; in the first interview in the garden, he had made her color come and go and brought tears to her eyes in a manner that interested his fancy, and he could not resist the impulse to experiment again. It was a new sensation to him, to find himself quietly studied and calmly measured by those thoughtful blue eyes; he felt, with his fine, instinctive tact, that the soul within was infolded in some crystalline sphere of protection, transparent, but adamantine, so that he could not touch it. What was that secret poise, that calm, immutable centre on which she rested, that made her, in her rustic simplicity, so unapproachable and so strong?

Burr remembered once finding in his grandfather's study, among a mass of old letters, one
in which that great man, in early youth, described
his future wife, then known to him only by distant report. With his keen natural sense of everything fine and poetic, he had been struck with this
passage, as so beautifully expressing an ideal
womanhood, that he had in his earlier days copied it in his private *recueil*.

" They say," it ran, " that there is a young lady
who is beloved of that Great Being who made
and rules the world, and that there are certain
seasons in which this Great Being, in some way
or other invisible, comes to her and fills her mind
with such exceeding sweet delight, that she hardly
cares for anything except to meditate on him; that
she expects, after a while, to be received up where
he is, to be raised up out of the world and caught
up into heaven, being assured that he loves her too
well to let her remain at a distance from him
always. Therefore, if you present all the world
before her, with the richest of its treasures, she
disregards it. She has a strange sweetness in her
mind, and singular purity in her affections; and
you could not persuade her to do anything wrong
or sinful, if you should give her all the world.
She is of a wonderful sweetness, calmness, and
universal benevolence of mind, especially after this
great God has manifested himself to her mind.

12

She will sometimes go from place to place singing sweetly, and seems to be always full of joy and pleasure; and no one knows for what. She loves to be alone, walking in fields and groves, and seems to have some invisible one always conversing with her."

A shadowy recollection of this description crossed his mind more than once, as he looked into those calm and candid eyes. Was there, then, a truth in that inner union of chosen souls with God, of which his mother and her mother before her had borne meek witness, — their souls shining out as sacred lamps through the alabaster walls of a temple?

But then, again, had he not logically.met and demonstrated, to his own satisfaction, the nullity of the religious dogmas on which New England faith was based? There could be no such inner life, he said to himself, — he had demonstrated it as an absurdity. What was it, then, — this charm, so subtile and so strong, by which this fair child, his inferior in age, cultivation, and knowledge of the world, held him in a certain awe, and made him feel her spirit so unapproachable? His curiosity was piqued. He felt stimulated to employ all his powers of pleasing. He was determined, that, sooner or later, she should feel his power.

With Mrs. Scudder his success was immediate; she was completely won over by the deferential

manner with which he constantly referred himself
to her matronly judgments; and, on returning to
the house, she warmly pressed him to stay to
dinner.

Burr accepted the invitation with a frank and
almost boyish *abandon*, declaring that he had not
seen anything, for years, that so reminded him of
old times. He praised everything at table, — the
smoking brown-bread, the baked beans steaming
from the oven, where they had been quietly sim-
mering during the morning walk, and the Indian
pudding, with its gelatinous softness, matured by
long and patient brooding in the motherly old
oven. He declared that there was no style of
living to be compared with the simple, dignified
order of a true New England home, where servants were excluded, and everything came direct
from the polished and cultured hand of a lady.
It realized the dreams of Arcadian romance. A
man, he declared, must be unworthy the name,
who did not rise to lofty sentiments and heroic
deeds, when even his animal wants were provided
for by the ministrations of the most delicate and
exalted portion of the creation.

After dinner he would be taken into all the
family interests. Gentle and pliable as oil, he
seemed to penetrate every joint of the *ménage* by
a subtile and seductive sympathy. He was interested in the spinning, in the weaving, — and in

fact, nobody knows how it was done, but, before the afternoon shadows had turned, he was sitting in the cracked arm-chair of Mary's garret-boudoir, gravely giving judgment on several specimens of her spinning, which Mrs. Scudder had presented to his notice.

With that ease with which he could at will glide into the character of the superior and elder brother, he had, without seeming to ask questions, drawn from Mary an account of her reading, her studies, her acquaintances.

"You read French, I presume?" he said to her, with easy negligence.

Mary colored deeply, and then, as one who recollects one's self, answered, gravely, —

"No, Mr. Burr, I know no language but my own."

"But you should learn French, my child," said Burr, with that gentle dictatorship which he could at times so gracefully assume.

"I should be delighted to learn," said Mary, "but have no opportunity."

"Yes," said Mrs. Scudder, — "Mary has always had a taste for study, and would be glad to improve in any way."

"Pardon me, Madam, if I take the liberty of making a suggestion. There is a most excellent man, the Abbé Léfon, now in Newport, driven here by the political disturbances in France; he is anxious to obtain a few scholars, and I am interested that he should succeed, for he is a most worthy man."

"Is he a Roman Catholic?"

"He is, Madam; but there could be no manner of danger with a person so admirably instructed as your daughter. If you please to see him, Madam, I will call with him some time."

"Mrs. Marvyn will, perhaps, join me," said Mary. "She has been studying French by herself for some time, in order to read a treatise on astronomy, which she found in that language. I will go over to-morrow and see her about it."

Before Colonel Burr departed, the Doctor requested him to step a moment with him into his study. Burr, who had had frequent occasions during his life to experience the sort of paternal freedom which the clergy of his country took with him in right of his clerical descent, began to summon together his faculties of address for the avoidance of a kind of conversation which he was not disposed to meet. He was agreeably disappointed, however, when, taking a paper from the table, and presenting it to him, the Doctor said, —

"I feel myself, my dear Sir, under a burden of obligation for benefits received from your family, so that I never see a member of it without casting about in my own mind how I may in some measure express my good-will towards him. You are aware that the papers of your distinguished grandfather have fallen into my hands, and from them I have taken the liberty to make a copy of those maxims by which he guided a life which was a blessing to his country and to the world. May I ask the favor that you will read them with attention? and if you find anything contrary to right reason or sober sense, I shall be happy to hear of it on a future occasion."

"Thank you, Doctor," said Burr, bowing. "I shall always be sensible of the kindness of the motive which has led you to take this trouble on my account. Believe me, Sir, I am truly obliged to you for it."

And thus the interview terminated.

That night, the Doctor, before retiring, offered fervent prayers for the grandson of his revered master and friend, praying that his father's and mother's God might bless him and make him a living stone in the Eternal Temple.

Meanwhile, the object of these prayers was sitting by a table in dressing-gown and slippers, thinking over the events of the day. The paper which Doctor Hopkins had handed him contained the celebrated "Resolutions" by which his ancestor led a life nobler than any mere dogmas can possibly be. By its side lay a perfumed note from Madame de Frontignac, — one of those womanly notes, so beautiful, so sacred in themselves, but so mournful to a right-minded person who sees whither they are tending. Burr opened and perused it,—laid it by,—opened the document that the Doctor had given, and thoughtfully read the first of the " Resolutions " : —

" Resolved, That I will do whatsoever I think to be most to God's glory, and my own good profit and pleasure *in the whole of my duration*, without any consideration of time, whether now or never so many myriad ages hence.

" Resolved, To do whatever I think to be my duty and most for the good and advantage of mankind in general.

" Resolved, To do this, whatsoever difficulties I meet with, and how many and how great soever."

Burr read the whole paper through attentively once or twice, and paused thoughtfully over many parts of it. He sat for some time after, lost in reflection ; the paper dropped from his hand, and then followed one of those long, deep seasons of fixed reverie, when the soul thinks by pictures and goes over endless distances in moments. In him, originally, every moral faculty and sensibility was as keenly strung as in any member of that remarkable family from which he was descended, and which has, whether in good or ill, borne no common stamp. Two possible lives flashed before his mind at that moment, rapidly as when a train sweeps by with flashing lamps in the

night. The life of worldly expediency, the life of
eternal rectitude,—the life of seventy years, and
that life eternal in which the event of death is no
disturbance. Suddenly he roused himself, picked
up the paper, filed and dated it carefully, and laid
it by; and in that moment was renewed again
that governing purpose which sealed him, with
all his beautiful capabilities, as the slave of the
fleeting and the temporary, which sent him at
last, a shipwrecked man, to a nameless, dishonored
grave.

He took his pen and gave to a friend his own
views of the events of the day.

"My dear,—— We are still in Newport, conju-
gating the verb *s'ennuyer*, which I, for one, have
put through all the moods and tenses. *Pour
passer le temps*, however, I have *la belle Française* and my sweet little Puritan. I visited there
this morning. She lives with her mother, a little
walk out toward the seaside, in a cottage quite
prettily sequestered among blossoming apple-trees,
and the great hierarch of modern theology, Dr.
Hopkins, keeps guard over them. No chance here
for any indiscretions, you see.

"By-the-by, the good Doctor astonished our
monde here on Sunday last, by treating us to a
solemn onslaught on slavery and the slave-trade.
He had all the chief captains and counsellors to

hear him, and smote them hip and thigh, and pursued them even unto Shur.

"He is one of those great, honest fellows, without the smallest notion of the world we live in, who think, in dealing with men, that you must go to work and prove the right or the wrong of a matter; just as if anybody cared for that! Supposing he is right,—which appears very probable to me,—what is he going to do about it? No moral argument, since the world began, ever prevailed over twenty-five per cent. profit.

"However, he is the spiritual director of *la belle Puritaine*, and was a resident in my grandfather's family, so I did the agreeable with him as well as such an uncircumcised Ishmaelite could. I discoursed theology,—sat with the most docile air possible while he explained to me all the ins and outs in his system of the universe, past, present, and future,—heard him dilate calmly on the Millennium, and expound prophetic symbols, marching out before me his whole apocalyptic menagerie of beasts and dragons with heads and horns innumerable, to all which I gave edifying attention, taking occasion now and then to turn a compliment in favor of the ladies,—never lost, you know.

"Really, he is a worthy old soul, and actually believes all these things with his whole heart, attaching unheard-of importance to the most abstract ideas, and embarking his whole being in his ideal view of a grand Millennial *finale* to the human race. I look at him and at myself, and ask, Can human beings be made so unlike?

" My little Mary to-day was in a mood of 'sweet austere composure' quite becoming to her style of beauty; her *naïve nonchalance* at times is rather stimulating. What a contrast between her and *la belle Française!* — all the difference that there is between a diamond and a flower. I find the little thing has a cultivated mind, enriched by reading, and more by a still, quaint habit of think-ing, which is new and charming. But a truce to this.

" I have seen our friends at last. We have had three or four meetings, and are waiting to hear from Philadelphia, — matters are getting in train. If Messrs. T. and S. dare to repeat what they said again, let me know; they will find in me a man not to be trifled with. I shall be with you in a week or ten days at farthest. Meanwhile stand to your guns.

" Ever yours,

" BURR."

CHAPTER XVII.

POLEMICS IN THE KITCHEN.

THE next morning, before the early dews had yet dried off the grass, Mary started to go and see her friend Mrs. Marvyn. It was one of those charming, invigorating days, familiar to those of Newport experience, when the sea lies shimmering and glittering in deep blue and gold, and the sky above is firm and cloudless, and every breeze that comes landward seems to bear health and energy upon its wings.

As Mary approached the house, she heard loud sounds of discussion from the open kitchen-door, and, looking in, saw a rather original scene acting.

Candace, armed with a long oven-shovel, stood before the open door of the oven, whence she had just been removing an army of good things which appeared ranged around on the dresser. Cato, in the undress of a red flannel shirt and tow-cloth trousers, was cuddled, in a consoled and protected attitude, in the corner of the wooden settle, with

a mug of flip in his hand, which Candace had
prepared, and, calling him in from his work, authoritatively ordered him to drink, on the showing
that he had kept her awake the night before with
his cough, and she was sure he was going to be
sick. Of course, worse things may happen to a
man than to be vigorously taken care of by his
wife, and Cato had a salutary conviction of this
fact, so that he resigned himself to his comfortable corner and his flip with edifying serenity.

Opposite to Candace stood a well-built, corpulent negro man, dressed with considerable care,
and with the air of a person on excellent terms
with himself. This was no other than Digo, the
house-servant and factotum of Dr. Stiles, who
considered himself as the guardian of his master's
estate, his title, his honor, his literary character,
his professional position, and his religious creed.

Digo was ready to assert before all the world,
that one and all of these were under his special
protection, and that whoever had anything to say
to the contrary of any of these must expect to
take issue with him. Digo not only swallowed
all his master's opinions whole, but seemed to
have the stomach of an ostrich in their digestion.
He believed everything, no matter what, the moment he understood that the Doctor held it. He
believed that Hebrew was the language of heaven,
— that the ten tribes of the Jews had reappeared

in the North American Indians, — that there was no such thing as disinterested benevolence, and that the doings of the unregenerate had some value, — that slavery was a divine ordinance, and that Dr. Hopkins was a radical, who did more harm than good, — and, finally, that there never was so great a man as Dr. Stiles; and as Dr. Stiles belonged to him in the capacity of master, why, he, Digo, owned the greatest man in America. Of course, as Candace held precisely similar opinions in regard to Dr. Hopkins, the two never could meet without a discharge of the opposite electricities. Digo had, it is true, come ostensibly on a mere worldly errand from his mistress to Mrs. Marvyn, who had promised to send her some turkeys' eggs, but he had inly resolved with himself that he would give Candace his opinion, — that is, what Dr. Stiles had said at dinner the day before about Dr. Hopkins' Sunday's discourse. Dr. Stiles had not heard it, but Digo had. He had felt it due to the responsibilities of his position to be present on so very important an occasion.

Therefore, after receiving his, eggs, he opened hostilities by remarking, in a general way, that he had attended the Doctor's preaching on Sunday, and that there was quite a crowded house. Candace immediately began mentally to bristle her feathers like a hen who sees a hawk in the distance, and responded with decision: —

" Den you *heard* sometin', for once in your life ! "

" I must say," said Digo, with suavity, " dat I can't give my 'proval to such sentiments."

" More shame for you," said Candace, grimly. " *You* a man, and not stan' by your color, and flunk under to mean white ways ! Ef you was *half* a man, your heart would 'a' bounded like a cannon-ball at dat ar' sermon."

" Dr. Stiles and me we talked it over after church," said Digo, — " and de Doctor was of my 'pinion, dat Providence didn't intend " ——

" Oh, you go 'long wid your Providence ! Guess, ef white folks had let us alone, Providence wouldn't trouble us."

" Well," said Digo, " Dr. Stiles is clear dat dis yer's a-fulfillin' de prophecies and bringin' in de fulness of the Gentiles."

" Fulness of de fiddlesticks ! " said Candace, irreverently. " Now what a way dat ar' is of talkin' ! Go look at one o' dem ships we come over in, — sweatin' and groanin', — in the dark and dirt, — cryin' and dyin', — howlin' for breath till de sweat run off us, — livin' and dead chained together, — prayin' like de rich man in hell for a drop o' water to cool our tongues ! Call dat ar' a-bringin' de fulness of de Gentiles, do ye ? Ugh ! "

And Candace ended with a guttural howl, and

stood frowning and gloomy over the top of her long kitchen-shovel, like a black Bellona leaning on her spear of battle.

Digo recoiled a little, but stood too well in his own esteem to give up ; so he shifted his attack.

" Well, for my part, I must say I never was 'clined to your Doctor's 'pinions. Why, now, Dr. Stiles says, notin' couldn't be more absurd dan what he says 'bout disinterested benevolence. *My* Doctor says, dere a'n't no such ting ! "

" I should tink it's likely ! " said Candace, drawing herself up with superb disdain. " *Our* Doctor knows dere *is*, — and why ? 'cause he's got it IN HERE," said she, giving her ample chest a knock which resounded like the boom from a barrel.

" Candace," said Cato, gently, " you's gittin' too hot."

" Cato, you shut up ! " said Candace, turning sharp round. " What did I make you dat ar' flip for, 'cept you was so hoarse you oughtn' for to say a word ? Pooty business, you go to agitatin' *your*self wid dese yer! Ef you wear out your poor old throat talkin', you may get de 'sumption ; and den what 'd become o' me ? "

Cato, thus lovingly pitched *hors de combat*, sipped the sweetened cup in quietness of soul, while Candace returned to the charge.

" Now, I tell ye what," she said to Digo, — " jest cause you wear your master's old coats and hats,

you tink you must go in for all dese yer old, mean
white 'pinions. A'n't ye 'shamed — you, a black
man — to have no more pluck and make cause wid
de Egyptians? Now, 'ta'n't what my Doctor gives
me, — he never giv' me the snip of a finger-nail, —
but it's what he does for *mine;* and when de poor
critturs lands dar, tumbled out like bales on de
wharves, ha'n't dey seen his great cocked hat, like
a lighthouse, and his big eyes lookin' sort o' pitiful
at 'em as ef he felt o' one blood wid 'em? Why,
de very looks of de man is worth everyting; and
who ever thought o' doing anyting for deir souls, or
cared ef dey had souls, till he begun it?"

"Well, at any rate," said Digo, brightening up,
"I don't believe his doctrine about de doings of de
unregenerate, — it's quite clear he's wrong dar."

"Who cares?" said Candace, — "generate or
unregenerate, it's all one to me. I believe a man
dat *acts* as he does. Him as stands up for the
poor, — him as pleads for de weak, — he's my man.
I'll believe straight through anyting he's a mind to
put at me."

At this juncture, Mary's fair face appearing at the
door put a stop to the discussion.

"Bress *you,* Miss Mary! comin' here like a fresh
June rose! it makes a body's eyes dance in deir
head! Come right in! I got Cato up from de lot,
'cause he's rader poorly dis mornin'; his cough
makes me a sight o' concern; he's allers a-pullin'

off his jacket de wrong time, or doin' sometin' I tell him not to, — and it just keeps him hack, hack, hackin', all de time."

During this speech, Cato stood meekly bowing, feeling that he was being apologized for in the best possible manner; for long years of instruction had fixed the idea in his mind, that he was an ignorant sinner, who had not the smallest notion how to conduct himself in this world, and that, if it were not for his wife's distinguishing grace, he would long since have been in the shades of oblivion.

" Missis is spinnin' up in de north chamber," said Candace ; " but I'll run up and fetch her down."

Candace, who was about the size of a puncheon, was fond of this familiar manner of representing her mode of ascending the stairs ; but Mary, suppressing a smile, said, " Oh, no, Candace! don't for the world disturb her. I know just where she is." And before Candace could stop her, Mary's light foot was on the top step of the staircase that led up from the kitchen.

The north room was a large chamber, overlooking a splendid reach of sea-prospect. A moving panorama of blue water and gliding sails was unrolled before its three windows, so that stepping into the room gave one an instant and breezy sense of expansion. Mrs. Marvyn was standing at the large wheel, spinning wool, — a reel and basket of spools on her side. Her large brown eyes had an eager

joy in them when Mary entered; but they seemed
to calm down again, and she received her only with
that placid, sincere air which was her habit. Everything about this woman showed an ardent soul,
repressed by timidity and by a certain dumbness in
the faculties of outward expression; but her eyes
had, at times, that earnest, appealing language
which is so pathetic in the silence of inferior animals. — One sometimes sees such eyes, and wonders
whether the story they intimate will ever be spoken
in mortal language.

Mary began eagerly detailing to her all that had
interested her since they last met: — the party, —
her acquaintance with Burr, — his visit to the cottage, — his inquiries into her education and reading,
— and, finally, the proposal, that they should study
French together.

" My dear," said Mrs. Marvyn, "let us begin at
once; — such an opportunity is not to be lost. I
studied a little with James, when he was last at
nome."

" With James?" said Mary, with an air of timid
surprise.

" Yes, — the dear boy has become, what I never
expected, quite a student. He employs all his spare
time now in reading and studying; — the second
mate is a Frenchman, and James has got so that
he can both speak and read. He is studying Span
ish, too."

Ever since the last conversation with her mother on the subject of James, Mary had felt a sort of guilty constraint when any one spoke of him; — instead of answering frankly, as she once did, when anything brought his name up, she fell at once into a grave, embarrassed silence.

Mrs. Marvyn was so constantly thinking of him, that it was difficult to begin on any topic that did not in some manner or other knit itself into the one ever present in her thoughts. None of the peculiar developments of the female nature have a more exquisite vitality than the sentiment of a frail, delicate, repressed, timid woman for a strong, manly, generous son. There is her ideal expressed; there is the out-speaking and out-acting of all she trembles to think, yet burns to say or do; here is the hero that shall speak for her, the heart into which she has poured her's, and that shall give to her tremulous and hidden aspirations a strong and victorious expression. " I have gotten a *man* from the Lord," she · says to herself; and each outburst of his manliness, his vigor, his self-confidence, his superb vitality, fills her with a strange, wondering pleasure, and she has a secret tenderness and pride even in his wilfulness and waywardness. " What a creature he is!" she says, when he flouts at sober argument and pitches all received opinions hither and thither in the wild capriciousness of youthful paradox. She looks grave and reproving; but he reads the concealed

triumph in her eyes, — he knows that in her heart
she is full of admiration all the time.   First love
of womanhood is something wonderful and mysterious, — but in this second love it rises again,
idealized and refined; she loves the father and herself united and made one in this young heir of life
and hope.

Such was Mrs. Marvyn's still intense, passionate
love for her son.   Not a tone of his manly voice,
not a flash of his dark eyes, not one of the deep,
shadowy dimples that came and went as he laughed,
not a ring of his glossy black hair, that was not
studied, got by heart, and dwelt on in the inner
shrine of her thoughts; he was the romance of her
life.   His strong, daring nature carried her with
it beyond those narrow, daily bounds where her
soul was weary of treading; and just as his voyages had given to the trite prose of her *ménage*
a poetry of strange, foreign perfumes, of quaint
objects of interest, speaking of many a far-off
shore, so his mind and life were a constant chan-
nel of outreach through which her soul held
converse with the active and stirring world.   Mrs.
Marvyn had known all the story of her son's
love, and to no other woman would she have been
willing to resign him; but her love to Mary was
so deep, that she thought of his union with her
more as gaining a daughter than as losing a son.
She would not speak of the subject; she knew

the feelings of Mary's mother; and the name of
James fell so often from her lips, simply because
it was so ever-present in her heart that it could
not be helped.

Before Mary left, it was arranged that they
should study together, and that the lessons should
be given alternately at each other's houses; and
with this understanding they parted.

CHAPTER XVIII.

EVIDENCES.

THE Doctor sat at his study-table. It was even
ing, and the slant beams of the setting sun shot
their golden arrows through the healthy purple
clusters of lilacs that veiled the windows. There
had been a shower that filled them with drops of
rain, which every now and then tattooed with a
slender rat-tat on the window-sill, as a breeze
would shake the leaves and bear in perfume on
its wings. Sweet, fragrance-laden airs tripped stir-
ringly to and fro about the study-table, making
gentle confusions, fluttering papers on moral ability, agitating treatises on the great end of creation, mixing up subtile distinctions between amiable instincts and true holiness, and, in short,
conducting themselves like very unappreciative and
unphilosophical little breezes.

The Doctor patiently smoothed back and rearranged, while opposite to him sat Mary, bending
over some copying she was doing for him. One
stray sunbeam fell on her light brown hair, tinging

it to gold; her long, drooping lashes lay over the wax-like pink of her cheeks, as she wrote on.

"Mary," said the Doctor, pushing the papers from him.

"Sir," she answered, looking up, the blood just perceptibly rising in her cheeks.

"Do you ever have any periods in which your evidences seem not altogether clear?"

Nothing could show more forcibly the grave, earnest character of thought in New England at this time than the fact that this use of the term "evidences" had become universally significant and understood as relating to one's right of citizenship in a celestial, invisible commonwealth.

So Mary understood it, and it was with a deepening flush she answered gently, "No, Sir."

"What! never any doubts?" said the Doctor.

"I am sorry," said Mary, apologetically; "but I do not see how I *can* have; I never could."

"Ah!" said the Doctor, musingly, "would I could say so! There are times, indeed, when I hope I have an interest in the precious Redeemer, and behold an infinite loveliness and beauty in Him, apart from anything I expect or hope. But even then how deceitful is the human heart! how insensibly might a mere selfish love take the place of that disinterested complacency which regards Him for what He is in Himself, apart from what He is to us! Say, my dear friend,

does not this thought sometimes make you tremble ? "

Poor Mary was truth itself, and this question
distressed her; she must answer the truth. The
fact was, that it had never come into her blessed
little heart to tremble, for she was one of those
children of the bride-chamber who cannot mourn
because the bridegroom is ever with them ; but
then, when she saw the man for whom her reverence was almost like that for her God thus dis-
trustful, thus lowly, she could not but feel that
her too calm repose might, after all, be the shallow, treacherous calm of an ignorant, ill-grounded
spirit, and therefore, with a deep blush and a fal-
tering voice, she said, —

" Indeed, I am afraid something must be wrong
with me.   I *cannot* have any fears, — I never
could; I try sometimes, but the thought of God's
goodness comes all around me, and I am so happy before I think of it!"

" Such exercises, my dear friend, I have also
had," said the Doctor; "but before I rest on them
as evidences, I feel constrained to make the following inquiries : — Is this gratitude that swells
my bosom the result of a mere natural sensibility?
Does it arise in a particular manner because God
has done me good? or do I love God for what
He *is*, as well as for what He has done? and for
what he has done for others, as well as for what

He has done for me ? Love to God which is built on nothing but good received is not incompatible with a disposition so horrid as even to curse God to His face. If God is not to be loved except when He does good, then in affliction we are free. If doing *us* good is all that renders God lovely to us, then not doing us good divests Him of His glory, and dispenses us from obligation to love Him. But there must be, undoubtedly, some permanent reason why God is to be loved by all; and if not doing us good divests Him of His glory so as to free *us* from our obligation to love, it equally frees the universe ; so that, in fact, the universe of happiness, if ours be not included, reflects no glory on its Author."

The Doctor had practised his subtile mental analysis till his instruments were so fine-pointed and keen-edged that he scarce ever allowed a flower of sacred emotion to spring in his soul without picking it to pieces to see if its genera and species were correct. Love, gratitude, reverence, benevolence, — which all moved in mighty tides in his soul, — were all compelled to pause midway while he rubbed up his optical instruments to see whether they were rising in right order. Mary, on the contrary, had the blessed gift of womanhood, — that vivid life in the soul and sentiment which resists the chills of analysis, as a healthful human heart resists cold; yet still, all

13

humbly, she thought this perhaps was a defect in herself, and therefore, having confessed, in a depreciating tone, her habits of unanalyzed faith and love, she added, —

"But, my dear Sir, you are my best friend. I trust you will be faithful to me. If I am deceiving myself, undeceive me; you cannot be too severe with me."

"Alas!" said the Doctor, "I fear that I may be only a blind leader of the blind. What, after all, if I be only a miserable self-deceiver? What if some thought of self has come in to poison all my prayers and strivings? It is true, I think, — yes, I *think*," said the Doctor, speaking very slowly, and with intense earnestness, — "I think, that, if I knew at this moment that my name never would be written among those of the elect, I could still see God to be infinitely amiable and glorious, and could feel sure that He *could* not do me wrong, and that it was infinitely becoming and right that He should dispose of me according to His sovereign pleasure. I *think* so; — but still my deceitful heart! — after all, I might find it rising in rebellion. Say, my dear friend, are you sure, that, should you discover yourself to be forever condemned by His justice, you would not find your heart rising up against Him?"

"Against *Him?*" said Mary, with a tremulous, sorrowful expression on her face, — "against my Heavenly Father?"

Her face flushed, and faded; her eyes kindled eagerly, as if she had something to say, and then grew misty with tears. At last she said, —

"Thank you, my dear, faithful friend! I will think about this; *perhaps* I may have been deceived. How very difficult it must be to know one's self perfectly!"

Mary went into her own little room, and sat leaning for a long time with her elbow on the window-seat, watching the pale shells of the apple-blossoms as they sailed and fluttered downward into the grass, and listened to a chippering conversation in which the birds in the nest above were settling up their small housekeeping accounts for the day.

After awhile, she took her pen and wrote the following, which the Doctor found the next morning lying on his study-table · · —

"My dear, honored friend, — How can I sufficiently thank you for your faithfulness with me? All you say to me seems true and excellent; and yet, my dear Sir, permit me to try to express to you some of the many thoughts to which our conversation this evening has given rise. To love God because He is good to me you seem to think is not a right kind of love; and yet every moment of my life I have experienced His goodness. When recollection brings back the past, where can I look that I see not His goodness? What mo

ment of my life presents not instances of merciful
kindness to me, as well as to every creature, more
and greater than I can express, than my mind is
able to take in? How, then, can I help loving
God because He is good to me? Were I not an
object of God's mercy and goodness, I cannot
have any conception what would be my feeling.
Imagination never yet placed me in a situation not
to experience the goodness of God in some way or
other; and if I do love Him, how can it be but because He is good, and to me good? Do not God's
children love Him because He first loved them?

"If I called nothing goodness which did not
happen to suit my inclination, and could not believe the Deity to be gracious and merciful except
when the course of events was so ordered as to
agree with my humor, so far from imagining that
I had any love to God, I must conclude myself
wholly destitute of anything good. A love founded
on nothing but good received is not, you say, in
compatible with a disposition so horrid as even to
curse God. I am not sensible that I ever in my
life imagined anything *but* good could come from
the hand of God. From a Being infinite in goodness everything *must* be good, though we do not
always comprehend how it is so. Are not afflictions good? Does He not even in judgment remember mercy? Sensible that ' afflictions are but
blessings in disguise,' I would bless the hand that,

with infinite kindness, wounds only to heal, and love and adore the goodness of God equally in suffering as in rejoicing.

" The disinterested love to God, which you think is a.one the genuine love, I see not how we can be certain we possess, when our love of happiness and our love of God are so inseparably connected. The joys arising from a consciousness that God is a benefactor to me and my friends, (and when I think of God, every creature is my friend,) if arising from a selfish motive, it does not seem to me possible could be changed into hate, even sup- posing God my enemy, whilst I regarded Him as a Being infinitely just as well as good. If God is my enemy, it must be because I deserve that He should be such; and it does not seem to me *possible* that I should hate Him, even if I knew He would always be so.

" In what you say of willingness to suffer eter- nal punishment, I don't know that I understand what the feeling is. Is it wickedness in me that I do not feel a willingness to be left to eternal sin ? Can any one joyfully acquiesce in being thus left ? When I pray for a new heart and a right spirit, must I be willing to be denied, and rejoice that my prayer is not heard ? Could any real Christian rejoice in this ? But he fears it not, — he knows it will never be, — he therefore can cheerfully leave it with God; and so can I

" Such, my dear friend, are my thoughts, poor
and unworthy ; yet they seem to me as certain as
my life, or as anything I see.   Am I unduly confident ?   I ask your prayers that I may be guided
aright.

" Your affectionate friend,

" MARY."

There are in this world two kinds of natures,—
those that have wings, and those that have feet,—
the winged and the walking spirits.   The walking
are the logicians ; the winged are the instinctive
and poetic.   Natures that must always walk find
many a bog, many a thicket, many a tangled
brake, which God's happy little winged birds flit
over by one noiseless flight.   Nay, when a man
has toiled till his feet weigh too heavily with the
mud of earth to enable him to walk another step,
these little birds will often cleave the air in a right
line towards the bosom of God, and show the way
where he could never have found it.

The Doctor paused in his ponderous and heavy
reasonings to read this real woman's letter; and
being a loving man, he felt as if he could have
kissed the hem of her garment who wrote it.   He
recorded it in his journal, and after it this significant passage from Canticles : —

" I charge you, O ye daughters of Jerusalem,
by the roes, and by the hinds of the field, that ye

stir not up nor awake this lovely one till she please."

Mrs. Scudder's motherly eye noticed, with satisfaction, these quiet communings. " Let it alone," she said to herself; " before she knows it, she will find herself wholly under his influence."   Mrs. Scudder was a wise woman.

CHAPTER XIX.

MADAME DE FRONTIGNAC.

In the course of a day or two, a handsome carriage drew up in front of Mrs. Scudder's cottage, and a brilliant party alighted. They were Colonel and Madame de Frontignac, the Abbé Léfon, and Colonel Burr. Mrs. Scudder and her daughter, being prepared for the call, sat in afternoon dignity and tranquillity, in the best room, with their knitting-work.

Madame de Frontignac had divined, with the lightning-like tact which belongs to women in the positive, and to French women in the superlative degree, that there was something in the cottage-girl, whom she had passingly seen at the party, which powerfully affected the man whom she loved with all the jealous intensity of a strong nature, and hence she embraced eagerly the opportunity to see her,—yes, to see her, to study her, to dart her keen French wit through her, and detect the secret of her charm, that she, too, might practise it.

Madame de Frontignac was one of those women

whose beauty is so striking and imposing, that they seem to kindle up, even in the most prosaic apartment, an atmosphere of enchantment. All the pomp and splendor of high life, the wit, the refinements, the nameless graces and luxuries of courts, seemed to breathe in invisible airs around her, and she made a Faubourg St. Germain of the darkest room into which she entered. Mary thought, when she came in, that she had never seen anything so splendid. She was dressed in a black velvet riding-habit, buttoned to the throat with coral; her riding-hat drooped with its long plumes so as to cast a shadow over her animated face, out of which her dark eyes shone like jewels, and her pomegranate cheeks glowed with the rich shaded radiance of one of Rembrandt's pictures. Something quaint and foreign, something poetic and strange, marked each turn of her figure, each article of her dress, down to the sculptured hand on which glittered singular and costly rings, — and the riding-glove, embroidered with seed-pearls, that fell carelessly beside her on the floor.

In Antwerp one sees a picture in which Rubens, who felt more than any other artist the glory of the physical life, has embodied his conception of the Madonna, in opposition to the faded, cold ideals of the Middle Ages, from which he revolted with such a bound. *His* Mary is a superb Oriental sultana, with lustrous dark eyes, redundant

13 *

form, jewelled turban, standing leaning on the balustrade of a princely terrace, and bearing on her hand, *not* the silver dove, but a gorgeous paroquet. The two styles, in this instance, were both in the same room; and as Burr sat looking from one to the other, he felt, for a moment, as one would who should put a sketch of Overbeck's beside a splendid painting of Titian's.

For a few moments, everything in the room seemed faded and cold, in contrast with the tropical atmosphere of this regal beauty. Burr watched Mary with a keen eye, to see if she were dazzled and overawed. He saw nothing but the most innocent surprise and delight. All the slumbering poetry within her seemed to awaken at the presence of her beautiful neighbor,—as when one, for the first time, stands before the great revelations of Art. Mary's cheek glowed, her eyes seemed to grow deep with the enthusiasm of admiration, and, after a few moments, it seemed as if her delicate face and figure reflected the glowing loveliness of her visitor, just as the virgin snows of the Alps become incarnadine as they stand opposite the glorious radiance of a sunset sky.

Madame de Frontignac was accustomed to the effect of her charms; but there was so much love in the admiration now directed towards her, that her own warm nature was touched, and she threw out the glow of her feelings with a magnetic power. Mary never felt the cold, habitual reserve of her education so suddenly melt, never felt herself so naturally falling into language of confidence and endearment with a stranger; and as her face, so delicate and spiritual, grew bright with love, Madame de Frontignac thought she had never seen anything so beautiful, and, stretching out her hands towards her, she exclaimed, in her own language,—

" *Mais, mon Dieu! mon enfant, que tu es belle!* "

Mary's deep blush, at her ignorance of the language in which her visitor spoke, recalled her to herself;—she laughed a clear, silvery laugh, and laid her jewelled little hand on Mary's with a caressing movement.

" *He* shall not teach you French, *ma toute belle,*" she said, indicating the Abbé, by a pretty, wilful gesture; " *I* will teach you;—and you shall teach me English. Oh, I shall try *so* hard to learn!" she said.

There was something inexpressibly pretty and quaint in the childish lisp with which she pronounced English. Mary was completely won over. She could have fallen into the arms of this wondrously beautiful fairy princess, expecting to be carried away by her to Dream-land.

Meanwhile, Mrs. Scudder was gravely discoursing with Colonel Burr and M. de Frontignac; and the Abbé, a small and gentlemanly personage, with

clear black eye, delicately-cut features, and powdered hair, appeared to be absorbed in his efforts
to follow the current of a conversation imperfectly
understood. Burr, the while, though seeming to be
entirely and politely absorbed in the conversation
he was conducting, lost not a glimpse of the picturesque aside which was being enacted between
the two fair ones whom he had thus brought together. He smiled quietly when he saw the effect
Madame de Frontignac produced on Mary.

"After all, the child has flesh and blood!" he
thought, "and may feel that there are more things
in heaven and earth than she has dreamed of yet.
A few French ideas won't hurt her."

The arrangements about lessons being completed,
the party returned to the carriage. Madame de
Frontignac was enthusiastic in Mary's praise.

" *Cependant*," she said, leaning back, thoughtfully,
after having exhausted herself in superlatives, —
" *cependant elle est dévote, — et à dix-neuf comment
cela se peut il?* "

" It is the effect of her austere education," said
Burr. " It is not possible for you to conceive how
young people are trained in the religious families
of this country."

" But yet," said Madame, " it gives her a grace
altogether peculiar; something in her looks went
to my heart. I could find it very easy to love her,
because she is really good."

" The Queen of Hearts should know all that is possible in loving," said Burr.

Somehow, of late, the compliments which fell so readily from those graceful lips had brought with them an unsatisfying pain. Until a woman really *loves*, flattery and compliment are often like her native air; but when that deeper feeling has once awakened in her, her instincts become marvellously acute to detect the false from the true. Madame de Frontignac longed for one strong, unguarded, real, earnest word from the man who had stolen from her her whole being. She was beginning to feel in some dim wise what an untold treasure she was daily giving for tinsel and dross. She leaned back in the carriage, with a restless, burning cheek, and wondered why she was born to be so miserable. The thought of Mary's saintly face and tender eyes rose before her as the moon rises on the eyes of some hot and fevered invalid, inspiring vague yearnings after an unknown, unattainable peace.

Could some friendly power have made her at that time clairvoyant and shown her the *reality* of the man whom she was seeing through the prismatic glass of her own enkindled ideality! Could she have seen the calculating quietness in which, during the intervals of a restless and sleepess ambition, he played upon her heart-strings, as one uses a musical instrument to beguile a pass-

ing hour, — how his only embarrassment was the
fear that the feelings he was pleased to excite
might become too warm and too strong, while as
yet his relations to her husband were such as to
make it dangerous to arouse his jealousy! And
if he could have seen that pure ideal conception
of himself which alone gave him power in the
heart of this woman, — that spotless, glorified image of a hero without fear, without reproach, —
would he have felt a moment's shame and abase-
ment at its utter falsehood?

The poet says that the Evil Spirit stood abashed
when he saw virtue in an angel form! How
would a man, then, stand, who meets face to face
his own glorified, spotless ideal, made living by
the boundless faith of some believing heart? The
best must needs lay his hand on his mouth at
this apparition; but woe to him who feels no redeeming power in the sacredness of this believing
dream, — who with calculating shrewdness *uses* this
most touching miracle of love only to corrupt and
destroy the loving! For him there is no sacrifice
for sin, no place for repentance. His very mother
might shrink in her grave to have him laid beside
her.

Madame de Frontignac had the high, honorable
nature of the old blood of France, and a touch
of its romance. She was strung heroically, and
educated according to the notions of her caste

and church, purely and religiously. True it is,
that one can scarcely call *that* education which
teaches woman everything except herself,—*except*
the things that relate to her own peculiar womanly destiny, and, on plea of the holiness of
ignorance, sends her without one word of just
counsel into the temptations of life. Incredible
as it may seem, Virginie de Frontignac had never
read a romance or work of fiction of which love
was the staple; the *régime* of the convent in this
regard was inexorable; at eighteen she was more
thoroughly a child than most American girls at
thirteen. On entrance into life, she was at first
so dazzled and bewildered by the mere contrast
of fashionable excitement with the quietness of
the scenes in which she had hitherto grown up,
that she had no time for reading or thought,—all
was one intoxicating frolic of existence, one dazzling, bewildering dream.

He whose eye had measured her for his victim
verified, if ever man did, the proverbial expression
of the iron hand under the velvet glove. Under
all his gentle suavities there was a fixed, inflexible will, a calm self-restraint, and a composed philosophical measurement of others, that fitted him
to bear despotic rule over an impulsive, unguarded
nature. The position, at once accorded to him,
of her instructor in the English language and literature, gave him a thousand daily opportunities

to touch and stimulate all that class of finer fac‑
ulties, so restless and so perilous, and which a
good man approaches always with a certain awe.
It is said that he once asserted that he never be‑
guiled a woman who did not come half-way to
meet him, — an observation much the same as a
serpent might make in regard to his birds.

The visit of the morning was followed by sev‑
eral others. Madame de Frontignac seemed to
conceive for Mary one of those passionate attach‑
ments which women often conceive for anything
fair and sympathizing, at those periods when their
whole inner being is made vital by the approaches
of a grand passion. It took only a few visits to
make her as familiar as a child at the cottage;
and the whole air of the Faubourg St. Germain
seemed to melt away from her, as, with the pli‑
ability peculiar to her nation, she blended herself
with the quiet pursuits of the family. Sometimes,
in simple straw hat and white wrapper, she would
lie down in the grass under the apple-trees, or
join Mary in an expedition to the barn for hen's
eggs, or a run along the sea-beach for shells; and
her childish eagerness and delight on these occa‑
sions used to arouse the unqualified astonishment
of Mrs. Katy Scudder.

The Doctor she regarded with a *naïve* astonish‑
ment, slightly tinctured with apprehension. She
knew he was very religious, and stretched her

comprehension to imagine what he might be like.
She thought of Bossuet's sermons walking about
under a Protestant coat, and felt vaguely alarmed
and sinful in his presence, as she used to when
entering under the shadows of a cathedral. In
her the religious sentiment, though vague, was
strong. Nothing in the character of Burr had ever
awakened so much disapprobation as his occasional sneers at religion. On such occasions she
always reproved him with warmth, but excused
him in her heart, because he was brought up a
heretic. She held a special theological conversation
with the Abbé, whether salvation were possible to
one outside of the True Church, — and had added
to her daily prayer a particular invocation to the
Virgin for him.

The French lessons, with her assistance, proceeded prosperously. She became an inmate in
Mrs. Marvyn's family also. The brown-eyed, sensitive woman loved her as a new poem; she felt
enchanted by her; and the prosaic details of her
household seemed touched to poetic life by her
innocent interest and admiration. The young Madame insisted on being taught to spin at the great
wheel; and a very pretty picture she made of it,
too, with her earnest gravity of endeavor, her
deepening cheek, her graceful form, with some
strange foreign scarf or jewelry waving and flashing in odd contrast with her work.

"Do you know," she said, one day, while thus employed in the north room at Mrs. Marvyn's,— "do you know Burr told me that princesses used to spin? He read me a beautiful story from the 'Odyssey,' about how Penelope cheated her lovers with her spinning, while she was waiting for her husband to come home;— *he* was gone to sea, Mary,— her *true* love,— you understand."

She turned on Mary a wicked glance, so full of intelligence that the snowdrop grew red as the inside of a sea-shell.

"*Mon enfant!* thou hast a thought *deep in here!*" she said to Mary, one day, as they sat together in the grass under the apple-trees.

"Why, what?" said Mary, with a startled and guilty look.

"Why, what? *petite!*" said the fairy princess, whimsically mimicking her accent. "*Ah! ah! ma belle!* you think I have no eyes;— Virginic sees deep in here!" she said, laying her hand playfully on Mary's heart. "*Ah, petite!*" she said, gravely, and almost sorrowfully, "if you love him, wait for him,— *don't marry another!* It is dreadful not to have one's heart go with one's duty."

"I shall never marry anybody," said Mary.

"Nevare marrie anybodie!" said the lady, imitating her accents in tones much like those of a bobolink. "Ah! ah! my little saint, you cannot always live on nothing but the prayers, though

prayers are verie good. But, *ma chère*," she added,
in a low tone, " don't you ever marry that good
man in there; priests should not marry."

" Ours are not priests, — they are ministers,"
said Mary. " But why do you speak of him? —
he is like my father."

" Virginie sees something! " said the lady, shaking her head gravely; " she sees he loves little
Mary."

" Of course he does! "

" Of-course-he-does? — ah, yes; and by-and-by
comes the mamma, and she takes this little hand,
and she says, ' Come, Mary!' and then she gives
it to him; and then the poor *jeune homme*, when
he comes back, finds not a bird in his poor little
nest. *Oh, c'est ennuyeux cela!*" she said, throwing herself back in the grass till the clover-heads
and buttercups closed over her.

" I do assure you, dear Madame! "——

" I do assure you, dear Mary, *Virginie knows*.
So lock up her words in your little heart; you
will want them some day."

There was a pause of some moments, while the
lady was watching the course of a cricket through
the clover. At last, lifting her head, she spoke
very gravely, —

" My little cat! it is *dreadful* to be married to
a good man, and want to be good, and want to
love him, and yet never like to have him take

your hand, and be more glad when he is away
than when he is at home; and then to think how
different it would all be, if it was only somebody
else. That will be the way with you, if you let
them lead you into this; so don't you do it, *mon
enfant.*"

A thought seemed to cross Mary's mind, as
she turned to Madame de Frontignac, and said,
earnestly, —

"If a good man were my husband, I would
never think of another, — I wouldn't let myself."

"How could you help it, *mignonne?* Can you
stop your thinking?"

Mary said, after a moment's blush, —

"I can *try!*"

"Ah, yes! But to try all one's life, — oh, Mary,
that is too hard! Never do it, darling!"

And then Madame de Frontignac broke out
into a carolling little French song, which started
all the birds around into a general orchestral ac-
companiment.

This conversation occurred just before Madame
de Frontignac started for Philadelphia, whither her
husband had been summoned as an agent in some
of the ambitious intrigues of Burr.

It was with a sigh of regret that she parted
from her friends at the cottage. She made them
a hasty good-bye call, — alighting from a splendid
barouche with two white horses, and filling their

simple best-room with the light of her presence for a last half-hour.   When she bade good-bye to Mary, she folded her warmly to her heart, and her long lashes drooped heavily with tears.

After her absence, the lessons were still pursued with the gentle, quiet little Abbé, who seemed the most patient and assiduous of teachers; but, in both houses, there was that vague *ennui*, that sense of want, which follows the fading of one of life's beautiful dreams!   We bid her adieu for a season; — we may see her again.

CHAPTER XX.

TIDINGS FROM OVER SEA.

THE summer passed over the cottage, noiselessly as our summers pass. There were white clouds walking in saintly troops over blue mirrors of sea, — there were purple mornings, choral with bird-singing, — there were golden evenings, with long, eastward shadows. Apple-blossoms died quietly in the deep orchard-grass, and tiny apples waxed and rounded and ripened and gained stripes of gold and carmine; and the blue eggs broke into young robins, that grew from gaping, yellow-mouthed youth to fledged and outflying maturity. Came autumn, with its long Indian summer, and winter, with its flinty, sparkling snows, under which all Nature lay a sealed and beautiful corpse. Came once more the spring winds, the lengthening days, the opening flowers, and the ever-renewing miracle of buds and blossoms on the apple-trees around the cottage. A year had passed since the June afternoon when first we showed you Mary standing under the spotty shadows of the tree, with the

white dove on her hand,—a year in which not
many outward changes have been made in the relations of the actors of our story.

Mary calmly spun and read and thought; now
and then composing with care very English-French
letters, to be sent to Philadelphia to Madame de
Frontignac, and receiving short missives of very
French-English in return.

The cautions of Madame, in regard to the Doctor, had not rippled the current of their calm, confiding intercourse; and the Doctor, so very satisfied
and happy in her constant society and affection,
scarcely as yet meditated distinctly that he needed
to draw her more closely to himself. If he had a
passage to read, a page to be copied, a thought to
express, was she not ever there, gentle, patient, un-
selfish? and scarce by the absence of a day did
she let him perceive that his need of her was becoming so absolute that his hold on her must
needs be made permanent.

As to his salary and temporal concerns, they
had suffered somewhat for his unpopular warfare
with reigning sins,—a fact which had rather reconciled Mrs. Scudder to the dilatory movement
of her cherished hopes. Since James was gone,
what need to press imprudently to new arrangements? Better give the little heart time to grow
over before starting a subject which a certain
womanly instinct told her might be met with a

struggle. Somehow she never thought without a certain heart-sinking of Mary's look and tone the night she spoke with her about James; she had an awful presentiment that that tone of voice belonged to the things that cannot be shaken. But yet, Mary seemed so even, so quiet, her delicate form filled out and rounded so beautifully, and she sang so cheerfully at her work, and, above all, she was so entirely silent about James, that Mrs. Scudder had hope.

Ah, that silence! Do not listen to hear whom a woman praises, to know where her heart is! do not ask for whom she expresses the most earnest enthusiasm! but if there be one she once knew well, whose name she never speaks,—if she seem to have an instinct to avoid every occasion of its mention,—if, when you speak, she drops into silence and changes the subject,—why, look there for something! just as, when going through deep meadow-grass, a bird flies ostentatiously up before you, you may know her nest is not there, but far off, under distant tufts of fern and buttercup, through which she has crept with a silent flutter in her spotted breast, to act her pretty little falsehood before you.

Poor Mary's little nest was along the sedgy margin of the sea-shore, where grow the tufts of golden rod, where wave the reeds, where crimson, green, and purple seaweeds float up, like torn fringes of Nereid vestures, and gold and silver shells lie on the wet wrinkles of the sands.

The sea had become to her like a friend, with its ever-varying monotony. Somehow she loved this old, fresh, blue, babbling, restless giant, who had carried away her heart's love to hide him in some far-off palmy island, such as she had often heard him tell of in his sea-romances. Sometimes she would wander out for an afternoon's stroll on the rocks, and pause by the great Spouting Cave, now famous to Newport *dilettanti*, but then a sacred and impressive solitude. There the rising tide bursts with deafening strokes through a narrow opening into some inner cavern, which, with a deep thunder-boom, like the voice of an angry lion, casts it back in a high jet of foam into the sea.

Mary often sat and listened to this hollow noise, and watched the ever-rising columns of spray as they reddened with the transpiercing beams of the afternoon sun; and thence her eye travelled far, far off over the shimmering starry blue, where sails looked no bigger than miller's wings; and it seemed sometimes as if a door were opening by which her soul might go out into some eternity, — some abyss, so wide and deep, that fathomless lines of thought could not sound it. She was no longer a girl in a mortal body, but an infinite spirit, the adoring companion of Infinite Beauty and Infinite Love.

14

As there was an hour when the fishermen of Galilee saw their Master transfigured, his raiment white and glistening, and his face like the light, so are there hours when our whole mortal life stands forth in a celestial radiance. From our daily lot falls off every weed of care,—from our heart-friends every speck and stain of earthly infirmity. Our horizon widens, and blue, and amethyst, and gold touch every object. Absent friends and friends gone on the last long journey stand once more together, bright with an immortal glow, and, like the disciples who saw their Master floating in the clouds above them, we say, "Lord, it is good to be here!" How fair the wife, the husband, the absent mother, the gray-haired father, the manly son, the bright-eyed daughter! Seen in the actual present, all have some fault, some flaw; but absent, we see them in their permanent and better selves. Of our distant home we remember not one dark day, not one servile care, nothing but the echo of its holy hymns and the radiance of its brightest days,—of our father, not one hasty word, but only the fulness of his manly vigor and noble tenderness,—of our mother, nothing of mortal weakness, but a glorified form of love,—of our brother, not one teasing, provoking word of brotherly freedom, but the proud beauty of his noblest hours,—of our sister, our child, only what is fairest and sweetest.

This is to life the true ideal, the calm glass, wherein looking, we shall see, that, whatever defects cling to us, they are not, after all, permanent, and that we are tending to something nobler than we yet are; — it is "the earnest of our inheritance until the redemption of the purchased possession." In the resurrection we shall see our friends forever as we see them in these clairvoyant hours.

We are writing thus on and on, linking image and thought and feeling, and lingering over every flower, and listening to every bird, because just before us there lies a dark valley, and we shrink and tremble to enter it.

But it *must* come, and why do we delay ?

Towards evening, one afternoon in the latter part of June, Mary returned from one of these lonely walks by the sea, and entered the kitchen. It was still in its calm and sober cleanness ; — the tall clock ticked with a startling distinctness. From the half-closed door of her mother's bedroom, which stood ajar, she heard the chipper of Miss Prissy's voice. She stayed her light footsteps, and the words that fell on her ear were these : —

" Miss Marvyn fainted dead away ; — she stood it till it came to *that ;* but then she just clapped both hands together, as if she 'd been shot, and fell right forward on the floor in a faint ! "

What could this be? There was a quick, intense whirl of thoughts in Mary's mind, and then came one of those awful moments when the powers of life seem to make a dead pause and all things stand still; and then all seemed to fail under her, and the life to sink down, down, down, till nothing was but one dim, vague, miserable consciousness.

Mrs. Scudder and Miss Prissy were sitting, talking earnestly, on the foot of the bed, when the door opened noiselessly, and Mary glided to them, like a spirit, — no color in cheek or lip, — her blue eyes wide with calm horror; and laying her little hand, with a nervous grasp, on Miss Prissy's arm, she said, —

"Tell me, — what is it? — is it? — is he — dead?"

The two women looked at each other, and then Mrs. Scudder opened her arms.

"My daughter!"

"Oh! mother! mother!"

Then fell that long, hopeless silence, broken only by hysteric sobs from Miss Prissy, and answering ones from the mother; but *she* lay still and quiet, her blue eyes wide and clear, making an inarticulate moan.

"Oh! are they *sure?* — *can* it be? — *is* he dead?" at last she gasped.

"My child, it is too true; all we can say is, 'Be still, and know that I am God!'"

" I shall *try* to be still, mother," said Mary with a piteous, hopeless voice, like the bleat of a dying lamb; " but I did not think he *could* die! I never thought of that! — I never *thought* of it! — Oh! mother! mother! mother! oh! what shall I do?"

They laid her on her mother's bed, — the first and last resting-place of broken hearts, — and the mother sat down by her in silence. Miss Prissy stole away into the Doctor's study, and told him all that had happened.

" It's the same to her," said Miss Prissy, with womanly reserve, " as if he 'd been an own brother."

" What was his spiritual state?" said the Doctor, musingly.

Miss Prissy looked blank, and answered mournfully, —

" I don't know."

The Doctor entered the room where Mary was lying with closed eyes. Those few moments seemed to have done the work of years, — so pale, and faded, and sunken she looked; nothing but the painful flutter of the eyelids and lips showed that she yet breathed. At a sign from Mrs. Scudder, he kneeled by the bed, and began to pray, — " Lord, thou hast been our dwelling-place in all generations," — prayer deep, mournful, upheaving like the swell of the ocean, surging upward, under the pressure of mighty sorrows, towards an Almighty heart.

The truly good are of one language in prayer. Whatever lines or angles of thought may separate them in other hours, *when they pray in extremity*, all good men pray alike. The Emperor Charles V. and Martin Luther, two great generals of opposite faiths, breathed out their dying struggle in the self-same words.

There be many tongues and many languages of men, — but the language of prayer is one by itself, *in* all and *above* all. It is the inspiration of that Spirit that is ever working with our spirit, and constantly lifting us higher than we know, and, by our wants, by our woes, by our tears, by our yearnings, by our poverty, urging us, with mightier and mightier force, against those chains of sin which keep us from our God. We speak not of *things* conventionally called prayers, — vain mutterings of unawakened spirits talking drowsily in sleep, — but of such prayers as come when flesh and heart fail, in mighty straits; — *then* he who prays is a prophet, and a Mightier than he speaks in him; for the "*Spirit* helpeth our infirmities; for we know not what we should pray for as we ought; but the Spirit itself maketh intercession for us, with groanings which cannot be uttered."

So the voice of supplication, upheaving from

that great heart, so childlike in its humility, rose with a wisdom and a pathos beyond what he dreamed in his intellectual hours; it uprose even as a strong angel, whose brow is solemnly calm, and whose wings shed healing dews of paradise.

CHAPTER XXI.

THE BRUISED FLAX-FLOWER.

THE next day broke calm and fair. The robins sang remorselessly in the apple-tree, and were answered by bobolink, oriole, and a whole tribe of ignorant little bits of feathered happiness that danced among the leaves. Golden and glorious unclosed those purple eyelids of the East, and regally came up the sun; and the treacherous sea broke into ten thousand smiles, laughing and dancing with every ripple, as unconsciously as if no form dear to human hearts had gone down beneath it. Oh! treacherous, deceiving beauty of outward things! beauty, wherein throbs not one answering nerve to human pain!

Mary rose early and was about her morning work. Her education was that of the soldier, who must know himself no more, whom no personal pain must swerve from the slightest minutiæ of duty. So she was there, at her usual hour, dressed with the same cool neatness, her brown hair parted in satin bands, and only the colorless cheek and lip differing from the Mary of yesterday.

How strange this external habit of living! One thinks how to stick in a pin, and how to tie a string, — one busies one's self with folding robes, and putting away napkins, the day after some stroke that has cut the inner life in two, with the heart's blood dropping quietly at every step.

Yet it is better so! Happy those whom stern principle or long habit or hard necessity calls from the darkened room, the languid trance of pain, in which the wearied heart longs to indulge, and gives this trite prose of common life, at which our weak and wearied appetites so revolt! Mary never thought of such a thing as self-indulgence; — this daughter of the Puritans had her seed within her. Aerial in her delicacy, as the blue-eyed flax-flower with which they sowed their fields, she had yet its strong fibre, which no stroke of the flail could break; bruising and hackling only made it fitter for uses of homely utility. Mary, therefore, opened the kitchen-door at dawn, and, after standing one moment to breathe the freshness, began spreading the cloth for an early breakfast. Mrs. Scudder, the mean while, was kneading the bread that had been set to rise over-night; and the oven was crackling and roaring with a large-throated, honest garrulousness.

But, ever and anon, as the mother worked, she followed the motions of her child anxiously.

" Mary, my dear," she said, " the eggs are giv

14 *

ing out; hadn't you better run to the barn and get a few?"

Most mothers are instinctive philosophers. No treatise on the laws of nervous fluids could have taught Mrs. Scudder a better *rôle* for this morning, than her tender gravity, and her constant expedients to break and ripple, by changing employments, that deep, deadly under-current of thoughts which she feared might undermine her child's life.

Mary went into the barn, stopped a moment, and took out a handful of corn to throw to her hens, who had a habit of running towards her and cocking an expectant eye to her little hand, whenever she appeared. All came at once flying towards her, — speckled, white, and gleamy with hues between of tawny orange-gold, — the cocks, magnificent with the blade-like waving of their tails, — and, as they chattered and cackled and pressed and crowded about her, pecking the corn, even where it lodged in the edge of her little shoes, she said, " Poor things, I am glad they enjoy it!" — and even this one little act of love to the ignorant fellowship below her carried away some of the choking pain which seemed all the while suffocating her heart. Then, climbing into the hay, she sought the nest and filled her little basket with eggs, warm, translucent, pinky-white in their freshness. She felt, for a moment, the customary animation in surveying her new treasures; but suddenly, like a vision rising before her, came a remembrance of once when she and James were children together and had been seeking eggs just there. He flashed before her eyes, the bright boy with the long black lashes, the dimpled cheeks, the merry eyes, just as he stood and threw the hay over her when they tumbled and laughed together, —and she sat down with a sick faintness, and then turned and walked wearily in.

CHAPTER XXII.

THE HOUSE OF MOURNING.

MARY returned to the house with her basket of warm, fresh eggs, which she set down mournfully upon the table. In her heart there was one conscious want and yearning, and that was to go to the friends of him she had lost,—to go to his mother. The first impulse of bereavement is to stretch out the hands towards what was nearest and dearest to the departed.

Her dove came fluttering down out of the tree, and settled on her hand, and began asking in his dumb way to be noticed. Mary stroked his white feathers, and bent her head down over them, till they were wet with tears. " Oh, birdie, you live, but he is gone!" she said. Then suddenly putting it gently from her, and going near and throwing her arms around her mother's neck,— " Mother," she said, " I want to go up to Cousin Ellen's." (This was the familiar name by which she always called Mrs. Marvyn.) " Can't you go with me, mother?"

" My daughter, I have thought of it. I hurried

about my baking this morning, and sent word to
Mr. Jenkyns that he needn't come to see about the
chimney, because I expected to go as soon as
breakfast should be out of the way. So, hurry,
now, boil some eggs, and get on the cold beef and
potatoes; for I see Solomon and Amaziah coming
in with the milk. They'll want their breakfast immediately."

The breakfast for the hired men was soon arranged on the table, and Mary sat down to pre-
side while her mother was going on with her baking, — introducing various loaves of white and
brown bread into the capacious oven by means of
a long iron shovel, and discoursing at intervals
with Solomon, with regard to the different farming operations which he had in hand for the
day.

Solomon was a tall, large-boned man, brawny
and angular; with a face tanned by the sun, and
graven with those considerate lines which New
England so early writes on the faces of her sons.
He was reputed an oracle in matters of agricul-
ture and cattle, and, like oracles generally, was
prudently sparing of his responses. Amaziah was
one of those uncouth overgrown boys of eighteen
whose physical bulk appears to have so suddenly
developed that the soul has more matter than she
has learned to recognize, so that the hapless individual is always awkwardly conscious of too much

limb; and in Amaziah's case, this consciousness grew particularly distressing when Mary was in the room. He liked to have her there, he said,—"but, somehow, she was so white and pretty, she made him feel sort o' awful-like."

Of course, as such poor mortals always do, he must, on this particular morning, blunder into precisely the wrong subject.

"S'pose you've heerd the news that Jeduthun Pettibone brought home in the 'Flying Scud,' 'bout the wreck o' the 'Monsoon'; it's an awful providence, that 'ar' is,—a'n't it? Why, Jeduthun says she jest crushed like an egg-shell";—and with that Amaziah illustrated the fact by crushing an egg in his great brown hand.

Mary did not answer. She could not grow any paler than she was before; a dreadful curiosity came over her, but her lips could frame no question. Amaziah went on:—

"Ye see, the cap'en he got killed with a spar when the blow fust come on, and Jim Marvyn he commanded; and Jeduthun says that he seemed to have the spirit of ten men in him; he worked and he watched, and he was everywhere at once, and he kep' 'em all up for three days, till finally they lost their rudder, and went drivin' right onto the rocks. When they come in sight, he come up on deck, and says he, 'Well, my boys, we're headin' right into eternity,' says he, 'and our chances for this world a'n't worth mentionin', any on us, but we'll all have one try for our lives. Boys, I've tried to do my duty by you and the ship,— but God's will be done! All I have to ask now is, that, if any of you git to shore, you'll find my mother and tell her I died thinkin' of her and father and my dear friends.' That was the last Jeduthun saw of him; for in a few minutes more the ship struck, and then it was every man for himself. Laws! Jeduthun says there couldn't no-body have stood beatin' agin them rocks, unless they was all leather and inger-rubber like him. Why, he says the waves would take strong men and jest crush 'em against the rocks like smashin' a pie-plate!"

Here Mary's paleness became livid; she made a hasty motion to rise from the table, and Solomon trod on the foot of the narrator.

" You seem to forget that friends and relations has feelin's," he said, as Mary hastily went into her own room.

Amaziah, suddenly awakened to the fact that he had been trespassing, sat with mouth half open and a stupefied look of perplexity on his face for a moment, and then, rising hastily, said, " Well, Sol, I guess I'll go an' yoke up the steers."

At eight o'clock all the morning toils were over, the wide kitchen cool and still, and the one-horse wagon standing at the door, into which climbed

Mary, her mother, and the Doctor; for, though invested with no spiritual authority, and charged with no ritual or form for hours of affliction, the religion of New England always expects her minister as a first visitor in every house of mourning.

The ride was a sorrowful and silent one. The Doctor, propped upon his cane, seemed to reflect deeply.

" Have you been at all conversant with the exercises of our young friend's mind on the subject of religion?" he asked.

Mrs. Scudder did not at first reply. The remembrance of James's last letter flashed over her mind, and she felt the vibration of the frail child beside her, in whom every nerve was quivering. After a moment, she said,—" It does not become us to judge the spiritual state of any one. James's mind was in an unsettled way when he left; but who can say what wonders may have been effected by divine grace since then?"

This conversation fell on the soul of Mary like the sound of clods falling on a coffin to the ear of one buried alive;—she heard it with a dull, smothering sense of suffocation. *That* question to be raised?—and about one, too, for whom she could have given her own soul? At this moment she felt how idle is the mere hope or promise of personal salvation made to one who has passed beyond the life of self, and struck deep the roots of his existence in others. She did not utter a word; — how could she ? A doubt, — the faintest shadow of a doubt, — in such a case, falls on the soul with the weight of mountain certainty; and in that short ride she felt what an infinite pain may be locked in one small, silent breast.

The wagon drew up to the house of mourning. Cato stood at the gate, and came forward, officiously, to help them out. " Mass'r and Missis will be glad to see you," he said. " It's a drefful stroke has come upon 'em."

Candace appeared at the door. There was a majesty of sorrow in her bearing, as she received them. She said not a word, but pointed with her finger towards the inner room ; but as Mary lifted up her faded, weary face to hers, her whole soul seemed to heave towards her like a billow, and she took her up in her arms and broke forth into sobbing, and, carrying her in, as if she had been a child, set her down in the inner room and sat down beside her.

Mrs. Marvyn and her husband sat together, holding each other's hands, the open Bible between them. For a few moments nothing was to be heard but sobs and unrestrained weeping, and then all kneeled down to pray.

After they rose up, Mr. Zebedee Marvyn stood for a moment thoughtfully, and then said, — " If it had pleased the Lord to give me a sure evidence of my son's salvation, I could have given him up with all my heart; but now, whatever there may be, I have seen none." He stood in an attitude of hopeless, heart-smitten dejection, which contrasted painfully with his usual upright carriage and the firm lines of his face.

Mrs. Marvyn started as if a sword had pierced her, passed her arm round Mary's waist, with a strong, nervous clasp, unlike her usual calm self, and said,—" Stay with me, daughter, to-day!— stay with me!"

" Mary can stay as long as you wish, cousin," said Mrs. Scudder; " we have nothing to call her home."

" *Come* with me!" said Mrs. Marvyn to Mary opening an adjoining door into her bedroom, and drawing her in with a sort of suppressed vehemence,—" I want you!— I must have you!"

" Mrs. Marvyn's state alarms me," said her husband, looking apprehensively after her when the door was closed; " she has not shed any tears, nor slept any, since she heard this news. You know that her mind has been in a peculiar and unhappy state with regard to religious things for many years. I was in hopes she might feel free to open her exercises of mind to the Doctor."

" Perhaps she will feel more freedom with Mary," said the Doctor. " There is no healing for such

troubles except in unconditional submission to Infinite Wisdom and Goodness.   The Lord reign-
eth, and will at last bring infinite good out of
evil, whether *our* small portion of existence be
included or not."

After a few moments more of conference, Mrs.
Scudder and the Doctor departed, leaving Mary
alone in the house of mourning.

CHAPTER XXIII.

VIEWS OF DIVINE GOVERNMENT.

WE have said before, what we now repeat, that it is impossible to write a story of New England life and manners for superficial thought or shallow feeling.   They who would fully understand the springs which moved the characters with whom we now associate must go down with us to the very depths.

Never was there a community where the roots of common life shot down so deeply, and were so intensely grappled around things sublime and eternal.   The founders of it were a body of confessors and martyrs, who turned their backs on the whole glory of the visible, to found in the wilderness a republic of which the God of Heaven and Earth should be the sovereign power.   For the first hundred years grew this community, shut out by a fathomless ocean from the existing world, and divided by an antagonism not less deep from all the reigning ideas of nominal Christendom.

In a community thus unworldly must have arisén a mode of thought, energetic, original, and sublime. The leaders of thought and feeling were the ministry, and we boldly assert that the spectacle of the early ministry of New England was one to which the world gives no parallel. Living an intense, earnest, practical life, mostly tilling the earth with their own hands, they yet carried on the most startling and original religious investigations with a simplicity that might have been deemed audacious, were it not so reverential. All old issues relating to government, religion, ritual, and forms of church organization having for them passed away, they went straight to the heart of things, and boldly confronted the problem of universal being. They had come out from the world as witnesses to the most solemn and sacred of human rights. They had accustomed themselves boldly to challenge and dispute all sham pretensions and idolatries of past ages,— to question the right of kings in the State, and of prelates in the Church; and now they turned the same bold inquiries towards the Eternal Throne, and threw down their glove in the lists as authorized defenders of every mystery in the Eternal Government. The task they proposed to themselves was that of reconciling the most tremendous facts of sin and evil, present and eternal, with those conceptions of Infinite Power and Benevolence which

their own strong and generous natures enabled
them so vividly to realize. In the intervals of
planting and harvesting, they were busy with the
toils of adjusting the laws of a universe. Solemnly simple, they made long journeys in their
old one-horse chaises, to settle with each other
some nice point of celestial jurisprudence, and to
compare their maps of the Infinite. Their letters
to each other form a literature altogether unique.
Hopkins sends to Edwards the younger his scheme
of the universe, in which he starts with the proposition, that God is infinitely above all obligations
of any kind to his creatures. Edwards replies
with the brusque comment, — " This is wrong;
God has no more right to injure a creature than
a creature has to injure God;" and each probably about that time preached a sermon on his
own views, which was discussed by every farmer,
in intervals of plough and hoe, by every woman
and girl, at loom, spinning-wheel, or wash-tub.
New England was one vast sea, surging from
depths to heights with thought and discussion on
the most insoluble of mysteries. And it is to be
added, that no man or woman accepted any theory or speculation simply *as* theory or speculation;
all was profoundly real and vital, — a foundation
on which actual life was based with intensest
earnestness.

The views of human existence which resulted

from this course of training were gloomy enough
to oppress any heart which did not rise above
them by triumphant faith or sink below them by
brutish insensibility; for they included every moral
problem of natural or revealed religion, divested
of all those softening poetries and tender draperies which forms, ceremonies, and rituals had
thrown around them in other parts and ages of
Christendom. The human race, without exception,
coming into existence "under God's wrath and
curse," with a nature so fatally disordered, that,
although perfect free agents, men were infallibly
certain to do nothing to Divine acceptance until
regenerated by the supernatural aid of God's Spirit, — this aid being given only to a certain decreed number of the human race, the rest, with
enough free agency to make them responsible, but
without this indispensable assistance exposed to
the malignant assaults of evil spirits versed in
every art of temptation, were sure to fall hopelessly into perdition. The standard of what constituted a true regeneration, as presented in such
treatises as Edwards on the Affections, and others of
the times, made this change to be something so high,
disinterested, and superhuman, so removed from all
natural and common habits and feelings, that the
most earnest and devoted, whose whole life had
been a constant travail of endeavor, a tissue of
almost unearthly disinterestedness, often lived and

died with only a glimmering hope of its attain-
ment.

According to any views then entertained of the
evidences of a true regeneration, the number of
the whole human race who could be supposed as
yet to have received this grace was so small, that,
as to any numerical valuation, it must have been
expressed as an infinitesimal. Dr. Hopkins in many
places distinctly recognizes the fact, that the great-
ei part of the human race, up to his time, had
been eternally lost,— and boldly assumes the ground,
that this amount of sin and suffering, being the
best and most necessary means of the greatest
final amount of happiness, was not merely permitted, but distinctly chosen, decreed, and provided
for, as essential in the schemes of Infinite Benevolence. He held that this decree not only *permitted* each individual act of sin, but also took measures to make it certain, though, by an exercise of
infinite skill, it accomplished this result without
violating human free agency.

The preaching of those times was animated by
an unflinching consistency which never shrank
from carrying an idea to its remotest logical verge
The sufferings of the lost were not kept from
view, but proclaimed with a terrible power. Dr.
Hopkins boldly asserts, that "all the use which
God will have for them is to suffer; this is all the
end they can answer; therefore all their faculties

and their whole capacities, will be employed and used for this end. . . . . . The body can by omnipotence be made capable of suffering the greatest imaginable pain, without producing dissolution, or abating the least degree of life or sensibility. . . . . . One way in which God will show his power in punishing the wicked will be in strengthening and upholding their bodies and souls in torments which otherwise would be intolerable."

The sermons preached by President Edwards on this subject are so terrific in their refined poetry of torture, that very few persons of quick sensibility could read them through without agony; and it is related, that, when, in those calm and tender tones which never rose to passionate enunciation, he read these discourses, the house was often filled with shrieks and wailings, and that a brother minister once laid hold of his skirts, exclaiming, in an involuntary agony, " Oh! Mr. Edwards! Mr. Edwards! is God not a God of mercy?"

Not that these men were indifferent or insensible to the dread words they spoke; their whole lives and deportment bore thrilling witness to their sincerity. Edwards set apart special days of fasting, in view of the dreadful doom of the lost, in which he was wont to walk the floor, weeping and wringing his hands. Hopkins fasted every Saturday. David Brainerd gave up every refinement of

15

civilized life to weep and pray at the feet of hard-ened savages, if by any means he might save *one*. All, by lives of eminent purity and earnestness, gave awful weight and sanction to their words.

If we add to this statement the fact, that it was always proposed to every inquiring soul, as an evidence of regeneration, that it should truly and heartily accept all the ways of God thus declared right and lovely, and from the heart submit to Him as the only just and good, it will be seen what materials of tremendous internal conflict and agitation were all the while working in every bosom. Almost all the histories of religious experience of those times relate paroxysms of opposition to God and fierce rebellion, expressed in language which appalls the very soul, — followed, at length, by mysterious elevations of faith and reactions of confiding love, the result of Divine interposition, which carried the soul far above the region of the intellect, into that of direct spiritual intuition.

President Edwards records that he was once in this state of enmity, — that the facts of the Divine administration seemed horrible to him, — and that this opposition was overcome by no course of reasoning, but by an " *inward and sweet sense*," which came to him once when walking alone in the fields, and, looking up into the blue sky, he saw the blending of the Divine majesty with a calm, sweet, and almost infinite meekness.

The piety which grew up under such a system was, of necessity, energetic, — it was the uprousing of the whole energy of the human soul, pierced and wrenched and probed from her lowest depths to her topmost heights with every awful life-force possible to existence. He whose faith in God came clear through these terrible tests would be sure never to know greater ones. He might certainly challenge earth or heaven, things present or things to come, to swerve him from this grand allegiance.

But it is to be conceded, that these systems, so admirable in relation to the energy, earnestness, and acuteness of their authors, when received as absolute truth, and as a basis of actual life, had, on minds of a certain class, the effect of a slow poison, producing life-habits of morbid action very different from any which ever followed the simple reading of the Bible. They differ from the New Testament as the living embrace of a friend does from his lifeless body, mapped out under the knife of the anatomical demonstrator; — every nerve and muscle is there, but to a sensitive spirit there is the very chill of death in the analysis.

All systems that deal with the infinite are, besides, exposed to danger from small, unsuspected admixtures of human error, which become deadly when carried to such vast results. The smallest speck of earth's dust, in the focus of an infinite lens, appears magnified among the heavenly orbs as a frightful monster.

Thus it happened, that, while strong spirits walked, palm-crowned, with victorious hymns, along these sublime paths, feebler and more sensitive ones lay along the track, bleeding away in life-long despair. Fearful to them were the shadows that lay over the cradle and the grave. The mother clasped her babe to her bosom, and looked with shuddering to the awful coming trial of free agency, with its terrible responsibilities and risks; and, as she thought of the infinite chances against her beloved, almost wished it might die in infancy. But when the stroke of death came, and some young, thoughtless head was laid suddenly low, who can say what silent anguish of loving hearts sounded the dread depths of eternity with the awful question, *Where?*

In no other time or place of Christendom have so fearful issues been presented to the mind. Some church interposed its protecting shield; the Christian born and baptized child was supposed in some wise rescued from the curse of the fall, and related to the great redemption, — to be a member of Christ's family, and, if ever so sinful, still infolded in some vague sphere of hope and protection. Augustine solaced the dread anxieties of trembling love by prayers offered for the dead, in times when the Church above and on earth

presented itself to the eye of the mourner as a
great assembly with one accord lifting interceding
hands for the parted soul.

But the clear logic and intense individualism
of New England deepened the problems of the
Augustinian faith, while they swept away all those
softening provisions so earnestly clasped to the
throbbing heart of that great poet of theology.
No rite, no form, no paternal relation, no faith or
prayer of church, earthly or heavenly, interposed
the slightest shield between the trembling spirit
and Eternal Justice. The individual entered eternity alone, as if he had no interceding relation in
the universe.

This, then, was the awful dread which was constantly underlying life. This it was which caused
the tolling bell in green hollows and lonely dells
to be a sound which shook the soul and searched
the heart with fearful questions. And this it was
that was lying with mountain weight on the soul
of the mother, too keenly agonized to feel that
doubt in such a case was any less a torture than
the most dreadful certainty.

Hers was a nature more reasoning than creative and poetic; and whatever she believed bound
her mind in strictest chains to its logical results.
She delighted in the regions of mathematical
knowledge, and walked them as a native home,
but the commerce with abstract certainties fitted

her mind still more to be stiffened and enchained by glacial reasonings, in regions where spiritual intuitions are as necessary as wings to birds.

Mary was by nature of the class who never reason abstractly, whose intellections all begin in the heart which sends them colored with its warm .ife-tint to the brain. Her perceptions of the same subjects were as different from Mrs. Marvyn's as his who revels only in color from his who is busy with the dry details of mere outline. The one mind was arranged like a map, and the other like a picture. In all the system which had been explained to her, her mind selected points on which it seized with intense sympathy, which it dwelt upon and expanded till all else fell away. The sublimity of disinterested benevolence, — the harmony and order of a system tending in its final results to infinite happiness, — the goodness of God, — the love of a self-sacrificing Redeemer, — were all so many glorious pictures, which she revolved in her mind with small care for their logical relations.

Mrs. Marvyn had never, in all the course of their intimacy, opened her mouth to Mary on the subject of religion. It was not an uncommon incident of those times for persons of great elevation and purity of character to be familiarly known and spoken of as living under a cloud of religious gloom; and it was simply regarded as one more mysterious instance of the workings of that infinite decree which denied to them the special illumination of the Spirit.

When Mrs. Marvyn had drawn Mary with her into her room, she seemed like a person almost in frenzy. She shut and bolted the door, drew her to the foot of the bed, and, throwing her arms round her, rested her hot and throbbing forehead on her shoulder. She pressed her thin hand over her eyes, and then, suddenly drawing back, looked her in the face as one resolved to speak something long suppressed. Her soft brown eyes had a flash of despairing wildness in them, like that of a hunted animal turning in its death-struggle on its pursuer.

"Mary," she said, "I can't help it, — don't mind what I say, but I must speak or die! Mary, I cannot, will not, be resigned! — it is all hard, unjust, cruel! — to all eternity I will say so! To me there is no goodness, no justice, no mercy in anything! Life seems to me the most tremendous doom that can be inflicted on a helpless being! *What had we done*, that it should be· sent upon us? Why were we made to love so, to hope so, — our hearts so full of feeling, and all the laws of Nature marching over us, — never stopping for our agony? Why, we can suffer so in this life that we had better never have been born!

"But, Mary, think what a moment life is! think

of those awful ages of eternity! and then think of all God's power and knowledge used on the lost to make them suffer! think that all but the merest fragment of mankind have gone into this, — are in it now! The number of the elect is so small we can scarce count them for anything! Think what noble minds, what warm, generous hearts, what splendid natures are wrecked and thrown away by thousands and tens of thousands! How we love each other! how our hearts weave into each other! how more than glad we should be to die for each other! And all this ends —·— O God, how must it end? — Mary! it isn't *my* sorrow only! What right have I to mourn? Is *my* son any better than any other mother's son? Thousands of thousands, whose mothers loved them as I love mine, are gone there! — Oh, my wedding-day! Why did they rejoice? Brides should wear mourning, — the bells should toll for every wedding; every new family is built over this awful pit of despair, and only one in a thousand escapes!"

Pale, aghast, horror-stricken, Mary stood dumb, as one who in the dark and storm sees by the sudden glare of lightning a chasm yawning under foot. It was amazement and dimness of anguish; — the dreadful words struck on the very centre where her soul rested. She felt as if the point of a wedge were being driven between her life and her life's life, — between her and her God. She clasped her hands instinctively on her bosom, as if to hold there some cherished image, and said, in a piercing voice of supplication, " *My* God! *my* God! oh, where art Thou?"

Mrs. Marvyn walked up and down the room with a vivid spot of red in each cheek, and a baleful fire in her eyes, talking in rapid soliloquy, scarcely regarding her listener, absorbed in her own enkindled thoughts.

" Dr. Hopkins says that this is all best, — better than it would have been in any other possible way, — that God *chose* it because it was for a greater final good, — that He not only chose it, but took means to make it certain, — that He ordains every sin, and does all that is necessary to make it certain, — that He creates the vessels of wrath and fits them for destruction, and that He has an infinite knowledge by which He can do it without violating their free agency. — So much the worse! What a use of infinite knowledge! What if men should do so? What if a father should take means to make it certain that his poor little child should be an abandoned wretch, without violating his free agency? So much the worse, say! — They say He does this so that He may show to all eternity, by their example, the evil nature of sin and its consequences! This is all that the greater part of the human race

15*

have been used for yet; and it is all right, because an overplus of infinite happiness is yet to be wrought out by it! — It is *not* right! No possible amount of good to ever so many can make it right to deprave ever so few; — happiness and misery cannot be measured so! I never can think it right, — never! — Yet they say our salvation depends on our loving God, — loving Him better than ourselves, — loving Him better than our dearest friends. — It is impossible! — it is contrary to the laws of my nature! I can never love God! I can never praise Him! — I am lost! lost! lost! And what is worse, I cannot redeem my friends! Oh, I *could* suffer forever, — how willingly! — if I could save *him!* — But oh, eternity, eternity! Frightful, unspeakable woe! No end! — no bottom! — no shore! — no hope! — O God! O God!"

Mrs. Marvyn's eyes grew wilder, — she walked the floor, wringing her hands, — and her words, mingled with shrieks and moans, became whirling and confused, as when in autumn a storm drives the leaves in dizzy mazes.

Mary was alarmed, — the ecstacy of despair was just verging on insanity. She rushed out and called Mr. Marvyn.

"Oh! come in! do! quick! — I'm afraid her mind is going!" she said.

"It is what I feared," he said, rising from where

he sat reading his great Bible, with an air of heartbroken dejection. "Since she heard this news, she has not slept nor shed a tear. The Lord hath covered us with a cloud in the day of his fierce anger."

He came into the room, and tried to take his wife into his arms. She pushed him violently back, her eyes glistening with a fierce light. "Leave me alone!" she said,—"I am a lost spirit!"

These words were uttered in a shriek that went through Mary's heart like an arrow.

At this moment, Candace, who had been anxiously listening at the door for an hour past, suddenly burst into the room.

"Lor' bress ye, Squire Marvyn, we won't hab her goin' on dis yer way," she said. "Do talk *gospel* to her, can't ye?—ef you can't, I will.

"Come, ye poor little lamb," she said, walking straight up to Mrs. Marvyn, "come to ole Candace!"—and with that she gathered the pale form to her bosom, and sat down and began rocking her, as if she had been a babe. "Honey, darlin', ye a'n't right,—dar's a drefful mistake somewhar," she said. "Why, de Lord a'n't like what ye tink,—He *loves* ye, honey! Why, jes' feel how *I* loves ye,—poor ole black Candace,—an' I a'n't better'n Him as made me! Who was it wore de crown o' thorns, lamb?—who was it sweat great

drops o' blood? — who was it said, 'Father, forgive dem'? Say, honey! — wasn't it de Lord dat
made ye? — Dar, dar, now ye'r' cryin'! — cry away,
and ease yer poor little heart! He died for Mass'r
Jim, — loved him and *died* for him, — jes' give up
his sweet, precious body and soul for him on de
cross! Laws, jes' *leave* him in Jesus's hands!
Why, honey, dar's de very print o' de nails in
his hands now!"

The flood-gates were rent; and healing sobs and
tears shook the frail form, as a faded lily shakes
under the soft rains of summer. All in the room
wept together.

"Now, honey," said Candace, after a pause of
some minutes, "I knows our Doctor's a mighty
good man, an' larned, — an' in fair weather I ha'n't
no 'bjection to yer hearin' all about dese yer great
an' mighty tings he's got to say. But, honey, dey
won't do for you now; sick folks mus'n't hab
strong meat; an' times like dese, dar jest a'n't but
one ting to come to, an' dat ar's *Jesus*. Jes' come
right down to whar poor ole black Candace has
to stay allers, — it's a good place, darlin'! *Look
right at Jesus.* Tell ye, honey, ye can't live no
other way now. Don't ye 'member how He looked
on His mother, when she stood faintin' an' trem-
blin' under de cross, jes' like you? He knows all
about mothers' hearts; He won't break yours. It
was jes' 'cause He know'd we'd come into straits

like dis yer, dat he went through all dese tings, —
Him, de Lord o' Glory! Is dis Him you was a-
talkin' about? — Him you can't love? Look at
Him, an' see ef you can't. Look an' see what
He is! — don't ask no questions, and don't go to
no reasonin's, — jes' look at *Him*, hangin' dar, so
sweet and patient, on de cross! All dey could do
couldn't stop his lovin' 'em ; he prayed for 'em
wid all de breath he had. Dar's a God you can
love, a'n't dar? Candace loves Him, — poor, ole,
foolish, black, wicked Candace, — and she knows
He loves her," — and here Candace broke down
into torrents of weeping.

They laid the mother, faint and weary, on her
bed, and beneath the shadow of that suffering
cross came down a healing sleep on those weary
eyelids.

" Honey," said Candace, mysteriously, after she
had drawn Mary out of the room, " don't ye go
for to troublin' yer mind wid dis yer. I'm clar
Mass'r James is one o' de 'lect ; and I'm clar dar's
consid'able more o' de 'lect dan people tink. Why,
Jesus didn't die for nothin', — all dat love a'n't
gwine to be wasted. De 'lect is more'n you or I
knows, honey! Dar's de *Spirit*, — He'll give it to
'em ; and ef Mass'r James *is* called an' took, depend upon it de Lord has got him ready, — course
He has, — so don't ye go to layin' on your poor
heart what no mortal creetur can live under ;

'cause, as we's got to live in dis yer world, it's quite clar de Lord must ha' fixed it so we *can;* and ef tings was as some folks suppose, why, we *couldn't* live, and dar wouldn't be no sense in anyting dat goes on."

The sudden shock of these scenes was followed, in Mrs. Marvyn's case, by a low, lingering fever. Her room was darkened, and she lay on her bed, a pale, suffering form, with scarcely the ability to raise her hand. The shimmering twilight of the sick-room fell on white napkins, spread over stands, where constantly appeared new vials, big and little, as the physician made his daily visit, and prescribed now this drug and now that, for a wound that had struck through the soul.

Mary remained many days at the white house, because, to the invalid, no step, no voice, no hand was like hers. We see her there now, as she sits in the glimmering by the bed-curtains, — her head a little drooped, as droops a snowdrop over a grave; — one ray of light from a round hole in the closed shutters falls on her smooth-parted hair, her small hands are clasped on her knees, her mouth has lines of sad compression, and in her eyes are infinite questionings.

CHAPTER XXIV.

MYSTERIES.

WHEN Mrs. Marvyn began to amend, Mary returned to the home cottage, and resumed the details of her industrious and quiet life.

Between her and her two best friends had fallen a curtain of silence. The subject that filled all her thoughts could not be named between them. The Doctor often looked at her pale cheeks and drooping form with a face of honest sorrow, and heaved deep sighs as she passed; but he did not find any power within himself by which he could approach her. When he would speak, and she turned her sad, patient eyes so gently on him, the words went back again to his heart, and there, taking a second thought, spread upward wing in prayer.

Mrs. Scudder sometimes came to her room after she was gone to bed, and found her weeping; and when gently she urged her to sleep, she would wipe her eyes so patiently and turn her head with such obedient sweetness, that her mother's heart utterly failed her. For hours Mary sat in her room with James's last letter spread out before her. How anxiously had she studied every word and phrase in it, weighing them to see if the hope of eternal life were in them! How she dwelt on those last promises! Had he kept them? Ah! to die without one word more! Would no angel tell her?— would not the loving God, who knew all, just whisper one word? He must have read the little Bible! What had he thought? What did he feel in that awful hour when he felt himself drifting on to that fearful eternity? Perhaps he had been regenerated,— perhaps there had been a sudden change; —who knows?— she had read of such things;— *perhaps* —— Ah, in that perhaps lies a world of anguish! Love will not hear of it. Love *dies* for certainty. Against an uncertainty who can brace the soul? We put all our forces of faith and prayer against it, and it goes down just as a buoy sinks in the water, and the next moment it is up again. The soul fatigues itself with efforts which come and go in waves; and when with laborious care she has adjusted all things in the light of hope, back flows the tide, and sweeps all away. In such struggles life spends itself fast; an inward wound does not carry one deathward more surely than this worst wound of the soul. God has made us so mercifully that there is no *certainty*, however dreadful, to which life-forces do not in time adjust themselves,—but to uncertainty there is no possible adjustment. Where is he? Oh, question of questions!—question which we suppress, but which a power of infinite force still urges on the soul, who feels a part of herself torn away.

Mary sat at her window in evening hours, and watched the slanting sunbeams through the green blades of grass, and thought one year ago he stood there, with his well-knit, manly form, his bright eye, his buoyant hope, his victorious mastery of life! And where was he now? Was his heart as sick, longing for her, as hers for him? Was he looking back to earth and its joys with pangs of unutterable regret? or had a divine power interpenetrated his soul, and lighted there the flame of a celestial love which bore him far above earth? If he were among the lost, in what age of eternity could she ever be blessed? Could Christ be happy, if those who were one with Him were sinful and accursed? and could Christ's own loved ones be happy, when those with whom they have exchanged being, in whom they live and feel, are as wandering stars, for whom is reserved the mist of darkness forever? She had been taught that the agonies of the lost would be forever in sight of the saints, without abating in the least their eternal joys; nay, that they would find in it increasing motives to praise and adoration. Could

it be so? Would the last act of the great Bridegroom of the Church be to strike from the heart
of his purified Bride those yearnings of self-devot-
ing love which His whole example had taught her,
and in which she reflected, as in a glass, His own
nature? If not, is there not some provision by
which those roots of deathless love which Christ's
betrothed ones strike into other hearts shall have
a divine, redeeming power? Question vital as
life-blood to ten thousand hearts,—fathers, mothers, wives, husbands,—to all who feel the infinite
sacredness of love!

After the first interview with Mrs. Marvyn, the
subject which had so agitated them was not renewed. She had risen at last from her sick-bed,
as thin and shadowy as a faded moon after sunrise. Candace often shook her head mournfully, as
her eyes followed her about her daily tasks. Once
only, with Mary, she alluded to the conversation
which had passed between them;—it was one day
when they were together, spinning, in the north
upper room that looked out upon the sea. It was
a glorious day. A ship was coming in under full
sail, with white gleaming wings. Mrs. Marvyn
watched it a few moments,—the gay creature, so
full of exultant life,—and then smothered down
an inward groan, and Mary thought she heard her
saying, "Thy will be done!"

"Mary," she said, gently, "I hope you will forget all I said to you that dreadful day. It had to be said, or I should have died. Mary, I begin to think that it is not best to stretch our minds with reasonings where we are so limited, where we can know so little. I am quite sure there must be dreadful mistakes somewhere.

" It seems to me irreverent and shocking that a child should oppose a father, or a creature its Creator. I never should have done it, only that, where direct questions are presented to the judgment, one cannot help judging. If one is required to praise a being as just and good, one must judge of his actions by some standard of right,—and we have no standard but such as our Creator has placed in us. I have been told it was my duty to attend to these subjects, and I have tried to,—and the result has been that the facts presented seem wholly irreconcilable with any notions of justice or mercy that I am able to form. If these be the facts, I can only say that my nature is made entirely opposed to them. If I followed the standard of right they present, and acted according to my small mortal powers on the same principles, I should be a very bad person. Any father, who should make such use of power over his children as they say the Deity does with regard to us, would be looked upon as a monster by our very imperfect moral sense. Yet I cannot say that the facts are not so. When I heard the Doctor's sermons on ' Sin a

Necessary Means of the Greatest Good,' I could not extricate myself from the reasoning.

" I have thought, in desperate moments, of giving up the Bible itself. But what do I gain? Do I not see the same difficulty in Nature? I see everywhere a Being whose main ends seem to be beneficent, but whose good purposes are worked out at terrible expense of suffering, and apparently by the total sacrifice of myriads of sensitive creatures. I see unflinching order, general good-will, but no sympathy, no mercy. Storms, earthquakes, volcanoes, sickness, death, go on without regarding us. Everywhere I see the most hopeless, unrelieved suffering,—and for aught I see, it may be eternal. Immortality is a dreadful chance, and I would rather never have been.—The Doctor's dreadful system is, I confess, much like the laws of Nature,—about what one might reason out from them.

" There is but just one thing remaining, and that is, as Candace said, the cross of Christ. If God so loved us,—if He died for us,—greater love hath no man than this. It seems to me that love is shown here in the two highest forms possible to our comprehension. We see a Being who gives himself for us,—and more than that, harder than that, a Being who consents to the suffering of a dearer than self. Mary, I feel that I must love more, to give up one of my children to suffer, than to consent to suffer myself. There is a world of comfort to me in the words, ' He that spared not his own Son, but delivered him up for us all, how shall he not with him also freely give us all things?' These words speak to my heart. I can interpret them by my own nature, and I rest on them. If there is a fathomless mystery of sin and sorrow, there is a deeper mystery of God's love. So, Mary, I try Candace's way,— I look at Christ,— I pray to Him. If he that hath seen Him hath seen the Father, it is enough. I rest there,— I wait. What I know not now I shall know hereafter."

Mary kept all things and pondered them in her heart. She could speak to no one,— not to her mother, nor to her spiritual guide; for had she not passed to a region beyond theirs? As well might those on the hither side of mortality instruct the souls gone beyond the veil as souls outside a great affliction guide those who are struggling in it. That is a mighty baptism, and only Christ can go down with us into those waters.

Mrs. Scudder and the Doctor only marked that she was more than ever conscientious in every duty, and that she brought to life's daily realities something of the calmness and disengagedness of one whose soul has been wrenched by a mighty shock from all moorings here below. Hopes did not excite, fears did not alarm her; life had no force strong enough to awaken a thrill within; and the only subjects on which she ever spoke with any degree of ardor were religious subjects.

One who should have seen moving about the daily ministrations of the cottage a pale girl, whose steps were firm, whose eye was calm, whose hands were ever busy, would scarce imagine that through that silent heart were passing tides of thought that measured a universe; but it was even so. Through that one gap of sorrow flowed in the whole awful mystery of existence, and silently, as she spun and sewed, she thought over and over again all that she had ever been taught, and compared and revolved it by the light of a dawning inward revelation.

Sorrow is the great birth-agony of immortal powers,—sorrow is the great searcher and revealer of hearts, the great test of truth; for Plato has wisely said, sorrow will not endure sophisms,—all shams and unrealities melt in the fire of that awful furnace. Sorrow reveals forces in ourselves we never dreamed of. The soul, a bound and sleeping prisoner, hears her knock on her cell-door, and wakens. Oh, how narrow the walls! oh, how close and dark the grated window! how the long useless wings beat against the impassable barriers! Where are we? What *is* this prison? What *is* beyond? Oh for more air, more light! When will the door be opened? The soul seems

to itself to widen and deepen; it trembles at its
own dreadful forces; it gathers up in waves that
break with wailing only to flow back into the
everlasting void. The calmest and most centred
natures are sometimes thrown by the shock of a
great sorrow into a tumultuous amazement. All
things are changed. The earth no longer seems
solid, the skies no longer secure; a deep abyss
seems underlying every joyous scene of life. The
soul, struck with this awful inspiration, is a mournful Cassandra; she sees blood on every threshold,
and shudders in the midst of mirth and festival
with the weight of a terrible wisdom.

Who shall dare be glad any more, that has
once seen the frail foundations on which love and
joy are built? Our brighter hours, have they
only been weaving a network of agonizing remembrances for this day of bereavement? The heart
is pierced with every past joy, with every hope of
its ignorant prosperity. Behind every scale in
music, the gayest and cheeriest, the grandest, the
most triumphant, lies its dark relative minor; the
notes are the same, but the change of a semitone
changes all to gloom; — all our gayest hours are
tunes that have a modulation into these dreary
keys ever possible; at any moment the key-note
may be struck.

The firmest, best-prepared natures are often beside themselves with astonishment and dismay,

when they are called to this dread initiation
They thought it a very happy world before, — a
glorious universe. Now it is darkened with the
shadow of insoluble mysteries. Why this everlasting tramp of inevitable laws on quivering life?
If the wheels must roll, why must the crushed be
so living and sensitive?

And yet sorrow is godlike, sorrow is grand and
great, sorrow is wise and far-seeing. Our own
instinctive valuations, the intense sympathy which
we give to the tragedy which God has inwoven
into the laws of Nature, show us that it is with
no slavish dread, no cowardly shrinking, that we
should approach her divine mysteries. What are
the natures that cannot suffer? Who values them?
From the fat oyster, over which the silver tide
rises and falls without one pulse upon its fleshy
ear, to the hero who stands with quivering nerve
parting with wife and child and home for country
and God, all the way up is an ascending scale,
marked by increasing power to suffer; and when
we look to the Head of all being, up through
principalities and powers and princedoms, with
dazzling orders and celestial blazonry, to behold
by what emblem the Infinite Sovereign chooses
to reveal himself, we behold, in the midst of the
throne, " a lamb as it had been slain."

Sorrow is divine. Sorrow is reigning on the
throne of the universe, and the crown of all

crowns has been one of thorns. There have been
many books that treat of the mystery of sorrow,
but only one that bids us glory in tribulation, and
count it all joy when we fall into divers afflictions, that so we may be associated with that
great fellowship of suffering of which the Incar-
nate God is the head, and through which He is
carrying a redemptive conflict to a glorious victory over evil. If we suffer with Him, we shall
also reign with Him.

Even in the very making up of our physical
nature, God puts suggestions of such a result.
" Weeping may endure for a night, but joy com-
eth in the morning." There are victorious powers
in our nature which are all the while working for
us in our deepest pain. It is said, that, after the
sufferings of the rack, there ensues a period in
which the simple repose from torture produces a
beatific trance; it is the reaction of Nature, asserting the benignant intentions of her Creator.
So, after great mental conflicts and agonies must
come a reaction, and the Divine Spirit, co-working
with our spirit, seizes the favorable moment, and,
interpenetrating natural laws with a celestial vitality, carries up the soul to joys beyond the ordinary possibilities of mortality.

It is said that gardeners, sometimes, when they
would bring a rose to richer flowering, deprive it,
for a season, of light and moisture. Silent and

16

dark it stands, dropping one fading leaf after another, and seeming to go down patiently to death.
But when every leaf is dropped, and the plant
stands stripped to the uttermost, a new life is
even then working in the buds, from which shall
spring a tender foliage and a brighter wealth of
flowers. So, often in celestial gardening, every
leaf of earthly joy must drop, before a new and
divine bloom visits the soul.

Gradually, as months passed away, the floods
grew still; the mighty rushes of the inner tides
ceased to dash. There came first a delicious
calmness, and then a celestial inner clearness, in
which the soul seemed to lie quiet as an untroubled ocean, reflecting heaven. Then came the fulness of mysterious communion given to the pure
in heart, — that advent of the Comforter in the
soul, teaching all things and bringing all things
to remembrance; and Mary moved in a world
transfigured by a celestial radiance. Her face, so
long mournfully calm, like some chiselled statue
of Patience, now wore a radiance, as when one
places a light behind some alabaster screen sculptured with mysterious and holy emblems, and
words of strange sweetness broke from her, as if
one should hear snatches of music from a door
suddenly opened in heaven. Something wise and
strong and sacred gave an involuntary impression
of awe in her looks and words; — it was not the

childlike loveliness of early days, looking with dovelike, ignorant eyes on sin and sorrow; but the victorious sweetness of that great multitude who have come out of great tribulation, having washed their robes and made them white in the blood of the Lamb. In her eyes there was that nameless depth that one sees with awe in the Sistine Madonna, — eyes that have measured infinite sorrow and looked through it to an infinite peace.

"My dear Madam," said the Doctor to Mrs. Scudder, "I cannot but think that there must be some uncommonly gracious exercises passing in the mind of your daughter; for I observe, that, though she is not inclined to conversation, she seems to be much in prayer; and I have, of late, felt the sense of a Divine Presence with her in a most unusual degree. Has she opened her mind to you?"

"Mary was always a silent girl," said Mrs. Scudder, "and not given to speaking of her own feelings; indeed, until she gave you an account of her spiritual state, on joining the church, I never knew what her exercises were. Hers is a most singular case. I never knew the time when she did not seem to love God more than anything else. It has disturbed me sometimes, — because I did not know but it might be mere natural sensibility, instead of gracious affection"

"Do not disturb yourself, Madam," said the Doctor. "The Spirit worketh when, where, and how He will; and, undoubtedly, there have been cases where His operations commence exceedingly early. Mr. Edwards relates a case of a young person who experienced a marked conversion when three years of age; and Jeremiah was called from the womb. (Jeremiah, i. 5.) In all cases we must test the quality of the evidence without relation to the time of its commencement. I do not generally lay much stress on our impressions, which are often uncertain and delusive; yet I have had an impression that the Lord would be pleased to make some singular manifestations of His grace through this young person. In the economy of grace there is neither male nor female; and Peter says (Acts, ii. 17) that the Spirit of the Lord shall be poured out and your sons and your daughters shall prophesy. Yet if we consider that the Son of God, as to his human nature, was made of a woman, it leads us to see that in matters of grace God sets a special value on woman's nature and designs to put special honor upon it. Accordingly, there have been in the Church, in all ages, holy women who have received the Spirit and been called to a ministration in the things of God,—such as Deborah, Huldah, and Anna, the prophetess. In our own days, most uncommon manifestations of divine grace have been given to noly women. It was my privilege to be in the family of President Edwards at a time when Northampton was specially visited, and his wife seemed and spoke more like a glorified spirit than a mortal woman,— and multitudes flocked to the house to hear her wonderful words. She seemed to have such a sense of the Divine love as was almost beyond the powers of nature to endure. Just to speak the words, ' Our Father who art in heaven,' would overcome her with such a manifestation that she would become cold and almost faint; and though she uttered much, yet she told us that the divinest things she saw could not be spoken. These things could not be fanaticism, for she was a person of a singular evenness of nature, and of great skill and discretion in temporal matters, and of an exceeding humility, sweetness, and quietness of disposition."

" I have observed of late," said Mrs. Scudder, " that, in our praying circles, Mary seemed much carried out of herself, and often as if she would speak, and with difficulty holding herself back. I have not urged her, because I thought it best to wait till she should feel full liberty."

" Therein you do rightly, Madam," said the Doctor; " but I am persuaded you will hear from her yet."

It came at length, the hour of utterance. And one day, in a praying circle of the women of

the church, all were startled by the clear silver
tones of one who sat among them and spoke with
the unconscious simplicity of an angel child, calling God her Father, and speaking of an ineffable
union in Christ, binding all things together in one,
and making all complete in Him. She spoke of a
love passing knowledge,—passing all love of lovers or of mothers,—a love forever spending, yet
never spent,—a love ever pierced and bleeding,
yet ever constant and triumphant, rejoicing with
infinite joy to bear in its own body the sins and
sorrows of a universe,—conquering, victorious love,
rejoicing to endure, panting to give, and offering
its whole self with an infinite joyfulness for our
salvation. And when, kneeling, she poured out
her soul in prayer, her words seemed so many
winged angels, musical with unearthly harpings
of an untold blessedness. They who heard her had
the sensation of rising in the air, of feeling a celestial light and warmth descending into their
souls; and when, rising, she stood silent and with
downcast drooping eyelids, there were tears in all
eyes, and a hush in all movements as she passed,
as if something celestial were passing out.

Miss Prissy came rushing homeward, to hold a
private congratulatory talk with the Doctor and
Mrs. Scudder, while Mary was tranquilly setting
the tea-table and cutting bread for supper.

"To see her now, certainly," said Miss Prissy,

"moving round so thoughtful, not forgetting anything, and doing everything so calm, you wouldn't
'a' thought it could be her that spoke those blessed
words and made that prayer! Well, certainly
that prayer seemed to take us all right up and
put us down in heaven! and when I opened my
eyes, and saw the roses and asparagus-bushes on
the manteltree-piece, I had to ask myself, ' Where
have I been?' Oh, Miss Scudder, her afflictions
have been sanctified to her!—and really, when I
see her going on so, I feel she can't be long for
us. They say, dying grace is for dying hours,
and I'm sure this seems more like dying grace
than anything that I ever yet saw."

"She is a precious gift," said the Doctor; "let
us thank the Lord for his grace through her. She
has evidently had a manifestation of the Beloved,
and feedeth among the lilies (Canticles, vi. 3);
and we will not question the Lord's further dis
pensations concerning her."

"Certainly," said Miss Prissy, briskly, "it's never
best to borrow trouble; 'sufficient unto the day' is
enough, to be sure.—And now, Miss Scudder, I
thought I'd just take a look at that dove-colored
silk of yours to-night, to see what would have to
be done with it, because I must make every min
ute tell; and you know I lose half a day every
week for the prayer-meeting. Though I ought not
to say I lose it, either; for I was telling Miss

General Wilcox I wouldn't give up that meeting
for bags and bags of gold. She wanted me to
come and sew for her one Wednesday, and says
I, 'Miss Wilcox, I'm poor and have to live by
my work, but I a'n't so poor but what I have
some comforts, and I can't give up my prayer-
meeting for any money,—for you see, if one gets
a little lift there, it makes all the work go lighter,
—but then I have to be particular to save up
every scrap and end of time."

Mrs. Scudder and Miss Prissy crossed the kitchen
and entered the bedroom, and soon had the dove-
colored silk under consideration.

" Well, Miss Scudder," said Miss Prissy, after
mature investigation, " here's a broad hem, not cut
at all on the edge, as I see, and that might be
turned down, and so cut off the worn spot up by
the waist,—and then, if it is turned, it will look
every bit and grain as well as a· new silk;—I'll
sit right down now and go to ripping. I put my
ripping-knife into my pocket when I put on this
dress to go to prayer-meeting, because, says I to
myself, there'll be something to do at Miss Scudder's to-night. You just get an iron to the fire,
and we'll have it all ripped and pressed out before
dark."

Miss Prissy seated herself at the open window
as cheery as a fresh apple-blossom, and began
busily plying her knife, looking at the garment she

was ripping with an astute air, as if she were about to circumvent it into being a new dress by some surprising act of legerdemain. Mrs. Scudder walked to the looking-glass and began changing her bonnet cap for a tea-table one.

Miss Prissy, after a while, commenced in a mysterious tone.

" Miss Scudder, I know folks like me shouldn't have their eyes open too wide, but then I can't help noticing some things. Did you see the Doctor's face when we was talking to him about Mary? Why, he colored all up and the tears came into his eyes. It's my belief that that blessed man worships the ground she treads on. I don't mean *worships*, either, — 'cause that would be wicked, and he's too good a man to make a graven image of anything, — but it's clear to see that there a'n't anybody in the world like Mary to him. I always did think so; but I used to think Mary was such a little poppet — that she'd do better for—— Well, you know, I thought about some younger man; — but, laws, now I see how she rises up to be ahead of every body, and is so kind of solemn-like. I can't but see the leadings of Providence. What a minister's wife she'd be, Miss Scudder! — why, all the ladies coming out of prayer-meeting were speaking of it. You see, they want the Doctor to get married; — it seems more comfortable-like to have ministers married; one

16 *

feels more free to open their exercises of mind and as Miss Deacon Twitchel said to me,—'If the Lord had made a woman o' purpose, as he did for Adam, he wouldn't have made her a bit different from Mary Scudder.' Why, the oldest of us would follow her lead,—'cause she goes before us without knowing it."

"I feel that the Lord has greatly blessed me in such a child," said Mrs. Scudder, "and I feel disposed to wait the leadings of Providence."

"Just exactly," said Miss Prissy, giving a shake to her silk; "and as Miss Twitchel said, in this case every providence seems to p'int. I felt dreadfully for her along six months back; but now I see how she's been brought out, I begin to see that things are for the best, perhaps, after all. I can't help feeling that Jim Marvyn is gone to heaven, poor fellow! His father is a deacon, — and such a good man! — and Jim, though he did make a great laugh wherever he went, and sometimes laughed where he hadn't ought to, was a noble-hearted fellow. Now, to be sure, as the Doctor says, 'amiable instincts a'n't true holiness'; but then they are better than unamiable ones, like Simeon Brown's. I do think, if that man is a Christian, he is a dreadful ugly one; he snapped me short up about my change, when he settled with me last Tuesday; and if I hadn't felt that it was a sinful rising, I should have told him

I'd never put foot in his house again; I'm glad, for my part, he's gone out of our church. Now Jim Marvyn was like a prince to poor people; and I remember once his mother told him to settle with me, and he gave me 'most double, and wouldn't let me make change. ' Confound it all, Miss Prissy,' says he, ' I wouldn't stitch as you do from morning to night for double that money.' Now I know we can't do anything to recommend ourselves to the Lord, but then I can't help feeling some sorts of folks must be by nature more pleasing to Him than others. David was a man after God's own heart, and he was a generous, whole-souled fellow, like Jim Marvyn, though he did get carried away by his spirits sometimes and do wrong things; and so I hope the Lord saw fit to make Jim one of the elect. We don't ever know what God's grace has done for folks. I think a great many are converted when we know nothing about it, as Miss Twitchel told poor old Miss Tyrel, who was mourning about her son, a dreadful wild boy, who was killed falling from mast-head; she says, that from the mast-head to the deck was time enough for divine grace to do the work."

" I have always had a trembling hope for poor James," said Mrs. Scudder, — " not on account of any of his good deeds or amiable traits, because election is without foresight of any good works, — but I felt he was a child of the covenant, at

least by the father's side, and I hope the Lord
has heard his prayer. These are dark providences;
the world is full of them; and all we can do is
to have faith that the Lord will bring infinite
good out of finite evil, and make everything better than if the evil had not happened. That's
what our good Doctor is always repeating; and
we must try to rejoice, in view of the happiness
of the universe, without considering whether we
or our friends are to be included in it or not."

"Well, dear me!" said Miss Prissy, "I hope,
if that is necessary, it will please the Lord to
give it to me; for I don't seem to find any powers in me to get up to it. But all's for the best,
at any rate, — and that's a comfort."

Just at this moment Mary's clear voice at the
door announced that tea was on the table.

"Coming, this very minute," said Miss Prissy,
bustling up and pulling off her spectacles. Then,
running across the room, she shut the door mysteriously, and turned to Mrs. Scudder with the air
of an impending secret. Miss Prissy was subject
to sudden impulses of confidence, in which she
was so very cautious that not the thickest oak-
plank door seemed secure enough, and her voice
dropped to its lowest key. The most important
and critical words were entirely omitted, or supplied by a knowing wink and a slight stamp of
the foot.

In this mood she now approached Mrs. Scudder, and, holding up her hand on the door-side to prevent consequences, if, after all, she should be betrayed into a loud word, she said, " I thought I'd just say, Miss Scudder, that, in case Mary should —— the Doctor, — in case, you know, there should be a —— in the house, you *must* just contrive it so as to give me a month's notice, so that I could give you a whole fortnight to fix her up as such a good man's —— ought to be. Now I know how spiritually-minded our blessed Doctor is; but bless you, Ma'am, he's got eyes. I tell you, Miss Scudder, these men, the best of 'em, *feel* what's what, though they don't *know* much. I saw the Doctor look at Mary that night I dressed her for the wedding-party. I tell you he'd like to have his wife look pretty well, and he'll get up some blessed text or other about it, just as he did that night about being brought unto the king in raiment of needle-work. That is an encouraging thought to us sewing-women.

" But this thing was spoken of after the meeting. Miss Twitchel and Miss Jones were talking about it; and they all say that there would be the best setting-out got for her that was ever seen in Newport, if it should happen. Why, there's reason in it. She ought to have at least two real good India silks that will stand alone, — and you'll see she'll have 'em too; you let me alone for that, and I was thinking, as I lay awake last night, of a new way of making up, that you will say is just the sweetest that ever you did see. And Miss Jones was saying that she hoped there wouldn't anything happen without her knowing it, because her husband's sister in Philadelphia has sent her a new receipt for cake, and she has tried it and it came out beautifully, and she says she'll send some in."

All the time that this stream was flowing, Mrs. Scudder stood with the properly reserved air of a discreet matron, who leaves all such matters to Providence, and is not supposed unduly to anticipate the future; and, in reply, she warmly pressed Miss Prissy's hand, and remarked, that no one could tell what a day might bring forth, — and other general observations on the uncertainty of mortal prospects, which form a becoming shield when people do not wish to say more exactly what they are thinking of.

CHAPTER XXV.

A GUEST AT THE COTTAGE.

Nⱼᴛʜɪɴɢ is more striking, in the light and shadow of the human drama, than to compare the inner life and thoughts of elevated and silent natures with the thoughts and plans which those by whom they are surrounded have of and for them. Little thought Mary of any of the speculations that busied the friendly head of Miss Prissy, or that lay in the provident forecastings of her prudent mother. When a life into which all our life-nerves have run is cut suddenly away, there follows, after the first long bleeding is stanched, an internal paralysis of certain portions of our nature. It was so with Mary: the thousand fibres that bind youth and womanhood to earthly love and life were all in her as still as the grave, and only the spiritual and divine part of her being was active. Her hopes, desires, and aspirations were all such as she could have had in greater perfection as a disembodied spirit than as a mortal woman. The small stake for self which she had invested in life was gone, — and henceforward all personal matters were to her so indifferent that she scarce was conscious of a wish in relation to her own individual happiness. Through the sudden crush of a great affliction, she was in that state of self-abnegation to which the mystics brought themselves by fastings and self-imposed penances, — a state not purely healthy, nor realizing the divine ideal of a perfect human being made to exist in the relations of human life, — but one of those exceptional conditions, which, like the hours that often precede dissolution, seem to impart to the subject of them a peculiar aptitude for delicate and refined spiritual impressions. We could not afford to have it always night, — and we must think that the broad, gay morning-light, when meadow-lark and robin and bobolink are singing in chorus with a thousand insects and the waving of a thousand breezes, is on the whole the most in accordance with the average wants of those who have a material life to live and material work to do. But then we reverence that clear-obscure of midnight, when everything is still and dewy; — then sing the nightingales, which cannot be heard by day; then shine the mysterious stars. So when all earthly voices are hushed in the soul, all earthly lights darkened, music and color float in from a higher sphere.

No veiled nun, with her shrouded forehead and downcast eyes, ever moved about a convent with a spirit more utterly divided from the world than

Mary moved about her daily employments. Her care about the details of life seemed more than ever minute; she was always anticipating her mother in every direction, and striving by a thousand gentle preveniences to save her from fatigue and care; there was even a tenderness about her ministrations, as if the daughter had changed feelings and places with the mother.

The Doctor, too, felt a change in her manner towards him, which, always considerate and kind, was now invested with a tender thoughtfulness and anxious solicitude to serve which often brought tears to his eyes. All the neighbors who had been in the habit of visiting at the house received from her, almost daily, in one little form or another, some proof of her thoughtful remembrance.

She seemed in particular to attach herself to Mrs. Marvyn, — throwing her care around that fragile and wounded nature, as a generous vine will sometimes embrace with tender leaves and flowers a dying tree.

But her heart seemed to have yearnings beyond even the circle of home and friends. She longed for the sorrowful and the afflicted, — she would go down to the forgotten and the oppressed, — and made herself the companion of the Doctor's secret walks and explorings among the poor victims of the slave-ships, and entered with zeal as teacher among his African catechumens

Nothing but the limits of bodily strength could confine her zeal to do and suffer for others; a river of love had suddenly been checked in her heart, and it needed all these channels to drain off the waters that must otherwise have drowned her in the suffocating agonies of repression.

Sometimes, indeed, there would be a returning thrill of the old wound,—one of those overpowering moments when some turn in life brings back anew a great anguish. She would find unexpectedly in a book a mark that he had placed there,—or a turn in conversation would bring back a tone of his voice,—or she would see on some thoughtless young head curls just like those which were swaying to and fro down among the wavering seaweeds,—and then her heart gave one great throb of pain, and turned for relief to some immediate act of love to some living being. They who saw her in one of these moments felt a surging of her heart towards them, a moisture of the eye, a sense of some inexpressible yearning, and knew not from what pain that love was wrung, nor how that poor heart was seeking to still its own throbbings in blessing them.

By what name shall we call this beautiful twilight, this night of the soul, so starry with heavenly mysteries? *Not* happiness,—but blessedness. They who have it walk among men "as sorrowful, yet alway rejoicing,—as poor, yet making many rich,— as having nothing, and yet possessing all things."

The Doctor, as we have seen, had always that reverential spirit towards women which accompanies a healthy and great nature; but in the constant converse which he now held with a beautiful being, from whom every particle of selfish feeling or mortal weakness seemed sublimed, he appeared to yield his soul up to her leading with a wonderful humility, as to some fair, miraculous messenger of Heaven. All questions of internal experience, all delicate shadings of the spiritual history with which his pastoral communings in his flock made him conversant, he brought to her to be resolved with the purest simplicity of trust.

" She is one of the Lord's rarities," he said, one day to Mrs. Scudder, " and I find it difficult to maintain the bounds of Christian faithfulness in talking with her. It is a charm of the Lord's hidden ones that they know not their own beauty, and God forbid that I should tempt a creature made so perfect by divine grace to self-exaltation, or lay my hand unadvisedly, as Uzzah did, upon the ark of God, by my inconsiderate praises!"

" Well, Doctor," said Miss Prissy, who sat in the corner, sewing on the dove-colored silk, " I do wish you could come into one of our meetings and hear those blessed prayers. I don't think you nor anybody else ever heard anything like 'em."

" I would, indeed, that I might with propriety enjoy the privilege," said the Doctor.

" Well, I'll tell you what," said Miss Prissy, " next week they're going to meet here; and I'll leave the door just ajar, and you can hear every word, just by standing in the entry."

" Thank you, Madam," said the Doctor; " it would certainly be a blessed privilege, but I cannot persuade myself that such an act would be consistent with Christian propriety."

" Ah, now do hear that good man!" said Miss Prissy, after he had left the room; " if he ha'n't got the making of a real gentleman in him, as well as a real Christian! — though I always did say, for my part, that a real Christian will be a gentleman. But I don't believe all the temptations in the world could stir that blessed man one jot or grain to do the least thing that he thinks is wrong or out of the way. Well, I must say, I never saw such a good man; he is the only man I ever saw good enough for our Mary."

Another spring came round, and brought its roses, and the apple-trees blossomed for the third time since the commencement of our story; and the robins had rebuilt their nest, and began to lay their blue eggs in it; and Mary still walked her calm course, as a sanctified priestess of the great worship of sorrow. Many were the hearts now dependent on her, the spiritual histories, the threads of which were held in her loving hand,— many the souls burdened with sins, or oppressed with sorrow, who found in her bosom at once confessional and sanctuary. So many sought her prayers, that her hours of intercession were full, and often needed to be lengthened to embrace all for whom she would plead. United to the good Doctor by a constant friendship and fellowship, she had gradually grown accustomed to the more and more intimate manner in which he regarded her, — which had risen from a simple "dear child," and "dear Mary," to "dear friend," and at last "dearest of all friends," which he frequently called her, encouraged by the calm, confiding sweetness of those still, blue eyes, and that gentle smile, which came without one varying flutter of the pulse or the rising of the slightest flush on the marble cheek.

One day a letter was brought in, post-marked "Philadelphia." It was from Madame de Frontignac; it was in French, and ran as follows: —

"My dear little White Rose: —

"I am longing to see you once more, and before long I shall be in Newport. Dear little Mary, I am sad, very sad; — the days seem all of them too long; and every morning I look out of my window and wonder why I was born. I am not so happy as I used to be, when I cared for nothing but to sing and smooth my feathers like the birds. That is the best kind of life for us women; — if we love anything better than our clothes, it is sure to bring us great sorrow. For all that, I can't help thinking it is very noble and beautiful to love; — love is very beautiful, but very, very sad. My poor dear little white cat, I should like to hold you a little while to my heart; — it is so cold all the time, and aches so, I wish I were dead; but then I am not good enough to die. The Abbé says, we must offer up our sorrow to God as a satisfaction for our sins. I have a good deal to offer, because my nature is strong and I can feel a great deal.

"But I am very selfish, dear little Mary, to think only of myself, when I know how you must suffer. Ah! but you knew he loved you truly, the poor dear boy! — that is something. I pray daily for his soul; don't think it wrong of me; you know it is our religion; — we should all do our best for each other.

"Remember me tenderly to Mrs. Marvyn. Poor mother! — the bleeding heart of the Mother of God alone can understand such sorrows.

"I am coming in a week or two, and then I have many things to say to *ma belle rose blanche*; till then I kiss her little hands.

"VIRGINIE DE FRONTIGNAC."

One beautiful afternoon, not long after, a car
riage stopped at the cottage, and Madame de
Frontignac alighted. Mary was spinning in her
garret-boudoir, and Mrs. Scudder was at that moment at a little distance from the house, sprinkling
some linen, which was laid out to bleach on the
green turf of the clothes-yard.

Madame de Frontignac sent away the carriage,
and ran up the stairway, pursuing the sound of
Mary's spinning-wheel, mingled with her song; and
in a moment, throwing aside the curtain, she seized
Mary in her arms, and kissed her on either cheek,
laughing and crying both at once.

" I knew where I should find you, *ma blanche !* I
heard the wheel of my poor little princess! It's
a good while since we spun together, *mimi !* Ah,
Mary, darling, little do we know what we spin!
life is hard and bitter, is'n't it? Ah, how white
your cheeks are, poor child!"

Madame de Frontignac spoke with tears in her
own eyes, passing her hand caressingly over the
fair cheeks.

" And you have grown pale, too, dear Madame,"
said Mary, looking up, and struck with the change
in the once brilliant face.

" Have I, *petite ?* I don't know why not. We
women have secret places where our life runs out.
At home I wear *rouge ;* that makes all right; —
but I don't put it on for you, Mary ; you see me
just as I am."

Mary could not but notice the want of that brilliant color and roundness in the cheek, which once made so glowing a picture; the eyes seemed larger and tremulous with a pathetic depth, and around them those bluish circles that speak of languor and pain. Still, changed as she was, Madame de Frontignac seemed only more strikingly interesting and fascinating than ever. Still she had those thousand pretty movements, those nameless graces of manner, those wavering shades of expression, that irresistibly enchained the eye and the imagination, — true Frenchwoman as she was, always in one rainbow shimmer of fancy and feeling, like one of those cloud-spotted April days which give you flowers and rain, sun and shadow, and snatches of bird-singing, all at once.

"I have sent away my carriage, Mary, and come to stay with you. You want me, — *n'est ce pas?*" she said, coaxingly, with her arms round Mary's neck; "if you don't, *tant pis!* for I am the bad penny you English speak of, — you cannot get me off."

"I am sure, dear friend," said Mary, earnestly, "we don't want to put you off."

"I know it; you are true; you *mean* what you say; you are all good real gold, down to your hearts; that is why I love you. But you, my poor Mary, your cheeks are very white; poor little heart, you suffer!"

"No," said Mary; "I do not suffer now. Christ has given me the victory over sorrow."

There was something sadly sublime in the manner in which this was said, — and something so sacred in the expression of Mary's face that Madame de Frontignac crossed herself, as she had been wont before a shrine; and then said, "Sweet Mary, pray for me; I am not at peace; I cannot get the victory over sorrow."

"What sorrow can you have?" said Mary, — "you, so beautiful, so rich, so admired, whom everybody must love?

"That is what I came to tell you; I came to confess to you. But you must sit down *there*," she said, placing Mary on a low seat in the garret-window; "and Virginie will sit here," she said, drawing a bundle of uncarded wool towards her, and sitting down at Mary's feet.

"Dear Madame," said Mary, "let me get you a better seat."

"No, no, *mignonne*, this is best; I want to lay my head in your lap"; — and she took off her riding-hat with its streaming plume, and tossed it. carelessly from her, and laid her head down on Mary's lap. "Now don't call me Madame any more. Do you know," she said, raising her head with a sudden brightening of cheek and eye, " do you know that there are two *mes* to this person? — one is Virginie, and the other is Madame de Fron-

17

tignac. Everybody in Philadelphia knows Madame
de Frontignac ; — she is very gay, very careless,
very happy ; she never has any serious hours, or
any sad thoughts ; she wears powder and diamonds,
and dances all night, and never prays ; — that is
Madame. But Virginie is quite another thing.
She is tired of all this, — tired of the balls, and
the dancing, and the diamonds, and the beaux ;
and she likes true people, and would like to live
very quiet with somebody that she loved. She is
very unhappy ; and she prays, too, sometimes, in
a poor little way, — like the birds in your nest out
there, who don't know much, but chipper and cry
because they are hungry. This is your Virginie.
Madame never comes here, — never call me Madame."

"Dear Virginie," said Mary, "how I love
you!".

"Do you Mary, — *bien sûr?* You are my good
angel! I felt a good impulse from you when I
first saw you, and have always been stronger to
do right when I got one of your pretty little letters. Oh, Mary, darling, I have been very foolish
and very miserable, and sometimes tempted to be
very, very bad! Oh, sometimes I thought I would
not care for God or anything else! — it was very
bad of me, — but I was like a foolish little fly
caught in a spider's net before he knows it."

Mary's eyes questioned her companion with an

expression of eager sympathy, somewhat blended with curiosity.

"I can't make you understand me quite," said Madame de Frontignac, "unless I go back a good many years. You see, dear Mary, my dear angel mamma died when I was very little, and I was sent to be educated at the Sacré Cœur in Paris I was very happy and very good in those days; the sisters loved me, and I loved them; and I used to be so pious, and loved God dearly. When I took my first communion, Sister Agatha prepared me. She was a true saint, and is in heaven now; and I remember, when I came to her, all dressed like a bride, with my white crown and white veil, that she looked at me so sadly, and said she hoped I would never love anybody better than God, and then I should be happy. I didn't think much of those words then; but, oh, I have since, many times! They used to tell me always that I had a husband who was away in the army, and who would come to marry me when I was seventeen, and that he would give me all sorts of beautiful things, and show me everything I wanted to see in the world, and that I must love and honor him.

"Well, I was married at last; and Monsieur de Frontignac is a good brave man, although he seemed to me very old and sober; but he was always kind to me, and gave me nobody knows

how many sets of jewelry, and let me do everything I wanted to, and so I liked him very much;
but I thought there was no danger I should love
him, or anybody else, better than God. I didn't
love anybody in those days; I only liked people,
and some people more than others. All the men
I saw professed to be lovers, and I liked to lead
them about and see what foolish things I could
make them do, because it pleased my vanity; but
I laughed at the very idea of love.

" Well, Mary, when we came to Philadelphia,
I heard everybody speaking of Colonel Burr, and
what a fascinating man he was; and I thought it
would be a pretty thing to have him in my train,
— and so I did all I could to charm him. I tried
all my little arts, — and if it is a sin for us wom-
en to do such things, I am sure I have been pun-
ished for it. Mary, he was stronger than I was.
These men, they are not satisfied with having the
whole earth under their feet, and having all the
strength and all the glory, but they must even
take away our poor little reign; — it's too bad!

" I can't tell you how it was; I didn't know
myself; but it seemed to me that he took my
very life away from me; and it was all done
before I knew it. He called himself my friend,
my brother; he offered to teach me English; he
read with me; and by-and-by he controlled my
whole life. I, that used to be so haughty, so

proud, — I, that used to laugh to think how independent I was of everybody, — I was entirely
under his control, though I tried not to show it.
I didn't well know where I was; for he talked
friendship, and I talked friendship; he talked about
sympathetic natures that are made for each other,
and I thought how beautiful it all was; it was
living in a new world. Monsieur de Frontignac
was as much charmed with him as I was; he
often told me that he was his best friend, — that
he was his hero, his model man; and I thought, ——
oh, Mary, you would wonder to hear me say what
I thought! I thought he was a Bayard, a Sully,
a Montmorenci, — everything grand and noble and
good. I loved him with a religion; I would have
died for him; I sometimes thought how I might
lay down my life to save his, like women I read
of in history. I did not know myself; I was astonished I could feel so; and I did not dream that
this could be wrong. How could I, when it made
me feel more religious than anything in my whole
life? Everything in the world seemed to grow sacred. I thought, if men could be so good and
admirable, life was a holy thing, and not to be
trifled with.

"But our good Abbé is a faithful shepherd,
and when I told him these things in confession,
he told me I was in great danger, — danger of
falling into mortal sin. Oh, Mary, it was as if

the earth had opened under me! He told me, too, that this noble man, this man so dear, was a heretic, and that, if he died, he would go to dreadful pains. Oh, Mary, I dare not tell you half what he told me, — dreadful things that make me shiver when I think of them! And then he said that I must offer myself a sacrifice for him; that, if I would put down all this love and overcome it, God would perhaps accept it as a satisfaction, and bring him into the True Church at last.

"Then I began to try. Oh, Mary, we never know how we love till we try to unlove! It seemed like taking my heart out of my breast, and separating life from life. How can one do it? I wish any one would tell me. The Abbé said I must do it by prayer; but it seemed to me prayer only made me think the more of him.

"But at last I had a great shock; everything broke up like a great, grand, noble dream, — and I waked out of it just as weak and wretched as one feels when one has overslept. Oh, Mary, I found I was mistaken in him, — all, all, wholly!"

Madame de Frontignac laid her forehead on Mary's knee, and her long chestnut hair drooped down over her face.

"He was going somewhere with my husband to explore, out in the regions of the Ohio, where he had some splendid schemes of founding a state; and I was all interest. And one day, as they

were preparing, Monsieur de Frontignac gave me
a quantity of papers to read and arrange, and
among them was a part of a letter; — I never
could imagine how it got there; it was from Burr
to one of his confidential friends. I read it, at
first, wondering what it meant, till I came to two
or three sentences about me."

Madame de Frontignac paused a moment, and
then said, rising with sudden energy, —

" Mary, that man never loved me; he cannot
love; he does not know what love is. What I
felt he cannot know; he cannot even dream of it,
because he never felt anything like it. Such men
never know us women; we are as high as heaven
above them. It is true enough that my heart was
wholly in his power, — but why ? Because I
adored him as something divine, incapable of dishonor, incapable of selfishness, incapable of even
a thought that was not perfectly noble and heroic.
If he had been all that, I should have been proud
to be even a poor little flower that should exhale
away to give him an hour's pleasure; I would
have offered my whole life to God as a sacrifice
for such a glorious soul; — and all this time what
was he thinking of me ?

" He was *using* my feelings to carry his plans;
he was admiring me like a picture; he was considering what he should do with me; and but for
his interests with my husband, he would have

tried his power to make me sacrifice this world and the next to his pleasure. But he does not know me. My mother was a Montmorenci, and I have the blood of her house in my veins; we are princesses; — we can give all; but he must be a god that we give it for."

Mary's enchanted eye followed the beautiful narrator, as she enacted before her this poetry and tragedy of real life, so much beyond what dramatic art can ever furnish. Her eyes grew splendid in their depth and brilliancy; sometimes they were full of tears, and sometimes they flashed out like lightnings; her whole form seemed to be a plastic vehicle which translated every emotion of her soul; and Mary sat and looked at her with the intense absorption that one gives to the highest and deepest in Art or Nature.

" *Enfin,* — *que faire!* " she said at last, suddenly stopping, and drooping in every limb. " Mary, I have lived on this dream so long! — never thought of anything else! — now all is gone, and what shall I do?

" I think, Mary," she added, pointing to the nest in the tree, " I see my life in many things. My heart was once still and quiet, like the round little eggs that were in your nest; — now it has broken out of its shell, and cries with cold and hunger. I want my dream again, — I wish it all back, — or that my heart could go back into its shell. If I only could drop this year out of my life, and care for nothing, as I used to! I have tried to do that; I can't; I cannot get back where I was before."

"*Would* you do it, dear Virginie?" said Mary; "would you, if you could?"

"It was very noble and sweet, all that," said Virginie; "it gave me higher thoughts than ever I had before; I think my feelings were beautiful; — but now they are like little birds that have no mother; they kill me with their crying."

"Dear Virginie, there is a real Friend in heaven, who is all you can ask or think, — nobler, better, purer, — who cannot change, and cannot die, and who loved you and gave himself for you."

"You mean Jesus," said Virginie. "Ah, I know it; and I say the offices to him daily, but my heart is very wild and starts away from my words. I say, 'My God, I give myself to you!' — and after all, I don't give myself, and I don't feel com-forted. Dear Mary, you must have suffered, too, — for you loved really, — I saw it; — when we feel a thing ourselves, we can see very quick the same in others; — and it was a dreadful blow to come so all at once."

"Yes, it was," said Mary; "I thought I must die; but Christ has given me peace."

These words were spoken with that long-breathed sigh with which we always speak of peace, — a

17 *

sigh that told of storms and sorrows past, — the
sighing of the wave that falls spent and broken on
the shores of eternal rest.

There was a little pause in the conversation
and then Virginie raised her head and spoke in a
sprightlier tone.

"Well, my little fairy cat, my white doe, I have
come to you. Poor Virginie wants something to
hold to her heart; let me have you," she said,
throwing her arms round Mary.

"Dear, dear Virginie, indeed you shall!" said
Mary. "I will love you dearly, and pray for you.
I always have prayed for you, ever since the first
day I knew you."

"I knew it, — I felt your prayers in my heart.
Mary, I have many thoughts that I dare not tell
to any one, lately, — but I cannot help feeling that
some are real Christians who are not in the True
Church. You are as true a saint as Saint Catharine; indeed, I always think of you when I think
of our dear Lady; and yet they say there is no
salvation out of the Church."

This was a new view of the subject to Mary,
who had grown up with the familiar idea that the
Romish Church was Babylon and Antichrist, and
who, during the conversation, had been revolving
the same surmises with regard to her friend. She
turned her grave, blue eyes on Madame de Frontignac with a somewhat surprised look, which

melted into a half-smile. But the latter still went
on with a puzzled air, as if trying to talk herself
out of some mental perplexity.

"Now, Burr is a heretic,—and more than that,
he is an infidel; he has no religion in his heart,
—I saw that often,—it made me tremble for him,
—it ought to have put me on my guard. But
you, dear Mary, you love Jesus as your life. I
think you love him just as much as Sister Agatha,
who was a saint. The Abbé says that there is
nothing so dangerous as to begin to use our reason in religion,—that, if we once begin, we never
know where it may carry us; but I can't help
using mine a very little. I must think there are
some saints that are not in the True Church."

"All are one who love Christ," said Mary; "we
are one in Him."

"I should not dare to tell the Abbé," said
Madame de Frontignac; and Mary queried in her
heart, whether Dr. Hopkins would feel satisfied that
she could bring this wanderer to the fold of Christ
without undertaking to batter down the walls of
her creed ; and yet, there they were, the Catholic
and the Puritan, each strong in her respective faith,
yet melting together in that embrace of love and
sorrow, joined in the great communion of suffering. Mary took up her Testament, and read the
fourteenth chapter of John : —

"Let not your heart be troubled; ye believe in

God, believe also in me. In my Father's house
are many mansions; if it were not so, I would
have told you. I go to prepare a place for you;
and if I go and prepare a place for you, I will
come again and receive you unto myself, that
where I am, there ye may be also."

Mary read on through the chapter, — through
the next wonderful prayer; her face grew solemnly
transparent, as of an angel; for her soul was lifted
from earth by the words, and walked with Christ
far above all things, over that starry pavement
where each footstep is on a world.

The greatest moral effects are like those of music, — not wrought out by sharp-sided intellectual
propositions, but melted in by a divine fusion, by
words that have mysterious, indefinite fulness of
meaning, made living by sweet voices, which seem
to be the out-throbbings of angelic hearts. So one
verse in the Bible read by a mother in some hour
of tender prayer has a significance deeper and
higher than the most elaborate of sermons, the
most acute of arguments.

Virginie Frontignac sat as one divinely enchanted, while that sweet voice read on; and
when the silence fell between them, she gave a
long sigh, as we do when sweet music stops.
They heard between them the soft stir of summer
leaves, the distant songs of birds, the breezy hum
when the afternoon wind shivered through many

branches, and the silver sea chimed in. Virginie
rose at last, and kissed Mary on the forehead.

" That is a beautiful book," she said, " and to
read it all by one's self must be lovely. I cannot
understand why it should be dangerous; it has not
injured you.

" Sweet saint," she added, " let me stay with
you; you shall read to me every day. Do you
know I came here to get you to take me? I
want you to show me how to find peace where
you do; will you let me be your sister?"

" Yes, indeed," said Mary, with a cheek brighter
than it had been for many a day; her heart feeling a throb of more real human pleasure than for
long months.

" Will you get your mamma to let me stay?"
said Virginie, with the bashfulness of a child;
" haven't you a little place like yours, with white
curtains and sanded floor, to give to poor little
Virginie to learn to be good in?"

" Why, do you really want to stay here with
us," said Mary, " in this little house?"

" Do I really?" said Virginie, mimicking her
voice with a start of her old playfulness; — " *don't*
I really? Come now, *mimi*, coax the good mamma
for me, — tell her I shall try to be very good. I
shall help you with the spinning, — you know I
spin beautifully, — and I shall make butter, and

milk the cow, and set the table. Oh, I will be so useful, you can't spare me!"

"I should love to have you dearly," said Mary, warmly; "but you would soon be dull for want of society here."

"*Quelle idée! ma petite drôle!*" said the lady, — who, with the mobility of her nation, had already recovered some of the saucy mocking grace that was habitual to her, as she began teasing Mary with a thousand little childish motions. "Indeed, *mimi*, you must keep me hid up here, or may be the wolf will find me and eat me up; who knows?"

Mary looked at her with inquiring eyes.

"What do you mean?"

"I mean, Mary, — I mean, that, when *he* comes back to Philadelphia, he thinks he shall find me there; he thought I should stay while my husband was gone; and when he finds I am gone, he may come to Newport; and I never want to see him again without you; — you must let me stay with you."

"Have you told him," said Mary, "what you think?"

"I wrote to him, Mary, — but, oh, I can't trust my heart! I want so much to believe him, it kills me so to think evil of him, that it will never do for me to see him. If he looks at me with those eyes of his, I am all gone; I shall believe anything he tells me; he will draw me to him as a great magnet draws a poor little grain of steel."

" But now you know his unworthiness, his base-ness," said Mary, " I should think it would break all his power."

" *Should* you think so? Ah, Mary, we cannot unlove in a minute; love is a great while dying. I do not worship him now as I did. I know what he is. I know he is bad, and I am sorry for it. I should like to cover it from all the world, — even from you, Mary, since I see it makes you dislike him; it hurts me to hear any one else blame him. But sometimes I do so long to think I am mistaken, that I know, rf I should see him, I should catch at anything he might tell me, as a drowning man at straws; I should shut my eyes, and think, after all, that it was all my fault, and ask a thousand pardons for all the evil he has done. No, — Mary, you must keep your blue eyes upon me, or I shall be gone."

At this moment Mrs. Scudder's voice was heard, calling Mary below.

" Go down now, darling, and tell mamma; make a good little talk to her, *ma reine!* Ah, you are queen here! all do as you say, — even the good priest there; you have a little hand, but it leads all; so go, *petite.*"

Mrs. Scudder was somewhat flurried and dis-composed at the proposition; — there were the *pros* and the *cons* in her nature, such as we all have. In the first place, Madame de Frontignac belonged to high society,— and that was *pro;* for Mrs. Scudder prayed daily against worldly vanities, because she felt a little traitor in her heart that was ready to open its door to them, if not constantly talked down. In the second place, Madame de Frontignac was French,— there was a *con;* for Mrs. Scudder had enough of her father John Bull in her heart to have a very wary lookout on anything French. But then, in the third place, she was out of health and unhappy,— and there was a *pro* again; for Mrs. Scudder was as kind and motherly a soul as ever breathed. But then she was a Catholic,— *con.* But the Doctor and Mary might convert her,— *pro.* And then Mary wanted her,— *pro.* And she was a pretty, bewitching, lovable creature,— *pro.*— The *pros* had it; and it was agreed that Madame de Frontignac should be installed as proprietress of the spare chamber, and she sat down to the tea-table that evening in the great kitchen.

CHAPTER XXVI.

THE DECLARATION.

THE domesticating of Madame de Frontignac as an inmate of the cottage added a new element of vivacity to that still and unvaried life. One of the most beautiful traits of French nature is that fine gift of appreciation, which seizes at once the picturesque side of every condition of life, and finds in its own varied storehouse something to assort with it. As compared with the Anglo-Saxon, the French appear to be gifted with a *naïve* childhood of nature, and to have the power that children have of gilding every scene of life with some of their own poetic fancies.

Madame de Frontignac was in raptures with the sanded floor of her little room, which commanded, through the apple-boughs, a little morsel of a sea view. She could fancy it was a nymph's cave, she said.

" Yes, *ma Marie*, I will play Calypso, and you shall play Telemachus, and Dr. Hopkins shall be Mentor. Mentor was so very, very good! — only a bit— *dull*," she said, pronouncing the last word with a wicked accent, and lifting her hands with a whimsical gesture like a naughty child who expects a correction.

Mary could not but laugh ; and as she laughed, more color rose in her waxen cheeks than for many days before.

Madame de Frontignac looked as triumphant as a child who has made its mother laugh, and went on laying things out of her trunk into her drawers with a zeal that was quite amusing to see.

" You see, *ma blanche*, I have left all Madame's clothes at Philadelphia, and brought only those that belong to Virginie, — no *tromperie*, no feathers, no gauzes, no diamonds, — only white dresses, and my straw hat *en bergère*. I brought one string of pearls that was my mother's; but pearls, you know, belong to the sea-nymphs. I will trim my hat with seaweed and buttercups together, and we will go out on the beach to-night and get some gold and silver shells to dress *mon miroir*."

" Oh, I have ever so many now," said Mary, running into her room, and coming back with a little bag.

They both sat on the bed together, and began pouring them out, — Madame de Frontignac showering childish exclamations of delight.

Suddenly Mary put her hand to her heart as if

she had been struck with something; and Madame de Frontignac heard her say, in a low voice of sudden pain, "Oh, dear!"

"What is it, *mimi?*" she said, looking up quickly.

"Nothing," said Mary, turning her head.

Madame de Frontignac looked down, and saw among the sea-treasures a necklace of Venetian shells, that she knew never grew on the shores of Newport. She held it up.

"Ah, I see," she said. "He gave you this. Ah, *ma pauvrette*," she said, clasping Mary in her arms, "thy sorrow meets thee everywhere! May I be a comfort to thee! — just a little one!"

"Dear, dear friend!" said Mary, weeping. "I know not how it is. Sometimes I think this sorrow is all gone; but then, for a moment, it comes back again. But I am at peace; it is all right, all right; I would not have it otherwise. But, oh, if he could have spoken one word to me before! He gave me this," she added, "when he came home from his first voyage to the Mediterranean. I did not know it was in this bag. I had looked for it everywhere."

"Sister Agatha would have told you to make a rosary of it," said Madame de Frontignac; "but you pray without a rosary. It is all one," she added; "there will be a prayer for every shell, though you do not count them. But come, *ma chère*, get your bonnet, and let us go out on the beach."

That evening, before going to bed, Mrs. Scudder came into Mary's room. Her manner was grave and tender; her eyes had tears in them; and although her usual habits were not caressing, she came to Mary and put her arms around her and kissed her. It was an unusual manner, and Mary's gentle eyes seemed to ask the reason of it.

" My daughter," said her mother, " I have just had a long and very interesting talk with our dear good friend, the Doctor; ah, Mary, very few people know how good he is! "

" True, mother," said Mary, warmly; " he is the best, the noblest, and yet the humblest man in the world."

" You love him very much, do you not? " said her mother.

" Very dearly," said Mary.

" Mary, he has asked me, this evening, if you would be willing to be his wife."

" His *wife*, mother? " said Mary, in the tone of one confused with a new and strange thought.

" Yes, daughter; I have long seen that he was preparing to make you this proposal."

" You have, mother? "

" Yes, daughter; have you never thought of it? "

" Never, mother."

There was a long pause, — Mary standing, just as she had been interrupted, in her night toilette, with her long, light hair streaming down over her white dress, and the comb held mechanically in her hand. She sat down after a moment, and, clasping her hands over her knees, fixed her eyes intently on the floor ; and there fell between the two a silence so profound, that the tickings of the clock in the next room seemed to knock upon the door. Mrs. Scudder sat with anxious eyes watching that silent face, pale as sculptured marble.

" Well, Mary," she said at last.

A deep sigh was the only answer. The violent throbbings of her heart could be seen undulating the long hair as the moaning sea tosses the rockweed.

" My daughter," again said Mrs. Scudder.

Mary gave a great sigh, like that of a sleeper awakening from a dream, and, looking at her mother, said, — " Do you suppose he really *loves* me, mother ? "

" Indeed he does, Mary, as much as man ever loved woman ! "

" Does he indeed ? " said Mary, relapsing into thoughtfulness.

" And you love him, do you not ? " said her mother.

"Oh, yes, I love him."

"You love him better than any man in the world, don't you?"

"Oh, mother, mother! yes!" said Mary, throwing herself passionately forward, and bursting into sobs; "yes, there is no one else now that I love better, — no one! — no one!"

"My darling! my daughter!" said Mrs. Scudder, coming and taking her in her arms.

"Oh, mother, mother!" she said, sobbing distressfully, "let me cry, just for a little, — oh, mother, mother, mother!"

What was there hidden under that despairing wail? — It was the parting of the last strand of the cord of youthful hope.

Mrs. Scudder soothed and caressed her daughter, but maintained still in her breast a tender pertinacity of purpose, such as mothers will, who think they are conducting a child through some natural sorrow into a happier state.

Mary was not one, either, to yield long to emotion of any kind. Her rigid education had taught her to look upon all such outbursts as a species of weakness, and she struggled for composure, and soon seemed entirely calm.

"If he really loves me, mother, it would give him great pain if I refused," said Mary thoughtfully.

"Certainly it would; and, Mary, you have allowed him to act as a very near friend for a long time; and it is quite natural that he should have hopes that you loved him."

"I do love him, mother, — better than anybody in the world except you. Do you think that will do?"

"Will do?" said her mother; "I don't understand you."

"Why, is that loving enough to marry? I shall love him more, perhaps, after, — shall I, mother?"

"Certainly you will; every one does."

"I wish he did not want to marry me, mother," said Mary, after a pause. "I liked it a great deal better as we were before."

"All girls feel so, Mary, at first; it is very natural."

"Is that the way you felt about father, mother?"

Mrs. Scudder's heart smote her when she thought of her own early love, — that great love that asked no questions, — that had no doubts, no fears, no hesitations, — nothing but one great, outsweeping impulse, which swallowed her life in that of another. She was silent; and after a moment, she said, —

"I was of a different disposition from you, Mary. I was of a strong, wilful, positive nature. I either liked or disliked with all my might. And besides, Mary, there never was a man like your father."

The matron uttered this first article in the great confession of woman's faith with the most unconscious simplicity.

"Well, mother, I will do whatever is my duty. I want to be guided. If I can make that good man happy, and help him to do some good in the world —— After all, life is short, and the great thing is to do for others."

"I am sure, Mary, if you could have heard how he spoke, you would be sure you could make him happy. He had not spoken before, because he felt so unworthy of such a blessing; he said I was to tell you that he should love and honor you all the same, whether you could be his wife or not,— but that nothing this side of heaven would be so blessed a gift,— that it would make up for every trial that could possibly come upon him. And you know, Mary, he has a great many discouragements and trials;—people don't appreciate him; his efforts to do good are misunderstood and misconstrued; they look down on him, and despise him, and tell all sorts of evil things about him; and sometimes he gets quite discouraged."

"Yes, mother, I will marry·him," said Mary;— "yes, I will."

"My darling daughter!" said Mrs. Scudder,— "this has been the hope of my life!"

"Has it, mother?" said Mary, with a faint smile; "I shall make you happier then?"

" Yes, dear, you will. And think what a prospect of usefulness opens before you! You can take a position, as his wife, which will enable you to do even more good than you do now; and you will have the happiness of seeing, every day, how much you comfort the hearts and encourage the hands of God's dear people."

" Mother, I ought to be very glad I can do it," said Mary; " and I trust I am. God orders all things for the best."

" Well, my child, sleep to-night, and to-morrow we will talk more about it."

18

CHAPTER XXVII.

SURPRISES.

Mrs. Scudder kissed her daughter, and left her.
After a moment's thought, Mary gathered the long
silky folds of hair around her head, and knotted
them for the night. Then leaning forward on her
toilet-table, she folded her hands together, and
stood regarding the reflection of herself in the
mirror.

Nothing is capable of more ghostly effect than
such a silent, lonely contemplation of that mysterious image of ourselves which seems to look out
of an infinite depth in the mirror, as if it were
our own soul beckoning to us visibly from unknown regions. Those eyes look into our own
with an expression sometimes vaguely sad and
inquiring. The face wears weird and tremulous
lights and shadows; it asks us mysterious questions, and troubles us with the suggestions of our
relations to some dim unknown. The sad, blue
eyes that gazed into Mary's had that look of calm
initiation, of melancholy comprehension, peculiar

to eyes made clairvoyant by "great and critical" sorrow. They seemed to say to her, "Fulfil thy mission; life is made for sacrifice; the flower must fall before fruit can perfect itself." A vague shuddering of mystery gave intensity to her reverie. It seemed as if those mirror-depths were another world; she heard the far-off dashing of sea-green waves; she felt a yearning impulse towards that dear soul gone out into the infinite unknown.

Her word just passed had in her eyes all the sacred force of the most solemnly attested vow; and she felt as if that vow had shut some till then open door between her and him; she had a kind of shadowy sense of a throbbing and yearning nature that seemed to call on her, — that seemed surging towards her with an imperative, protesting force that shook her heart to its depths.

Perhaps it is so, that souls, once intimately related, have ever after this a strange power of affecting each other, — a power that neither absence nor death can annul. How else can we interpret those mysterious hours in which the power of departed love seems to overshadow us, making our souls vital with such longings, with such wild throbbings, with such unutterable sighings, that a little more might burst the mortal bond? Is it not deep calling unto deep? the free soul singing outside the cage to her mate beating against the bars within?

Mary even, for a moment, fancied that a voice called her name, and started, shivering. Then the habits of her positive and sensible education returned at once, and she came out of her reverie as one breaks from a dream, and lifted all these sad thoughts with one heavy sigh from her breast; and opening her Bible, she read: " They that trust in the Lord shall be as Mount Zion, which cannot be removed, but abideth forever. As the mountains are round about Jerusalem, so the Lord is round about his people from henceforth, even forever."

Then she kneeled by her bedside, and offered her whole life a sacrifice to the loving God who had offered his life a sacrifice for her. She prayed for grace to be true to her promise, — to be faithful to the new relation she had accepted. She prayed that all vain regrets for the past might be taken away, and that her soul might vibrate without discord in unison with the will of Eternal Love. So praying, she rose calm, and with that clearness of spirit which follows an act of uttermost self-sacrifice ; and so calmly she laid down and slept, with her two hands crossed upon her breast, her head slightly turned on the pillow, her cheek pale as marble, and her long dark lashes lying drooping, with a sweet expression, as if under that mystic veil of sleep the soul were seeing things forbidden to the waking eye. Only the gentlest heaving of the quiet breast told that the heavenly spirit within had not gone whither it was hourly aspiring to go.

Meanwhile Mrs. Scudder had left Mary's room, and entered the Doctor's study, holding a candle in her hand. The good man was sitting alone in the dark, with his head bowed upon his Bible. When Mrs. Scudder entered, he rose, and regarded her wistfully, but did not speak. He had something just then in his heart for which he had no words; so he only looked as a man does who hopes and fears for the answer of a decisive question.

Mrs. Scudder felt some of the natural reserve which becomes a matron coming charged with a gift in which lies the whole sacredness of her own existence, and which she puts from her hands with a jealous reverence. She therefore measured the man with her woman's and mother's eye, and said, with a little stateliness, —

"My dear Sir, I come to tell you the result of my conversation with Mary."

She made a little pause, — and the Doctor stood before her as humbly as if he had not weighed and measured the universe; because he knew, that, though he might weigh the mountains in scales and the hills in a balance, yet it was a far subtiler power which must possess him of one small woman's heart. In fact, he felt to himself

like a great, awkward, clumsy mountainous earth-
ite asking of a white-robed angel to help him up
a ladder of cloud. He was perfectly sure, for the
moment, that he was going to be refused; and he
looked humbly firm, — he would take it like a
man. His large blue eyes, generally so misty in
their calm, had a resolute clearness, rather mournful than otherwise. Of course, no such celestial
experience was going to happen to him.

He cleared his throat, and said, —

" Well, Madam ? "

Mrs. Scudder's womanly dignity was appeased;
she reached out her hand, cheerfully, and said, —

" *She has accepted.*"

The Doctor drew his hand suddenly away,
turned quickly round, and walked to the window,
— although, as it was ten o'clock at night and
quite dark, there was evidently nothing to be seen
there. He stood there, quietly, swallowing very
hard, and raising his handkerchief several times to
his eyes. There was enough going on under the
black coat just then to make quite a little figure
in a romance, if it had been uttered; but he belonged to a class who *lived* romance, but never
spoke it. In a few moments he returned to Mrs.
Scudder, and said, —

" I trust, dear Madam, that this very dear friend
may never have reason to think me ungrateful for
her wonderful goodness; and whatever sins my

evil heart may lead me into, I *hope* I may never fall so low as to forget the undeserved mercy of this hour. If ever I shrink from duty or murmur at trials, while so sweet a friend is mine, I shall be vile indeed."

The Doctor, in general, viewed himself on the discouraging side, and had berated and snubbed himself all his life as a most flagitious and evil-disposed individual, — a person to be narrowly watched, and capable of breaking at any moment into the most flagrant iniquity; and therefore it was that he received his good fortune in so different a spirit from many of the lords of creation in similar circumstances.

" I am sensible," he added, " that a poor minister, without much power of eloquence, and commissioned of the Lord to speak unpopular truths, and whose worldly condition, in consequence, is never likely to be very prosperous, — that such an one could scarcely be deemed a suitable partner for so very beautiful a young woman, who might expect proposals, in a temporal point of view, of a much more advantageous nature; and I am there-fore the more struck and overpowered with this blessed result."

These last words caught in the Doctor's throat, as if he were overpowered in very deed.

" In regard to *her* happiness," said the Doctor, with a touch of awe in his voice, " I would not have presumed to become the guardian of it, were it not that I am persuaded it is assured by a Higher Power; for 'when He giveth quietness, who then can make trouble?' (Job, xxxiv. 29.) But I trust I may say no effort on my part shall be wanting to secure it."

Mrs. Scudder was a mother, and had come to that stage in life where mothers always feel tears rising behind their smiles. She pressed the Doctor's hand silently, and they parted for the night.

We know not how we can acquit ourselves to our friends of the great world for the details of such an unfashionable courtship, so well as by giving them, before they retire for the night, a dip into a more modish view of things.

The Doctor was evidently green, — green in his faith, green in his simplicity, green in his general belief of the divine in woman, green in his particular humble faith in one small Puritan maiden, whom a knowing fellow might at least have manœuvred so skilfully as to break up her saintly superiority, discompose her, rout her ideas, and lead her up and down a swamp of hopes and fears and conjectures, till she was wholly bewildered and ready to take him at last—if he made up his mind to have her at all — as a great bargain, for which she was to be sensibly grateful.

Yes, the Doctor was green, — *immortally* green, as a cedar of Lebanon, which, waving its broad archangel wings over some fast-rooted, eternal old solitude, and seeing from its sublime height the vastness of the universe, veils its kingly head with humility before God's infinite majesty.

He has gone to bed now,—simple old soul!—first apologizing to Mrs. Scudder for having kept her up to so dissipated and unparalleled an hour as ten o'clock on his personal matters.

Meanwhile our Asmodeus shall transport us to a handsomely furnished apartment in one of the most fashionable hotels of Philadelphia, where Colonel Aaron Burr, just returned from his trip to the then aboriginal wilds of Ohio, is seated before a table covered with maps, letters, books, and papers. His keen eye runs over the addresses of the letters, and he eagerly seizes one from Madame de Frontignac, and reads it; and as no one but ourselves is looking at him now, his face has no need to wear its habitual mask. First comes an expression of profound astonishment; then of chagrin and mortification; then of deepening concern; there were stops where the dark eyelashes flashed together, as if to brush a tear out of the view of the keen-sighted eyes; and then a red flush rose even to his forehead, and his delicate lips wore a sarcastic smile. He laid down the letter, and made one or two turns through the room.

The man had felt the dashing against his own

18*

of a strong, generous, indignant woman's heart
fully awakened, and speaking with that impassioned
vigor with which a French regiment charges in
battle. There were those picturesque, winged words,
those condensed expressions, those subtile piercings
of meaning, and, above all, that simple pathos, for
which the French tongue has no superior; and for
the moment the woman had the victory; she
shook his heart. But Burr resembled the marvel
with which chemists amuse themselves. His heart
was a vase filled with boiling passions,—while his
will, a still, cold, unmelted lump of ice, lay at the
bottom.

Self-denial is not 'peculiar to Christians. He
who goes downward often puts forth as much
force to kill a noble nature as another does to
annihilate a sinful one. There was something in
this letter so keen, so searching, so self-revealing,
that it brought on one of those interior crises in
which a man is convulsed with the struggle of
two natures, the godlike and the demoniac, and
from which he must pass out more wholly to the
dominion of the one or the other.

Nobody knew the true better than Burr. He
knew the godlike and the pure; he had *felt* its
beauty and its force to the very depths of his
being, as the demoniac knew at once the fair
Man of Nazareth; and even now he felt the
voice within that said, " What have I to do with

thee?" and the rending of a struggle of heavenly
life with fast-coming eternal death.

That letter had told him what he might be, and
what he was. It was as if his dead mother's
hand had held up before him a glass in which he
saw himself white-robed and crowned, and so
dazzling in purity that he loathed his present self.

As he walked up and down the room perturbed,
he sometimes wiped tears from his eyes, and then
set his teeth and compressed his lips. At last his
face grew calm and settled in its expression, his
mouth wore a sardonic smile; he came and took
the letter, and, folding it leisurely, laid it on the
table, and put a heavy paper-weight over it, as if
to hold it down and bury it. Then drawing to
himself some maps of new territories, he set himself vigorously to some columns of arithmetical
calculations on the margin; and thus he worked
for an hour or two, till his mind was as dry and
his pulse as calm as a machine; then he drew the
inkstand towards him, and scribbled hastily the
following letter to his most confidential associate,
— a letter which told no more of the conflict that
preceded it than do the dry sands and the civil
gossip of the sea-waves to-day of the storm and
wreck of last week.

" Dear ———. *Nous voici* — once more in Phil
adelphia. Our schemes in Ohio prosper. Fron-

tignac remains there to superintend. He answers our purpose *passablement*. On the whole, I don't see that we could do better than retain him; he is, besides, a gentlemanly, agreeable person, and wholly devoted to me, — a point certainly not to be overlooked.

" As to your railleries about the fair Madame, I must say, in justice both to her and myself, that any grace with which she has been pleased to honor me is not to be misconstrued. You are not to imagine any but the most Platonic of *liaisons*. She is as high-strung as an Arabian steed, — proud, heroic, romantic, and *French!* and such must be permitted to take their own time and way, which we in our *gaucherie* can only humbly wonder at. I have ever professed myself her abject slave, ready to follow any whim, and obeying the slightest signal of the jewelled hand. As that is her sacred pleasure, I have been inhabiting the most abstract realms of heroic sentiment, living on the most diluted moonshine, and spinning out elaborately all those charming and seraphic distinctions between tweedle-dum and tweedle-dee with which these ecstatic creatures delight themselves in certain stages of *affaires du cœur*.

" The last development, on the part of my goddess, is a fit of celestial anger, of the cause of which I am in the most innocent ignorance. She writes me three pages of French sublimities, writ-

ing as only a French woman can, — bids me an
eternal adieu, and informs me she is going to
Newport.

"Of course the affair becomes stimulating. I
am not to presume to dispute her sentence, or
doubt a lady's perfect sincerity in wishing never
to see me again; but yet I think I shall try to
pacify the

'tantas in animis cœlestibus iras.'

If a woman hates you, it is only her love turned
wrong side out, and you may turn it back with
due care. The pretty creatures know how becoming a *grande passion* is, and take care to keep
themselves in mind; a quarrel serves their turn,
when all else fails.

"To another point. I wish you to advertise
S——, that his insinuations in regard to me in
the 'Aurora' have been observed, and that I require that they be promptly retracted. He knows
me well enough to attend to this hint. I am in
earnest when I speak; if the word does nothing,
the blow will come, — and if I strike once, no
second blow will be needed. Yet I do not wish
to get him on my hands needlessly; a duel and
a love affair and hot weather, coming on together,
might prove too much even for me. — N. B. Thermometer stands at 85. I am resolved on Newport next week.

"Yours ever,   BURR.

" P. S.   I forgot to say, that, oddly enough, my
goddess has gone and placed herself under the
wing of the pretty Puritan I saw in Newport.
Fancy the *mélange !*   Could anything be more
piquant ? — that cart-load of goodness, the old
Doctor, that sweet little saint, and Madame Faubourg St. Germain shaken up together! Fancy
her listening with well-bred astonishment to a *cri-
tique* on the doings of the unregenerate, or flirting
that little jewelled fan of hers in Mrs. Scudder's
square pew of a Sunday!   Probably they will
carry her to the weekly prayer-meeting, which of
course she will contrive some fine French subtilty
for admiring, and find *ravissant.*   I fancy I see it."

When Burr had finished this letter, he had actually written himself into a sort of persuasion of
its truth.   When a finely constituted nature wishes
to go into baseness, it has first to bribe itself.
Evil is never embraced undisguised, as evil, but
under some fiction which the mind accepts and
with which it has the singular power of blinding
itself in the face of daylight.   The power of imposing on one's self is an essential preliminary to
imposing on others.   The man first argues himself
down, and then he is ready to put the whole
weight of his nature to deceiving others.   This
letter ran so smoothly, so plausibly, that it produced on the writer of it the effect of a work of

fiction, which we *know* to be unreal, but *feel* to be true. Long habits of this kind of self-delusion in time produce a paralysis in the vital nerves of truth, so that one becomes habitually unable to see things in their verity, and realizes the awful words of Scripture,— "He feedeth on ashes; a deceived heart hath turned him aside, that he cannot deliver his soul, nor say, Is there not a lie in my right hand?"

CHAPTER XXVIII.

THE BETROTHED.

BETWEEN three and four the next morning, the robin in the nest above Mary's window stretched out his left wing, opened one eye, and gave a short and rather drowsy chirp, which broke up his night's rest and restored him to the full consciousness that he was a bird with wings and feathers, with a large apple-tree to live in, and all heaven for an estate, — and so, on these fortunate premises, he broke into a gush of singing, clear and loud, which Mary, without waking, heard in her slumbers.

Scarcely conscious, she lay in that dim clairvoyant state, when the half-sleep of the outward senses permits a delicious dewy clearness of the soul, that perfect ethereal rest and freshness of faculties, comparable only to what we imagine of the spiritual state, — season of celestial enchantment, in which the heavy weight " of all this unintelligible world" drops off, and the soul, divinely charmed, nestles like a wind-tossed bird in the protecting bosom of the One All-Perfect, All-Beautiful. What visions then come to the inner eye have often no words corresponding in mortal vocabularies. The poet, the artist, and the prophet in such hours become possessed of divine certainties which all their lives they struggle with pencil or song or burning words to make evident to their fellows. The world around wonders; but they are unsatisfied, because they have seen the glory and know how inadequate the copy.

And not merely to selectest spirits come these hours, but to those humbler poets, ungifted with utterance, who are among men as fountains sealed, whose song can be wrought out only by the harmony of deeds, the patient, pathetic melodies of tender endurance, or the heroic chant of undiscouraged labor. The poor slave-woman, last night parted from her only boy, and weary with the cotton-picking, — the captive pining in his cell, — the patient wife of the drunkard, saddened by a consciousness of the growing vileness of one so dear to her once, — the delicate spirit doomed to harsh and uncongenial surroundings, — all in such hours feel the soothings of a celestial harmony, the tenderness of more than a mother's love.

It is by such seasons as these, more often. than by reasonings or disputings, that doubts are resolved in the region of religious faith. The All-Father treats us as the mother does her " infant crying in the dark;" He does not reason with our fears, or demonstrate their fallacy, but draws us silently to His bosom, and we are at peace. Nay, there have been those, undoubtedly, who have known God falsely with the intellect, yet felt Him truly with the heart, — and there be many, principally among the unlettered little ones of Christ's flock, who positively know that much that is dogmatically propounded to them of their Redeemer is cold, barren, unsatisfying, and utterly false, who yet can give no account of their certainties better than that of the inspired fisherman, "We know Him, and have seen Him." It was in such hours as these that Mary's deadly fears for the soul of her beloved had passed all away, — passed out of her, — as if some warm, healing nature of tenderest vitality had drawn out of her heart all pain and coldness, and warmed it with the breath of an eternal summer.

So, while the purple shadows spread their gauzy veils inwoven with fire along the sky, and the gloom of the sea broke out here and there into lines of light, and thousands of birds were answering to each other from apple-tree and meadow-grass, and top of jagged rock, or trooping in bands hither and thither, like angels on loving messages, Mary lay there with the flickering light through the leaves fluttering over her face, and the glow of dawn warming the snow-white draperies of the bed and giving a tender rose-hue to the calm cheek. She lay half-conscious, smiling the while, as one who sleeps while the heart waketh, and who hears in dreams the voice of the One Eternally Beautiful and Beloved.

Mrs. Scudder entered her room, and, thinking that she still slept, stood and looked down on her. She felt as one does who has parted with some precious possession, a sudden sense of its value coming over her; she queried in herself whether any living mortal were worthy of so perfect a gift; and nothing but a remembrance of the Doctor's prostrate humility at all reconciled her to the sacrifice she was making.

" Mary, dear!" she said, bending over her, with an unusual infusion of emotion in her voice, — "darling child!"

The arms moved instinctively, even before the eyes unclosed, and drew her mother down to her with a warm, clinging embrace. Love in Puritan families was often like latent caloric, — an all-pervading force, that affected no visible thermometer, shown chiefly by a noble silent confidence, a ready helpfulness, but seldom outbreathed in caresses; yet natures like Mary's always craved these outward demonstrations, and leaned towards them as a trailing vine sways to the nearest support. It was delightful for once fully to feel how much her mother loved her, as well as to know it.

"Dear, precious mother! do you love me so very much?"

"I live and breathe in you, Mary!" said Mrs. Scudder, — giving vent to herself in one of those trenchant shorthand expressions, wherein positive natures incline to sum up everything, if they must speak at all.

Mary held her mother silently to her breast, her heart shining through her face with a quiet radiance.

"Do you feel happy this morning?" said Mrs. Scudder.

"Very, very, very happy, mother!"

"I am so glad to hear you say so!" said Mrs. Scudder, — who, to say the truth, had entertained many doubts on her pillow the night before.

Mary began dressing herself in a state of calm exaltation. Every trembling leaf on the tree, every sunbeam, was like a living smile of God, — every fluttering breeze like His voice, full of encouragement and hope.

"Mother, did you tell the Doctor what I said last night?"

"I did, my darling."

"Then, mother, I would like to see him a few moments alone."

"Well, Mary, he is in his study, at his morning devotions."

"That is just the time. I will go to him."

The Doctor was sitting by the window; and the honest-hearted, motherly lilacs, abloom for the third time since our story began, were filling the air with their sweetness.

Suddenly the door opened, and Mary entered, in her simple white short-gown and skirt, her eyes calmly radiant, and her whole manner having something serious and celestial. She came directly towards him and put out both her little hands, with a smile half childlike, half angelic; and the Doctor bowed his head and covered his face with his hands.

"Dear friend," said Mary, kneeling and taking his hands, "if you want me, I am come. Life is but a moment, — there is an eternal blessedness just beyond us, — and for the little time between I will be all I can to you, if you will only show me how."

And the Doctor ——

No, young man, — the study-door closed just then, and no one heard those words from a quaint old Oriental book which told that all the poetry of that grand old soul had burst into flower, as the aloe blossoms once in a hundred years. The feelings of that great heart might have fallen unconsciously into phrases from that one love-poem of the Bible which such men as he read so purely and devoutly, and which warm the icy clearness of their intellection with the myrrh and spices of ardent lands, where earthly and heavenly love meet and blend in one indistinguishable horizon-line, like sea and sky.

"Who is she that looketh forth as the morning, fair as the moon, clear as the sun? My dove, my undefiled, is but one; she is the only one of her mother. Thou art all fair, my love; there is no spot in thee!"

The Doctor might have said all this; we will not say he did, nor will we say he did not; all we know is, that, when the breakfast-table was ready, they came out cheerfully together. Madame de Frontignac stood in a fresh white wrapper, with a few buttercups in her hair, waiting for the breakfast. She was startled to see the Doctor entering all-radiant, leading in Mary by the hand, and looking as if he thought she were some dream-miracle which might dissolve under his eyes, unless he kept fast hold of her.

The keen eyes shot their arrowy glance, which went at once to the heart of the matter. Madame de Frontignac knew they were affianced, and regarded Mary with attention.

The calm, sweet, elevated expression of her face struck her; it struck her also that *that* was not the light of any earthly love,—that it had no thrill, no blush, no tremor, but only the calmness of a soul that knows itself no more; and she sighed involuntarily

She looked at the Doctor, and seemed to study attentively a face which happiness made this morning as genial and attractive as it was generally strong and fine.

There was little said at the breakfast-table; and yet the loud singing of the birds, the brightness of the sunshine, the life and vigor of all things, seemed to make up for the silence of those who were too well pleased to speak.

"*Eh bien, ma chère*," said Madame, after breakfast, drawing Mary into her little room,—"*c'est donc fini?*"

"Yes," said Mary, cheerfully.

"Thou art content?" said Madame, passing her arm around her. "Well, then, I should be. But, Mary, it is like a marriage with the altar, like taking the veil, is it not?"

"No," said Mary; "it is not taking the veil; it is beginning a cheerful, reasonable life with a kind, noble friend, who will always love me truly, and whom I hope to make as happy as he deserves."

"I think well of him, my little cat," said Madame, reflectively; but she stopped something she was going to say, and kissed Mary's forehead. After a moment's pause, she added, "One must have love or refuge, Mary;— this is thy refuge, child; thou wilt have peace in it." She sighed again. "*Enfin*," she said, resuming her gay tone,

"what shall be *la toilette de noces?* Thou shalt
have Virginie's pearls, my fair one, and look like
a sea-born Venus. *Tiens*, let me try them in thy
hair."

And in a few moments she had Mary's long
hair down, and was chattering like a blackbird,
wreathing the pearls in and out, and saying a
thousand pretty little nothings, — weaving grace
and poetry upon the straight thread of Puritan
life.

CHAPTER XXIX.

BUSTLE IN THE PARISH.

THE announcement of the definite engagement of two such bright particular stars in the hemisphere of the Doctor's small parish excited the interest that such events usually create among the faithful of the flock.

There was a general rustle and flutter, as when a covey of wild pigeons has been started; and all the little elves who rejoice in the name of "says he" and "says I" and "do tell" and "have you heard" were speedily flying through the consecrated air of the parish.

The fact was discussed by matrons and maidens, at the spinning-wheel, in the green clothes-yard, and at the foamy wash-tub, out of which rose weekly a new birth of freshness and beauty. Many a rustic Venus of the foam, as she splashed her dimpled elbows in the rainbow-tinted froth, talked of what should be done for the forthcoming solemnities, and wondered what Mary would have on when she was married, and whether she

19

(the Venus) should get an invitation to the wedding, and whether Ethan would go, — not, of
course, that she cared in the least whether he did
or not.

Grave, elderly matrons talked about the prosperity of Zion, which they imagined intimately
connected with the event of their minister's marriage; and descending from Zion, speculated on
bed-quilts and table-cloths, and rummaged their
own clean, sweet-smelling stores, fragrant with
balm and rose-leaves, to lay out a bureau-cover,
or a pair of sheets, or a dozen napkins for the wedding outfit.

The solemnest of. solemn quiltings was resolved
upon. Miss Prissy declared that she fairly couldn't
sleep nights with the responsibility of the wedding-
dresses on her mind, but yet she must give one
day to getting on that quilt.

The *grand monde* also was in motion. Mrs.
General Wilcox called in her own particular carriage, bearing present of a Cashmere shawl for the
bride, with the General's best compliments, — also
an oak-leaf pattern for quilting, which had been
sent her from England, and which was authenti-
cally established to be that used on a petticoat
belonging to the Princess Royal. And Mrs. Major
Seaforth came also, bearing a scarf of wrought
India muslin; and Mrs. Vernon sent a splendid
China punch-bowl. Indeed, to say the truth, the

notables high and mighty of Newport, whom the Doctor had so unceremoniously accused of build ing their houses with blood and establishing their city with iniquity, considering that nobody seemed to take his words to heart, and that they were making money as fast as old Tyre, rather assumed the magnanimous, and patted themselves on the shoulder for this opportunity to show the Doctor that after all they were good fellows, though they did make money at the expense of thirty *per cent.* on human life.

Simeon Brown was the only exception. He stood aloof, grim and sarcastic, and informed some good middle-aged ladies who came to see if he would, as they phrased it, " esteem it a privilege to add his mite" to the Doctor's outfit, that he would give him a likely negro boy, if he wanted him, and, if he was too conscientious to keep him, he might sell him at a fair profit,— a happy stroke of humor which he was fond of relating many years after.

The quilting was in those days considered the most solemn and important recognition of a betrothal. And for the benefit of those not to the manner born, a little preliminary instruction may be necessary.

The good wives of New England, impressed with that thrifty orthodoxy of economy which forbids to waste the merest trifle, had a habit of saving every scrap clipped out in the fashioning of household garments, and these they cut into fanciful patterns and constructed of them rainbow shapes and quaint traceries, the arrangement of which became one of their few fine arts. Many a maiden, as she sorted and arranged fluttering bits of green, yellow, red, and blue, felt rising in her breast a passion for somewhat vague and unknown, which came out at length in a new pattern of patchwork. Collections of these tiny fragments were always ready to fill an hour when there was nothing else to do; and as the maiden chattered with her beau, her busy flying needle stitched together those pretty bits, which, little in themselves, were destined, by gradual unions and accretions, to bring about at last substantial beauty, warmth, and comfort,— emblems thus of that household life which is to be brought to stability and beauty by reverent economy in husbanding and tact in arranging the little useful and agreeable morsels of daily existence.

When a wedding was forthcoming, there was a solemn review of the stores of beauty and utility thus provided, and the patchwork-spread best worthy of such distinction was chosen for the quilting. Thereto, duly summoned, trooped all intimate female friends of the bride, old and young; and the quilt being spread on a frame, and wadded with cotton, each vied with the others in the

delicacy of the quilting she could put upon it.
For the quilting also was a fine art, and had its
delicacies and nice points, — which grave elderly
matrons discussed with judicious care. The quilting generally began at an early hour in the afternoon, and ended at dark with a great supper and
general jubilee, at which that ignorant and incapable sex which could not quilt was allowed to
appear and put in claims for consideration of
another nature. It may, perhaps, be surmised that
this expected reinforcement was often alluded to
by the younger maidens, whose wickedly coquet-
tish toilettes exhibited suspicious marks of that
willingness to get a chance to say " No " which
has been slanderously attributed to mischievous
maidens.

In consideration of the tremendous responsibilities involved in this quilting, the reader will not
be surprised to learn, that, the evening before, Miss
Prissy made her appearance at the brown cottage,
armed with thimble, scissors, and pincushion, in
order to relieve her mind by a little preliminary
confabulation.

" You see me, Miss Scudder, run 'most to
death," she said; " but I thought I would just
run up to Miss Major Seaforth's and see her best
bedroom quilt, 'cause I wanted to have all the
ideas we possibly could, before I decided on the
pattern. Her's is in shells, — just common shells, —

nothing to be compared with Miss Wilcox's oak-leaves; and I suppose there isn't the least doubt that Miss Wilcox's sister, in London, did get that from a lady who had a cousin who was governess in the royal family; and I just quilted a little bit to-day on an old piece of silk, and it comes out beautiful; and so I thought I would just come and ask you if you did not think it was best for us to have the oak-leaves."

"Well, certainly, Miss Prissy, if you think so," said Mrs. Scudder, who was as pliant to the opinions of this wise woman of the parish as New England matrons generally are to a reigning dressmaker and *factotum*.

Miss Prissy had the happy consciousness, always, that her early advent under any roof was considered a matter of especial grace; and therefore it was with rather a patronizing tone that she announced that she would stay and spend the night with them.

"I knew," she added, "that your spare chamber was full, with that Madame de ———, what do you call her? — if I was to die, I could not remember the woman's name. Well, I thought I could curl in with you, Mary, 'most anywhere."

"That's right, Miss Prissy," said Mary; "you shall be welcome to half my bed any time."

"Well, I knew you would say so, Mary; I never saw the thing you would not give away

one half of, since you was that high," said Miss
Prissy,— illustrating her words by placing her hand
about two feet from the floor.

Just at this moment, Madame de Frontignac
entered and asked Mary to come into her room
and give her advice as to a piece of embroidery.
When she was gone out, Miss Prissy looked after
her and sunk her voice once more to the confidential whisper which we before described.

"I have heard strange stories about that French
woman," she said; "but as she is here with you
and Mary, I suppose there cannot be any truth in
them. Dear me! the world is so censorious about
women! But then, you know, we don't expect
much from French women. I suppose she is a
Roman Catholic, and worships pictures and stone
images; but then, after all, she has got an immortal soul, and I can't help hoping Mary's influence may be blest to her. They say, when she
speaks French, she swears every few minutes; and
if that is the way she was brought up, may-be
she isn't accountable. I think we can't be too
charitable for people that a'n't privileged as we
are. Miss Vernon's Polly told me she had seen
her sew Sundays, — sew Sabbath-day! She came
into her room sudden, and she was working on
her embroidery there; and she never winked nor
blushed, nor offered to put it away, but sat there
just as easy! Polly said she never was so beat

in all her life; she felt kind o' scared, every time she thought of it. But now she has come here, who knows but she may be converted?"

"Mary has not said much about her state of mind," said Mrs. Scudder; "but something of deep interest has passed between them. Mary is such an uncommon child, that I trust everything to her."

We will not dwell further on the particulars of this evening, — nor describe how Madame de Frontignac reconnoitred Miss Prissy with keen, amused eyes, — nor how Miss Prissy assured Mary, in the confidential solitude of her chamber, that her fingers just itched to get hold of that trimming on Madame de Frog— something's dress, because she was pretty nigh sure she could make some just like it, for she never saw any trimming she could not make.

The robin that lived in the apple-tree was fairly outgeneralled the next morning; for Miss Prissy was up before him, tripping about the chamber on the points of her toes, knocking down all the movable things in the room, in her efforts to be still, so as not to wake Mary; and it was not until she had finally upset the stand by the bed, with the candlestick, snuffers, and Bible on it, that Mary opened her eyes.

"Miss Prissy! dear me! what is it you are doing?"

"Why, I am trying to be still, Mary, so as not to wake you up; and it seems to me as if everything was possessed, to tumble down so. But it is only half past three, — so you turn over and go to sleep."

"But, Miss Prissy," said Mary, sitting up in bed, "you are all dressed; where are you going?"

"Well, to tell the truth, Mary, I am just one of those people that can't sleep when they have got responsibility on their minds; and I have been lying awake more than an hour here, thinking about that quilt. There is a new way of getting it on to the frame that I want to try; 'cause, you know, when we quilted Cerinthy Stebbins's, it *would* trouble us in the rolling; and I have got a new way that I want to try, and I mean just to get it on to the frame before breakfast. I was in hopes I should get out without waking any of you. I am in hopes I shall get by your mother's door without waking her, — 'cause I know she works hard and needs her rest, — but that bedroom door squeaks like a cat, enough to raise the dead!

"Mary," she added, with sudden energy, "If I had the least drop of oil in a teacup, and a bit of quill, I'd stop that door making such a noise." And Miss Prissy's eyes glowed with resolution.

"I don't know where you could find any at this time," said Mary.

"Well, never mind; I'll just go and open the door as slow and careful as I can," said Miss Prissy, as she trotted out of the apartment.

The result of her carefulness was very soon announced to Mary by a protracted sound resembling the mewing of a hoarse cat, accompanied by sundry audible grunts from Miss Prissy, terminating in a grand finale of clatter, occasioned by her knocking down all the pieces of the quilting-frame that stood in the corner of the room, with a concussion that roused everybody in the house.

"What is that?" called out Mrs. Scudder, from her bedroom.

She was answered by two streams of laughter, —one from Mary, sitting up in bed, and the other from Miss Prissy, holding her sides, as she sat dissolved in merriment on the sanded floor.

CHAPTER XXX.

THE QUILTING.

By six o'clock in the morning, Miss Prissy came out of the best room to the breakfast-table, with the air of a general who has arranged a campaign, — her face glowing with satisfaction. All sat down together to their morning meal. The outside door was open into the green, turfy yard, and the apple-tree, now nursing stores of fine yellow jeannetons, looked in at the window. Every once in a while, as a breeze shook the leaves, a fully ripe apple might be heard falling to the ground, at which Miss Prissy would bustle up from the table and rush to secure the treasure.

As the meal waned to its close, the rattling of wheels was heard at the gate, and Candace was discerned, seated aloft in the one-horse wagon, with her usual complement of baskets and bags.

" Well, now, dear me! if there isn't Candace!" said Miss Prissy; "I do believe Miss Marvyn has sent her with something for the quilting!" and out she flew as nimble as a humming-bird, while those in the house heard various exclamations of admiration, as Candace, with stately dignity, disinterred from the wagon one basket after another, and exhibited to Miss Prissy's enraptured eyes sly peeps under the white napkins with which they were covered. And then, hanging a large basket on either arm, she rolled majestically towards the house, like a heavy-laden Indiaman, coming in after a fast voyage.

"Good-mornin', Miss Scudder! good-mornin', Doctor!" she said, dropping her curtsy on the door-step; "good-mornin', Miss Mary! Ye see our folks was stirrin' pootty early dis mornin', an' Miss Marvyn sent me down wid two or tree little tings."

Setting down her baskets on the floor, and seating herself between them, she proceeded to develop their contents with ill-concealed triumph. One basket was devoted to cakes of every species, from the great Mont-Blanc loaf-cake, with its snowy glaciers of frosting, to the twisted cruller and puffy doughnut. In the other basket lay pots of golden butter curiously stamped, reposing on a bed of fresh, green leaves,—while currants, red and white, and delicious cherries and raspberries, gave a final finish to the picture. From a basket which Miss Prissy brought in from the rear appeared cold fowl and tongue delicately prepared, and shaded with feathers of parsley. Candace, whose rollicking delight in the good things of this life was conspicuous in every emotion, might have furnished to a painter, as she sat in her brilliant turban, an idea for an African Genius of Plenty.

" Why, really, Candace," said Mrs. Scudder, " you are overwhelming us!"

" Ho! ho! ho!" said Candace, " I's tellin' Miss Marvyn folks don't git married but once in der lives, (gin'ally speakin', dat is,) an' den dey oughter hab plenty to do it wid."

" Well, I must say," said Miss Prissy, taking out the loaf-cake with busy assiduity, — " I must say, Candace, this does beat all!"

" I should rader tink it oughter," said Candace, bridling herself with proud consciousness; " ef it don't, 'ta'n't 'cause ole Candace ha'n't put enough into it. I tell ye, I didn't do nothin' all day yisterday but jes' make dat ar cake. Cato, when he got up, he begun to talk someh'n' 'bout his shirt-buttons, an' I jes' shet him right up. Says I, ' Cato, when I's r'ally got cake to make for a great 'casion, I wants my mind *jest* as quiet an' *jest* as serene as ef I was a-goin' to de sacra-ment. I don't want no 'arthly cares on't. Now,' says I, ' Cato, de ole Doctor's gwine to be mar-ried, an' dis yer's his quiltin'-cake, — an' Miss Mary, she's gwine to be married, an' dis yer's *her* quiltin'-cake. An' dar'll be eberybody to dat ar quiltin'; an' ef de cake a'n't right, why, 'twould be puttin' a candle under a bushel. An' so,' says I, ' Cato, your buttons mus' wait.' An' Cato, he sees de 'priety ob it, 'cause, dough he can't make cake like me, he's a 'mazin' good judge on't, an' is dre'ful tickled when I slips out a little loaf for his supper."

"How is Mrs. Marvyn?" said Mrs. Scudder.

"Kinder thin and shimmery; but she's about, —habin' her eyes eberywar 'n' lookin' into eberyting. She jes' touches tings wid de tips ob her fingers an' dey seem to go like. She'll be down to de quiltin' dis arternoon. But she tole me to take de tings an' come down an' spen' de day here; for Miss Marvyn an' I both knows how many steps mus' be taken sech times, an' we agreed you oughter favor yourselves all you could."

"Well, now," said Miss Prissy, lifting up her hands, "if that a'n't what 'tis to have friends! Why, that was one of the things I was thinking of, as I lay awake last night; because, you know, at times like these, people run their feet off before the time begins, and then they are all limpsey and lop-sided when the time comes. Now, I say, Candace, all Miss Scudder and Mary have to do is to give everything up to us, and we'll put it through straight."

"Dat's what we will!" said Candace. "Jes' show me what's to be done, an' I'll do it."

Candace and Miss Prissy soon disappeared to

gether into the pantry with the baskets, whose contents they began busily to arrange. Candace shut the door, that no sound might escape, and began a confidential outpouring to Miss Prissy.

" Ye see," she said, " I's *feelin's* all de while for Miss Marvyn; 'cause, ye see, she was expectin', ef eber Mary was married, — well — dat 'twould be to somebody else, ye know."

Miss Prissy responded with a sympathetic groan.

" Well," said Candace, " ef 't had ben anybody but de Doctor, *I* wouldn't 'a' been resigned. But arter all he has done for my color, dar a'n't nothin' I could find it in my heart to grudge him. But den I was tellin' Cato t'oder day, says I, ' Cato, I dunno 'bout de rest o' de world, but I ha'n't neber felt it in my bones dat Mass'r James is r'ally dead, for sartin.' Now I feels tings *gin'-ally*, but *some* tings I feels *in my bones*, and dem allers comes true. And dat ar's a feelin' I ha'n't had 'bout Mass'r Jim yit, an' dat ar's what I'm waitin' for 'fore I clar make up my mind. Though I know, 'cordin' to all white folks' way o' tinkin', dar a'n't no hope, 'cause Squire Marvyn he had dat ar Jeduth Pettibone up to his house, a-questionin' on him, off an' on, nigh about tree hours. An' r'ally I didn't see no hope no way, 'xcept jes' dis yer, as I was tellin' Cato, — *I can't feel it in my bones*."

Candace was not versed enough in the wisdom

of the world to know that she belonged to a large and respectable school of philosophers in this particular mode of testing evidence, which, after all, the reader will perceive has its conveniences.

"Anoder ting," said Candace, "as much as a dozen times, dis yer last year, when I's been a-scourin' knives, a fork has fell an' stuck straight up in de floor; an' de las' time I pinted it out to Miss Marvyn, an' she on'y jes' said, ' Why, what o' dat, Candace?'"

"Well," said Miss Prissy, "I don't believe in *signs*, but then strange things do happen. Now about dogs howling under windows, — why, I don't believe in it a bit, but I never knew it fail that there was a death in the house after."

"Ah, I tell ye what," said Candace, looking mysterious, " dogs knows a heap more'n dey likes to tell!"

"Jes' so," said Miss Prissy. " Now I remember, one night, when I was watching with Miss Colonel Andrews, after Marthy Ann was born, that we heard the *mournfulest* howling that ever you did hear. It seemed to come from right under the front stoop; and Miss Andrews she just dropped the spoon in her gruel, and says she, ' Miss Prissy, do, for pity's sake, just go down and see what that noise is.' And I went down and lifted up one of the loose boards of the stoop, and what should I see there but their Newfoundland pup? — there that creature had dug a grave and was a-sitting by it, crying!"

Candace drew near to Miss Prissy, dark with expressive interest, as her voice, in this awful narration, sank to a whisper.

"Well," said Candace, after Miss Prissy had made something of a pause.

"Well, I told Miss Andrews I didn't think there was anything in it," said Miss Prissy; "but," she added, impressively, "she lost a very dear brother, six months after, and I laid him out with my own hands, — yes, laid him out in white flannel."

"Some folks say," said Candace, "dat dreamin' 'bout white horses is a sartin sign. Jinny Styles is berry strong 'bout dat. Now she come down one mornin' cryin', 'cause she'd been dreamin' 'bout white horses, an' she was sure she should hear some friend was dead. An' sure enough, a man come in dat bery day an' tole her her son was drownded out in de harbor. An' Jinny said, 'Dar! she was sure dat sign neber would fail.' But den, ye see, dat night he come home. Jinny wa'n't r'ally disappinted, but she allers insisted he was *as good as drownded*, any way, 'cause he sunk tree times."

"Well, I tell you," said Miss Prissy, "there are a great many more things in this world than folks know about."

"So dey are," said Candace. "Now, I ha'n't

neber opened my mind to nobody; but dar's a dream I's had, tree mornin's runnin', lately. I dreamed I see Jim Marvyn a-sinkin' in de water, an' stretchin' up his hands. An' den I dreamed I see de Lord Jesus come a-walkin' on de water an' take hold ob his hand, an' says he, ' O thou of little faith, wherefore didst thou doubt?' An' den he lifted him right out. An' I ha'n't said nothin' to nobody, 'cause, you know, de Doctor, he says people mus'n't mind nothin' 'bout der dreams, 'cause dreams belongs to de ole 'spensation."

" Well, well, well!" said Miss Prissy, "I am sure I don't know what to think. What time in the morning was it that you dreamed it?"

" Why," said Candace, "it was jest arter bird-peep. I kinder allers wakes myself den, an' turns ober, an' what comes arter dat is apt to run clar."

" Well, well, well!" said Miss Prissy, "I don't know what to think. You see, it may have reference to the state of his soul."

" I know dat," said Candace; "but as nigh as I could judge in my dream," she added, sinking her voice and looking mysterious, " as nigh as I can judge, *dat boy's soul was in his body!*"

" Why, how do you know?" said Miss Prissy, looking astonished at the confidence with which Candace expressed her opinion.

" Well, ye see," said Candace, rather mysteriously, " de Doctor, he don't like to hab us talk much 'bout dese yer tings, 'cause he tinks it's kind o' heathenish. But den, folks as is used to seein' sech tings knows de look ob a sperit *out* o' de body from de look ob a sperit *in* de body, jest as easy as you can tell Mary from de Doctor."

At this moment Mrs. Scudder opened the pantry-door and put an end to this mysterious conversation, which had already so affected Miss Prissy, that, in the eagerness of her interest, she had rubbed up her cap border and ribbon into rather an elfin and goblin style, as if they had been ruffled up by a breeze from the land of spirits; and she flew around for a few moments in a state of great nervous agitation, upsetting dishes, knocking down plates, and huddling up contrary suggestions as to what ought to be done first, in such impossible relations that Mrs. Katy Scudder stood in dignified surprise at this strange freak of conduct in the wise woman of the parish.

A dim consciousness of something not quite canny in herself seemed to strike her, for she made a vigorous effort to appear composed; and facing Mrs. Scudder, with an air of dignified suavity, inquired if it would not be best to put Jim Marvyn in the oven now, while Candace was getting the pies ready,—meaning, of course, a large turkey. which was to be the first in an indefinite series to be baked that morning; and discovering, by Mrs.

Scudder's dazed expression and a vigorous pinch from Candace, that somehow she had not improved matters, she rubbed her spectacles into a diagonal position across her eyes, and stood glaring, half through, half over them, with a helpless expression, which in a less judicious person might have suggested the idea of a state of slight' intoxication.

But the exigencies of an immediate temporal dispensation put an end to Miss Prissy's unwonted vagaries, and she was soon to be seen flying round like a meteor, dusting, shaking curtains, counting napkins, wiping and sorting china, all with such rapidity as to give rise to the notion that she actually existed in forty places at once.

Candace, whom the limits of her corporeal frame restricted to an altogether different style of locomotion, often rolled the whites of her eyes after her and gave vent to her views of her proceedings in sententious expressions.

"Do you know why *dat ar* neber was married?" she said to Mary, as she stood looking after her. Miss Prissy had made one of those rapid transits through the apartment.

"No," answered Mary, innocently. "Why wasn't she?"

"'Cause neber was a man could run fast enough to cotch her," said Candace; and then her portly person shook with the impulse of her own wit.

By two o'clock a goodly company began to assemble. Mrs. Deacon Twitchel arrived, soft, pillowy, and plaintive as ever, accompanied by Cerinthy Ann, a comely damsel, tall and trim, with a bright black eye, and a most vigorous and determined style of movement. Good Mrs. Jones, broad, expansive, and solid, having vegetated tranquilly on in the cabbage-garden of the virtues since three years ago, when she graced our tea-party, was now as well preserved as ever, and brought some fresh butter, a tin pail of cream, and a loaf of cake made after a new Philadelphia receipt. The tall, spare, angular figure of Mrs. Simeon Brown alone was wanting; but she patronized Mrs. Scudder no more, and tossed her head with a becoming pride when her name was mentioned.

The quilt-pattern was gloriously drawn in oak-leaves, done in indigo; and soon all the company, young and old, were passing busy fingers over it and conversation went on briskly.

Madame de Frontignac, we must not forget to say, had entered with hearty *abandon* into the spirit of the day. She had dressed the tall china vases on the mantel-pieces, and, departing from the usual rule of an equal mixture of roses and asparagus-bushes, had constructed two quaint and graceful bouquets, where garden-flowers were mingled with drooping grasses and trailing wild vines, forming a graceful combination which excited the surprise of all who saw it.

"It's the very first time in my life that I ever saw grass put into a flower-pot," said Miss Prissy; "but I must say it looks as handsome as a picture. Mary, I must say," she added, in an aside, "I think that Madame de Frongenac is the sweetest dressing and appearing creature I ever saw; she don't dress up nor put on airs, but she seems to see in a minute how things ought to go; and if it's only a bit of grass, or leaf, or wild vine, that she puts in her hair, why, it seems to come just right. I should like to make her a dress, for I know she would understand my fit; do speak to her, Mary, in case she should want a dress fitted here, to let me try it."

At the quilting, Madame de Frontignac would have her seat, and soon won the respect of the party by the dexterity with which she used her needle; though, when it was whispered that she learned to quilt among the nuns, some of the elderly ladies exhibited a slight uneasiness, as being rather doubtful whether they might not be encouraging Papistical opinions by allowing her an equal share in the work of getting up their minister's bed-quilt; but the younger part of the company were quite captivated by her foreign air, and the pretty manner in which she lisped her English; and Cerinthy Ann even went so far as to horrify her mother by saying that she wished she'd been educated in a convent herself,—a declaration which arose less from native depravity than from a certain vigorous disposition, which often shows itself in young people, to shock the current opinions of their elders and betters. Of course, the conversation took a general turn, somewhat in unison with the spirit of the occasion; and whenever it flagged, some allusion to a forthcoming wedding, or some sly hint at the future young Madame of the parish, was sufficient to awaken the dormant animation of the company.

Cerinthy Ann contrived to produce an agreeable electric shock by declaring, that, for her part, she never could see into it, how any girl could marry a minister,—that she should as soon think of setting up housekeeping in a meeting-house.

"Oh, Cerinthy Ann!" exclaimed her mother, "how can you go on so?"

"It's a fact," said the adventurous damsel; "now other men let you have some peace,—but a minister's always round under your feet."

"So you think, the less you see of a husband, the better?" said one of the ladies.

"Just my views," said Cerinthy, giving a decided snip to her thread with her scissors; "I like the Nantucketers, that go off on four-years' voyages, and leave their wives a clear field. If ever I get married, I'm going up to have one of those fellows."

It is to be remarked, in passing, that Miss Cerinthy Ann was at this very time receiving surreptitious visits from a consumptive-looking, conscientious, young theological candidate, who came
occasionally to preach in the vicinity, and put up
at the house of the Deacon, her father. This good
young man, being violently attacked on the doctrine of Election by Miss Cerinthy, had been
drawn on to illustrate it in a most practical manner, to her comprehension; and it was the consciousness of the weak and tottering state of the
internal garrison that added vigor to the young
lady's tones. As Mary had been the chosen confidante of the progress of this affair, she was
quietly amused at the demonstration.

"You'd better take care, Cerinthy Ann," said
her mother; "they say that 'those who sing before breakfast will cry before supper.' Girls talk
about getting married," she said, relapsing into a
gentle didactic melancholy, "without realizing its
awful responsibilities."

"Oh, as to that," said Cerinthy, "I've been practising on my pudding now these six years, and I
shouldn't be afraid to throw one up chimney with
any girl."

This speech was founded on a tradition, current
in those times, that no young lady was fit to be
married till she could construct a boiled Indian-
pudding of such consistency that it could be

thrown up chimney and come down on the ground, outside, without breaking; and the consequence of Cerinthy Ann's sally was a general laugh.

"Girls a'n't what they used to be in my day," sententiously remarked an elderly lady. "I remember my mother told me when she was thirteen she could knit a long cotton stocking in a day."

"I haven't much faith in these stories of old times,— have you, girls?" said Cerinthy, appealing to the younger members at the frame.

"At any rate," said Mrs. Twitchel, "our minister's wife will be a pattern; I don't know anybody that goes beyond her either in spinning or fine stitching."

Mary sat as placid and disengaged as the new moon, and listened to the chatter of old and young with the easy quietness of a young heart that has early outlived life, and looks on everything in the world from some gentle, restful eminence far on towards a better home. She smiled at everybody's word, had a quick eye for everybody's wants, and was ready with thimble, scissors, or thread, whenever any one needed them; but once, when there was a pause in the conversation, she and Mrs. Marvyn were both discovered to have stolen away. They were seated on the bed in Mary's little room, with their arms

20

around each other, communing in low and gentle
tones.

"Mary, my dear child," said her friend, "this
event is very pleasant to me, because it places
you permanently near me. I did not know but
eventually this sweet face might lead to my losing
you, who are in some respects the dearest friend
I have."

"You might be sure," said Mary, "I never
would have married, except that my mother's happiness and the happiness of so good a friend
seemed to depend on it. When we renounce self
in anything, we have reason to hope for God's
blessing; and so I feel assured of a peaceful life
in the course I have taken. You will always be
as a mother to me," she added, laying her head
on her friend's shoulder.

"Yes," said Mrs. Marvyn; "and I must not let
myself think a moment how dear it might have
been to have you *more* my own. If you feel really, truly happy, — if you can enter on this life
without any misgivings —— "

"I can," said Mary, firmly.

At this instant, very strangely, the string which
confined a wreath of sea-shells around her glass,
having been long undermined by moths, suddenly
broke and fell down, scattering the shells upon the
floor.

Both women started, for the string of shells had

been placed there by James; and though neither was superstitious, this was one of those odd coincidences that make hearts throb.

"Dear boy!" said Mary, gathering the shells up tenderly; "wherever he is, I shall never cease to love him. It makes me feel sad to see this come down; but it is only an accident; nothing of him will ever fail out of my heart."

Mrs. Marvyn clasped Mary closer to her, with tears in her eyes.

"I'll tell you what, Mary; it must have been the moths did that," said Miss Prissy, who had been standing, unobserved, at the door for a moment back; "moths will eat away strings just so. Last week Miss Vernon's great family-picture fell down because the moths eat through the cord; people ought to use twine or cotton string always. But I came to tell you that the supper is all set, and the Doctor out of his study, and all the people are wondering where you are."

Mary and Mrs. Marvyn gave a hasty glance at themselves in the glass, to be assured of their good keeping, and went into the great kitchen, where a ong table stood exhibiting all that plenitude of provision which the immortal description of Washington Irving has saved us the trouble of recapitulating in detail.

The husbands, brothers, and lovers had come in, and the scene was redolent of gayety. When

Mary made her appearance, there was a moment's pause, till she was conducted to the side of the Doctor; when, raising his hand, he invoked a grace upon the loaded board.

Unrestrained gayeties followed. Groups of young men and maidens chatted together, and all the gallantries of the times were enacted. Serious matrons commented on the cake, and told each other high and particular secrets in the culinary art, which they drew from remote family-archives. One might have learned in that instructive assembly how best to keep moths out of blankets, — how to make fritters of Indian corn undistinguishable from oysters, — how to bring up babies by hand, — how to mend a cracked teapot, — how to take out grease from a brocade, — how to reconcile absolute decrees with free will, how to make five yards of cloth answer the purpose of six, — and how to put down the Democratic party. All were busy, earnest, and certain, — just as a swarm of men and women, old and young, are in 1859.

Miss Prissy was in her glory; every bow of her best cap was alive with excitement, and she presented to the eyes of the astonished Newport gentry an animated receipt-book. Some of the information she communicated, indeed, was so valuable and important that she could not trust the air with it, but whispered the most important portions in a confidential tone. Among the crowd, Cerin-

thy Ann's theological admirer was observed in
deeply reflective attitude ; and that high-spirited
young lady added further to his convictions of the
total depravity of the species by vexing and dis-
composing him in those thousand ways in which
a lively, ill-conditioned young woman will put to
rout a serious, well-disposed young man,—comforting herself with the reflection, that by-and-by
she would repent of all her sins in a lump together.

Vain, transitory splendors ! Even this evening,
so glorious, so heart-cheering, so fruitful in instruction and amusement, could not last forever. Gradually the company broke up; the matrons mount-
ed soberly on horseback behind their spouses ; and
Cerinthy consoled her clerical friend by giving him
an opportunity to read her a lecture on the way
home, if he found the courage to do so.

Mr. and Mrs. Marvyn and Candace wound their
way soberly homeward; the Doctor returned to his
study for nightly devotions ; and before long, sleep
settled down on the brown cottage.

"I'll tell you what, Cato," said Candace, before
composing herself to sleep, "I can't feel it in my
bones dat dis yer weddin's gwine to come off yit."

CHAPTER XXXI.

AN ADVENTURE.

A DAY or two after, Madame de Frontignac and Mary went out to gather shells and seaweed on the beach. It was four o'clock; and the afternoon sun was hanging in the sultry sky of July with a hot and vaporous stillness. The whole air was full of blue haze, that softened the outlines of objects without hiding them. The sea lay like so much glass; every ship and boat was double; every line and rope and spar had its counterpart; and it seemed hard to say which was the more real, the under or the upper world.

Madame de Frontignac and Mary had brought a little basket with them, which they were filling with shells and sea-mosses. The former was in high spirits. She ran, and shouted, and exclaimed, and wondered at each new marvel thrown out upon the shore, with the *abandon* of a little child. Mary could not but wonder whether this indeed were she whose strong words had pierced and wrung her sympathies the other night, and whether a deep life-wound could lie bleeding under those brilliant eyes and that infantine exuberance of gayety ; yet, surely, all that which seemed so strong, so true, so real could not be gone so soon, —and it could not be so soon consoled. Mary wondered at her, as the Anglo-Saxon constitution, with its strong, firm intensity, its singleness of nature, wonders at the mobile, many-sided existence of warmer races, whose versatility of emotion on the surface is not incompatible with the most intense persistency lower down.

Mary's was one of those indulgent and tolerant natures which seem to form the most favorable base for the play of other minds, rather than to be itself salient,— and something about her tender calmness always seemed to provoke the spirit of frolic in her friend. She would laugh at her, kiss her, gambol round her, dress her hair with fantastic coiffures, and call her all sorts of fanciful and poetic names in French or English, — while Mary surveyed her with a pleased and innocent surprise, as a revelation of character altogether new and different from anything to which she had been hitherto accustomed. She was to her a living pantomime, and brought into her unembellished life the charms of opera and theatre and romance.

After wearying themselves with their researches, they climbed round a point of rock that stretched some way out into the sea, and attained to a lit-

tle kind of grotto, where the high cliffs shut out
the rays of the sun. They sat down to rest upon
the rocks. A fresh breeze of declining day was
springing up, and bringing the rising tide landward,—each several line of waves with its white
crests coming up and breaking gracefully on the
hard, sparkling sand-beach at their feet.

Mary's eyes fixed themselves, as they were apt
to do, in a mournful reverie, on the infinite ex-
panse of waters, which was now broken and
chopped into a thousand incoming waves by the
fresh afternoon breeze. Madame de Frontignac
noticed the expression, and began to play with
her as if she had been a child. She pulled the
comb from her hair, and let down its long silky
waves upon her shoulders.

"Now," said she, "let us make a Miranda of
thee. This is our cave. I will be Prince Ferdinand. Burr told me all about that,—he reads
beautifully, and explained it all to me. What a
lovely story that is!—you must be so happy, who
know how to read Shakspeare without learning!
Tenez! I will put this shell on your forehead,—
it has a hole here, and I will pass this gold chain
through,—now! What a pity this seaweed will
not be pretty out of water! it has no effect; but
there is some green that will do;—let me fasten
it so. Now, fair Miranda, look at thyself!"

Where is the girl so angelic as not to feel a

slight curiosity to know how she shall look in a new and strange costume? Mary bent over the rock, where a little pool of water lay in a brown hollow above the fluctuations of the tide, dark and still, like a mirror,—and saw a fair face, with a white shell above the forehead and drooping wreaths of green seaweed in the silken hair; and a faint blush and smile rose on the cheek, giving the last finish to the picture.

"How do you find yourself?" said Madame. "Confess now that I have a true talent in coiffure. Now I will be Ferdinand."

She turned quickly, and her eye was caught by something that Mary did not see; she only saw the smile fade suddenly from Madame de Frontignac's cheek, and her lips grow deadly white, while her heart beat so that Mary could discern its flutterings under her black silk bodice.

"Will the sea-nymphs punish the rash presumption of a mortal who intrudes?" said Colonel Burr, stepping before them with a grace as invincible and assured as if he had never had any past history with either.

Mary started with a guilty blush, like a child detected in an unseemly frolic, and put her hand to her head to take off the unwonted adornments.

"Let me protest, in the name of the Graces," said Burr, who by that time stood with easy calmness at her side; and as he spoke, he stayed her hand with that gentle air of authority which made it the natural impulse of most people to obey him. "It would be treason against the picturesque," he added, "to spoil that toilette, so charmingly unit ing the wearer to the scene."

Mary was taken by surprise, and discomposed as every one is who finds himself masquerading in attire foreign to his usual habits and character; and therefore, when she would persist in taking it to pieces, Burr found sufficient to alleviate the embarrassment of Madame de Frontignac's utter silence in a playful run of protestations and compliments.

"I think, Mary," said Madame de Frontignac, "that we had better be returning to the house."

This was said in the haughtiest and coolest tone imaginable, looking at the place where Burr stood, as if there were nothing there but empty air. Mary rose to go; Madame de Frontignac offered her arm.

"Permit me to remark, ladies," said Burr, with the quiet suavity which never forsook him, "that your very agreeable occupations have caused time to pass more rapidly than you are aware. I think you will find that the tide has risen so as to in-tercept the path by which you came here. You will hardly be able to get around the point of rocks without some assistance."

Mary looked a few paces ahead, and saw, a

little before them, a fresh afternoon breeze driving the rising tide high on to the side of the rocks, at whose foot their course had lain. The nook in which they had been sporting formed part of a shelving ledge which inclined over their heads, and which it was just barely possible could be climbed by a strong and agile person, but which would be wholly impracticable to a frail, unaided woman.

" There is no time to be lost," said Burr, coolly, measuring the possibilities with that keen eye that was never discomposed by any exigency. " I am at your service, ladies; I can either carry you in my arms around this point, or assist you up these rocks."

He paused and waited for their answer.

Madame de Frontignac stood pale, cold, and silent, hearing only the wild beating of her heart.

" I think," said Mary, " that we should try the rocks."

" Very well," said Burr; and placing his gloved hand on a fragment of rock somewhat above their heads, he swung himself up to it with an easy agility; from this he stretched himself down as far as possible towards them, and, extending his hand, directed Mary, who stood foremost, to set her foot on a slight projection, and give him both her hands; she did so, and he seemed to draw her up as easily as if she had been a feather. He placed her by him on a shelf of rock, and turned again to Madame de Frontignac; she folded her arms and turned resolutely away towards the sea.

Just at that moment a coming wave broke at her feet.

" There is no time to be lost," said Burr; "there's a tremendous surf coming in, and the next wave may carry you out."

" *Tant mieux!*" she responded, without turning her head.

" Oh, Virginie! Virginie!" exclaimed Mary, kneeling and stretching her arms over the rock; but another voice called Virginie, in a tone which went to her heart. She turned and saw those dark eyes full of tears.

" Oh, come!" he said, with that voice which she never could resist.

She put her cold, trembling hands into his, and he drew her up and placed her safely beside Mary. A few moments of difficult climbing followed, in which his arm was thrown now around one and then around the other, and they felt themselves carried with a force as if the slight and graceful form were strung with steel.

Placed in safety on the top of the bank, there was a natural gush of grateful feeling towards their deliverer. The severest resentment, the coolest moral disapprobation, are necessarily somewhat softened, when the object of them has just laid one under a personal obligation.

Burr did not seem disposed to press his advantage, and treated the incident as the most matter-of-course affair in the world. He offered an arm to each lady, with the air of a well-bred gentleman who offers a necessary support; and each took it, because neither wished, under the circumstances, to refuse.

He walked along leisurely homeward, talking in that easy, quiet, natural way in which he excelled, addressing no very particular remark to either one, and at the door of the cottage took his leave, saying, as he bowed, that he hoped neither of them would feel any inconvenience from their exertions, and that he should do himself the pleasure to call soon and inquire after their health.

Madame de Frontignac made no reply; but curtsied with a stately grace, turned and went into her little room, whither Mary, after a few minutes, followed her.

She found her thrown upon the bed, her face buried in the pillow, her breast heaving as if she were sobbing; but when, at Mary's entrance, she raised her head, her eyes were bright and dry.

"It is just as I told you, Mary,—that man holds me. I love him yet, in spite of myself. It is in vain to be angry. What is the use of striking your right hand with your left? When we *love* one more than ourselves, we only hurt ourselves with our anger."

"But," said Mary, "love is founded on respect and esteem; and when that is gone"——

"Why, then," said Madame, "we are very sorry, —but we love yet. Do we stop loving ourselves when we have lost our own self-respect? No! it is so disagreeable to see, we shut our eyes and ask to have the bandage put on,—you know *that*, poor little heart! You can think how it would have been with you, if you had found that *he* was not what you thought."

The word struck home to Mary's consciousness, —but she sat down and took her friend in her arms with an air self-controlled, serious, rational.

"I see and feel it all, dear Virginie, but I must stand firm for you. You are in the waves, and I on the shore. If you are so weak at heart, you must not see this man any more."

"But he will call."

"I will see him for you."

"What will you tell him, my heart?—tell him that I am ill, perhaps?"

"No; I will tell him the truth,—that you do not wish to see him."

"That is hard;—he will wonder."

"I think not," said Mary, resolutely; "and furthermore, I shall say to him, that, while Madame de Frontignac is at the cottage, it will not be agreeable for us to receive calls from him."

"Mary, *ma chère*, you astonish me!"

"My dear friend," said Mary, "it is the only way. This man—this cruel, wicked, deceitful man —must not be allowed to trifle with you in this way. I will protect you."

And she rose up with flashing eye and glowing cheek, looking as her father looked when he protested against the slave-trade.

"Thou art my Saint Catharine," said Virginie, rising up, excited by Mary's enthusiam, "and hast the sword as well as the palm; but, dear saint, don't think so very, very badly of him;—he has a noble nature; he has the angel in him."

"The greater his sin," said Mary; "he sins against light and love."

"But I think his heart is touched,—I think he is sorry. Oh, Mary, if you had only seen how he looked at me when he put out his hands on the rocks!—there were tears in his eyes."

"Well there might be!" said Mary; "I do not think he is quite a fiend; no one could look at those cheeks, dear Virginie, and not feel sad, that saw you a few months ago."

"Am I so changed?" she said, rising and looking at herself in the mirror. "Sure enough,—my neck used to be quite round;—now you can see those two little bones, like rocks at low tide. Poor Virginie! her summer is gone, and the leaves are falling; poor little cat!"—and Virginie stroked her own chestnut head, as if she had been pitying

another, and began humming a little Norman air
with a refrain that sounded like the murmur of a
brook over the stones.

The more Mary was touched by these little
poetic ways, which ran just on an even line between the gay and the pathetic, the more indignant she grew with the man that had brought all
this sorrow. She felt a saintly vindictiveness, and
a determination to place herself as an adamantine
shield between him and her friend. There is no
courage and no anger like that of a gentle woman,
when once fully roused; if ever you have occasion
to meet it, you will certainly remember the hour.

CHAPTER XXXII.

PLAIN TALK.

MARY revolved the affairs of her friend in her mind, during the night. The intensity of the mental crisis through which she had herself just passed had developed her in many inward respects, so that she looked upon life no longer as a timid girl, but as a strong, experienced woman. She had thought, and suffered, and held converse with eternal realities, until thousands of mere earthly hesitations and timidities, that often restrain a young and untried nature, had entirely lost their hold upon her. Besides, Mary had at heart the true Puritan seed of heroism,—never absent from the souls of true New England women. Her essentially Hebrew education, trained in daily converse with the words of prophets and seers, and with the modes of thought of a people essentially grave and heroic, predisposed her to a kind of exaltation, which, in times of great trial, might rise to the heights of the religious-sublime, in which the impulse of self-devotion took a form essentially commanding. The very intensity of the repression under which her faculties had developed seemed, as it were, to produce a surplus of hidden strength, which came out in exigencies. Her reading, though restricted to a few volumes, had been of the kind that vitalized and stimulated a poetic nature, and laid up in its chambers vigorous words and trenchant phrases, for the use of an excited feeling,— so that eloquence came to her as a native gift. She realized, in short, in her higher hours, the last touch with which Milton finishes his portrait of an ideal woman:—

> " Greatness of mind and nobleness their seat
> Build in her loftiest, and create an awe
> About her as a guard angelic placed."

The next morning, Colonel Burr called at the cottage. Mary was spinning in the garret, and Madame de Frontignac was reeling yarn, when Mrs. Scudder brought this announcement.

" Mother," said Mary, " I wish to see Mr. Burr alone. Madame de Frontignac will not go down."

Mrs. Scudder looked surprised, but asked no questions. When she was gone down, Mary stood a moment reflecting; Madame de Frontignac looked eager and agitated.

" Remember and notice all he says, and just how he looks, Mary, so as to tell me; and be sure and say that I thank him for his kindness yesterday. We must own, he appeared very well there; did he not?"

"Certainly," said Mary; "but no man could have done less."

"Ah! but, Mary, not every man could have done it *as* he did. Now don't be too hard on him, Mary;—I have said dreadful things to him; I am afraid I have been too severe. After all, these distinguished men are so tempted! we don't know how much they are tempted; and who can wonder that they are a little spoiled? So, my angel, you must be merciful."

"Merciful!" said Mary, kissing the pale cheek, and feeling the cold little hands that trembled in hers.

"So you will go down in your little spinning-toilette, *mimi?* I fancy you look as Joan of Arc did, when she was keeping her sheep at Domremy. Go, and God bless thee!" and Madame de Frontignac pushed her playfully forward.

Mary entered the room where Burr was seated, and wished him good-morning, in a serious and placid manner, in which there was not the slightest trace of embarrassment or discomposure.

"Shall I have the pleasure of seeing your fair companion this morning?" said Burr, after some moments of indifferent conversation.

"No, Sir; Madame de Frontignac desires me to excuse ho to you."

"Is she ill?" said Burr, with a look of concern.

"No, Mr. Burr, she prefers not to see you."

Burr gave a start of well-bred surprise, and Mary added, —

"Madame de Frontignac has made me familiar with the history of your acquaintance with her; and you will therefore understand what I mean, Mr. Burr, when I say, that, during the time of her stay with us, we should prefer not to receive calls from you."

"Your language, Miss Scudder, has certainly the merit of explicitness."

"I intend it shall have, Sir," said Mary, tranquilly; "half the misery in the world comes of want of courage to speak and to hear the truth plainly and in a spirit of love."

"I am gratified that you add the last clause, Miss Scudder; I might not otherwise recognize the gentle being whom I have always regarded as the impersonation of all that is softest in woman. I have not the honor of understanding in the least the reason of this apparently capricious sentence, but I bow to it in submission."

"Mr. Burr," said Mary, walking up to him, and looking him full in the eyes, with an energy that for the moment bore down his practised air of easy superiority, "I wish to speak to you for a moment, as one immortal soul should to another, without any of those false glosses and deceits

which men call ceremony and good manners.
You have done a very great injury to a lovely
lady, whose weakness ought to have been sacred
in your eyes. Precisely because you are what
you are, — strong, keen, penetrating, and able to
control and govern all who come near you, — because you have the power to make yourself agreeable, interesting, fascinating, and to win esteem
and love, — just for that reason you ought to hold
yourself the guardian of every woman, and treat
her as you would wish any man to treat your own
daughter. I leave it to your conscience, whether
this is the manner in which you have treated
Madame de Frontignac."

"Upon my word, Miss Scudder," began Burr,
"I cannot imagine what representations our mutual friend may have been making. I assure you,
our intercourse has been as irreproachable as the
most scrupulous could desire."

"'Irreproachable! — scrupulous!' — Mr. Burr, you
know that you have taken the very life out of
her. You men can have everything, — ambition,
wealth, power; a thousand ways are open to you:
women have nothing but their heart; and when
that is gone, all is gone. Mr. Burr, you remember the rich man who had flocks and herds, but
nothing would do for him but he must have the
one little ewe-lamb which was all his poor neighbor had. Thou art the man! You have stolen all

the love she had to give,—all that she had to
make a happy home; and you can never give her
anything in return, without endangering her purity
and her soul,—and you knew you could not. I
know you men *think* this is a light matter; but it
is death to us. What will this woman's life be?
one long struggle to forget; and when you have
forgotten her, and are going on gay and happy,—
when you have thrown her very name away as a
faded flower, she will be praying, hoping, fearing
for you; though all men deny you, yet will not
she. Yes, Mr. Burr, if ever your popularity and
prosperity should leave you, and those who now
flatter should despise and curse you, she will always be interceding with her own heart and with
God for you, and making a thousand excuses
where she cannot deny; and if you die, as I fear
you have lived, unreconciled to the God of your
fathers, it will be in her heart to offer up her very
soul for you, and to pray that God will impute
all your sins to her, and give you heaven. Oh, I
know this, because I have felt it in my own heart!"
and Mary threw herself passionately down into a
chair, and broke into an agony of uncontrolled
sobbing.

Burr turned away, and stood looking through
the window; tears were dropping silently, unchecked
by the cold, hard pride which was the evil demon
of his life.

It is due to our human nature to believe that no man could ever have been so passionately and enduringly loved and revered by both men and women as he was, without a beautiful and lovable nature; — no man ever demonstrated more forcibly the truth, that it is not a man's natural constitution, but the *use* he makes of it, which stamps him as good or vile.

The diviner part of him was weeping, and the cold, proud demon was struggling to regain his lost ascendency. Every sob of the fair, inspired child who had been speaking to him seemed to shake his heart,—he felt as if he could have fallen on his knees to her; and yet that stoical habit which was the boast of his life, which was the sole wisdom he taught to his only and beautiful daughter, was slowly stealing back round his heart, — and he pressed his lips together, resolved that no word should escape till he had fully mastered himself.

In a few moments Mary rose with renewed calmness and dignity, and, approaching him, said, —

"Before I wish you good-morning, Mr. Burr, I must ask pardon for the liberty I have taken in speaking so very plainly."

"There is no pardon needed, my dear child," said Burr, turning and speaking very gently, and with a face expressive of a softened concern; "if you have told me harsh truths, it was with gentle intentions ; — I only hope that I may prove, at least by the future, that I am not altogether so bad as you imagine. As to the friend whose name has been passed between us, no man can go beyond me in a sense of her real nobleness; I am sensible how little I can ever deserve the sentiment with which she honors me. I am ready, in my future course, to obey any commands that you and she may think proper to lay upon me."

" The only kindness you can now do her," said Mary, " is to leave her. It is impossible that you should be merely friends; — it is impossible, without violating the holiest bonds, that you should be more. The injury done is irreparable; but you *can* avoid adding another and greater one to it."

Burr looked thoughtful.

" May I say one thing more ? " said Mary, the color rising in her cheeks.

Burr looked at her with that smile that always drew out the confidence of every heart.

" Mr. Burr," she said, " you will pardon me, but I cannot help saying this : You have, I am told, wholly renounced the Christian faith of your fathers, and build your whole life on quite another foundation. I cannot help feeling that this is a great and terrible mistake. I cannot help wishing that you would examine and reconsider "

"My dear child, I am extremely grateful to you for your remark, and appreciate fully the purity of the source from which it springs. Unfortunately, our intellectual beliefs are not subject to the control of our will. I have examined, and the examination has, I regret to say, not had the effect you would desire."

Mary looked at him wistfully; he smiled and bowed, — all himself again; and stopping at the door, he said, with a proud humility, —

"Do me the favor to present my devoted regard to your friend; believe me, that hereafter you shall have less reason to complain of me."

He bowed, and was gone.

An eye-witness of the scene has related, that, when Burr resigned his seat as President of his country's Senate, an object of peculiar political bitterness and obloquy, almost all who listened to him had made up their minds that he was an utterly faithless, unprincipled man; and yet, such was his singular and peculiar personal power, that his short farewell-address melted the whole assembly into tears, and his most embittered adversaries were charmed into a momentary enthusiasm of admiration.

It must not be wondered at, therefore, if our simple-hearted, loving Mary strangely found all her indignation against him gone, and herself little disposed to criticize the impassioned tenderness

21

with which Madame de Frontignac still regarded him.

We have one thing more that we cannot avoid saying, of two men so singularly in juxtaposition as Aaron Burr and Dr. Hopkins. Both had a perfect *logic* of life, and guided themselves with an inflexible rigidity by it. Burr assumed individual pleasure to be the great object of human existence; Dr. Hopkins placed it in a life altogether beyond self. Burr rejected all sacrifice; Hopkins considered sacrifice as the foundation of all existence. To live as far as possible without a disagreeable sensation was an object which Burr proposed to himself as the *summum bonum,* for which he drilled down and subjugated a nature of singular richness. Hopkins, on the other hand, smoothed the asperities of a temperament naturally violent and fiery by a rigid discipline which guided it entirely above the plane of self-indulgence; and, in the pursuance of their great end, the one watched against his better nature as the other did against his worse. It is but fair, then, to take their lives as the practical workings of their respective ethical creeds

CHAPTER XXXIII.

NEW ENGLAND IN FRENCH EYES.

WE owe our readers a digression at this point, while we return for a few moments to say a little more of the fortunes of Madame de Frontignac, whom we left waiting with impatience for the termination of the conversation between Mary and Burr.

"*Enfin, chère Sybille,*" said Madame de Frontignac, when Mary came out of the room, with her cheeks glowing and her eye flashing with a still unsubdued light, "*te voilà encore!* What did he say, *mimi?* — did he ask for me?"

"Yes," said Mary, "he asked for you."

"What did you tell him?"

"I told him that you wished me to excuse you."

"How did he look then? — did he look surprised?"

"A good deal so, I thought," said Mary.

"*Allons, mimi,* — tell me all you said, and all he said."

" Oh," said Mary, " I am the worst person in the world; in fact, I cannot remember anything that I have said; but I told him that he must leave you, and never see you any more."

" Oh, *mimi*, never!"

Madame de Frontignac sat down on the side of the bed with such a look of utter despair as went to Mary's heart.

" You know that it is best, Virginie; do you not?"

" Oh, yes, I know it; *mais pourtant, c'est dur comme la mort.* Ah, well, what shall Virginie do now?"

" You have your husband," said Mary.

" *Je ne l'aime point,*" said Madame de Frontignac.

" Yes, but he is a good and honorable man, and you should love him."

" Love is not in our power," said Madame de Frontignac.

" Not every kind of love," said Mary, " but some kinds. If you have a kind, indulgent friend who protects you and cares for you, you can be grateful to him, you can try to make him happy, and in time you may come to love him very much. He is a thousand times nobler man, if what you say is true, than the one who has injured you so."

" Oh, Mary!" said Madame de Frontignac,

" there are some cases where we find it too easy to love our enemies."

" More than that," said Mary; " I believe, that, if you go on patiently in the way of duty, and pray daily to God, He will at last take out of your heart this painful love, and give you a true and healthy one. As you say, such feelings are very sweet and noble; but they are not the only ones we have to live by; — we can find happiness in duty, in self-sacrifice, in calm, sincere, honest friendship. That is what you can feel for your husband."

" Your words cool me," said Madame de Frontignac; " thou art a sweet snow-maiden, and my heart is hot and tired. I like to feel thee in my arms," she said, putting her arms around Mary, and resting her head upon her shoulder. " Talk to me so every day, and read me good cool verses out of that beautiful Book, and perhaps by-and-by I shall grow still and quiet like you."

Thus Mary soothed her friend; but every few days this soothing had to be done over, as long as Burr remained in Newport. When he was finally gone, she grew more calm. The simple, homely ways of the cottage, the healthful routine of daily domestic toils, into which she delighted to enter, brought refreshment to her spirit. That fine tact and exquisite social sympathy, which distinguish the French above other nations, caused her at once to enter into the spirit of the life in which she moved; so that she no longer shocked any one's religious feelings by acts forbidden by the Puritan idea of Sunday, or failed in any of the exterior proprieties of religious life. She also read and studied with avidity the English Bible, which came to her with the novelty of a wholly new book in a new language; nor was she without a certain artistic appreciation of the austere precision and gravity of the religious life by which she was surrounded.

"It is sublime, but a little *glaciale*, like the Alps," she sometimes said to Mary and Mrs. Marvyn, when speaking of it; "but then," she added, playfully, "there are the flowers, — *les roses des Alpes*, — and the air is very strengthening, and it is near to heaven, — *faut avouer*."

We have shown how she appeared to the eye of New England life; it may not be uninteresting to give a letter to one of her friends, which showed how the same appeared to her. It was not a friend with whom she felt on such terms, that her intimacy with Burr would appear at all in the correspondence.

"You behold me, my charming Gabrielle, quite pastoral, recruiting from the dissipations of my Philadelphia life in a quiet cottage, with most worthy, excellent people, whom I have learned to love very much. They are good and true, as pious

as the saints themselves, although they do not belong to the Church, — a thing which I am sorry
for; but then let us hope, that, if the world is
wide, heaven is wider, and that all worthy people
will fin'd room at last.   This is Virginie's own
little, pet, private heresy; and when I tell it to the
Abbé, he only smiles, and so I think, somehow,
that it is not so very bad as it might be.

"We have had a very gay life in Philadelphia,
and now I am growing tired of the world, and
think I shall retire to my cheese, like Lafontaine's
rat.

"These people in the country here in America
have a character quite their own, very different
from the life of cities, where one sees, for the most
part, only a continuation of the forms of good
society which exist in the Old World.

"In the country, these people seem simple, grave,
severe, always industrious, and, at first, cold and
reserved in their manners towards each other, but
with great warmth of heart.   They are all obedient
to the word of their minister, who lives among
them just like any other man, and marries and
has children.

"Everything in their worship is plain and austere; their churches are perfectly desolate; they
have no chants, no pictures, no carvings, — only a
most disconsolate, bare-looking building, where they
meet together, and sing one or two hymns, and the

minister makes one or two prayers, all out of his own thoughts, and then gives them a long, long discourse about things which I cannot understand enough English to comprehend.

" There is a very beautiful, charming young girl here, the daughter of my hostess, who is as lovely and as saintly as St. Catharine, and has such a genius for religion, that, if she had been in our Church, she would certainly have been made a saint.

" Her mother is a good, worthy matron; and the good priest lives in the family. I think he is a man of very sublime religion, as much above this world as a great mountain; but he has the true sense of liberty and fraternity; for he has dared to oppose with all his might this detestable and cruel trade in poor negroes, which makes us, who are so proud of the example of America in asserting the rights of men, so ashamed for her inconsistencies.

" Well, now, there is a little romance getting up in the cottage; for the good priest has fixed his eyes on the pretty saint, and discovered, what he must be blind not to see, that she is very lovely, —and so, as he can marry, he wants to make her his wife; and her mamma, who adores him as if he were God, is quite set upon it. The sweet Marie, however, has had a lover of her own in her little heart, a beautiful young man, who went to sea, as heroes always do, to seek his fortune.

And the cruel sea has drowned him; and the poor little saint has wept and prayed, till she is so thin and sweet and mournful that it makes one's heart ache to see her smile. In our Church, Gabrielle, she would have gone into a convent; but she makes a vocation of her daily life, and goes round the house so sweetly, doing all the little work that is to be done, as sacredly as the nuns pray at the altar. For you must know, here in New England, the people, for the most part, keep no servants, but perform all the household work themselves, with no end of spinning and sewing besides. It is the true Arcadia, where you find cultivated and refined people busying themselves with the simplest toils. For these people are well-read and well-bred, and truly ladies in all things. And so my little Marie and I, we feed the hens and chickens together, and we search for eggs in the hay in the barn. And they have taught me to spin at their great wheel, and at a little one too, which makes a noise like the humming of a bee.

"But where am I? Oh, I was telling about the romance. Well, so the good priest has proposed for my Marie, and the dear little soul has accepted him as the nun accepts the veil; for she only loves him filially and religiously. And now they are going on, in their way, with preparations for the wedding. They had what they call 'a quilting

21 *

here the other night, to prepare the bride's quilt, —
and all the friends in the neighborhood came; — it
was very amusing to see.

"The morals of this people are so austere, that
young men and girls are allowed the greatest freedom. They associate and talk freely together, and
the young men walk home alone with the girls
after evening parties. And most generally, the
young people, I am told, arrange their marriages
among themselves before the consent of the parents
is asked. This is very strange to us. I must not
weary you, however, with the details. I watch my
little romance daily, and will let you hear further
as it progresses.

"With a thousand kisses, I am, ever, your loving
"VIRGINIE."

CHAPTER XXXIV.

CONSULTATIONS AND CONFIDENCES.

MEANWHILE, the wedding-preparations were going on at the cottage with that consistent vigor
with which Yankee people always drive matters
when they know precisely what they are about.

The wedding-day was definitely fixed for the first
of August; and each of the two weeks between
had its particular significance and value precisely
marked out and arranged in Mrs. Katy Scudder's
comprehensive and systematic schemes.

It was settled that the newly wedded pair were,
for a while at least, to reside at the cottage.   It
might have been imagined, therefore, that no great
external changes were in contemplation; but it is
astonishing, the amount of discussion, the amount
of advising, consulting, and running to and fro,
which can be made to result out of an apparently
slight change in the relative position of two people in the same house.

Dr. Hopkins really opened his eyes with calm
amazement. Good, modest soul! he had never

imagined himself the hero of so much preparation.
From morning to night, he heard his name constantly occurring in busy consultations that seemed
to be going on between Miss Prissy and Mrs.
Deacon Twitchel and Mrs. Scudder and Mrs. Jones,
and quietly wondered what they could have so
much more than usual to say about him. For a
while it seemed to him that the whole house was
about to be torn to pieces. He was even requested to step out of his study, one day, into
which immediately entered, in his absence, two of
the most vigorous women of the parish, who proceeded to uttermost measures, — first pitching everything into pi, so that the Doctor, who returned
disconsolately to look for a book, at once gave up
himself and his system of divinity as entirely lost,
until assured by one of the ladies, in a condescending manner, that he knew nothing about the
matter, and that, if he would return after half a
day, he would find everything right again, — a
declaration in which he tried to have unlimited
faith, and which made him feel the advantage of
a mind accustomed to believing in mysteries.
And it is to be remarked, that on his return he
actually found his table in most perfect order,
with not a single one of his papers missing; in
fact, to his ignorant eye the room looked exactly
as it did before; and when Miss Prissy eloquently
demonstrated to him, that every inch of that paint

had been scrubbed, and the windows taken out, and washed inside and out, and rinsed through three waters, and that the curtains had been taken down, and washed, and put through a blue water, and starched, and ironed, and put up again, — he only innocently wondered, in his ignorance, what there was in a man's being married that made all these ceremonies necessary. But the Doctor was a wise man, and in cases of difficulty kept his mind to himself; and therefore he only informed these energetic practitioners that he was extremely obliged to them, accepting it by simple faith, — an example which we recommend to all good men in similar circumstances.

The house throughout was subjected to similar renovation. Everything in every chest or box was vigorously pulled out and hung out on lines in the clothes-yard to air; for when once the spirit of enterprise has fairly possessed a group of women, it assumes the form of a " prophetic fury," and carries them beyond themselves. Let not any ignorant mortal of the masculine gender, at such hours, rashly dare to question the promptings of the genius that inspires them. Spite of all the treatises that have lately appeared, to demonstrate that there are no particular inherent diversities between men and women, we hold to the opinion that one thorough season of house-cleaning is sufficient to prove the existence of awful and mysterious difference between the sexes, and of subtile and reserved forces in the female line, before which the lords of creation can only veil their faces with a discreet reverence, as our Doctor has done.

In fact, his whole deportment on the occasion was characterized by humility so edifying as really to touch the hearts of the whole synod of matrons; and Miss Prissy rewarded him by declaring impressively her opinion, that he was worthy to have a voice in the choosing of the wedding-dress; and she actually swooped him up, just in a very critical part of a distinction between natural and moral ability, and conveyed him bodily, as fairy sprites knew how to convey the most ponderous of mortals, into the best room, where three specimens of brocade lay spread out upon a table for inspection.

Mary stood by the side of the table, her pretty head bent reflectively downward, her cheek just resting upon the tip of one of her fingers, as she stood looking thoughtfully *through* the brocades at something deeper that seemed to lie under them; and when the Doctor was required to give judgment on the articles, it was observed by the matrons that his large blue eyes were resting upon Mary, with an expression that almost glorified his face; and it was not until his elbow was repeatedly shaken by Miss Prissy, that he gave a sudden start, and fixed his attention, as was requested, upon the silks. It had been one of Miss Prissy's favorite theories, that " *that dear blessed man had taste enough, if he would only give his mind to things* "; and, in fact, the Doctor rather verified the remark on the present occasion, for he looked very conscientiously and soberly at the silks, and even handled them cautiously and respectfully with his fingers, and listened with grave attention to all that Miss Prissy told him of their price and properties, and then laid his finger down on one whose snow-white ground was embellished with a pattern representing lillies of the valley on a background of green leaves. " This is the one," he said, with an air of decision; and then he looked at Mary, and smiled, and a murmur of universal approbation broke out.

" *Il a de la délicatesse,*" said Madame de Frontignac, who had been watching this scene with bright, amused eyes, — while a chorus of loud acclamations, in which Miss Prissy's voice took the lead, conveyed to the innocent-minded Doctor the idea, that in some mysterious way he had distinguished himself in the eyes of his feminine friends; whereat he retired to his study slightly marvelling, but on the whole well pleased, as men generally are when they do better than they expect; and Miss Prissy, turning out all profaner persons from the apartment, held a solemn consultation, to which only Mary, Mrs. Scudder, and Madame de Frontignac were admitted. For it is to be observed that the latter had risen daily and hourly in Miss Prissy's esteem, since her entrance into the cottage; and she declared, that, if she only would give her a few hints, she didn't believe but that she could make that dress look just like a Paris one; and rather intimated that in such a case she might almost be ready to resign all mortal ambitions.

The afternoon of this day, just at that cool hour when the clock ticks so quietly in a New England kitchen, and everything is so clean and put away that there seems to be nothing to do in the house, Mary sat quietly down in her room to hem a ruffle. Everybody had gone out of the house on various errands. The Doctor, with implicit faith, had surrendered himself to Mrs. Scudder and Miss Prissy, to be conveyed up to Newport, and attend to various appointments in relation to his outer man, which he was informed would be indispensable in the forthcoming solemnities. Madame de Frontignac had also gone to spend the day with some of her Newport friends. And Mary, quite well pleased with the placid and orderly stillness which reigned through the house, sat pleasantly murmuring a little tune to her sewing, when suddenly the trip of a very brisk foot was heard in the kitchen, and Miss Cerinthy Ann

Twitchel made her appearance at the door, her healthy glowing cheek wearing a still brighter color from the exercise of a three-mile walk in a July day.

" Why, Cerinthy," said Mary, " how glad I am to see you!"

" Well," said Cerinthy, " I have been meaning to come down all this week, but there's so much to do in haying-time, — but to-day I told mother I *must* come. I brought these down," she said, unfolding a dozen snowy damask napkins, "that I spun myself, and was thinking of you almost all the while I spun them, so I suppose they aren't quite so wicked as they might be."

We will observe here, that Cerinthy Ann, in virtue of having a high stock of animal spirits and great fulness of physical vigor, had very small proclivities towards the unseen and spiritual, but still always indulged a secret resentment at being classed as a sinner above many others, who, as church-members, made such professions, and were, as she remarked, " not a bit better than she was." She had always, however, cherished an unbounded veneration for Mary, and had made her the confidante of most of her important secrets. It soon became very evident that she had come with one on her mind now.

" Don't you want to come and sit out in the lot?" she said, after sitting awhile, twirling her bonnet-strings with the air of one who has something to say and doesn't know exactly how to begin upon it.

Mary cheerfully gathered up her thread, scissors, and ruffling, and the two stepped over the window-sill, and soon found themselves seated cozily under the boughs of a large apple-tree, whose descending branches, meeting the tops of the high grass all around, formed a seclusion as perfect as heart could desire.

They sat down, pushing away a place in the grass; and Cerinthy Ann took off her bonnet, and threw it among the clover, exhibiting to view her black hair, always trimly arranged in shining braids, except where some glossy curls fell over the rich high color of her cheeks. Something appeared to discompose her this afternoon. There were those evident signs of a consultation impending, which, to an experienced eye, are as unmistakable as the coming up of a shower in summer.

Cerinthy began by passionately demolishing several heads of clover, remarking, as she did so, that she "didn't see, for her part, how Mary could keep so calm when things were coming so near." And as Mary answered to this only with a quiet smile, she broke out again:—

"I don't see, for my part, how a young girl *could* marry a minister, anyhow; but then I think *you* are just cut out for it. But what would anybody say, if *I* should do such a thing?"

"I don't know," said Mary, innocently.

"Well, I suppose everybody would hold up their hands; and yet, if I *do* say it myself," — she added, coloring, — "there are not many girls who could make a better minister's wife than I could, if I had a mind to try."

"That I am sure of," said Mary, warmly.

"I guess you are the only one that ever thought so," said Cerinthy, giving an impatient toss. "There's father and mother all the while mourning over me; and yet I don't see but what I do pretty much all that is done in the house, and they say I am a great comfort in a temporal point of view. But, oh, the groanings and the sighings that there are over me! I don't think it is pleasant to know that your best friends are thinking such awful things about you, when you are working your fingers off to help them. It is kind o' discouraging, but I don't know what to do about it;" — and for a few moments Cerinthy sat demolishing buttercups, and throwing them up in the air till her shiny black head was covered with golden flakes, while her cheeks grew redder with something that she was going to say next.

"Now, Mary, there is *that creature.* Well, you know, he won't take '*No*' for an answer. What shall I do?"

" Suppose, then, you try ' *Yes*,' " said Mary, rather archly.

" Oh, pshaw ! Mary Scudder, you know better than that, now. I look like it, don't I ? "

" Why, yes," said Mary, looking at Cerinthy, deliberately; " on the whole, I think you do."

" Well ! one thing I must say," said Cerinthy, — " I can't see what *he* finds in me. I think he is a thousand times too good for me. Why, you have no idea, Mary, how I *have* plagued him. I believe that man *really is a Christian*," she added, while something like a penitent tear actually glistened in those sharp, saucy, black eyes. "Besides," she added, " I have told him everything I could think of to discourage him. I told him that I had a bad temper, and didn't believe the doctrines, and couldn't promise that I ever should ; and after all, that creature keeps right on, and I don't know what to tell him."

" Well," said Mary, mildly, " do you think you really love him ? "

" Love him ? " said Cerinthy, giving a great flounce, " to be sure I don't ! Catch me loving any man ! I told him last night I didn't ; but it didn't do a bit of good. I used to think that man was bashful, but I declare I have altered my mind ; he will talk and talk till I don't know what to do. I tell you, Mary, he talks beautifully, too, sometimes."

Here Cerinthy turned quickly away, and began reaching passionately after clover-heads. After a few moments, she resumed:—

"The fact is, Mary, that man *needs* somebody to take care of him; for he never thinks of himself. They say he has got the consumption; but he hasn't, any more than I have. It is just the way he neglects himself,—preaching, talking, and visiting; nobody to take care of him, and see to his clothes, and nurse him up when he gets a little hoarse and run down. Well, I suppose if I *am* unregenerate, I do know how to keep things in order; and if I should keep *such* a man's soul in his body, I should be doing some good in the world; because, if ministers don't live, of course they can't convert anybody. Just think of his saying that I could be a comfort to *him!* I told him that it was perfectly ridiculous. 'And besides,' says I, 'what will everybody think?' I thought that I had really talked him out of the notion of it last night; but there he was in again this morning, and told me he had derived great encouragement from what I had said. Well, the poor man really is lonesome,—his mother's dead, and he hasn't any sisters. I asked him why he didn't go and take Miss Olladine Slocum : everybody says she would make a first-rate minister's wife."

"Well, and what did he say to that?" said Mary.

"Well, something really silly, — about my looks," said Cerinthy, looking down.

Mary looked up, and remarked the shining black hair, the long dark lashes lying down over the glowing cheek, where two arch dimples were nestling, and said, quietly, —

"Probably he is a man of taste, Cerinthy; I advise you to leave the matter entirely to his judgment."

"You don't, really, Mary!" said the damsel, looking up. "Don't you think it would injure *him*, if I should?"

"I think not, materially," said Mary.

"Well," said Cerinthy, rising, "the men will be coming home from the mowing, before I get home, and want their supper. Mother has got one of her headaches on this afternoon, so I can't stop any longer. There isn't a soul in the house knows where anything is, when I am gone. If I should ever take it into my head to go off, I don't know what would become of father and mother. I was telling mother, the other day, that I thought unregenerate folks were of some use in *this* world, any way."

"Does your mother know anything about it?" said Mary.

"Oh, as to mother, I believe she has been hoping and praying about it these three months. She thinks that I am such a desperate case, it is the

only way I am to be brought in. as she calls it.
That's what set me against him at first; but the
fact is, if girls will let a man argue with them,
he always contrives to get the best of it. I am
kind of provoked about it, too. But, mercy on
us! he is so meek, there is no use of getting provoked at him. Well, I guess I will go home and
think about it."

As she turned to go, she looked really pretty.
Her long lashes were wet with a twinkling moisture, like meadow-grass after a shower; and there
was a softened, childlike expression stealing over
the careless gayety of her face.

Mary put her arms round her with a gentle ca-
essing movement, which the other returned with
a hearty embrace. They stood locked in each
other's arms, — the glowing, vigorous, strong-hearted
girl, with that pale, spiritual face resting on her
breast, as when the morning, songful and radiant,
clasps the pale silver moon to her glowing bosom.

"Look here now, Mary," said Cerinthy; "your
folks are all gone. You may as well walk with
me. It's pleasant now."

"Yes, I will," said Mary; "wait a minute, till
I get my bonnet."

In a few moments the two girls were walking
together in one of those little pasture foot-tracks
which run so cozily among huckleberry and juni-

per bushes, while Cerinthy eagerly pursued the subject she could not leave thinking of. Their path now wound over high ground that overlooked the distant sea, now lost itself in little copses of cedar and pitch-pine, and now there came on the air the pleasant breath of new hay, which mowers were harvesting in adjoining meadows.

They walked on and on, as girls will; because, when a young lady has once fairly launched into the enterprise of telling another all that *he* said, and just how *he* looked, for the last three months, walks are apt to be indefinitely extended.

Mary was, besides, one of the most seductive little confidantes in the world. She was so pure from selfishness, so heartily and innocently interested in what another was telling her, that people in talking with her found the subject constantly increasing in interest, — although, if they really had been called upon afterwards to state the exact portion in words which she added to the conversation, they would have been surprised to find it so small.

In fact, before Cerinthy Ann had quite finished her confessions, they were more than a mile from the cottage, and Mary began to think of returning, saying that her mother would wonder where she was, when she came home.

CHAPTER XXXV.

OLD LOVE AND NEW DUTY.

THE sun was just setting, and the whole air and sea seemed flooded with rosy rays. Even the crags and rocks of the sea-shore took purple and lilac tints, and savins and junipers, had a painter been required to represent them, would have been found not without a suffusion of the same tints. And through the tremulous rosy sea of the upper air, the silver full-moon looked out like some calm superior presence which waits only for the flush of a temporary excitement to die away, to make its tranquillizing influence felt.

Mary, as she walked homeward with this dreamy light around her, moved with a slower step than when borne along by the vigorous arm and determined motion of her young friend.

It is said that a musical sound uttered with decision by one instrument always makes the corresponding chord of another vibrate; and Mary felt, as she left her positive but warm-hearted friend, a plaintive vibration of something in her own self, of which she was conscious her calm

22

friendship for her future husband had no part. She fell into one of those reveries which she thought she had forever forbidden to herself, and there rose before her mind the picture of a marriage-ceremony, — but the eyes of the bridegroom were dark, and his curls were clustering in raven ringlets, and her hand throbbed in his as it had never throbbed in any other.

It was just as she was coming out of a little grove of cedars, where the high land overlooks the sea, and the dream which came to her overcame her with a vague and yearning sense of pain. Suddenly she heard footsteps behind her, and some one said, " Mary!" It was spoken in a choked voice, as one speaks in the crises of a great emotion ; and she turned and saw those very eyes, that very hair, yes, and the cold little hand throbbed with that very throb in that strong, living, manly hand ; and, whether in the body or out of the body God knoweth, she felt herself borne in those arms, and words that spoke themselves in her inner heart, words profaned by being repeated, were on her ear.

" Oh! is this a dream? is this a dream? James! are we in heaven? Oh, I have lived through such an agony! I have been so worn out! Oh, I thought you never would come!" And then the eyes closed, and heaven and earth faded away together in a trance of blissful rest.

But it was no dream;' for an hour later you might have seen a manly form sitting in that self-same place, bearing in his arms a pale figure which he cherished as tenderly as a mother her babe. And they were talking together, — talking in low tones; and in all this wide universe neither of them knew or felt anything but the great joy of being thus side by side.

They spoke of love mightier than death, which many waters cannot quench. They spoke of yearnings, each for the other, — of longing prayers, — of hopes deferred, — and then of this great joy, — for *one* had hardly yet returned to the visible world.

Scarce wakened from deadly faintness, she had not come back fully to the realm of life, — only to that of love, — to love which death cannot quench. And therefore it was, that, without knowing that she spoke, she had said all, and compressed the history of those three years into one hour.

But at last, thoughtful of her health, provident of her weakness, he rose up and passed his arm around her to convey her home. And as he did so, he spoke *one* word that broke the whole charm.

" You will allow me, Mary, the right of a future husband, to watch over your life and health."

Then came back the visible world, — recollection, consciousness, and the great battle of duty, — and Mary drew away a little, and said, —

"Oh, James, you are too late! that can never be!"

He drew back from her.

"Mary, are you married?"

"Before God, I am," she said. "My word is pledged. I cannot retract it. I have suffered a good man to place his whole faith upon it, — a man who loves me with his whole soul."

"But, Mary, you do not love *him*. *That* is impossible!" said James, holding her off from him, and looking at her with an agonized eagerness. "After what you have just said, it is not possible."

"Oh, James! I am sure I don't know what I have said, — it was all so sudden, and I didn't know what I was saying, — but things that I must never say again. The day is fixed for next week. It is all the same as if you had found me his wife."

"Not quite," said James, his voice cutting the air with a decided manly ring. "I have some words to say to that yet."

"Oh, James, will you be selfish? will *you* tempt me to do a mean, dishonorable thing? to be false to my word deliberately given?"

"But," said James, eagerly, "you know, Mary,

you *never* would have given it, if you had known that I was living."

"That is true, James; but I *did* give it. I have suffered him to build all his hopes of life upon it. I *beg* you not to tempt me, — help me to do right!"

"But, Mary, did you not get my letter?"

"Your letter?"

"Yes, — that long letter that I wrote you."

"I never got any letter, James."

"Strange!" he said. "No wonder it seems sudden to you!"

"Have you seen your mother?" said Mary, who was conscious this moment only of a dizzy instinct to turn the conversation from where she felt too weak to bear it.

"No; do you suppose I should see anybody before you?"

"Oh, then, you must go to her!" said Mary. "Oh, James, you don't know how she has suffered!"

They were drawing near to the cottage-gate.

"Do, pray!" said Mary. "Go, hurry to your mother! Don't be too sudden, either, for she's very weak; she is almost worn out with sorrow. Go, my dear brother! *Dear* you always will be to me."

James helped her into the house, and they parted. All the house was yet still. The open kitchen-door let in a sober square of moonlight on the floor. The very stir of the leaves on the trees could be heard. Mary went into her little room, and threw herself upon the bed, weak, weary, yet happy, — for deep and high above all other feelings was the great relief that *he* was living still. After a little while she heard the rattling of the wagon,.and then the quick patter of Miss Prissy's feet, and her mother's considerate tones, and the Doctor's grave voice, — and quite unexpectedly to herself, she was shocked to find herself turning with an inward shudder from the idea of meeting him. " How very wicked! " she thought, — " how ungrateful! " — and she prayed that God would give her strength to check the first rising of such feelings.

Then there was her mother, so ignorant and innocent, busy putting away baskets of things that she had bought in provision for the wedding-ceremony.

Mary almost felt as if she had a guilty secret. But when she looked back upon the last two hours, she felt no wish to take them back again. Two little hours of joy and rest they had been, — so pure, so perfect! she thought God must have given them to her as a keepsake to remind her of His love, and to strengthen her in the way of duty.

Some will, perhaps, think it an unnatural thing

that Mary should have regarded her pledge to the
Doctor as of so absolute and binding force; but
they must remember the rigidity of her education.
Self-denial and self-sacrifice had been the daily
bread of her· life. Every prayer, hymn, and sermon, from her childhood, had warned her to dis-
trust her inclinations, and regard her feelings as
traitors. In particular had she been brought up
to regard the sacredness of a promise with a superstitious tenacity; and in this case the promise
involved so deeply the happiness of a friend whom
she had loved and revered all her life, that she
never thought of any way of escape from it. She
had been taught that there was no feeling so
strong but that it might be immediately repressed
at the call of duty; and if the thought arose to her
of this great love to another, she immediately answered it by saying, "How would it have been
if I had been married? As I could have overcome then, so I can now."

Mrs. Scudder came into her room with a candle in her hand, and Mary, accustomed to read
the expression of her mother's face, saw at a
glance a visible discomposure there. She held the
light so that it shone upon Mary's face.

"Are you asleep?" she said.

"No, mother."

"Are you unwell?"

"No, mother,—only a little tired."

Mrs. Scudder set down the candle, and shut the door, and, after a moment's hesitation, said,—

"My daughter, I have some news to tell you, which I want you to prepare your mind for. Keep yourself quite quiet."

"Oh, mother!" said Mary, stretching out her hands towards her, "I know it. James has come home."

"How did you hear?" said her mother, with astonishment.

"I have seen him, mother."

Mrs. Scudder's countenance fell.

"Where?"

"I went to walk home with Cerinthy Twitchel, and as I was coming back he came up behind me, just at Savin Rock."

Mrs. Scudder sat down on the bed and took her daughter's hand.

"I trust, my dear child," she said. She stopped.

"I think I know what you are going to say, mother. It is a great joy, and a great relief; but of course I shall be true to my engagement with the Doctor."

Mrs. Scudder's face brightened.

"That is my own daughter! I might have known that you would do so. You would not, certainly, so cruelly disappoint a noble man who has set his whole faith upon you."

"No, mother, I shall not disappoint him.

I told James that I should be true to my word."

"He will probably see the justice of it," said Mrs. Scudder, in that easy tone with which elderly people are apt to dispose of the feelings of young persons. "Perhaps it may be something of a trial at first."

Mary looked at her mother with incredulous blue eyes. The idea that feelings which made her hold her breath when she thought of them could be so summarily disposed of! She turned her face wearily to the wall, with a deep sigh, and said, —

"After all, mother, it is mercy enough and comfort enough to think that he is living. Poor Cousin Ellen, too, — what a relief to her! It is like life from the dead. Oh, I shall be happy enough; no fear of that!"

"And you know," said Mrs. Scudder, "that there has never existed any engagement of any kind between you and James. He had no right to found any expectations on anything you ever told him."

"That is true also, mother," said Mary. "I had never thought of such a thing as marriage, in relation to James."

"Of course," pursued Mrs. Scudder, "he will always be to you as a near friend."

Mary assented.

22 *

" There is but a week now, before your wedding," continued Mrs. Scudder; " and I think Cousin James, if he is reasonable, will see the propriety of your mind being kept as quiet as possible. I heard the news this afternoon in town," pursued Mrs. Scudder, " from Captain Staunton, and, by a curious coincidence, I received from him this letter from James, which came from New York by post. The brig that brought it must have been delayed out of the harbor."

" Oh, please, mother, give it to me!" said Mary, rising up with animation; " he mentioned having sent me one."

" Perhaps you had better wait till morning," said Mrs. Scudder; " you are tired and excited."

" Oh, mother, I think I shall be more composed when I know all that is in it," said Mary, still stretching out her hand.

" Well, my daughter, you are the best judge," said Mrs. Scudder; and she set down the candle on the table, and left Mary alone.

It was a very thick letter of many pages, dated in Canton, and ran as follows: —

CHAPTER XXXVI.

JACOB'S VOW.

"My dearest Mary:—

"I have lived through many wonderful scenes since I saw you last. My life has been so adventurous, that I scarcely know myself when I think of it. But it is not of *that* I am going now to write. I have written all that to mother, and she will show it to you. But since I parted from you, there has been another history going on within me; and that is what I wish to make you understand, if I can.

"It seems to me that I have been a changed man from that afternoon when I came to your window, and where we parted. I have never forgot how you looked then, nor what you said. Nothing in my life ever had such an effect upon me. I thought that I loved you before; but I went away feeling that love was something so deep and high and sacred, that I was not worthy to name it to you. I cannot think of the man in the world who is worthy of what you said you felt for me.

" From *that* hour there was a new purpose in
my soul, — a purpose which has led me upward
ever since. I thought to myself in this way:
' There is some secret source from whence this
inner life springs,' — and I knew that it was connected with the Bible which you gave me; and
so I thought I would read it carefully and deliberately, to see what I could make of it.

" I began with the beginning. It impressed me
with a sense of something quaint and strange, —
something rather fragmentary; and yet there were
spots all along that went right to the heart of a
man who had to deal with life and things as I
did. Now I must say that the Doctor's preaching,
as I told you, never impressed me much in any
way. I could not make any connection between
it and the men I had to manage and the things
I had to do in my daily life. But there were
things in the Bible that struck me otherwise.
There was *one* passage in particular, and that was
where Jacob started off from all his friends to go
off and seek his fortune in a strange country, and
laid down to sleep all alone in the field, with
only a stone for his pillow. It seemed to me exactly the image of what every young man is like,
when he leaves his home and goes out to shift
for himself in this hard world. I tell you, Mary,
that one man alone on the great ocean of life
feels himself a very weak thing. We are held up

by each other more than we know till we go off by ourselves into this great experiment. Well, there he was as lonesome as *I* upon the deck of my ship. And so lying with the stone under his head, he saw a ladder in his sleep between him and heaven, and angels going up and down. That was a sight which came to the very point of his necessities. He saw that there was a way between him and God, and that there were those above who did care for him, and who could come to him to help him. Well, so the next morning he got up, and set up the stone to mark the place; and it says Jacob vowed a vow, saying, 'If God will be with me, and will keep me in this way that I go, and will give me bread to eat and raiment to put on, so that I come again to my father's house in peace, *then* shall the Lord be my God.' Now *there* was something that looked to me like a tangible foundation to begin upon.

"If I understand Dr. Hopkins, I believe he would have called that all selfishness. At first sight it does look a little so; but then I thought of it in this way: 'Here he was all alone. God was entirely invisible to him; and how could he feel certain that He really existed, unless he could come into some kind of connection with Him? the point that he wanted to be sure of, more than merely to know that there was a God who made the world;—he wanted to know whether He cared

anything about men, and would do anything to
help them. And so, in fact, it was saying, ' If
there is a God who interests Himself at all in
me, and will be my Friend and Protector, I will
obey Him, so far as I can find out His will.'

" I thought to myself, ' This is the great experiment, and I will try it.' I made in my heart
exactly the same resolution, and just quietly resolved to assume for a while as a fact that there
was such a God, and, whenever I came to a place
where I could not help myself, just to ask His
help honestly in so many words, and see what
would come of it.

" Well, as I went on reading through the Old
Testament, I was more and more convinced that
all the men of those times had tried this experiment, and found that it would bear them ; and in
fact, I did begin to find, in my own experience, a
great many things happening so remarkably that
I could not but think that *Somebody* did attend
even to my prayers, — I began to feel a trembling faith that *Somebody* was guiding me, and
that the events of my life were not happening
by accident, but working themselves out by His
will.

" Well, as I went on in this way, there were
other and higher thoughts kept rising in my mind.
I wanted to be better than I was. I had a sense
of a life much nobler and purer than anything I

had ever lived, that I wanted to come up to. But
in the world of men, as I found it, such feelings
are always laughed down as romantic, and impracticable, and impossible. But about this time
I began to read the New Testament, and then
the idea came to me, that the same Power that
helped me in the lower sphere of life would help
me carry out those higher aspirations. Perhaps
the Gospels would not have interested me so
much, if I had begun with them first; but my
Old Testament life seemed to have schooled me,
and brought me to a place where I wanted something higher; and I began to notice that my
prayers now were more that I might be noble,
and patient, and self-denying, and constant in my
duty, than for any other kind of help. And then
I understood what met me in the very first of
Matthew: ' Thou shalt call his name Jesus, for he
shall save his people from their sins.'

"I began now to live a new life, — a life in
which I felt myself coming into sympathy with
you; for, Mary, when I began to read the Gospels, I took knowledge of you, that you had been
with Jesus.

"The crisis of my life was that dreadful night
of the shipwreck. It was as dreadful as the Day
of Judgment. No words of mine can describe to
you what I felt when I knew that our rudder was
gone, and saw those hopeless rocks before us,

What I felt for our poor men! But, in the midst of it all, the words came into my mind, 'And Jesus was in the hinder part of the ship asleep on a pillow,' and at once I felt He *was* there; and when the ship struck I was only conscious of an intense going out of my soul to Him, like Peter's when he threw himself from the ship to meet Him in the waters.

"I will not recapitulate what I have already written,— the wonderful manner in which I was saved, and in which friends and help and prosperity and worldly success came to me again, after life had seemed all lost; but now I am ready to return to my country, and I feel as Jacob did when he said, 'With my staff I passed over this Jordan, and now I am become two bands.'

"I do not need any arguments now to convince me that the Bible is from above. There is a great deal in it that I cannot understand, a great deal that seems to me inexplicable; but all I can say is, that I have tried its directions, and find that in my case they do work,— that it is a book that I can live by; and that is enough for me.

"And now, Mary, I am coming home again, quite another man from what I went out,— with a whole new world of thought and feeling in my heart, and a new purpose, by which, please God, I mean to shape my life. All this, under God, I owe to you; and if you will let me devote my whole life to you, it will be a small return for what you have done for me.

"You know I left you wholly free. Others must have seen your loveliness, and felt your worth; and you may have learnt to love some better man than me. But I know not what hope tells me that this will not be; and I shall find true what the Bible says of love, that 'many waters cannot quench it, nor floods drown.' In any case, I shall be always, from my very heart, yours, and yours only.

"JAMES MARVYN."

Mary rose, after reading this letter, rapt into a divine state of exaltation, — the pure joy, in contemplating an infinite good to another, in which the question of self was utterly forgotten.

He was, then, what she had always hoped and prayed he would be, and she pressed the thought triumphantly to her heart. He was that true and victorious man, that Christian able to subdue life, and to show, in a perfect and healthy manly nature, a reflection of the image of the superhuman excellence. Her prayers that night were aspirations and praises, and she felt how possible it might be so to appropriate the good and the joy and the nobleness of others as to have in them an eternal and satisfying treasure. And with this came the dearer thought, that she, in her weakness and solitude, had been permitted to put her hand to the beginning of a work so noble. The consciousness of good done to an immortal spirit is wealth that neither life nor death can take away.

And so, having prayed, she lay down to that sleep which God giveth to his beloved.

CHAPTER XXXVII.

THE QUESTION OF DUTY.

IT is a hard condition of our existence here, that every exaltation must have its depression. God will not let us have heaven here below, but only such glimpses and faint showings as parents sometimes give to children, when they show them beforehand the jewelry and pictures and stores of rare and curious treasures which they hold for the possession of their riper years. So it very often happens that the man who has gone to bed an angel, feeling as if all sin were forever vanquished, and he himself immutably grounded in love, may wake the next morning with a sick-headache and, if he be not careful, may scold about his breakfast like a miserable sinner.

We will not say that our dear little Mary rose in this condition next morning, — for, although she had the headache, she had one of those natures in which, somehow or other, the combative element seems to be left out, so that no one ever knew her to speak a fretful word. But still, as we have observed, she had the headache and the depression, — and there came the slow, creeping sense of waking up, through all her heart and soul, of a thousand, thousand things that could be said only to one person, and that person one that it would be temptation and danger to say them to.

She came out of her room to her morning work with a face resolved and calm, but expressive of languor, with slight signs of some inward struggle.

Madame de Frontignac, who had already heard the intelligence, threw two or three of her bright glances upon her at breakfast, and at once divined how the matter stood. She was of a nature so delicately sensitive to the most refined shades of honor, that she apprehended at once that there must be a conflict, — though, judging by her own impulsive nature, she made no doubt that all would at once go down before the mighty force of re-awakened love.

After breakfast she would insist upon following Mary about through all her avocations. She possessed herself of a towel, and would wipe the teacups and saucers, while Mary washed. She clinked the glasses, and rattled the cups and spoons, and stepped about as briskly as if she had two or three breezes to carry her train, and chattered half English and half French, for the sake of bringing into Mary's cheek the shy, slow dimples that she liked to watch. But still Mrs. Scudder was around, with an air as provident and forbidding as that of a sitting hen who watches her nest; nor was it till after all things had been cleared away in the house, and Mary had gone up into her little attic to spin, that the long-sought opportunity came of diving to the bottom of this mystery.

" *Enfin, Marie, nous voici!* Are you not going to tell me anything, when I have turned my heart out to you like a bag? *Chère enfant!* how happy you must be!" she said, embracing her.

" Yes, I am very happy," said Mary, with calm gravity.

" *Very happy!*" said Madame de Frontignac, mimicking her manner. "Is that the way you American girls show it, when you are very happy? Come, come, *ma belle!* tell little Virginie something. Thou hast seen this hero, this wandering Ulysses. He has come back at last; the tapestry will not be quite as long as Penelope's? Speak to me of him. Has he beautiful black eyes, and hair that curls like a grape-vine? Tell me, *ma belle!*"

" I only saw him a little while," said Mary, " and I felt a great deal more than I saw. He could not have been any clearer to me than he always has been in my mind."

"But I think," said Madame de Frontignac, seating Mary, as was her wont, and sitting down at her feet,—"I think you are a little *triste* about this. Very likely you pity the good priest. It is sad for him; but a good priest has the Church for his bride, you know."

"You do not think," said Mary, speaking seriously, "that I shall break my promise given before God to this good man?"

"*Mon Dieu, mon enfant!* you do not mean to marry the priest, after all? *Quelle idée!*"

"But I *promised* him," said Mary.

Madame de Frontignac threw up her hands with an expression of vexation.

"What a pity, my little one, you are not in the True Church! Any good priest could dispense you from that."

"I do not believe," said Mary, "in any earthly power that can dispense us from solemn obligations which we have assumed before God, and on which we have suffered others to build the most precious hopes. If James had won the affections of some girl, thinking as I do, I should not think it right for him to leave her and come to me. The Bible says, that the just man is 'he that sweareth to his own hurt, and changeth not.'"

"*C'est le sublime de devoir!*" said Madame de Frontignac, who, with the airy frailty of her race never lost her appreciation of the fine points of

anything that went on under her eyes. But, nev
ertheless, she was inwardly resolved, that, picturesque as this "sublime of duty" was, it must not
be allowed to pass beyond the limits of a fine art,
and so she recommenced.

"*Mais c'est absurde.* This beautiful young man,
with his black eyes, and his curls, — a real hero,
— a Theseus, Mary, — just come home from killing
a Minotaur, — and loves you with his whole heart,
— and this dreadful promise! Why, haven't you
any sort of people in your Church that can un-
bind you from promises? I should think the good
priest himself would do it!"

"Perhaps he would," said Mary, "if I should
ask him; but that would be equivalent to a breach
of it. Of course, no man would marry a woman
that asked to be dispensed."

"You are an angel of delicacy, my child; *c'est
admirable!* but, after all, Mary, this is not well.
Listen now to me. You are a very sweet saint,
and very strong in goodness. I think you must
have a very strong angel that takes care of you.
But think, *chère enfant,* — think what it is to marry
one man, while you love another!"

"But I love the Doctor," said Mary, evasively.

"*Love!*" said Madame de Frontignac. "Oh,
Marie! you may love him well, but you and I
both know that there is something deeper than
that. What will you *do* with this young man?

Must he move away from this place, and not be with his poor mother any more? Or can you see him, and hear him, and be with him, after your marriage, and not feel that you love him more than your husband?"

"I should hope that God would help me to feel right," said Mary.

"I am very much afraid He will not, *ma chère*. I asked Him a great many times to help *me*, when I found how wrong it all was; and He did not. You remember what you told me the other day, — that, if I would do right, I must not *see* that man any more. You will have to ask him to go away from this place; you can never see him; for this love will never die till you die; — that you may be sure of. Is it wise? is it right, dear little one? *Must* he leave his home forever for you? or must you struggle always, and grow whiter and whiter, and fall away into heaven, like the moon this morning, and nobody know what is the matter? People will say you have the liver-complaint, or the consumption, or something. Nobody ever knows what we women die of."

Poor Mary's conscience was fairly posed. This appeal struck upon her sense of right as having its grounds. She felt inexpressibly confused and distressed.

"Oh, I wish somebody would tell me exactly what is right!" she said.

"Well, *I* will," said Madame de Frontignac. "Go down to the dear priest, and tell him the whole truth. My dear child, do you think, if he should ever find it out after your marriage, he would think you used him right?"

"And yet *mother* does not think so; mother does not wish me to tell him."

"*Pauvrette, toujours les mères!* Yes, it is always the mothers that stand in the way of the lovers. Why cannot she marry the priest herself?" she said between her teeth, and then looked up, startled and guilty, to see if Mary had heard her.

"I *cannot*," said Mary,—"I cannot go against my conscience, and my mother, and my best friend."

At this moment, the conference was cut short by Mrs. Scudder's provident footsteps on the garret-stairs. A vague suspicion of something French had haunted her during her dairy-work, and she resolved to come and put a stop to the interview, by telling Mary that Miss Prissy wanted her to come and be measured for the skirt of her dress.

Mrs. Scudder, by the use of that sixth sense peculiar to mothers, had divined that there had been some agitating conference, and, had she been questioned about it, her guesses as to what it might have been would probably have given no

23

bad *résumé* of the real state of the case. She was inwardly resolved that there should be no more such for the present, and kept Mary employed about various matters relating to the dresses, so scrupulously that there was no opportunity for anything more of the sort that day.

In the evening James Marvyn came down, and was welcomed with the greatest demonstrations of joy by all but Mary, who sat distant and embarrassed, after the first salutations had passed.

The Doctor was innocently paternal; but we fear that on the part of the young man there was small reciprocation of the sentiments he expressed.

Miss Prissy, indeed, had had her heart somewhat touched, as good little women's hearts are apt to be by a true love-story, and had hinted something of her feelings to Mrs. Scudder, in a manner which brought such a severe rejoinder as quite humbled and abashed her, so that she coweringly took refuge under her former declaration, that, "to be sure, there couldn't be any man in the world better *worthy* of Mary than the Doctor," while still at her heart she was possessed with that troublesome preference for unworthy people which stands in the way of so many excellent things. But she went on vigorously sewing on the wedding-dress, and pursing up her small mouth into the most perfect and guarded expression of non committal; though she said afterwards, "it went to her heart to see how that poor young man did look, sitting there just as noble and as handsome as a picture. She didn't see, for *her* part, how anybody's heart *could* stand it; though, to be sure, as Miss Scudder said, the poor Doctor ought to be thought about, dear blessed man! What a pity it was things *would* turn out so! Not that it was a pity that Jim came home, — that was a great providence, — but a pity they hadn't known about it sooner. Well, for her part, she didn't pretend to say; the path of duty did have a great many hard places in it."

As for James, during his interview at the cottage, he waited and tried in vain for one moment's private conversation. Mrs. Scudder was immovable in her motherly kindness, sitting there, smiling and chatting with him, but never stirring from her place by Mary.

Madame de Frontignac was out of all patience, and determined, in her small way, to do something to discompose the fixed state of things. So, retreating to her room, she contrived, in very desperation, to upset and break a water-pitcher, shrieking violently in French and English at the deluge which came upon the sanded floor and the little piece of carpet by the bedside.

What housekeeper's instincts are proof against the crash of breaking china?

Mrs. Scudder fled from her seat, followed by Miss Prissy.

"Ah! then and there was hurrying to and fro," while Mary sat quiet as a statue, bending over her sewing, and James, knowing that it must be now or never, was, like a flash, in the empty chair by her side, with his black moustache very near to the bent brown head.

"Mary," he said, "you *must* let me see you once more. All is not said, is it? Just hear me, — hear me once alone!"

"Oh, James, I am too weak! — I dare not! — I am afraid of myself!"

"You think," he said, "that you *must* take this course, because it is right. But *is* it right? Is it right to marry one man, when you love another better? I don't put this to your inclination, Mary, — I know it would be of no use, — I put it to your conscience."

"Oh, I was never so perplexed before!" said Mary. "I don't know what I *do* think. I must have time to reflect. And you, — oh, James! — you *must* let me do right! There will never be any happiness for me, if I do wrong, — nor for you, either."

All this while the sounds of running and hurrying in Madame de Frontignac's room had been unintermitted; and Miss Prissy, not without some glimmerings of perception, was holding tight on

to Mrs. Scudder's gown, detailing to her a most
capital receipt for mending broken china, the history of which she traced regularly through all the
families in which she had ever worked, varying
the details with small items of family history, and
little incidents as to the births, marriages, and
deaths of different people for whom it had been
employed, with all the particulars of how, where,
and when, so that the time of James for conversation was by this means indefinitely extended.

"Now," he said to Mary, "let me propose one
thing. Let *me* go to the Doctor, and tell him the
truth."

"James, it does not seem to me that I can. A
friend who has been so considerate, so kind, so
self-sacrificing and disinterested, and whom I have
allowed to go on with this implicit faith in me
so long. Should you, James, think of *yourself*
only?"

"I do not, I trust, think of myself only," said
James; "I hope that I am calm enough, and have
a heart to think for others. But, I ask you, is it
doing right to *him* to let him marry you in ignorance of the state of your feelings? Is it a kindness to a good and noble man to give yourself to
him only seemingly, when the best and noblest
part of your affections is gone wholly beyond your
control? I am quite sure of *that*, Mary. I know
you do love him very well,—that you would make

a most true, affectionate, constant wife to him,
but what I know you feel for me is something
wholly out of your power to give to him, — is it
not, now?"

"I think it is," said Mary, looking gravely and
deeply thoughtful. "But then, James, I ask myself, 'What if this had happened a week hence?'
My feelings would have been just the same, because they are feelings over which I have no
more control than over my existence. I can only
control the expression of them. But in *that* case
you would not have asked me to break my mar-
riage-vow; and why now shall I break a solemn
vow deliberately made before God? If what I
can give him will content him, and he never knows
that which would give him pain, what wrong is
done him?"

"I should think the deepest possible wrong
done me," said James, "if, when I thought I had
married a wife with a whole heart, I found that
the greater part of it had been before that given
to another. If you tell him, or if I tell him, or
your mother, — who is the proper person, — and he
chooses to hold you to your promise, then, Mary,
I have no more to say. I shall sail in a few
weeks again, and carry your image forever in my
heart; — nobody can take that away; that dear
shadow will be the only wife I shall ever know.

At this moment Miss Prissy came rattling

along towards the door, talking — we suspect designedly — on quite a high key. Mary hastily said, —

" Wait, James, — let me think, — to-morrow is the Sabbath-day. Monday I will send you word, or see you."

And when Miss Prissy returned into the best room, James was sitting at one window and Mary at another, — he making remarks, in a style of most admirable commonplace, on a copy of Milton's " Paradise Lost," which he had picked up in the confusion of the moment, and which, at the time Mrs. Katy Scudder entered, he was declaring to be a most excellent book, — a really, truly, valuable work.

Mrs. Scudder looked keenly from one to the other, and saw that Mary's cheek was glowing like the deepest heart of a pink shell, while, in all other respects, she was as cold and calm. On the whole, she felt satisfied that no mischief had been done.

We hope our readers will do Mrs. Scudder justice. It is true that she yet wore on her third finger the marriage-ring of a sailor lover, and his memory was yet fresh in her heart; but even mothers who have married for love themselves somehow so blend a daughter's existence with their own as to conceive that she must marry their love, and not her own. Besides this, Mrs.

Scudder was an Old Testament woman, brought up with that scrupulous exactitude of fidelity in relation to promises which would naturally come from familiarity with a book in which covenant-keeping is represented as one of the highest attributes of Deity, and covenant-breaking as one of the vilest sins of humanity. To break the word that had gone forth out of one's mouth was to lose self-respect, and all claim to the respect of others, and to sin against eternal rectitude.

As we have said before, it is almost impossible to make our light-minded times comprehend the earnestness with which those people lived. It was, in the beginning, no vulgar nor mercenary ambition that made her seek the Doctor as a husband for her daughter. He was poor, and she had had offers from richer men. He was often unpopular; but he was the man in the world she most revered, the man she believed in with the most implicit faith, the man who embodied her highest ideas of the good; and therefore it was that she was willing to resign her child to him.

As to James, she had felt truly sympathetic with his mother, and with Mary, in the dreadful hour when they supposed him lost; and had it not been for the great perplexity occasioned by his return, she would have received him, as a relative, with open arms. But now she felt it her duty to be on the defensive, — an attitude not the most favorable for cherishing pleasing associations in regard to another. She had read the letter giving an account of his spiritual experience with very sincere pleasure, as a good woman should, but not without an internal perception how very much it endangered her favorite plans. When Mary, however, had calmly reiterated her determination, she felt sure of her; for had she ever known her to say a thing she did not do?

The uneasiness she felt at present was not the doubt of her daughter's steadiness, but the fear that she might have been unsuitably harassed or annoyed.

CHAPTER XXXVIII.

THE TRANSFIGURED.

THE next morning rose calm and fair. It was the Sabbath-day, — the last Sabbath in Mary's maiden life, if her promises and plans were fulfilled.

Mary dressed herself in white, — her hands trembling with unusual agitation, her sensitive nature divided between two opposing consciences and two opposing affections. Her devoted filial love toward the Doctor made her feel the keenest sensitiveness at the thought of giving him pain. At the same time, the questions which James had proposed to her had raised serious doubts in her mind whether it was altogether right to suffer him blindly to enter into this union. So, after she was all prepared, she bolted the door of her chamber, and, opening her Bible, read, " If any of you lack wisdom, let him ask of God, that giveth to all men liberally, and upbraideth not, and it shall be given him"; and then, kneeling down by the bedside, she asked that God would give her some immediate light in her present perplexity. So praying, her mind grew calm and steady, and she rose up at the sound of the bell, which marked that it was time to set forward for church.

Everybody noticed, as she came into church that morning, how beautiful Mary Scudder looked. It was no longer the beauty of the carved statue, the pale alabaster shrine, the sainted virgin, but a warm, bright, living light, that spoke of some summer breath breathing within her soul.

When she took her place in the singers' seat, she knew, without turning her head, that *he* was in his old place, not far from her side; and those whose eyes followed her to the gallery marvelled at her face there, —

> "her pure and eloquent blood
> Spoke in her cheeks, and so distinctly wrought
> That you might almost say her body thought;"

for a thousand delicate nerves were becoming vital once more, — the holy mystery of womanhood had wrought within her.

When they rose to sing, the tune must needs be one which they had often sung together, out of the same book, at the singing-school, — one of those wild, pleading tunes, dear to the heart of New England, — born, if we may credit the report, in the rocky hollows of its mountains, and whose notes have a kind of grand and mournful triumph in their warbling wail, and in which different parts of the harmony, set contrary to all the canons of musical Pharisaism, had still a singular and romantic effect, which a true musical genius would not have failed to recognize. The four parts, tenor, treble, bass, and counter, as they were then called, rose and swelled and wildly mingled, with the fitful strangeness of an Æolian harp, or of winds in mountain-hollows, or the vague moanings of the sea on lone, forsaken shores. And Mary, while her voice rose over the waves of the treble, and trembled with a pathetic richness, felt, to her inmost heart, the deep accord of that other voice which rose to meet hers, so wildly melancholy, as if the soul in that manly breast had come to meet her soul in the disembodied, shadowy verity of eternity. The grand old tune, called by our fathers " China," never, with its dirge-like melody, drew two souls more out of themselves, and entwined them more nearly with each other.

The last verse of the hymn spoke of the resurrection of the saints with Christ, —

> " Then let the last dread trumpet sound
>   And bid the dead arise;
>   Awake, ye nations under ground!
>   Ye saints, ascend the skies!"

And as Mary sang, she felt sublimely upborne with the idea that life is but a moment and love is immortal, and seemed, in a shadowy trance, to feel herself and him past this mortal fane, far over on the shores of that other life, ascending with Christ, all-glorified, all tears wiped away, and with full permission to love and to be loved forever. And as she sang, the Doctor looked upward, and marvelled at the light in her eyes and the rich bloom on her cheek; for where she stood, a sun-beam, streaming aslant through the dusty panes of the window, touched her head with a kind of glory, and the thought he then received out-breathed itself in the yet more fervent adoration of his prayer

CHAPTER XXXIX.

THE ICE BROKEN.

Our fathers believed in special answers to prayer. They were not stumbled by the objection about the inflexibility of the laws of Nature; because they had the idea, that, when the Creator of the world promised to answer human prayers, He probably understood the laws of Nature as well as they did. At any rate, the laws of Nature were His affair, and not theirs. They were men, very apt, as the Duke of Wellington said, to "look to their marching-orders,"— which, being found to read, "Be careful for nothing, but in everything by prayer and supplication with thanksgiving let your requests be made known unto God," they did it. "They looked unto Him and were lightened, and their faces were not ashamed." One reads, in the Memoirs of Dr. Hopkins, of Newport Gardner, one of his African catechumens, a negro of singular genius and ability, who, being desirous of his freedom, that he might be a missionary to Africa, and having long worked without being able to raise the amount required, was counselled by Dr. Hopkins that it might be a shorter way to seek his freedom from the Lord, by a day of solemn fasting and prayer. The historical fact is, that, on the evening of a day so consecrated, his master returned from church, called Newport to him, and presented him with his freedom. Is it not possible that He who made the world may have established laws for prayer as invariable as those for the sowing of seed and raising of grain? Is it not as legitimate a subject of inquiry, when petitions are not answered, which of these laws has been neglected?

But be that as it may, certain it is, that Candace, who on this morning in church sat where she could see Mary and James in the singers' seat, had certain thoughts planted in her mind which bore fruit afterwards in a solemn and select consultation held with Miss Prissy at the end of the horse-shed by the meeting-house, during the intermission between the morning and afternoon services.

Candace sat on a fragment of granite boulder which lay there, her black face relieved against a clump of yellow mulleins, then in majestic altitude. On her lap was spread a checked pocket-handkerchief, containing rich slices of cheese, and a store of her favorite brown doughnuts.

"Now, Miss Prissy," she said, "dar's *reason* in all tings, an' a good deal *more* in some tings dan dar is in oders. Dar's a good deal more reason in two young, handsome folks comin' togeder dan dar is in " ——

Candace finished the sentence by an emphatic flourish of her doughnut.

"Now, as long as eberybody thought Jim Marvyn was dead, dar wa'n't nothin' else in de world *to* be done *but* marry de Doctor. But, good lan! I hearn him a-talkin' to Miss Marvyn las' night; it kinder 'mos' broke my heart. Why, dem two poor creeturs, dey's jest as onhappy's dey can be! An' she's got too much feelin' for de Doctor to say a word; an' *I* say *he oughter be told on't!* dat's what *I* say," said Candace, giving a decisive bite to her doughnut.

"I say so, too," said Miss Prissy. "Why, I never had such bad feelings in my life as I did yesterday, when that young man came down to our house. He was just as pale as a cloth. I tried to say a word to Miss Scudder, but she snapped me up so! She's an awful decided woman when her mind's made up. I was telling Cerinthy Ann Twitchel, — she came round me this noon, — that it didn't exactly seem to me right that things should go on as they are going. And says I, 'Cerinthy Ann, I don't know anything what to do.' And says she, 'If I was you, I know what *I'd* do, — I'd tell the Doctor,' says she. 'Nobody ever takes offence at anything *you* do,

Miss Prissy.' To be sure," added Miss Prissy, "I have talked to people about a good many things that it's rather strange I should; 'cause I a'n't one, somehow, that can let things go that seem to want doing. I always told folks that I should spoil a novel before it got half-way through the first volume, by blurting out some of those things that they let go trailing on so, till everybody gets so mixed up they don't know what they're doing."

"Well, now, honey," said Candace, authoritatively, "ef you's got any notions o' dat kind, I tink it mus' come from de good Lord, an' I 'dvise you to be 'tendin' to't, right away. You jes' go 'long an' tell de Doctor yourself all you know, an' den le's see what'll come on't. I tell you, I b'liebe it'll be one o' de bes' day's works you eber did in your life!"

"Well," said Miss Prissy, "I guess to-night, before I go to bed, I'll make a dive at him. When a thing's once out, it's out, and can't be got in again, even if people don't like it; and that's a mercy, anyhow. It really makes me feel 'most wicked to think of it, for he is the most blessedest man!"

"Dat's what he *is*," said Candace. "But de blessedest man in de world oughter know de truth; dat's what *I* tink!"

"Yes,—true enough!" said Miss Prissy. "I'll tell him, anyway."

Miss Prissy was as good as her word; for that evening, when the Doctor had retired to his study, she took her life in her hand, and, walking swiftly as a cat, tapped rather timidly at the study-door, which the Doctor opening said, benignantly, —

"Ah, Miss Prissy!"

"If you please, Sir," said Miss Prissy, "I'd like a little conversation."

The Doctor was well enough used to such requests from the female members of his church, which, generally, were the prelude to some disclosures of internal difficulties or spiritual experiences. He therefore graciously motioned her to a chair.

"I thought I must come in," she began, busily twirling a bit of her Sunday gown. "I thought — that is — I felt it my duty — I thought — perhaps — I ought to tell you — that perhaps you ought to know."

The Doctor looked civilly concerned. He did not know but Miss Prissy's wits were taking leave of her. He replied, however, with his usual honest stateliness, —

"I trust, dear Madam, that you will feel at perfect freedom to open to me any exercises of mind that you may have."

"It isn't about myself," said Miss Prissy. "If you please, it's about you and Mary!"

The Doctor *now* looked awake in right earnest,

and very much astonished besides; and he looked eagerly at Miss Prissy, to have her go on.

"I don't know how you would view such a matter," said Miss Prissy; "but the fact is, that James Marvyn and Mary always did love each other, ever since they were children."

Still the Doctor was unawakened to the real meaning of the words, and he answered, simply, —

"I should be far from wishing to interfere with so very natural and universal a sentiment, which, I make no doubt, is all quite as it should be."

"No, — but," said Miss Prissy, "you don't understand what I mean. I mean that James Marvyn wanted to marry Mary, and that she was — well — she wasn't engaged to him, but" ——

"Madam!" said the Doctor, in a voice that frightened Miss Prissy out of her chair, while a blaze like sheet-lightning shot from his eyes, and his face flushed crimson.

"Mercy on us! Doctor, I hope you'll excuse me; but there the fact is, — I've said it out, — the fact is, they wa'n't engaged; but that Mary loved him ever since he was a boy, as she never will and never can love any man again in this world, is what I am just as sure of as that I'm standing here; and I've felt you ought to know it; 'cause I'm quite sure, that, if he'd been alive, she'd never given the promise she has, — the promise that she means to keep, if her heart breaks, and his too. They wouldn't anybody tell you, and I thought I must tell you; 'cause I thought you'd know what was right to do about it."

During all this latter speech the Doctor was standing with his back to Miss Prissy, and his face to the window, just as he did some time before, when Mrs. Scudder came to tell him of Mary's consent. He made a gesture backward, without speaking, that she should leave the apartment; and Miss Prissy left, with a guilty kind of feeling, as if she had been striking a knife into her pastor, and, rushing distractedly across the entry into Mary's little bedroom, she bolted the door, threw herself on the bed, and began to cry.

" Well, I've done it ! " she said to herself. " He's a very strong, hearty man," she soliloquized, " so I hope it won't put him in a consumption;— men do go into a consumption about such things sometimes. I remember Abner Seaforth did; but then he was always narrow-chested, and had the liver-complaint, or something. I don't know what Miss Scudder will say;—but I've done it. Poor man! such a good man, too! I declare, I feel just like Herod taking off John the Baptist's head Well, well! it's done, and can't be helped."

Just at this moment Miss Prissy heard a gentle tap at the door, and started, as if it had been a ghost, — not being able to rid herself of the impression, that, somehow, she had committed a great crime, for which retribution was knocking at the door.

It was Mary, who said, in her sweetest and most natural tones, " Miss Prissy, the Doctor would like to see you."

Mary was much astonished at the frightened, discomposed manner with which Miss Prissy received this announcement, and said, —

" I'm afraid I've waked you up out of sleep. I don't think there's the least hurry."

Miss Prissy didn't, either; but she reflected afterwards that she might as well get through with it at once ; and therefore, smoothing her tumbled cap-border, she went to the Doctor's study. This time he was quite composed, and received her with a mournful gravity, and requested her to be seated.

" I beg, Madam," he said, " you will excuse the abruptness of my manner in our late interview. I was so little prepared for the communication you had to make, that I was, perhaps, unsuitably discomposed. Will you allow me to ask whether you were requested by any of the parties to communicate to me what you did ? "

" No, Sir," said Miss Prissy.

" Have any of the parties ever communicated with you on the subject at all ? " said the Doctor

"No, Sir," said Miss Prissy.

"That is all," said the Doctor. "I will not detain you. I am very much obliged to you, Madam."

He rose, and opened the door for her to pass out, — and Miss Prissy, overawed by the stately gravity of his manner, went out in silence.

CHAPTER XL.

THE SACRIFICE.

WHEN Miss Prissy left the room, the Doctor sat down by the table and covered his face with his hands. He had a large, passionate, determined nature; and he had just come to one of those cruel crises in life in which it is apt to seem to us that the whole force of our being, all that we can hope, wish, feel, enjoy, has been suffered to gather itself into one great wave, only to break upon some cold rock of inevitable fate, and go back, moaning, into emptiness.

In such hours men and women have cursed God and life, and thrown violently down and trampled under their feet what yet was left of life's blessings, in the fierce bitterness of despair. " This, or nothing ! " the soul shrieks, in her frenzy. At just such points as these, men have plunged into intemperance and wild excess, — they have gone to be shot down in battle, — they have broken life, and thrown it away, like an empty goblet, and gone, like wailing ghosts, out into the dread unknown.

The possibility of all this lay in that heart
which had just received that stunning blow. Ex-
ercised and disciplined as he had been, by years
of sacrifice, by constant, unsleeping self-vigilance,
there was rising there, in that great heart, an
ocean-tempest of passion, and for a while his cries
unto God seemed as empty and as vague as the
screams of birds tossed and buffeted in the clouds
of mighty tempests.

The will that he thought wholly subdued seemed
to rise under him as a rebellious giant. A few
hours before, he thought himself established in an
invincible submission to God's will that nothing
could shake. Now he looked into himself as into
a seething vortex of rebellion, and against all the
passionate cries of his lower nature could, in the
language of an old saint, cling to God only by
the naked force of his will. That will rested unmelted amid the boiling sea of passion, waiting
its hour of renewed sway. He walked the room
for hours, and then sat down to his Bible, and
roused once or twice to find his head leaning on
its pages, and his mind far gone in thoughts, from
which he woke with a bitter throb. Then he determined to set himself to some definite work, and,
taking his Concordance, began busily tracing out
and numbering all the proof-texts for one of the
chapters of his theological system! till, at last, he
worked himself down to such calmness that he

could pray; and then he schooled and reasoned with himself, in a style not unlike, in its spirit, to that in which a great modern author has addressed suffering humanity : —

"What is it that thou art fretting and self-tormenting about? Is it because thou art not happy? Who told thee that thou wast to be happy? Is there any ordinance of the universe that thou shouldst be happy? Art thou nothing but a vulture screaming for prey? Canst thou not do without happiness? Yea, thou canst do without happiness, and, instead thereof, find blessedness."

The Doctor came, lastly, to the conclusion, that blessedness, which was all the portion his Master had on earth, might do for him also; and therefore he kissed and blessed that silver dove of happiness, which he saw was weary of sailing in his clumsy old ark, and let it go out of his hand without a tear.

He slept little that night; but when he came to breakfast, all noticed an unusual gentleness and benignity of manner, and Mary, she knew not why, saw tears rising in his eyes when he looked at her.

After breakfast he requested Mrs. Scudder to step with him into his study, and Miss Prissy shook in her little shoes as she saw the matron entering. The door was shut for a long time, and

24

two voices could be heard in earnest conversation.

Meanwhile James Marvyn entered the cottage, prompt to remind Mary of her promise that she would talk with him again this morning.

They had talked with each other but a few moments, by the sweetbrier-shaded window in the best room, when Mrs. Scudder appeared at the door of the apartment, with traces of tears upon her cheeks.

"Good morning, James," she said. "The Doctor wishes to see you and Mary a moment, together."

Both looked sufficiently astonished, knowing, from Mrs. Scudder's looks, that something was impending. They followed her, scarcely feeling the ground they trod on.

The Doctor was sitting at his table, with his favorite large-print Bible open before him. He rose to receive them, with a manner at once gentle and grave.

There was a pause of some minutes, during which he sat with his head leaning upon his hand.

"You all know," he said, turning toward Mary, who sat very near him, "the near and dear relation in which I have been expected to stand towards this friend. I should not have been worthy of that relation, if I had not felt in my heart the

true love of a husband, as set forth in the New
Testament, — who should love his wife even as
Christ loved the Church, and gave himself for it;
and in case any peril or danger threatened this
dear soul, and I could not give myself for her, I
had never been worthy the honor she has done
me. For, I take it, whenever there is a cross or
burden to be borne by one or the other, that the
man, who is made in the image of God as to
strength and endurance, should take it upon himself, and not lay it upon her that is weaker; for
he is therefore strong, not that he may tyrannize
over the weak, but bear their burdens for them,
even as Christ for his Church.

"I have just discovered," he added, looking
kindly upon Mary, "that there is a great cross
and burden which must come, either on this dear
child or on myself, through no fault of either of
us, but through God's good providence; and therefore let me bear it.

"Mary, my dear child," he said, "I will be to
thee as a father, but I will not force thy heart."

At this moment, Mary, by a sudden, impulsive
movement, threw her arms around his neck and
kissed him, and lay sobbing on his shoulder.

"No! no!" she said, — "I will marry you, as I
said!"

"Not if I will not," he replied, with a benign
smile. "Come here, young man;" he said, with

some authority, to James. "I give thee this maiden to wife." And he lifted her from his shoulder, and placed her gently in the arms of the young man, who, overawed and overcome, pressed her silently to his heart.

"There, children, it is over," he said. "God bless you!"

"Take her away," he added; "she will be more composed soon."

Before James left, he grasped the Doctor's hand in his, and said, —

"Sir, this tells on my heart more than any sermon you ever preached. I shall never forget it. God bless you, Sir!"

The Doctor saw them slowly quit the apartment, and, following them, closed the door; and thus ended THE MINISTER'S WOOING.

CHAPTER XLI.

THE WEDDING.

OF the events which followed this scene we are happy to give our readers more minute and graphic details than we ourselves could furnish, by transcribing for their edification an autograph letter of Miss Prissy's, still preserved in a black oaken cabinet of our great-grandmother's; and with which we take no further liberties than the correction of a somewhat peculiar orthography. It is written to that sister "Lizabeth," in Boston, of whom she made such frequent mention, and whom, it appears, it was her custom to keep well-informed in all the gossip of her immediate sphere.

"MY DEAR SISTER:—

"You wonder, I s'pose, why I haven't written you; but the fact is, I've been run just off my feet, and worked till the flesh aches so it seems as if it would drop off my bones, with this wedding of Mary Scudder's. And, after all, you'll be astonished to hear that she ha'n't married the

Doctor, but that Jim Marvyn that I told you about. You see, he came home a week before the wedding was to be, and Mary, she was so conscientious she thought 'twa'n't right to break off with the Doctor, and so she was for going right on with it; and Mrs. Scudder, she was for going on more yet; and the poor young man, he couldn't get a word in edgeways, and there wouldn't anybody tell the Doctor a word about it, and there 'twas drifting along, and both on 'em feeling dreadful, and so I thought to myself, 'I'll just take my life in my hand, like Queen Esther, and go in and tell the Doctor all about it.' And so I did. I'm scared to death always when I think of it. But that dear blessed man, he took it like a saint. He just gave her up as serene and calm as a psalm-book, and called Jim in and told him to take her.

"Jim was fairly overcrowed, — it really made him feel small, — and he says he'll agree that there is more in the Doctor's religion than most men's: which shows how important it is for professing Christians to bear testimony in their works, — as I was telling Cerinthy Ann Twitchel; and she said there wa'n't anything made her want to be a Christian so much, if that was what religion would do for people.

"Well, you see, when this came out, it wanted just three days of the wedding, which was to be

Thursday, and that wedding-dress I told you about
that had lilies of the valley on a white ground
was pretty much made, except puffing the gauze
round the neck, which I do with white satin pip
ing-cord, and it looks beautiful too; and so Mrs.
Scudder and I, we were thinking 'twould do just
as well, when in come Jim Marvyn, bringing the
sweetest thing you ever saw, that he had got in
China, and I think I never did see anything love-
lier. It was a white silk, as thick as a board, and
so stiff that it would stand alone, and overshot
with little fine dots of silver, so that it shone,
when you moved it, just like frostwork; and when
I saw it, I just clapped my hands, and jumped up
from the floor, and says I, ' If I have to sit up
all night, that dress shall be made, and made well,
too.' For, you know, I thought I could get Miss
Olladine Hocum to run the breadths and do such
parts, so that I could devote myself to the fine
work. And that French woman I told you about,
she said she'd help, and she's a master-hand for
touching things up. There seems to be work provided for all kinds of people, and French people
seem to have a gift in all sorts of dressy things,
and 'tisn't a bad gift either.

" Well, as I was saying, we agreed that this
was to be cut open with a train, and a petticoat
of just the palest, sweetest, loveliest blue that ever
you saw, and gauze puffings down the edgings

each side, fastened in, every once in a while, with lilies of the valley; and 'twas cut square in the neck, with puffings and flowers to match, and then tight sleeves, with full ruffles of that old Mechlin lace that you remember Mrs. Katy Scudder showed you once in that great camphor-wood trunk.

"Well, you see, come to get all things together that were to be done, we concluded to put off the wedding till Tuesday; and Madame de Frontignac, she would dress the best room for it herself, and she spent nobody knows what time in going round and getting evergreens and making wreaths, and putting up green boughs over the pictures, so that the room looked just like the Episcopal church at Christmas. In fact, Mrs. Scudder said, if it had been Christmas, she shouldn't have felt it right, but, as it was, she didn't think anybody would think it any harm.

"Well, Tuesday night, I and Madame de Frontignac, we dressed Mary ourselves, and, I tell you, the dress fitted as if it was grown on her; and Madame de Frontignac, she dressed her hair; and she had on a wreath of lilies of the valley, and a gauze veil that came a'most down to her feet, and came all around her like a cloud, and you could see her white shining dress through it every time she moved, and she looked just as white as a snow-berry; but there were two little pink spots that kept coming and going in her cheeks, that kind of lightened up when she smiled, and then faded down again. And the French lady put a string of real pearls round her neck, with a cross of pearls, which went down and lay hid in her bosom.

" She was mighty calm-like while she was being dressed; but just as I was putting in the last pin, she heard the rumbling of a coach down-stairs, for Jim Marvyn had got a real elegant carriage to carry her over to his father's in, and so she knew he was come. And pretty soon Mrs. Marvyn came in the room, and when she saw Mary, her brown eyes kind of danced, and she lifted up both hands, to see how beautiful she looked. And Jim Marvyn, he was standing at the door, and they told him it wasn't proper that he should see till the time come; but he begged so hard that he might just have one peep, that I let him come in, and he looked at her as if she was something he wouldn't dare to touch; and he said to me softly, says he, ' I'm 'most afraid she has got wings somewhere that will fly away from me, or that I shall wake up and find it is a dream.'

" Well, Cerinthy Ann Twitchel was the brides· maid, and she came next with that young man she is engaged to. It is all out now, that she is engaged, and she don't deny it. And Cerinthy, she looked handsomer than I ever saw her, in a white brocade, with rosebuds on it, which I guess

24 *

she got in reference to the future, for they say she is going to be married next month.

"Well, we all filled up the room pretty well, till Mrs. Scudder came in to tell us that the company were all together; and then they took hol⸱ of arms, and they had a little time practising how they must stand, and Cerinthy Ann's beau would always get her on the wrong side, 'cause he's rather bashful, and don't know very well what he's about; and Cerinthy Ann declared she was afraid that she should laugh out in prayer-time, 'cause she always did laugh when she knew she mus'n't. But finally Mrs. Scudder told us we must go in, and looked so reproving at Cerinthy that she had to hold her mouth with her pocket-handkerchief.

"Well, the old Doctor was standing there in the very silk gown that the ladies gave him to be married in himself, — poor, dear man! — and he smiled kind of peaceful on 'em when they came in, and walked up to a kind of bower of evergreens and flowers that Madame de Frontignac had fixed for them to stand in. Mary grew rather white, as if she was going to faint; but Jim Marvyn stood up just as firm, and looked as proud and handsome as a prince, and he kind of looked down at her, — 'cause, you know, he is a great deal taller, — kind of wondering, as if he wanted to know if it was really so. Well, when they got all placed, they let the doors stand open, and Cato and Candace came and stood in the door. And Candace had on her great splendid Mogadore turban, and a crimson and yellow shawl, that she seemed to take comfort in wearing, although it was pretty hot.

"Well, so when they were all fixed, the Doctor, he begun his prayer, — and as 'most all of us knew what a great sacrifice he had made, I don't believe there was a dry eye in the room; and when he had done, there was a great time, — people blowing their noses and wiping their eyes, as if it had been a funeral. Then Cerinthy Ann, she pulled off Mary's glove pretty quick; but that poor beau of hers, he made such work of James's that he had to pull it off himself, after all, and Cerinthy Ann, she liked to have laughed out loud. And so when the Doctor told them to join hands, Jim took hold of Mary's hand as if he didn't mean to let go very soon, and so they were married.

"I was the first one that kissed the bride after Mrs. Scudder, — I got that promise out of Mary when I was making the dress. And Jim Marvyn, he insisted upon kissing me, — "'Cause,' says he, 'Miss Prissy, you are as young and handsome as any of 'em'; and I told him he was a saucy fellow, and I'd box his ears, if I could reach them.

"That French lady looked lovely, dressed in

pale pink silk, with long pink wreaths of flowers in her hair; and she came up and kissed Mary, and said something to her in French.

"And after a while old Candace came up, and Mary kissed her; and then Candace put her arms round Jim's neck, and gave him a real hearty smack, so that everybody laughed.

"And then the cake and the wine was passed round, and everybody had good times till we heard the nine-o'clock-bell ring. And then the coach came up to the door, and Mrs. Scudder, she wrapped Mary up, kissing her, and crying over her, while Mrs. Marvyn stood stretching her arms out of the coach after her. And then Cato and Candace went after in the wagon behind, and so they all went off together; and that was the end of the wedding; and ever since then we ha'n't any of us done much but rest, for we were pretty much beat out. So no more at present from your affectionate sister,

"PRISSY.

" P.S. — I forgot to tell you that Jim Marvyn has come home quite rich. He fell in with a man in China who was at the head of one of their great merchant-houses, whom he nursed through a long fever, and took care of his business, and so, when he got well, nothing would do but he must have him for a partner; and now he is going to live in this country and at-

tend to the business of the house here. They
say he is going to build a house as grand as the
Vernons'. And we hope ne has experienced religion; and he means to join our church, which is a
providence, for he is twice as rich and generous
as that old Simeon Brown that snapped me up so
about my wages. I never believed in him, for all
his talk. I was down to Mrs. Scudder's when the
Doctor examined Jim about his evidences. At
first the Doctor seemed a little anxious, 'cause he
didn't talk in the regular way; for you know Jim
always did have his own way of talking, and
never could say things in other people's words;
and sometimes he makes folks laugh, when he
himself don't know what they laugh at, because
he hits the nail on the head in some strange way
they aren't expecting. If I was to have died, I
couldn't help laughing at some things he said; and
yet I don't think I ever felt more solemnized. He
sat up there in a sort of grand, straightforward,
noble way, and told all the way the Lord had
been leading of him, and all the exercises of his
mind, and all about the dreadful shipwreck, and
how he was saved, and the loving-kindness of the
Lord, till the Doctor's spectacles got all blinded
with tears, and he couldn't see the notes he made
to examine him by; and we all cried, Mrs. Scudder, and Mary, and I; and as to Mrs. Marvyn,
she just sat with her hands clasped, looking into

her son's eyes, like a picture of the Virgin Mary
And when Jim got through, there wa'n't nothing
to be heard for some minutes; and the Doctor he
wiped his eyes and wiped his glasses, and he
looked over his papers, but he couldn't bring out
a word, and at last says he, " Let us pray,"—for
that was all there was to be said; for I think
sometimes things so kind of fills folks up that
there a'n't nothing to be done but pray, which, the
Lord be praised, we are privileged to do always.
Between you and I, Martha, I never could understand all the distinctions our dear, blessed Doctor
sets up; but when he publishes his system, if I
work my fingers to the bone, I mean to buy one
and study it out, because he is such a blessed
man; though, after all's said, I have to come back
to my old place, and trust to the loving-kindness
of the Lord, who takes care of the sparrow on
the house-top, and all small, lone creatures like me;
though I can't say I'm lone either, because nobody
need say that, so long as there's folks to be done
for. So if I *don't* understand the Doctor's theology,
or don't get eyes to read it, on account of the fine
stitching on his shirt-ruffles I've been trying to do,
still I hope I may be accepted on account of the
Lord's great goodness; for if we can't trust that
it's all over with us all."

CHAPTER XLII.

LAST WORDS.

WE know it is fashionable to drop the curtain over a newly married pair, as they recede from the altar; but we cannot but hope our readers may by this time have enough of interest in our little history to wish for a few words on the lot of the personages whose acquaintance they have thereby made.

The conjectures of Miss Prissy in regard to the grand house which James was to build for his bride were as speedily as possible realized. On a beautiful elevation, a little out of the town of Newport, rose a fair and stately mansion, whose windows overlooked the harbor, and whose wide, cool rooms were adorned by the constant presence of the sweet face and form which has been the guiding star of our story. The fair poetic maiden, the seeress, the saint, has passed into that appointed shrine for woman, more holy than cloister, more saintly and pure than church or altar, — *a Christian home.* Priestess, wife, and mother, there she ministers daily in holy works of household peace, and by faith and prayer and love redeems from grossness and earthliness the common toils and wants of life.

The gentle guiding force that led James Marvyn from the maxims and habits and ways of this world to the higher conception of an heroic and Christ-like manhood was still ever present with him, gently touching the springs of life, brooding peacefully with dovelike wings over his soul, and he grew up under it noble in purpose and strong in spirit. He was one of the most energetic and fearless supporters of the Doctor in his life-long warfare against an inhumanity which was intrenched in all the mercantile interests of the day, and which at last fell before the force of conscience and moral appeal.

Candace in time transferred her allegiance to the growing family of her young master and mistress, and predominated proudly in gorgeous raiment with her butterfly turban over a rising race of young Marvyns. All the care not needed by them was bestowed on the somewhat querulous old age of Cato, whose never-failing cough furnished occupation for all her spare hours and thought.

As for our friend the Doctor, we trust our readers will appreciate the magnanimity with which he proved a real and disinterested love, in a point where so many men experience only the graspings of a selfish one. A mind so severely trained as his had been brings to a great crisis, involving severe self-denial, an amount of reserved moral force quite inexplicable to those less habituated to self-control. He was like a warrior whose sleep even was in armor, always ready to be roused to the conflict.

In regard to his feelings for Mary, he made the sacrifice of himself to her happiness so wholly and thoroughly that there was not a moment of weak hesitation, — no going back over the past, — no vain regret. Generous and brave souls find a support in such actions, because the very exertion raises them to a higher and purer plane of existence.

His diary records the event only in these very calm and temperate words: — " It was a trial to me, — a *very great* trial ; but as she did not deceive me, I shall never lose my friendship for her."

The Doctor was always a welcome inmate in the house of Mary and James, as a friend revered and dear. Nor did he want in time a hearthstone of his own, where a bright and loving face made him daily welcome ; for we find that he married at last a woman of a fair countenance, and that sons and daughters grew up around him.

In time, also, his theological system was pub-

lished. In that day, it was customary to dedicate
new or important works to the patronage of some
distinguished or powerful individual. The Doctor
had no earthly patron. Four or five simple lines
are found in the commencement of his work, in
which, in a spirit reverential and affectionate, he
dedicates it to our Lord Jesus Christ, praying Him
to accept the good, and to overrule the errors to
His glory.

Quite unexpectedly to himself, the work proved
a success, not only in public acceptance and esteem, but even in a temporal view, bringing to
him at last a modest competence, which he accepted with surprise and gratitude. To the last
of a very long life, he was the same steady, undiscouraged worker, the same calm witness against
popular sins and proclaimer of unpopular truths,
ever saying and doing what he saw to be eternally right, without the slightest consultation with
worldly expediency or earthly gain; nor did his
words cease to work in New England till the evils
he opposed were finally done away.

Colonel Burr leaves the scene of our story to
pursue those brilliant and unscrupulous political
intrigues so well known to the historian of those
times, and whose results were so disastrous to
himself. His duel with the ill-fated Hamilton, the
awful retribution of public opinion that followed, and the slow downward course of a doomed

life are all on record. Chased from society,
pointed at everywhere by the finger of hatred,
so accursed in common esteem that even the pub-
lican who lodged him for a night refused to accept his money when he knew his name, heart-
stricken in his domestic relations, his only daughter taken by pirates and dying amid untold hor-
rors, — one seems to see in a doom so much
above that of other men the power of an aveng-
ing Nemesis for sins beyond those of ordinary
humanity.

But we who have learned of Christ may humbly hope that these crushing miseries in this life
came not because he was a sinner above others, not
in wrath alone, — but that the prayers of the sweet
saint who gave him to God even before his birth
brought to him those friendly adversities, that thus
might be slain in his soul the evil demon of pride,
which had been the opposing force to all that was
noble within him. Nothing is more affecting than
the account of the last hours of this man, whom
a woman took in and cherished in his poverty
and weakness with that same heroic enthusiasm
with which it was his lot to inspire so many
women. This humble keeper of lodgings was told,
that, if she retained Aaron Burr, all her other lodg-
ers would leave. " Let them do it, then," she said;
" but he shall remain." In the same uncomplaining
and inscrutable silence in which he had borne the

reverses and miseries of his life did this singular
being pass through the shades of the dark valley
The New Testament was always under his pillow,
and when alone he was often found reading it attentively ; but of the result of that communion
with higher powers he said nothing. Patient, gentle, and grateful, he was, as to all his inner history, entirely silent and impenetrable. He died
with the request, which has a touching significance,
that he might be buried at the feet of those parents whose lives had finished so differently from
his own.

> "No farther seek his errors to disclose,
> Or draw his frailties from their dread abode."

Shortly after Mary's marriage, Madame de Fron
tignac sailed with her husband for home, where
they lived in a very retired way on a large estate
in the South of France. An intimate correspondence was kept up between her and Mary for many
years, from which we shall give our readers a few
extracts. Her first letter is dated shortly after her
return to France.

" At last, my sweet Marie, you behold us in
peace after our wanderings. I wish you could see
our lovely nest in the hills, which overlook the
Mediterranean, whose blue waters remind me of
Newport harbor and our old days there. Ah, my

sweet saint, blessed was the day I first learned to
know you! for it was you, more than anything
else, that kept me back from sin and misery. I
call you my Sibyl, dearest, because the Sibyl was
a prophetess of divine things out of the Church;
and so are you. The Abbé says, that all true, devout persons in all persuasions belong to the True
Catholic Apostolic Church, and will in the end be
enlightened to know it; what do you think of
that, *ma belle?* I fancy I see you look at me
with your grave, innocent eyes, just as you used
to; but you say nothing.

"I am far happier, *ma Marie*, than I ever thought
I could be. I took your advice, and told my husband all I had felt and suffered. It was a very
hard thing to do; but I felt how true it was, as you
said, that there could be no real friendship without
perfect truth at bottom; so I told him all, and he
was very good and noble and helpful to me; and
since then he has been so gentle and patient and
thoughtful, that no mother could be kinder; and I
should be a very bad woman, if I did not love
him truly and dearly, — as I do.

"I must confess that there is still a weak, bleeding place in my heart that aches yet, but I try to
bear it bravely; and when I am tempted to think
myself very miserable, I remember how patiently
you used to go about your house-work and spinning, in those sad days when you thought your

heart was drowned in the sea; and I try to do like you. I have many duties to my servants and tenants, and mean to be a good *châtelaine;* and I find, when I nurse the sick and comfort the poor, that my sorrows are lighter. For, after all, Mary, I have lost nothing that ever was mine,— only my foolish heart has grown to something that it should not, and bleeds at being torn away. Nobody but Christ and His dear Mother can tell what this sorrow is; but they know, and that is enough."

The next letter is dated some three years after.

"You see me now, my Marie, a proud and happy woman. I was truly envious, when you wrote me of the birth of your little son; but now the dear good God has sent a sweet little angel to me, to comfort my sorrows and lie close to my heart; and since he came, all pain is gone. Ah, if you could see him! he has black eyes and lashes like silk, and such little hands! — even his finger-nails are all perfect, like little gems; and when he puts his little hand on my bosom, I tremble with joy. Since he came, I pray always, and the good God seems very near to me. Now I realize, as I never did before, the sublime thought that God revealed Himself in the infant Jesus; and I bow before the manger of Bethlehem where the Holy Babe was laid. What comfort, what adorable condescension for us mothers in that scene! — My husband is so moved, he can scarce

stay an hour from the cradle. He seems to look
at me with a sort of awe, because I know how
to care for this precious treasure that he adores
without daring to touch. We are going to call
him Henri, which is my husband's name and that
of his ancestors for many generations back. I
vow for him an eternal friendship with the son of
my little Marie; and I shall try and train him up
to be a brave man and a true Christian. Ah,
Marie, this gives me something to live for! My
heart is full, — a whole new life opens before
me!"

Somewhat later, another letter announces the
birth of a daughter, — and later still, the birth of
another son; but we shall only add one more,
written some years after, on hearing of the great
reverses of popular feeling towards Burr, subsequently to his duel with the ill-fated Hamilton.

"*Ma chère Marie*, — Your letter has filled me
with grief. My noble Henri, who already begins
to talk of himself as my protector, (these boys
feel their manhood so soon, *ma Marie!*) saw by my
face, when I read your letter, that something pained me, and he would not rest till I told him something about it. Ah, Marie, how thankful I then
felt that I had nothing to blush for before my
son! how thankful for those dear children whose
little hands had healed all the morbid places of
my heart, so that I could think of all the past

without a pang! I told Henri that the letter brought bad news of an old friend, but that it pained me to speak of it; and you would have thought, by the grave and tender way he talked to his mamma, that the boy was an experienced man of forty, to say the least.

"But, Marie, how unjust is the world! how un-just both in praise and blame! Poor Burr was the petted child of society; yesterday she doted on him, flattered him, smiled on his faults, and let him do what he would without reproof; to-day she flouts and scorns and scoffs him, and refuses to see the least good in him. I know that man, Mary, — and I know, that, sinful as he may be before Infinite Purity, he is not so much more sinful than all the other men of his time. Have I not been in America? I know Jefferson; I knew poor Hamilton, — peace be with the dead! Neither of them had a life that could bear the sort of trial to which Burr's is subjected. When every secret fault, failing, and sin is dragged out, and held up without mercy, what man can stand?

"But I know what irritates the world is that proud, disdainful calm which will neither give sigh nor tear. It was not that he killed poor Hamil-ton, but that he never seemed to care! Ah, there is that evil demon of his life, — that cold, stoical pride, which haunts him like a fate! But I know he *does* feel; I know he is *not* as hard at heart as he tries to be; I have seen too many real acts of pity to the unfortunate, of tenderness to the weak, of real love to his friends, to believe that. Great have been his sins against our sex, and God forbid that the mothers of children should speak lightly of them; but is not so susceptible a temperament, and so singular a power to charm as he possessed, to be taken into account in estimating his temptations? Because he is a sinning man, it does not follow that he is a demon. If any should have cause to think bitterly of him, I should. He trifled inexcusably with my deepest feelings; he caused me years of conflict and anguish, such as he little knows; I was almost shipwrecked; yet I will still say to the last that what I loved in him was a better self, — something really noble and good, however concealed and perverted by pride, ambition, and self-will. Though all the world reject him, I still have faith in this better nature, and prayers that he may be led right at last. There is at least one heart that will always intercede with God for him."

It is well known, that, for many years after Burr's death, the odium that covered his name was so great that no monument was erected, lest it should become a mark for popular violence. Subsequently, however, in a mysterious manner, a plain granite slab marked his grave; by whom erected has been never known. It was placed in the night by some friendly, unknown hand. A laborer in the vicinity, who first discovered it, found lying near the spot a small *porte-monnaie*, which had perhaps been used in paying for the workmanship. It contained no papers that could throw any light on the subject, except the fragment of the address of a letter on which was written " Henri de Frontignac."

THE END.